Datsun Bluebird 160B, 180B, 1972-74 Autobook

By Kenneth Ball
Associate Member, Guild of Motoring Writers
and the Autopress Team of Technical Writers.

Datsun 160B, Series 610, 1595cc 1972-74
Datsun 180B, Series 610, 1770cc 1972-74
Datsun 180B SSS, Series 610, 1770cc 1972-74

Autobooks

Autopress Ltd. Golden Lane Brighton BN1 2QJ England

The AUTOBOOK series of Workshop Manuals is the largest in the world and covers the majority of British and Continental motor cars, as well as all major Japanese and Australian models. For a full list see the back of this manual.

CONTENTS

Acknowledgement

Introduction

Chapter 1	The Engine	9
Chapter 2	The Fuel System	31
Chapter 3	The Ignition System	45
Chapter 4	The Cooling System	53
Chapter 5	The Clutch	59
Chapter 6	The Gearbox	67
Chapter 7	Automatic Transmission	79
Chapter 8	The Propeller Shaft, Rear Axle and Rear Suspension	91
Chapter 9	Front Suspension and Hubs	105
Chapter 10	The Steering Gear	113
Chapter 11	The Braking System	121
Chapter 12	The Electrical Equipment	135
Chapter 13	The Bodywork	147
Appendix		159

ISBN 0 85147 376 8

First Edition 1974

823

Printed and bound in Brighton England for Autopress Ltd by G Beard & Son Ltd A

ACKNOWLEDGEMENT

My thanks are due to Datsun UK Ltd for their unstinted co-operation and also for supplying data and illustrations.

I am also grateful to a considerable number of owners who have discussed their cars at length and many of whose suggestions have been included in this manual.

Kenneth Ball
Associate Member Guild of Motoring Writers

Ditchling Sussex England.

INTRODUCTION

This do-it-yourself Workshop Manual has been specially written for the owner who wishes to maintain his car in first class condition and to carry out his own servicing and repairs. Considerable savings on garage charges can be made, and one can drive in safety and confidence knowing the work has been done properly.

Comprehensive step-by-step instructions and illustrations are given on all dismantling, overhauling and assembling operations. Certain assemblies require the use of expensive special tools, the purchase of which would be unjustified. In these cases information is included but the reader is recommended to hand the unit to the agent for attention.

Throughout the Manual hints and tips are included which will be found invaluable, and there is an easy to follow fault diagnosis at the end of each chapter.

Whilst every care has been taken to ensure correctness of information it is obviously not possible to guarantee complete freedom from errors or to accept liability arising from such errors or omissions.

Instructions may refer to the righthand or lefthand sides of the vehicle or the components. These are the same as the righthand or lefthand of an observer standing behind the car and looking forward.

CHAPTER 1

THE ENGINE

1:1 Description
1:2 Maintenance
1:3 Oil pump and filter
1:4 Adjusting valve clearances
1:5 Removing and fitting cylinder head
1:6 Servicing the cylinder head
1:7 Removing the engine
1:8 Dismantling the engine
1:9 Removing and fitting pistons and connecting rods
1:10 Pistons and rings
1:11 Connecting rods
1:12 Flywheel
1:13 Crankshaft and main bearings
1:14 Camshaft and camshaft drive
1:15 Distributor drive
1:16 Oil sump and strainer
1:17 Cylinder block
1:18 Assembling the engine
1:19 Installing the engine
1:20 Engine mountings
1:21 Emission control system
1:22 Fault diagnosis

1:1 Description

L16 engines of 1595 cc capacity are fitted to 160B models. L18 engines of 1770 cc capacity are fitted to 180B models. Both are four-cylinder, four-stroke, water-cooled, in-line engines. The L16 has a bore of 83 mm and a stroke of 73.7 mm. The L18 has a bore of 85 mm and a stroke of 78 mm. Either engine may be fitted with a single downdraught carburetter or with twin SU type side-draught carburetters. The compression ratio in the case of engines fitted with a single carburetter is 8.5:1. In the case of engines fitted with twin carburetters, the compression ratio is 9.5:1. Cross-sections through a single-carburetter L16 engine are shown in **FIG 1:1**. The following description covers both the L16 and the L18 engines since the design of both, with a few exceptions, is identical although they differ dimensionally in relevant respects.

The crankshaft runs in five shell type plain bearings carried in a monoblock cast cylinder block. The cylinder bores are machined directly into the block and liners are only fitted if, at overhaul, the bores cannot be refinished to suit the largest oversize pistons. The crankshaft is fully balanced. The forward, rear and two centre webs incorporate balance weights in the case of L16 engines while all webs carry balance weights in the case of L18 engines.

Connecting rod big-ends are fitted with shell type plain bearings and the gudgeon pins are a tight press fit in the little ends. Oil holes in the connecting rod webs adjacent to the big-ends provide 'squirt' lubrication to the thrust sides of the cylinder bores. The main and big-end bearings are pressure lubricated.

The overhead camshaft is chain driven from a sprocket which is keyed to the forward end of the crankshaft. The duplex chain is automatically tensioned and is provided with guides. The valves are operated through rocker arms and provision is made for routine valve clearance adjustment. Two springs are incorporated in each valve assembly. The diaphragm type fuel pump is actuated from an eccentric on the camshaft.

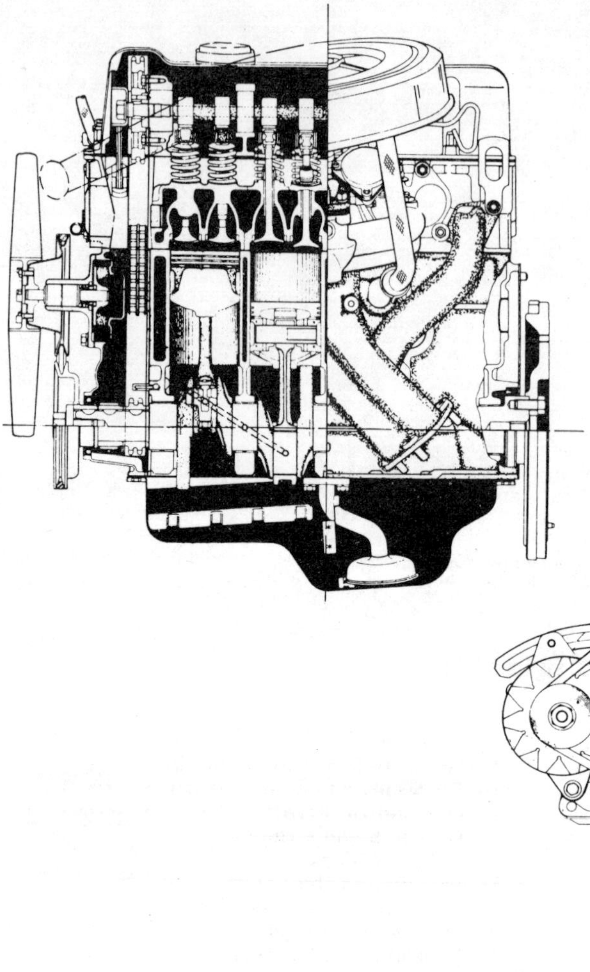

FIG 1:1 Cross-sections through an L16 type engine

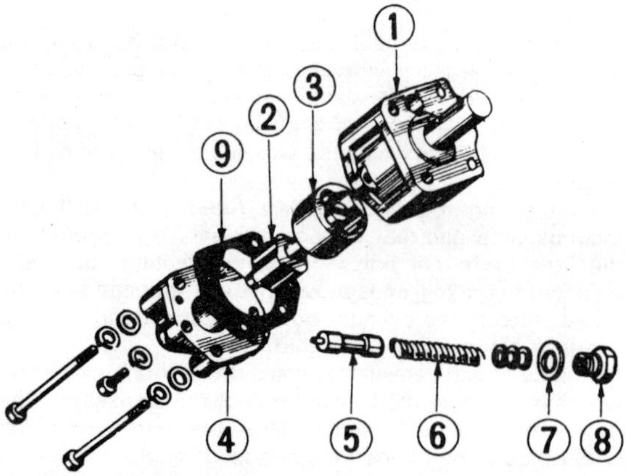

FIG 1:2 Components of the oil pump

Key to Fig 1:2 1 Pump body 2 Inner rotor and shaft 3 Outer rotor 4 Pump cover 5 Relief valve 6 Spring 7 Washer 8 Relief valve cap 9 Cover gasket

A skew gear on the forward end of the crankshaft drives the oil pump at half crankshaft speed and, via an extension of the oil pump drive shaft, the distributor. The pump draws oil from the sump through a gauze strainer.

The water pump, cooling fan and alternator are belt driven from a pulley on the extreme forward end of the crankshaft. On relevant models, the emission control system air pump is also belt driven from a pulley at the forward end of the crankshaft.

The flywheel is spigotted and bolted to the rear end of the crankshaft and a conventional ring gear with which the starter motor pinion engages is incorporated on its periphery.

The aluminium pistons are each provided with two compression rings and one oil control ring which is of a composite type.

The cylinder head may be lifted and the oil sump may be dropped with the engine in the vehicle. The firing order is 1, 3, 4, 2. The rear cylinder is No. 1.

1:2 Maintenance

Engine oil level:

Check the oil level with the car on level ground and, if the engine has been running, wait for at least a minute after the engine has stopped. Remove the dipstick, wipe it dry, re-insert fully, withdraw and check the level. If necessary, add oil to bring the level up to the **H** mark. Use the same grade and brand of oil as that already in use. Never allow the level to fall below the **L** mark.

Approximately 1¾ pints (1 litre) of oil is required to raise the level from the **L** mark to the **H** mark.

If the grade or brand of oil is to be changed, do so when the sump is being drained and the oil renewed.

Renewing engine oil:

Change the engine oil every 3000 miles (5000 km). Drain off the old oil when the engine is hot. After draining completely, refit the drain plug (the location is shown in **FIG 1:1**) and fill with appropriate approved oil up to the **H** level. Run the engine and check the oil level.

Depending upon the consistent climatic temperature, use oil of a reputable brand to whichever of the following specifications is relevant.

Multi-viscosity oils:

Ambient temperature	*Oil viscosity*
Below 10°C (14°F)	5 W-20
—24° to 30°C (—12° to 86°F)	10 W-30, 10 W-40
—20° to 40°C (—6° to 104°F)	20 W-40

Single viscosity oils:

Ambient temperature	*Oil viscosity*
Below 0°C (32°F)	10 W
—20° to 20°C (—6° to 68°F) ..	20 W
—10° to 30°C (14° to 86°F) ..	20
0° to 30°C (32° to 104°F) ..	30
Above 30°C (86°F)	40

Oil filter:

Every 6000 miles (10,000 km), that is every other engine oil change interval, renew the oil filter element as described in **Section 1:3**.

Valve clearances:

Every 6000 miles (10,000 km), check and adjust the valve clearance as described in **Section 1:4**.

General:

Refer to the relevant chapter for maintenance recommendations on the fuel, ignition and cooling systems.

1:3 Oil pump and filter

The components of the dual rotor oil pump and the relief valve are shown in **FIG 1:2**. A cross-section through an assembled relief valve is shown in **FIG 1:3**. Oil is drawn from the sump through a gauze screen (see **FIG 1:1**). The relief valve which opens at 50 to 70 lb/sq inch (3.5 to 5.0 kg/sq cm) is not adjustable and allows excess pressure oil to bypass to the pump inlet. Pressure oil is delivered to the engine main oil gallery through a fullflow, disposable element, canister type filter. A bypass valve is provided in the cylinder block at the centre of the filter location. If, through neglected maintenance, the filter becomes excessively clogged, the bypass valve opens and allows unfiltered oil to be fed to the main gallery.

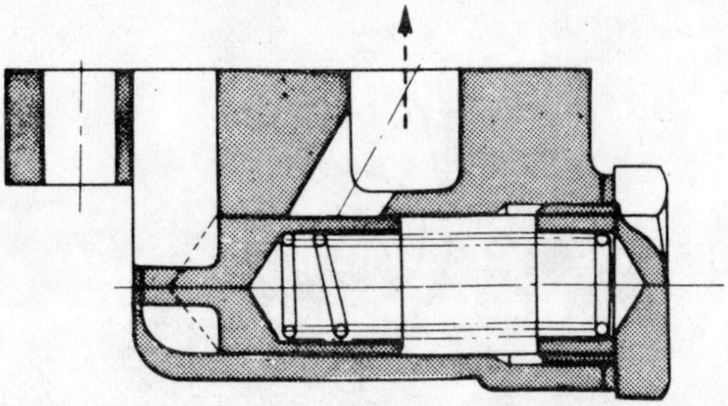

FIG 1:3 Cross-section through pump relief valve

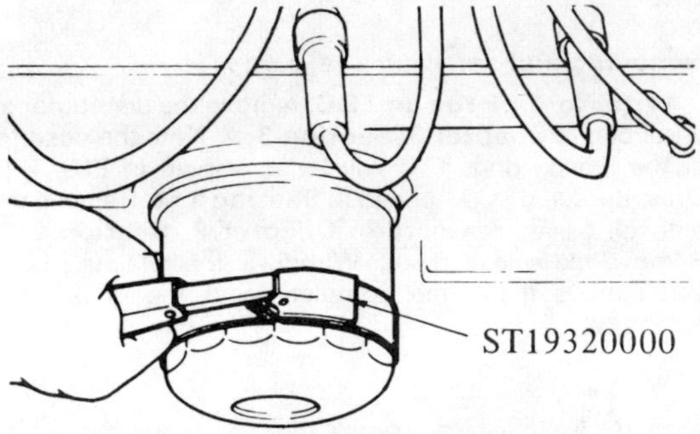

FIG 1:4 Removing the oil filter

The pump is driven at half engine speed from a skew gear at the forward end of the crankshaft. An extension of the pump drive shaft drives the distributor. An oil pressure transmitter is ganged with a pressure gauge in the instrument panel. Models not fitted with a gauge are provided with an oil pressure warning light which is actuated by a pressure senstive switch. The switch contacts are closed when there is no oil pressure and, with the ignition switched on, the warning light will be illuminated. When the engine is started and oil pressure rises, the contacts are opened and the warning light goes out.

Renewing the oil filter:

Renew the filter every 6000 miles (10,000 km). Use clamp ST19320000 as shown in **FIG 1:4** to remove the canister but, when installing, do so by hand. Overtightening may, by distorting the sealing joint, cause leakage. Approximately 1 pint (.5 litre) of oil will be required to top up the sump. Run the engine and check the oil level as described in **Section 1:2**.

Filter bypass valve:

Access to the valve requires removal of the filter as described earlier. If defective, pry it out with a screwdriver and tap in a new valve.

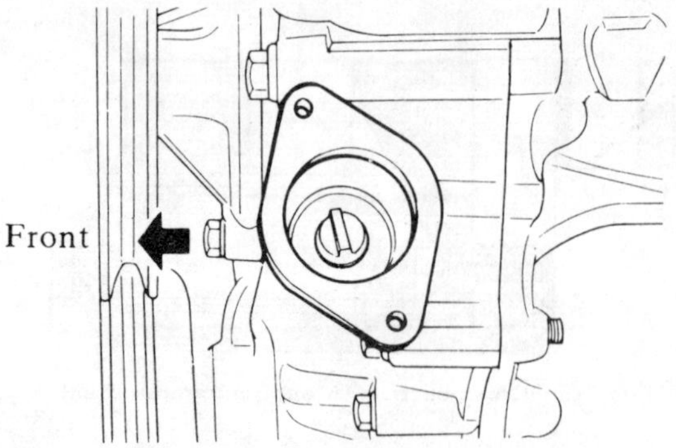

FIG 1:5 Distributor drive dog

Removing and refitting the pump:

With No. 1 piston on TDC, remove the distributor as described in **Chapter 3, Section 3:4**. Note the position of the driving dog. This will be as shown in **FIG 1:5**. Drain the sump as described in **Section 1:2**. Remove the anti-roll bar as described in **Chapter 9, Section 9:6**. Remove the splash shield. Withdraw the retaining bolts and remove the pump complete with the drive shaft assembly.

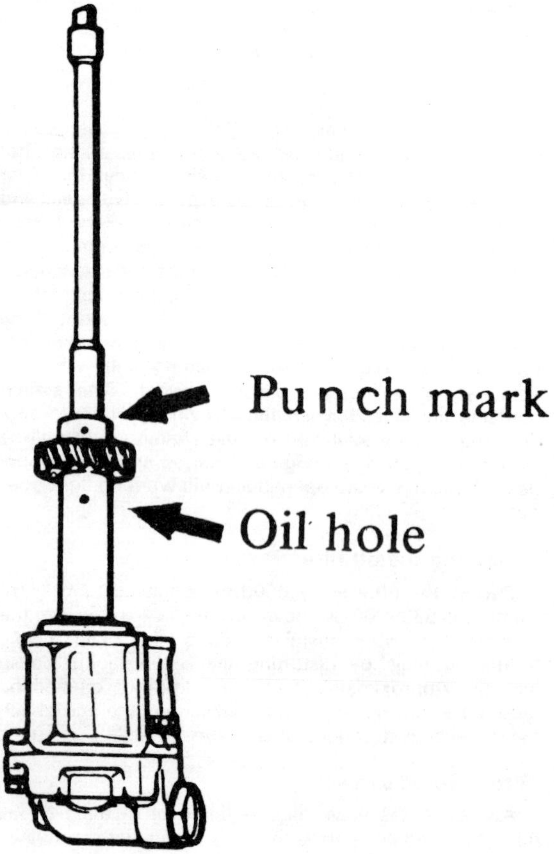

FIG 1:6 Pump and distributor drive

Fitment is the reverse of this sequence. **Ensure that No. 1 piston is on TDC.** Fill the pump housing with engine oil and, as shown in **FIG 1:6**, align the punch mark and the oil hole. Use a new gasket and install the pump as shown in **FIG 1:7**. Check that the distributor driving dog is, as shown in **FIG 1:5**, in its original position. If it is not, withdraw the pump, turn the shaft by an appropriate amount and refit. Torque tighten the retaining bolts to 8 to 11 lb ft (1.1 to 1.5 kgm). On completion of the installation, refill the sump as described in **Section 1:2** and check the ignition timing as described in **Chapter 3, Section 3:6**.

Dismantling and assembling the pump:

Refer to **FIG 1:2**. Withdraw the pump cover attachment bolts and remove the cover 4 and the gasket 9. Slide out the rotors 2 and 3. Remove the relief valve cup 8 and its sealing washer. Withdraw the valve 5, spring 6 and any shim washers that may be fitted. Wash all parts in petrol and dry off with compressed air.

Check the clearances as shown in **FIG 1:8**. 1, 2 and 4 should not exceed .008 inch (.2 mm). 3, the outer rotor to body clearance should not exceed .02 inch (.5 mm). Note that rotors and pump body are supplied only as a matched assembly and that they are not available as separate components. The free length of the relief valve spring is 2.067 inch (52.5 mm).

Assembly is the reverse of the dismantling sequence. Use a new gasket and assemble with the internal components wetted with engine oil. Torque tighten the cover retaining bolts to 5 to 7 lb ft (.7 to 1 kgm) and the relief valve cap to 29 to 36 lb ft (4 to 5 kgm).

1:4 Adjusting valve clearances

Valve clearances should be checked and adjusted if necessary every 6000 miles (10,000 km). Clearances should be checked with the engine cold and, for precise adjustment, rechecked with the engine warm. Proceed as follows:

1. With the engine cold, remove the breather pipe and unclip the sparking plug leads from the valve gear cover. Remove the retaining bolts and lift off the cover.
2. Turn the engine until the valve which is to be checked is in the fully closed position (TDC of the firing stroke).
3. Use feeler gauges between the rocker and the cam and check the clearance. The cold clearance should be .008 inch (.20 mm) for inlet valves and .010 inch (.25 mm) for exhaust valves.
4. Adjustment is made by loosening the locknut and turning the pivot post in the appropriate direction. **FIG 1:9** shows tool ST1060001 in use. When the clearance is correctly set, retighten the locknut to a torque of 36 to 43 lb ft (5 to 6 kgm).
5. Repeat operations 2, 3 and 4 until all valve clearances have been checked and adjusted.
6. Ensure that the valve cover gasket is in good condition and that it is correctly seated. Refit the cover.
7. Run the engine up to normal operating temperature and, with due regard to the temperature, check the valve clearances with the engine warm by following the procedure described earlier.

FIG 1:7 Fitting the pump and distributor drive

8 The warm clearances should be .010 inch (.25 mm) in the case of inlet valves and .012 inch (.30 mm) in the case of exhaust valves. Readjust the clearances if necessary.

1:5 Removing and fitting cylinder head

The cylinder head can be removed and refitted without removing the engine from the vehicle.

Removal:

1 Disconnect the battery earth cable. Dismount the bonnet as described in **Chapter 13, Section 13:2.**

2 Drain the cooling system as described in **Chapter 4, Section 4:2.** Loosen the hose clips and remove the radiator upper hose. Disconnect the heater piping. Disconnect the coolant temperature gauge transmitter unit.

3 Remove the leads from the sparking plugs and unclip them from the valve gear cover. Remove the vacuum pipe from the distributor. Remove the valve gear cover breather pipe.

4 Remove the air cleaner as described in **Chapter 2, Section 2:8.** Remove the fuel pump as described in **Chapter 2, Section 2:4.** Remove the carburetter(s) as described in **Chapter 2, Section 2:6** or **Section 2:7.**

5 Uncouple the exhaust pipe from the exhaust manifold.

6 Remove the valve gear cover. Refer to **Section 1:14**, withdraw the camshaft sprocket gear from the camshaft, remove the sprocket gear and fit the timing chain supporting tool ST1720001.

7 Refer to **FIG 1:10**. Starting with cylinder head holding down bolt No. 1, follow the numerical sequence and loosen off the bolts. There are two lengths of bolts.
Identify each bolt to the position from which it is removed.

8 Remove the cylinder head and lift it onto a clean smooth surface which will not damage the joint face. Remove and discard the joint gasket. Clean off old jointing compound from the top face of the front cover.

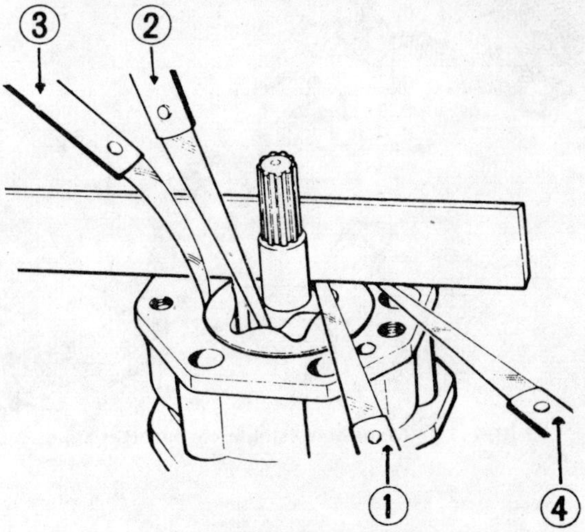

FIG 1:8 Oil pump clearances

Key to Fig 1:8 1 Inner rotor to outer rotor clearance 2 Inner rotor tip clearance 3 Outer rotor to body clearance 4 Rotor to cover clearance

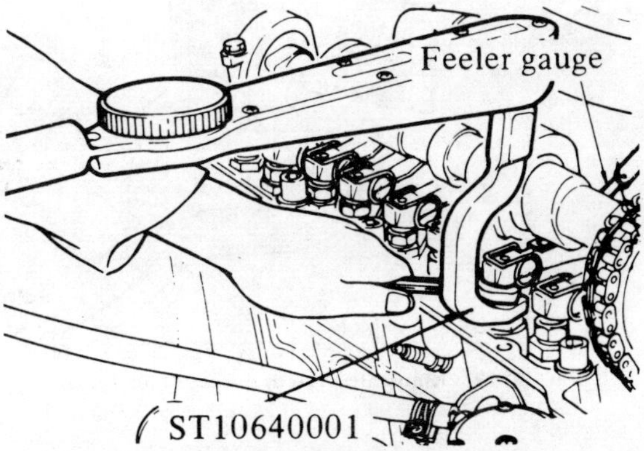

FIG 1:9 Adjusting valve clearances

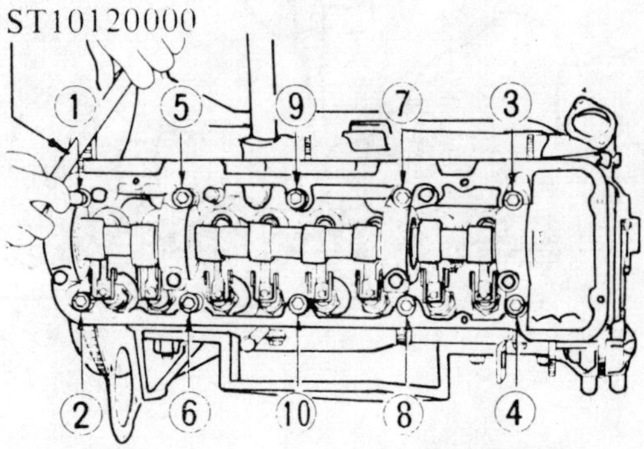

FIG 1:10 Removing cylinder head bolts

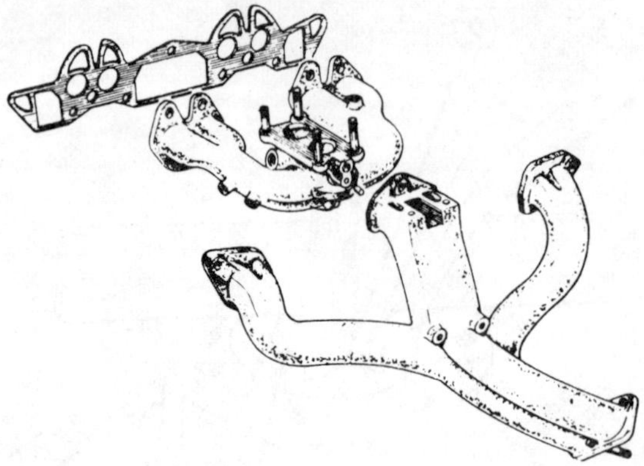

FIG 1:11 Manifolds (single carburetter type)

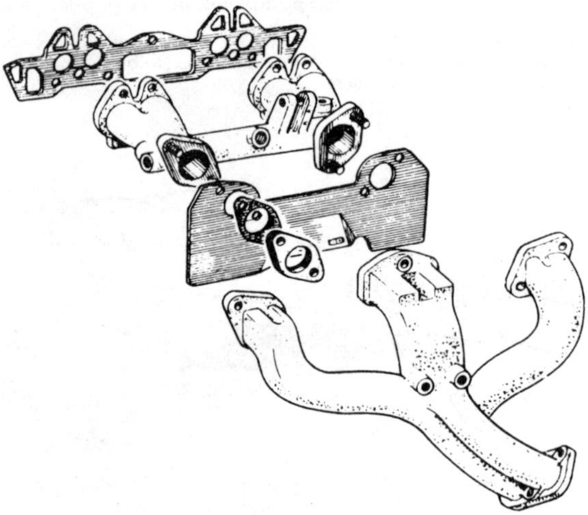

FIG 1:12 Manifolds (twin carburetter type)

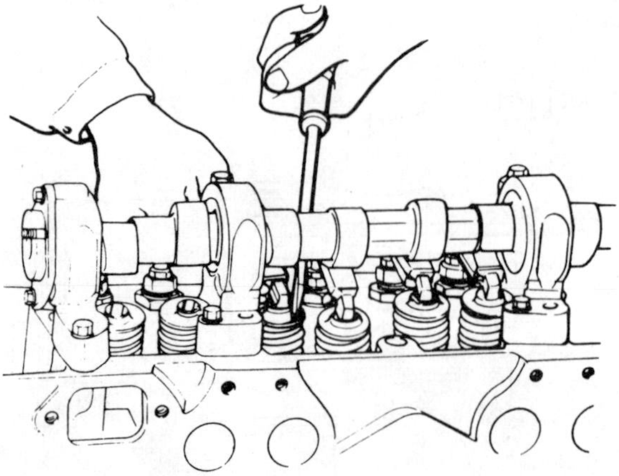

FIG 1:13 Rocker arm removal

Servicing the cylinder head:

Servicing of the cylinder head and valve gear is covered in **Section 1:6**.

Decarbonizing the piston crowns:

With the cylinder head removed, carbon deposits can be scraped from the crowns of the pistons. Use lint free rag in the coolant passages and round the camshaft drive chain to prevent ingress of foreign matter. Avoid the use of sharp tools which could damage the piston surfaces. When turning the engine to bring the piston which is to work on to the top of its stroke, take great care to keep tension on the camshaft drive chain to ensure that it does not become disengaged from the crankshaft sprocket. If the chain should inadvertantly slip from the crankshaft sprocket it will be necessary to refer to the timing procedure which is described in **Section 1:14**. Bring the piston which is to be worked on to the top of its stroke, work 'dry' (do not use paraffin) and remove the dislodged carbon carefully.

Fitment:

Refer to **Section 1:14. Bring the crankshaft to the datum position** at which the camshaft sprocket gear was removed from the camshaft in operation 6 of the cylinder head removal procedure.

Use a new cylinder head gasket and ensure that the joint faces of the gasket, head and cylinder block and front cover are clean. Apply jointing compound **only to the top face of the front cover** and not to the block or head faces.

Refitment is the reverse of the dismantling sequence. Tighten the cylinder head holding down bolts in three stages and, at each stage starting with bolt No. 10, follow the **inverse** numerical sequence to that shown in **FIG 1:10**. Firstly torque tighten all bolts to 28 lb ft (4 kgm), secondly to 43 lb ft (6 kgm) and finally to 47 to 61 lb ft (6.5 to 8.5 kgm). On completion of the refitment, adjust the valve clearances as described in **Section 1:4**.

600 miles (1000 km) after refitting the cylinder head, retighten the holding down bolts to the third stage torque figure. Follow the inverse numerical sequence to that shown in **FIG 1:10**.

1:6 Servicing the cylinder head

Removal and refitment of the cylinder head is described in **Section 1:5**.

Manifolds:

Remove the manifolds if the cylinder head is to be fully serviced. The components of the two types of manifolds are shown in **FIGS 1:11** and **1:12**. Use new gaskets when refitting and torque tighten the retaining nuts to 5.8 to 8.7 lb ft (.8 to 1.2 kgm).

Combustion chambers:

Before removing the valves, decarbonize the combustion chambers and valve heads. Decarbonizing at this stage protects the valve seats. Use a scraper and wire brush and avoid the use of sharply pointed tools. Be careful not to damage the joint face.

Rocker arms:

Remove the rocker arm springs, back off the pivot pillar locknuts, turn the pillars to increase the rocker arm to cam clearances until, when each valve is depressed against its spring load (using a screwdriver as shown in **FIG 1:13**), the rocker arm can be withdrawn. Collect the valve rocker guides. Ensure that the camshaft and not the cam faces are used as the fulcrums for the screwdriver.

Check that the rocker arm pads which contact the cams are not excessively worn. Similarly check the pivot recesses and the pivot pillars.

Camshaft:

Removal of the camshaft is described in **Section 1:14. Do not remove the camshaft bearing brackets.**

Valves and valve springs, removal:

A cylinder set of valves, spring seats, springs, collets rocker arms, etc., is shown in **FIG 1:14**. Use a suitable valve spring compressing tool (the official tool is ST12070000), compress each assembly in turn, remove the collets and spring seats and withdraw the valves. Unless new valves are being fitted, identify each valve to the position from which it was removed.

Valves:

FIG 1:15 gives the dimensions of new valves. Valve seat face blemishes which are minor may be corrected by lapping the valves to their seats. If necessary, valve seat faces may be reground provided that the seat face to head dimension at full valve diameter is not reduced below .020 inch (.5 mm). Pitting or cratering of the ends of the valve stems may be corrected by grinding provided that the length of the valve is not reduced by more than .020 inch (.5 mm).

Valve springs:

Springs should be square to within .063 inch (1.6 mm). The free length of the outer springs should be 1.968 inch (49.98 mm) and of the inner springs, 1.766 inch (44.85 mm). The valve spring rates differ for engines fitted with a single carburetter as against those fitted to twin carburetter engines. Check the springs against the rates given in the following tabulation.

	Valve spring rates, lb/inch (kg/mm)	
Spring	*Single carburetter*	*Twin carburetter*
Inlet, Outer ..	89 (1.59)	93 (1.66)
Inner ..	55.8 (1.0)	58.4 (1.04)
Exhaust, Outer ..	93 (1.66)	93 (1.66)
Inner ..	58.4 (1.04)	58.4 (1.04)

Valve seats:

Minor seat face blemishes may be corrected by lapping the valves to their seats. Seats which are too burned or worn to be corrected by lapping may be recut using tool ST11650001 which uses the valve guide as an axis. If new guides are required, they must be fitted as described later in this Section, before using this cutting tool. If the original valve seat inserts cannot be salvaged in this way, they may be machined out and new standard or oversize seat inserts shrunk in.

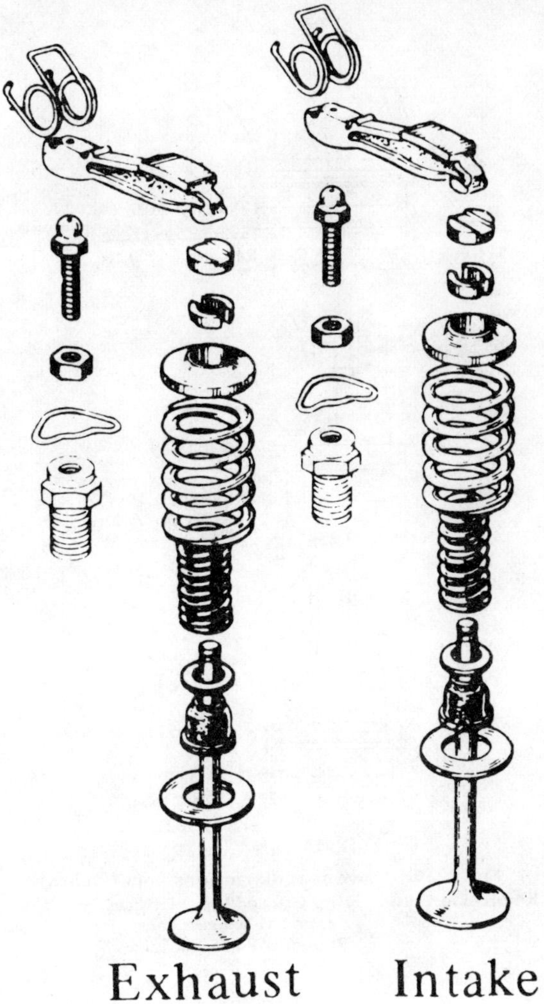

FIG 1:14 Valve gear components

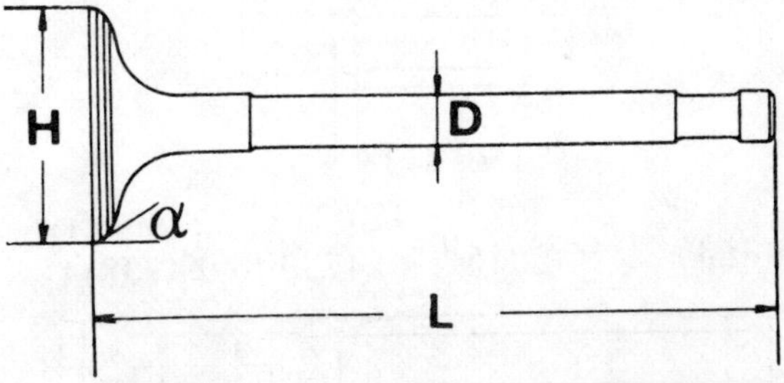

FIG 1:15 Valve dimensions, inches (mm)

Key to Fig 1:15 **H**, inlet (L16 and L18) 1.654 to 1.661 inch (42.0 to 42.2 mm) **H**, exhaust (L16) 1.299 to 1.307 inch (33.0 to 33.2 mm) **H**, exhaust (L18) 1.378 to 1.386 inch (35.0 to 35.2 mm) **L**, inlet (L16 and L18) 4.524 to 5.535 inch (114.9 to 115.2 mm) **L**, exhaust (L16 and L18) 4.555 to 4.567 inch (115.7 to 116.0 mm) **D**, inlet (L16 and L18) .3136 to .3142 inch (7.965 to 7.980 mm) **D**, exhaust (L16 and L18) .3128 to .3134 inch (7.945 to 7.960 mm) **d**, seat angle (L16 and L18) 45½ deg.

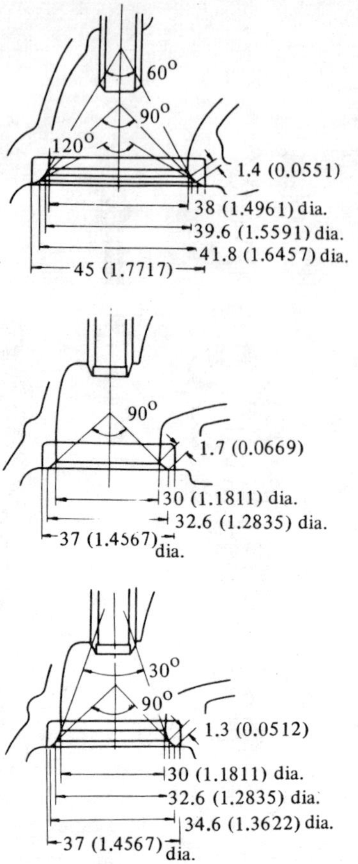

FIG 1:16 Valve seat dimensions, mm (inches)

Key to Fig 1:16 Top L16 and L18 inlet valves
Centre L16 exhaust valves
Bottom L18 exhaust valves

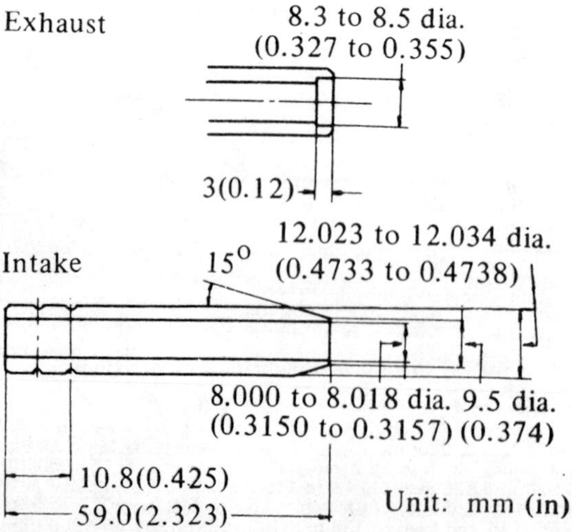

FIG 1:17 Standard valve guide dimensions, mm (inches)

Fitting valve seat inserts:

Standard and .020 inch (.5 mm) oversize seat inserts are available. When machining out the old insert(s), work to the dimensions given in the tabulation quoted later for a standard or an oversize insert as may apply. Ensure that the machined diameter is concentric with the valve guide and do not bore below the depth of the original insert. Heat the cylinder head to 150° to 200°C (300° to 390°F), fit the new insert and ensure that it bottoms completely in the recess. The shrinkage interference is .0025 to .0038 inch (.064 to .096 mm) for exhaust valve inserts and .0032 to .0044 inch (.081 to .113 mm) for inlet valve inserts. Cut and grind the seat face(s) to the angles and dimensions given in **FIG 1:16**.

Valve seat		*Insert recess diameter*
Inlet, Standard	. .	1.7717 to 1.7723 inch (45.000 to 45.016 mm)
Oversize	. .	1.7913 to 1.7920 inch (45.500 to 45.516 mm)
Exhaust, Standard	. .	1.4567 to 1.4573 inch (37.000 to 37.016 mm)
Oversize	. .	1.4764 to 1.4770 inch (37.500 to 37.516 mm)

Valve guides:

The dimensions of standard valve guides are given in **FIG 1:17**. Normal valve stem to guide clearances are .0008 to .0021 inch (.020 to .053 mm) for inlet valves and .0016 to .0029 inch (.040 to .073 mm) for exhaust valves. The maximum acceptable increase in clearance is .004 inch (.1 mm) for both inlet and exhaust positions.

Excessively worn guides should be pressed out (a load of approximately 2 tons will be required) from the combustion chamber side and towards the top of the head and the location reamed to take either a new standard guide or, if the location is oversize, a .008 inch (.2 mm) oversize guide. Heat the cylinder head to 150° to 200°C (300° to 390°F) and fit the new guides which must project by .4173 inch (10.6 mm) above the location faces as shown in **FIG 1:18**. The shrinkage interference required is .0009 to .0017 inch (.022 to .044 mm). The reaming diameters (**a** in **FIG 1:18**) for standard and oversize guides are:

Standard	. . . .	.4719 to .4723 inch (11.985 to 11.996 mm)
Oversize	. . . .	.4797 to .4802 inch (12.185 to 12.196 mm)

Cylinder head:

Measured with feeler gauges and a straightedge, the flatness of the joint face should not be more than .004 inch (.1 mm) out of true.

Measure the camshaft bearing bores and the camshaft journal diameters. The standard bearing bore diameter is 1.8898 to 1.8904 inch (48.000 to 48.016 mm) and the standard running clearance is .0015 to .0026 inch (.038 to .066 mm). The wear limit is .004 inch (.1 mm). If the clearance is excessive, a new cylinder head or a new camshaft will be required (or, in extreme cases, both).

Assembly:

Assembly is the reverse of the dismantling sequence. Wet working surfaces with engine oil. Set the rocker to cam clearances as described in **Section 1:4.**

1:7 Removing the engine

It is recommended that the engine and transmission are removed from the vehicle as a unit. Proceed as follows.

1 Disconnect the battery and lift it out of the vehicle. Remove the bonnet as described in **Chapter 13, Section 13:2.**

2 Drain the cooling system as described in **Chapter 4, Section 4:2.** On models fitted with automatic transmission, remove the under cover and disconnect the transmission fluid cooler piping. Remove the radiator as described in **Chapter 4, Section 4:3.**

3 Identify cables and wires before disconnecting them from the starter motor, the alternator, the HT at the ignition coil, the oil pressure transmitter (or switch) and the coolant temperature transmitter.

4 Uncouple the heater piping and the supply line to the fuel pump.

5 Refer to **Chapter 2, Section 2:6** or **Section 2:7** and release the carburetter choke and throttle controls.

6 Disconnect the handbrake cable at the adjuster. Remove the transmission control linkage. In the case of 3-speed gearbox models, disconnect the cross-shaft from the control linkage and the shaft from the second to top lever. In the case of floor gearchange models, detach the rubber boot, remove the locknut from the lever and remove the lever. In the case of automatic transmission models, uncouple the control lever from the selector rod.

7 Refer to **Chapter 5, Section 5:5** and remove the clutch actuating cylinder.

8 Uncouple the speedometer cable at the transmission. Disconnect the reversing light switch wiring and, in the case of automatic transmission models, disconnect the wiring from the kick-down switch and from the starting inhibitor switch.

9 Uncouple the front exhaust pipe from the exhaust manifold. Refer to **Chapter 13, Section 13:12** and dismount the front and centre exhaust pipes as an assembly.

10 Refer to **Chapter 8, Section 8:3** and uncouple the propeller shaft from the transmission. Plug the rear of the extension housing to prevent oil leakage.

11 Attach a suitable sling and just take the weight of the engine and transmission assembly. Refer to **Section 1:20.** Remove the rear mounting assembly. Remove the bolts which attach the front mountings to the suspension member.

12 Raise the engine, tilt and withdraw it forwards and upwards. Lower it onto a suitable cradle.

1:8 Dismantlind the engine

If the operator is not a skilled automobile engineer, it is suggested that he will find much useful information in Hints on Maintenance and Overhaul which is included in the Appendix at the end of this manual and that he should refer to it before proceeding with the engine dismantling procedure operations.

1 Remove the engine and transmission as described in **Section 1:7.** Separate the transmission from the engine as described in **Chapter 6, Section 6:3** or, in the case of automatic transmission models, in **Chapter 7, Section 7:5.** Drain off the engine oil if this was not done at an earlier stage.

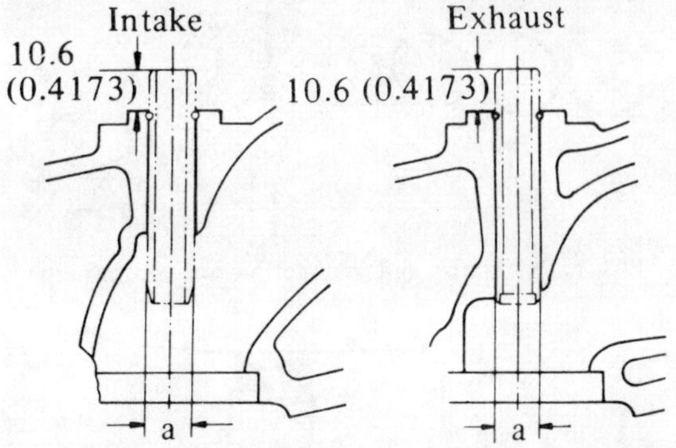

FIG 1:18 Valve guide fitment dimensions (L16 and L18)

Key to Fig 1:18 a Reaming diameter (standard and oversize reaming diameters are quoted in the text)

2 Refer to **Chapter 12, Sections 12:3** and **12:4** and remove the starter motor and the alternator. Refer to **Chapter 4, Sections 4:4** and **4:5** and remove the fan, drive pulley, water pump, thermostat housing and coolant temperature transmitter.

3 Withdraw the dipstick. Remove the oil filter, the distributor and the oil pump as described in **Section 1:3.** Remove the oil pressure transmitter (or switch if fitted).

4 Remove the HT cables and the sparking plugs.

5 Remove the fuel pump, the air cleaner and the carburetter(s) as described in **Chapter 2, Sections 2:4, 2:8** and either **2:6** or **2:7.** Remove the intake and exhaust manifolds.

6 Remove the front engine mountings. Remove the cylinder head as described in **Section 1:5** and dismantle the rockers and valves as described in **Section 1:6.**

7 Invert the engine. Make sure that the cylinder block face is positioned on a clean surface which will not damage the joint face. Remove the sump and oil strainer as described in **Section 1:16.**

8 Refer to **Section 1:14.** Remove the front cover, the camshaft drive chain tensioner and the drive chain. Remove the oil thrower, the skew gear and the sprocket gear from the crankshaft.

9 Remove the clutch or, in the case of automatic transmission models, the torque converter as described in **Chapter 5, Section 5:3** or **Chapter 7, Section 7:5** and dismount the flywheel as described in **Section 1:12.** Remove the rear cover.

10 Remove the piston/connecting rod assemblies and big-end bearings as described in **Section 1:9** and separate the pistons from the rods.

11 Remove the rear oil seal, the crankshaft and the main bearings as described in **Section 1:13.** Remove the baffle plate and gauze net.

12 After cleaning and washing off components in petrol, use compressed air to dry them off and, to prevent rust, brush clean engine oil over all steel parts.

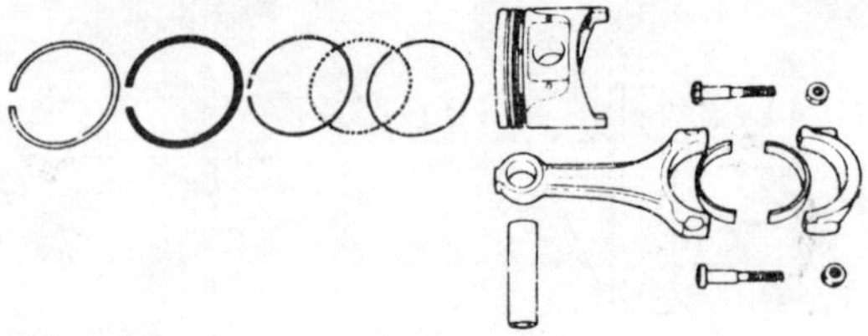

FIG 1:19 Piston and connecting rod components

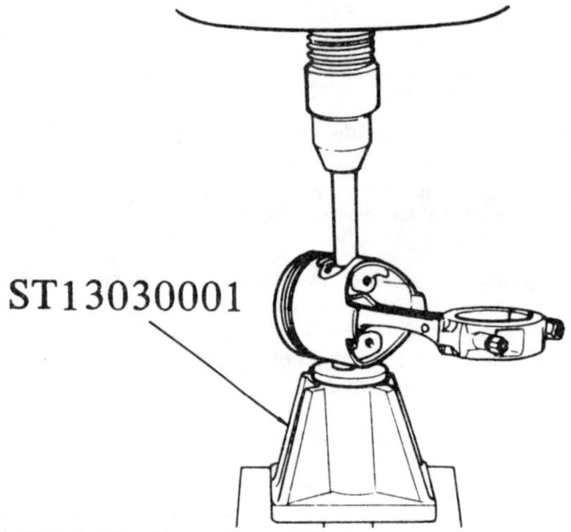

FIG 1:20 Removing and fitting a gudgeon pin

1:9 Removing and refitting pistons and connecting rods:

Pistons and rods can be removed and refitted with the engine in the vehicle after removing the sump and oil strainer and the cylinder head. The components of a piston and connecting rod assembly are shown in **FIG 1:19**.

Removal:

1 Drain off the engine oil as described in **Section 1:2**. Remove the sump and oil strainer as described in **Section 1:16** and remove the cylinder head as described in **Section 1:5**.

2 If all the pistons and rods are to be renewed, it will be found convenient to deal with them in pairs and, by turning the crankshaft, to bring the pair which are to be worked on to BDC. Ensure that, when turning the crankshaft, the camshaft drive chain does not slip from the crankshaft pulley (see **Section 1:5**).

3 Unless new rods are being fitted, confirm that the caps are marked to their rods and, if they are not, mark them. Remove the nuts from the cap retaining bolts, lift off the caps and the half bearing shells.

4 Remove the connecting rod bolts, push the pistons up their bores so that the remaining half shells may be removed and, after scraping away and ridge of carbon from round the top of the bores, push the rods and pistons up and out of the bores.

5 If the same rods are to be refitted, wire each cap to its rod and identify them to the cylinder from which they were removed. If the bearing shells are serviceable, identify them to their rods.

It will be appreciated that big-end bearing shells can be examined and changed without removing the pistons and rods and, consequently, without the need to remove the cylinder head. With that exception, proceed as described earlier but, when the connecting rod cap has been removed, lift the connecting rod off the crankpin and withdraw the second half shell. If there has been a big-end bearing failure, the crankpin must be examined for possible damage and for transfer of bearing metal to its surface. The oilway in the crankshaft must be checked to ensure that it is not obstructed.

Gudgeon pin removal:

The gudgeon pin is a tight press fit in the little-end of the rod. Press out the gudgeon pin and separate the piston from its rod. **FIG 1:20** shows fixture ST13030001 being used for this operation.

Servicing pistons and connecting rods:

Refer to **Sections 1:10** and **1:11**. Suitability of the original pistons or selections of new pistons to suit the cylinder bore is described in **Section 1:10**. Suitability of the original connecting rods and selection of big-end bearings to suit standard or reground crankpins is covered in **Section 1:11**.

Fitment:

Assemble the pistons to the connecting rods by pressing the gudgeon pins (wetted with engine oil) into the rod little-ends as shown in **FIG 1:20**. Use the same fixture (ST13030001) as when dismantling and ensure that, as shown in **FIG 1:21**, the connecting rod oil hole is towards the thrust side of the piston. A suitable piston ring clamp will be required (the official tool is EM347000). The pistons, rings, cylinder bores and big-end bearings must be liberally wetted with engine oil. Ensure that the fronts of the pistons (see **FIG 1:21** for the identification notches) are towards the front of the engine. The remaining operations are the reverse of the removal sequence. Torque tighten the cap retaining bolt nuts to 33 to 40 lb ft (4.5 to 5.5 kgm).

1:10 Pistons and rings

Pistons must be fitted with the notch mark (see **FIG 1:21**) towards the front of the engine. Pistons have three ring grooves. The two top grooves carry compression rings which must be fitted the correct way up (with the mark upwards). The top ring is chromium plated on its peripheral surface; the second compression ring has a peripheral surface which has more taper than has the top ring. The third groove carries a composite type of oil control ring; the upper rail is the same as the lower rail.

The gudgeon pin is a push fit in the piston and a tight press fit in the little-end of the connecting rod.

Overhaul:

The condition and extent of wear of the cylinder bores will decide whether pistons which may themselves be serviceable should be refitted. Before a conclusion can be reached regarding the pistons, the cylinder bores must be dealt with as described in **Section 1:17**. On completion of any necessary work on the cylinder bores, it will be evident whether new standard size pistons or oversize pistons will be required or whether the original pistons may be refitted. If the original pistons are being refitted, ensure that they are matched to their original positions as identified during dismantling.

Piston sizes:

The standard position at which piston skirts should be measured is .787 inch (20 mm) below the centre line of the gudgeon pin bore. The desired piston to cylinder bore diametrical clearance is .0010 to .0018 inch (.025 to .045 mm) and, with a recommended wear limit of .0079 inch (.2 mm), the maximum acceptable piston to bore clearance is .0089 to .0097 inch (.23 to .25 mm).

In addition to replacement standard size pistons, five sizes of oversize pistons are available for L16 engines and two sizes for L18 engines. Dimensions and tolerances of standard and oversize pistons are listed in **Technical Data** in the Appendix.

If a worn cylinder block has had sleeves fitted and these are finally honed to the relevant standard bore diameter, new standard size pistons may be fitted.

Where piston and cylinder bore measuring equipment is not available, the piston to bore clearance may be checked approximately by following the procedure shown in **FIG 1 : 22**. Standard clearance nominally requires a load of .44 to 3.3 lb (.2 to 1.5 kg) to withdraw a feeler gauge of .0016 inch (.04 mm) thickness from between the piston and the cylinder bore. If the load is less than the range quoted, the clearance is excessive. If the load is greater than the range quoted, the clearance is less than that which is acceptable.

Piston rings:

Piston rings are available to suit standard and all sizes of oversize pistons. If the original pistons are serviceable and diametrically suitable for refitment, check the ring groove clearances.

The standard clearance for the top compression ring is .0016 to .0031 inch (.04 to .08 mm) for L16 engine pistons and .0018 to .0031 inch (.045 to .08 mm) for L18 engine pistons. The standard clearance for the second compression ring is .0012 to .0028 inch (.03 to .07 mm) for both engines. The side clearance wear limit for both rings in both engines is .0039 inch (.1 mm).

Standard ring gaps, measured well down the bore and with the ring square in the bore (use a piston, crown down, to position the rings in the bore), are given in the following tabulation. The maximum acceptable wear limit is .0394 inch (1 mm) in all cases.

Standard piston ring gaps

Ring	*L16 engine*	*L18 engine*
Top compression	.0098 to .0157 inch (.25 to .40 mm)	.0138 to .0217 inch (.35 to .55 mm)
Second compression	.0059 to .0118 inch (.15 to .30 mm)	.0118 to .0197 inch (.30 to .50 mm)
Oil control	.0118 to .0354 inch (.30 to .90 mm)	.0118 to .0354 inch (.30 to .90 mm)

Fit compression rings with their gaps opposite to each other and at about 45 deg. to the gudgeon pin axis. Align the oil control ring gap with that of the top compression ring.

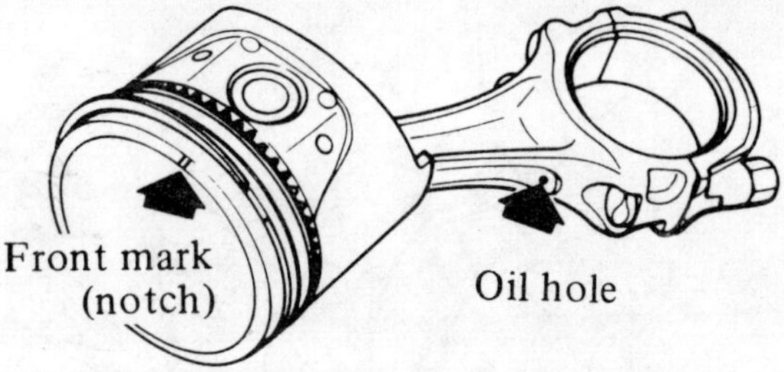

FIG 1:21 Assembled connecting rod and piston

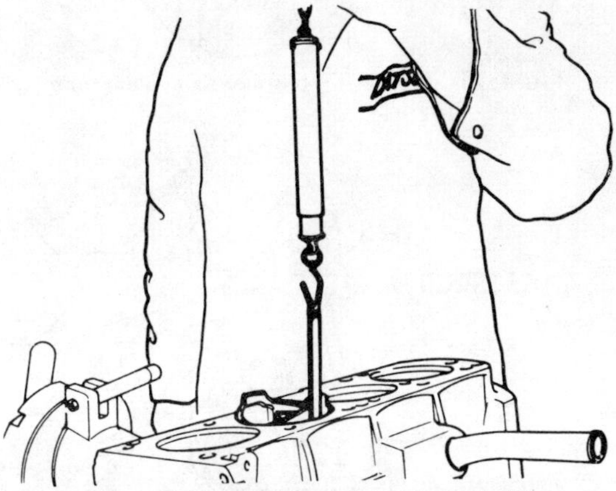

FIG 1:22 Measuring piston to bore fit

Gudgeon pin:

The standard gudgeon pin to piston bore clearance at ambient temperature is .0003 to .0004 inch (.008 to .010 mm). This corresponds to a firm thumb push fit.

The standard interference fit for a gudgeon pin in a connecting rod little-end bore is .0006 to .0013 inch (.015 to .033 mm). This corresponds to a tight press fit (see **Section 1 : 9**).

1:11 Connecting rods

A connecting rod and a pair of bearing shells are included in **FIG 1 : 19**. The rods are steel forgings. The big-end caps are retained by two nuts and bolts. The bearings are pressure lubricated and oil jet holes in the big-ends (see **FIG 1 : 21**) direct oil onto the thrust side of the cylinder bores. Gudgeon pins are a tight press fit in the little-ends.

Overhaul:

No attempt should be made to salvage a damaged connecting rod which should be rejected and replaced by a new part. Check rods which are apparently serviceable for bend and twist.

Bend and twist:

Neither bend nor twist should exceed .002 inch (.05 mm) per 3.94 inch (100 mm) of rod length. It is not advisable to attempt to correct these distortions and, if bend or twist is excessive, new rod(s) should be obtained.

A replacement rod should be within .25 oz (7 grm) weight of the rod which it is to replace.

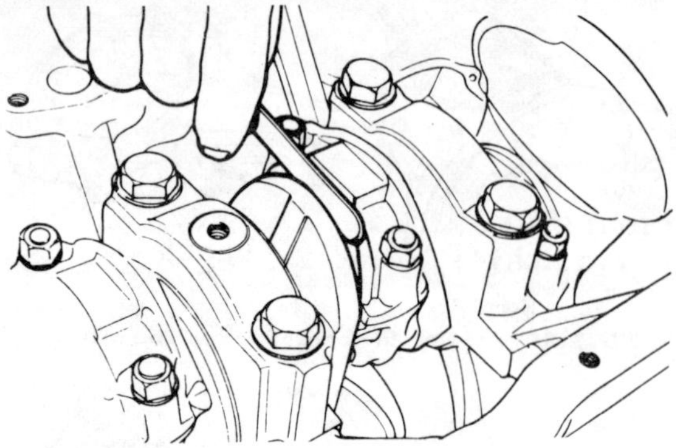

FIG 1:23 Measuring big-end axial clearance

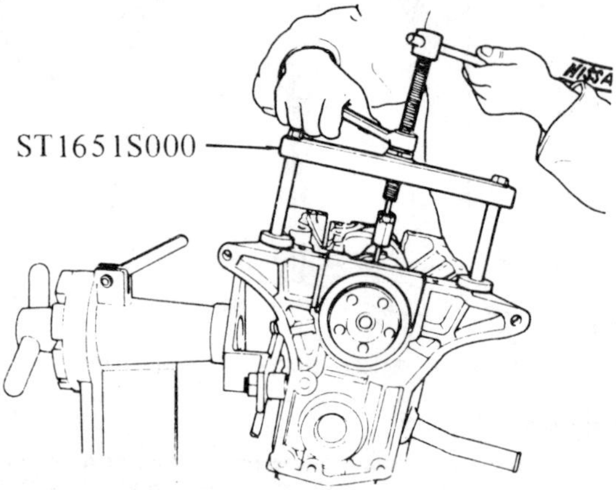

FIG 1:24 Removing rear main bearing cap

Side clearance:

When assembled to its crankpin (with the correct size of bearings fitted), side clearance should not exceed .016 inch (.4 mm). Standard side clearance is from .008 to .012 inch (.2 to .3 mm). **FIG 1:23** shows this clearance being checked.

Big-end bearings:

Before new shell bearings of appropriate size can be obtained, any regrinding of the crankpins which may be necessary must have been completed. Big-end bearings must therefore be selected after dealing with the crankshaft as described in **Section 1:13**. The desired big-end bearing to crankpin clearance is .0010 to .0022 inch (.025 to .055 mm) and, with worn components, .0047 inch (.1 mm) should be taken as a maximum.

Plastigage may be used to check the clearance and the procedure is described in **Section 1:13.** Tighten the rod cap retaining nuts to a torque of 33 to 40 lb ft (4.5 to 5.5 kgm) and **do not turn the rod on the crankpin while making the Plastigage check.** Remove the cap and note the clearance indicated. If the clearance is outside the range specified, select thicker or thinner shells and repeat the Plastigage check. In addition to standard bearing shells, six sizes of undersize (thicker than standard) shells are available to suit undersize crankpins. Details are tabulated in **Section 1:13**. When selection of the shells is finalized, identify them to their connecting rods and to their crankpins and, as described in **Section 1:13**, check that the 'bearing crush' is within the range of .006 to .0018 inch (.015 to .045 mm).

1:12 Flywheel

The flywheel is spigotted to the crankshaft and is retained by set bolts. A ring gear with which the starter pinion engages is shrunk onto its periphery. The flywheel carries the clutch assembly (see **Chapter 5**) or, in the case of automatic transmission models, the torque converter (see **Chapter 7**).

Removal and fitment:

Dismount the clutch or the torque converter as described in **Chapter 5, Section 5:3** or **Chapter 7, Section 7:5**, withdraw the retaining bolts. Dismount the flywheel.

When fitting, ensure that the crankshaft and flywheel faces are clean and free of burrs. Torque tighten the retaining bolts to 101 to 116 lb ft (14 to 16 kgm).

Note that, in the case of automatic transmission models, the flywheel (or drive plate) retaining bolts are provided with tabwashers to lock them.

Ring gear:

Minor damage to the teeth of the ring gear will require no more than blending. If a few teeth are badly chipped or broken, they may be built up by welding and dressed by hand to a close approximation of the tooth profile. Severe damage is best dealt with by machining off the old ring gear and shrinking on a new one or by fitting a new flywheel. To shrink fit a new ring gear requires that it be heated to 180° to 220°C (356° to 428°F).

1:13 Crankshaft and main bearings

The crankshaft is a steel forging. It runs in five main bearings and, at the flywheel end, carries an oil seal. The forward oil seal is carried in the front cover (see **Section 1:14**). The flywheel (or, in the case of automatic transmission models, the drive plate) is spigotted to the crankshaft and retained by set bolts. The forward end of the crankshaft carries the camshaft drive sprocket gear, the skew gear which drives the oil pump and the distributor and the pulley which drives the belt for the cooling fan and water pump and the alternator.

The shell type main bearings are retained by detachable caps which are secured by bolts to the cylinder block. The crankshaft end float is controlled by **flanged** bearing shells at the **centre** bearing position.

Crankshaft removal:

Check that the bearing caps are identified to their locations. Remove the retaining bolts and withdraw the caps. Puller ST1651S000 will be required, as shown in **FIG 1:24**, to remove the centre and rear caps. Lift out the shaft. Unless new bearings are being fitted, identify the bearing shells to the positions from which they were removed.

Overhaul:

Wash off the crankshaft in petrol and dry thoroughly. Check that the oil passages are clear and clean. Apply engine oil lightly to preclude rusting. Check the condition of the oil seal. It will be prudent to renew this irrespective of its apparent condition.

Mount the crankshaft in V-blocks and, using a dial indicator gauge, check the amount of bend at the centre bearing journal. Bend (half the indicator reading) over a complete revolution of the crankshaft should not exceed .004 inch (.1 mm).

Check the main bearing and crankpin journals for scores and cracks. If the shaft is acceptable from this point of view, measure the journal diameters at a number of points (round and along) so that, for each, a picture of ovality and taper may be obtained.

Main bearing and crankpin journal dimensions are quoted in **Technical Data** in the Appendix. The manufacturing tolerance for both ovality and taper is .004 inch (.01 mm). Correct by regrinding if either exceeds .0012 inch (.03 mm).

Crankpin journals:

Refer to **Section 1:11**. There are, in addition to standard big-end bearing shells, six sizes of undersize (thicker than standard) shells to cater for reground crankpin journals. The following tabulation lists the standard and undersize shells.

Crankpin diameter	*Bearing shell thickness*	*Bearing size*
1.9670 to 1.9675	.0588 to .0593	STD
(49.961 to 49.974)	(1.493 to 1.506)	
1.9646 to 1.9651	.0600 to .0605	6
(49.901 to 49.914)	(1.523 to 1.536)	
1.9622 to 1.9628	.0611 to .0617	12
(49.841 to 49.854)	(1.553 to 1.566)	
1.9571 to 1.9576	.0637 to .0642	25
(49.711 to 49.724)	(1.618 to 1.631)	
1.9473 to 1.9478	.0686 to .0691	50
(49.461 to 49.474)	(1.743 to 1.756)	
1.9374 to 1.9379	.0735 to .0741	75
(49.211 to 49.224)	(1.868 to 1.881)	
1.9276 to 1.9281	.0785 to .0790	100
(48.961 to 48.974)	(1.993 to 2.006)	

Dimensions are given in inches with mm equivalents in brackets.

Main journals:

There are, in addition to standard size main bearing shells, four sizes of undersize (thicker than standard) shells to cater for undersize main journals. Standard and undersize shells and journal diameters are listed in the following tabulation. Dimensions are in inches with mm equivalents in brackets.

Main journal diameter	*Bearing shell thickness*	*Bearing size*
2.1631 to 2.1636	.0717 to .0722	STD
(54.942 to 54.955)	(1.822 to 1.835)	
2.1532 to 2.1537	.0767 to .0772	25
(54.692 to 54.705)	(1.947 to 1.960)	
2.1434 to 2.1439	.0816 to .0821	50
(54.442 to 54.455)	(2.072 to 2.085)	
2.1335 to 2.1341	.0865 to .0870	75
(54.192 to 54.205)	(2.197 to 2.210)	
2.1237 to 2.1242	.0914 to .0919	100
(53.942 to 53.955)	(2.322 to 2.335)	

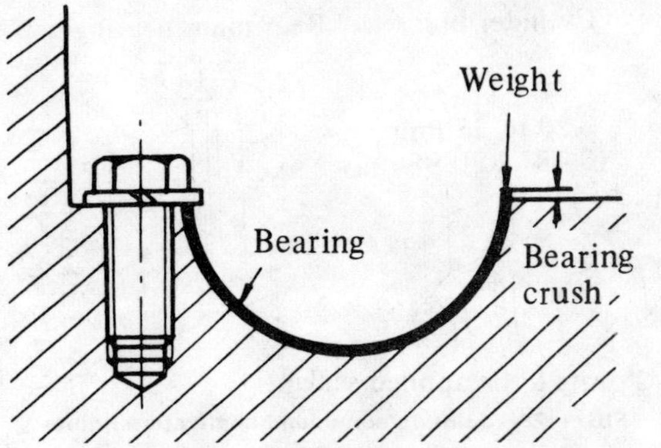

FIG 1:25 Measuring bearing 'crush'

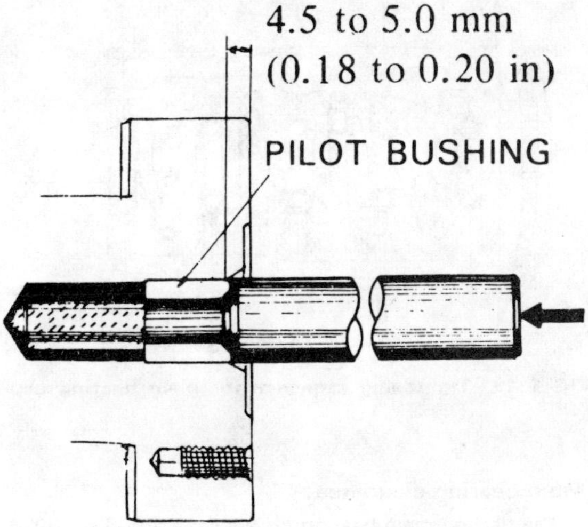

FIG 1:26 Fitting pilot bush

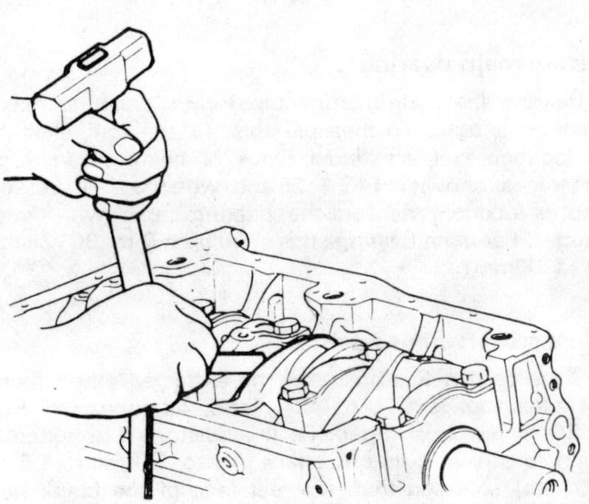
FIG 1:27 Measuring crankshaft axial clearance

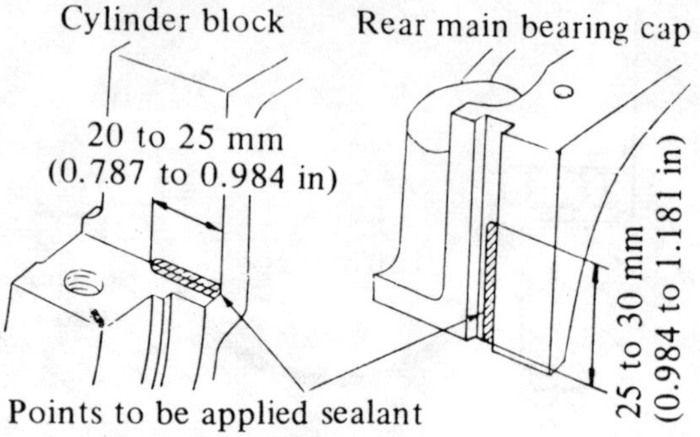

FIG 1:28 Jointing compound application points

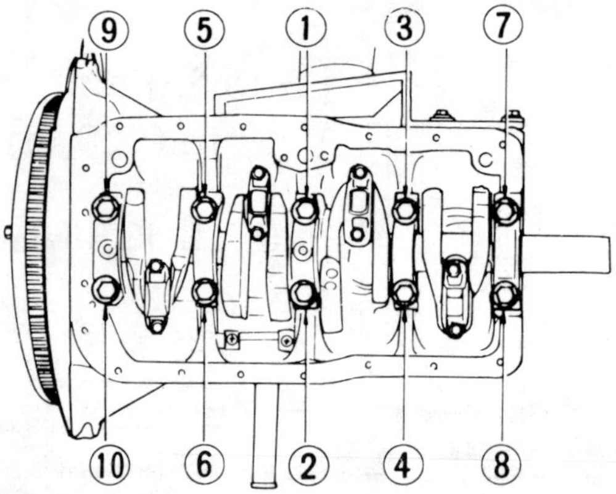

FIG 1:29 Tightening sequence for main bearing cap bolts

Main bearing clearance:

The desired main bearing clearance is .0008 to .0024 inch (.02 to .062 mm) with a wear limit of .0047 inch (.12 mm). These clearances apply to all main bearings and are best measured by using Plastigage as described at the end of this Section.

Fitting main bearings:

Bearing shells are manufactured with 'crush' to make them fit snugly. To measure this, fit the half shell to its location in the cylinder block or bearing cap, lock one joint as shown in **FIG 1:25** and, with the shell pressed into its location, measure the 'bearing crush' with feeler gauges. For main bearings this should be 0 to .0012 inch (0 to .03mm).

Clutch shaft pilot bush:

If necessary, this bush may be extracted (the official extractor tool is ST16610001) and, as shown in **FIG 1:26**, a new bush fitted. Fit the bush with its external diameter dry and its outer face .18 to .20 inch (4.5 to 5.0 mm) recessed from the rear face of the crankshaft flange.

Crankshaft fitment:

Install the baffle and gauze net to the crankcase before fitting the crankshaft. Without using jointing compound at the rear bearing, install the crankshaft temporarily as described later and, as shown in **FIG 1:27**, check that the end float is within the range of .0020 to .0071 inch (.05 to .18 mm). If this is in order, proceed with the final installation of the crankshaft as follows:

1 Position the bearing shells in the crankcase locations. Apply jointing compound to each side of the rear main bearing cap and each corner of the cylinder block as shown in **FIG 1:28**.

2 Apply engine oil to the crankshaft journals and bearing shells. Fit the upper shells. Install the crankshaft. Fit the caps and lower shells. Ensure that the caps are the correct way round (arrow marks towards the front).

3 Fit the cap retaining bolts. Apply axial pressure to the shaft in both directions before beginning to tighten the bolts.

4 Refer to **FIG 1:29**. Follow the numerical sequence and, in several stages graudally tighten the cap retaining bolts. Torque tighten them finally to 33 to 40 lb ft (4.5 to 5.5 kgm) and confirm that the shaft turns smoothly.

5 Apply jointing compound to the side seals and, as shown in **FIG 1:30**, drive these seals into position. Apply lithium grease to the lip of the rear oil seal and, using tool ST15310000, fit the seal. Fit the rear cover.

Plastigage:

The installed clearance of main and big-end bearings is best measured by using this proprietary 'thread' as follows:

1 Select the diameter of Plastigage which covers the clearance to be measured. Place a length of thread on the relevant journal across its full width and slightly off centre.

2 Fit the bearing shell and cap and tighten the retaining bolts or nuts to the torque specified for that bearing. The Plastigage will be squeezed down to the clearance dimension of the bearing and its width will increase. Do not turn the crankshaft or connecting rod while the Plastigage is in position.

3 Remove the bearing cap and shell and, using the Plastigage scale which is provided with the thread, read off the clearance. The maximum width of the Plastigage will indicate the minimum bearing clearance and the minimum width, the maximum clearance.

1:14 Camshaft and camshaft drive

The camshaft is chain driven from a sprocket gear at the forward end of the crankshaft. The duplex chain is controlled by a straight chain guide at the lefthand side (the taut side of the chain) and a curved guide at the righthand side. An automatic chain tensioner is provided immediately below the curved chain guide. These components are shown in **FIGS 1:31** and **1:32**. Timing adjustment is made at the camshaft sprocket gear. The camshaft runs in three pressure lubricated plain bearings which are carried in brackets **(which must not be dismounted)** on the cylinder head.

Precautions must be taken when removing and fitting the cylinder head to preclude the valve heads from fouling the crowns of the pistons. This can occur if, after uncoupling the camshaft sprocket, the crankshaft is rotated before the cylinder head is removed.

Uncoupling and recoupling the camshaft:

The following procedure applies when the cylinder head is to be removed and refitted but the camshaft drive is not being dismantled.

Turn the crankshaft to bring all pistons to approximately half-stroke (e.g. No. 1 cylinder valves closed and No. 1 piston coming up the compression stroke). Mark a mating sprocket tooth and chain link as a datum for recoupling and leave the crankshaft in this position until after the cylinder head has been removed.

Remove the bolt which retains the fuel pump actuating cam and the sprocket gear to the camshaft. Withdraw the cam. Mark which of the three holes in the sprocket is engaged with the driving dowel on the camshaft. Keeping the chain tensioned, disengage the chain from the sprocket and, as shown in **FIG 1:33**, fit the chain supporting tool ST17420001. Following removal of the cylinder head as described in **Section 1:5**, the crankshaft may be rotated as necessary. Ensure, however, that the chain does not become disengaged from the crankshaft sprocket gear while doing so.

Before refitting the cylinder head, bring the crankshaft back to the datum position. After fitting the head, remove the chain supporting tool, engage the marked sprocket tooth and the marked chain link and fit the sprocket so that the marked hole engages the driving dowel. Fit the fuel pump actuating cam. Fit the retaining bolt and torque tighten it to 87 to 116 lb ft (12 to 16 kgm).

Dismantling the camshaft drive:

With the engine removed from the vehicle, uncouple the camshaft sprocket as described earlier except for marking the sprocket and chain. Remove the cylinder head as described in **Section 1:5**.

Remove the bolt which retains the belt drive pulley to the crankshaft, pull off the pulley and collect the driving key. Remove the front cover. Remove the chain tensioner and the chain guides. Remove the chain. Remove the oil thrower and pull off the skew gear and the sprocket gear. Collect the driving keys. Withdraw the oil seal from the front cover and clean off old gasket material and jointing compound from the faces of the cover and from the cylinder block.

Assembling and timing the camshaft drive:

Before fitting the cylinder head, fit the crankshaft sprocket and bring No. 1 piston to the TDC of its compression stroke (the crankshaft sprocket drive key will be at the top). Turn the camshaft to the position at which both No. 1 cylinder valves are closed (the driving dowel will be at the top). Check that none of the valves will foul the pistons and, **without turning either the crankshaft or the camshaft from this set position,** fit the cylinder head. Proceed as described in **Section 1:5** but, at this stage, temporarily tighten only the two centre holding down bolts (Nos. 9 and 10 in **FIG 1:10**) to 14.5 lb ft (2 kgm).

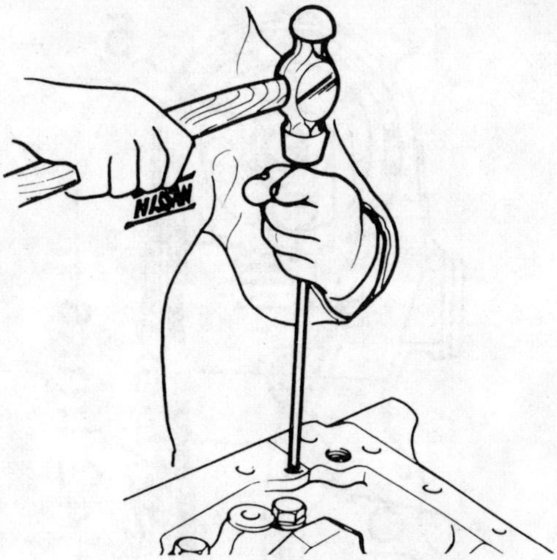

FIG 1:30 Driving in side oil seal

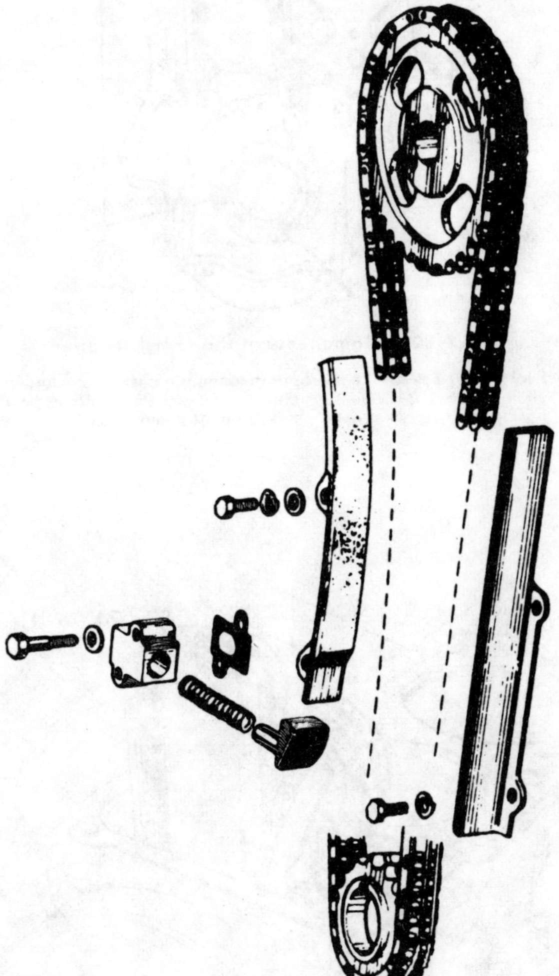

FIG 1:31 Components of the camshaft drive

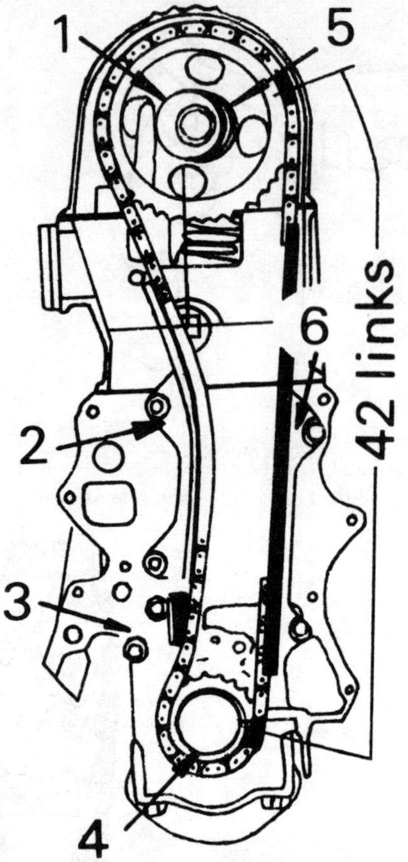

FIG 1:32 Components of the camshaft drive

Key to Fig 1:32 1 Fuel pump actuating cam 2 Curved chain guide 3 Chain tensioner 4 Crankshaft sproket gear 5 Camshaft sprocket gear 6 Straight chain guide

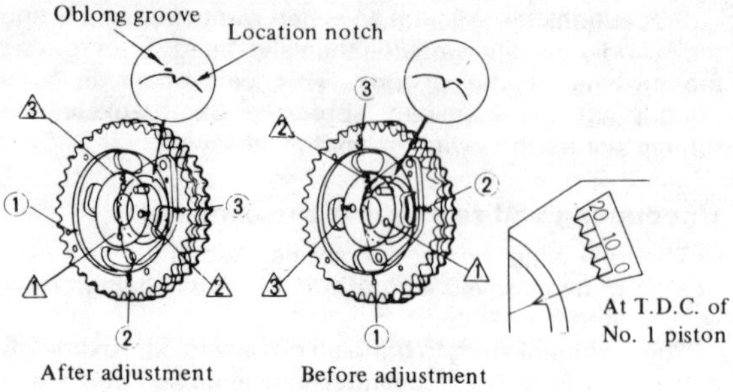

FIG 1:34 Camshaft timing adjustment

Key to Fig 1:34 1, 2 and 3 (in circles) Timing marks 1, 2 and 3 (in triangles) Dowel locating holes

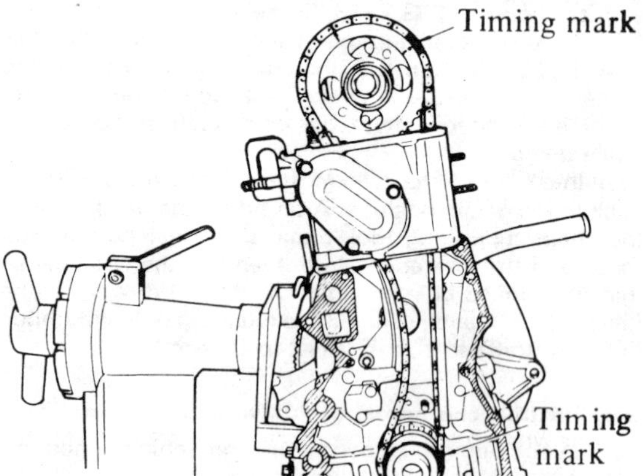

FIG 1:35 The assembled camshaft drive. The timing marks are 42 links apart

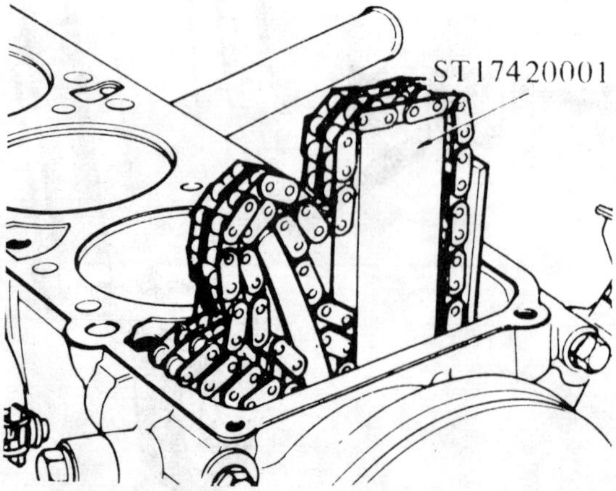

FIG 1:33 Supporting the camshaft drive chain

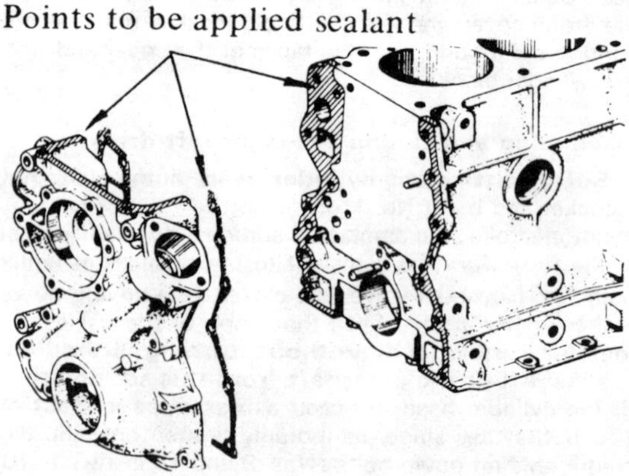

FIG 1:36 Fittind the front cover

The camshaft drive chain is provided with two marks which are 42 links apart. Refer to **FIG 1:32**. Fit the chain so that the lower mark aligns with the timing mark on the crankshaft sprocket gear. Engage the camshaft sprocket gear so that the centre (No. 2) of the three timing marks aligns with the upper chain mark. Fit the sprocket to the camshaft with the centre hole (No. 2 in **FIG 1:34**) engaging the dowel. Fit the chain guides and the tensioner. The assembly will now be as shown in **FIG 1:35**.

Fit the skew gear. Fit a new oil seal to the front cover. Use new gaskets and, using jointing compound over the areas shown in **FIG 1:36**, fit the front cover. Apply lithium grease to the lip of the oil seal, fit the pulley and torque tighten the retaining bolt to 87 to 116 lb ft (12 to 16 kgm). Torque tighten the front cover retaining bolts to 7.2 to 11.6 lb ft (1 to 1.6 kgm) in the case of .315 inch (M8) bolts and to 2.9 to 5.8 lb ft (.4 to .8 kgm) in the case of .236 inch (M6) bolts. Proceed now to tighten all the cylinder head holding down bolts in three stages and to the torques specified as described in **Section 1:5**.

Camshaft:

Four different camshafts are fitted to the engines covered by this manual depending upon the engine capacity (L16 or L18) and whether a single carburetter or twin carburetters are fitted. Details of valve timings are given in **Technical Data** in the Appendix. If a replacement camshaft is required, ensure that the correct type is obtained.

Camshaft removal and fitment:

The camshaft may be withdrawn after removing the two bolts which retain the locating plate to the forward bearing bracket. When refitting, torque tighten these two retaining bolts to 4.3 to 6.5 lb ft (.6 to .9 kgm). The camshaft end play should be within .003 to .015 inch (.08 to .40 mm).

Adjustment for chain stretch:

With a chain that has stretched, the camshaft will 'lag' and instead of the oblong groove in the location plate being substantially in the centre of the location notch when the crankshaft is **precisely at TDC** on the No. 1 compression stroke, it will be to the right of the notch as shown in the righthand (before adjustment) diagram in **FIG 1:34**.

Adjustment is made by uncoupling the camshaft sprocket as described earlier, rephasing the chain mark to align with the No. 3 sprocket timing mark and engaging the sprocket No. 3 hole with the camshaft dowel. The vernier effect 'advances' the camshaft and, as shown in the lefthand (after adjustment) diagram in **FIG 1:34**, the oblong groove will be to the left of the notch. This adjustment corresponds to 2 deg. of camshaft rotation (4 deg. crankshaft). If it is not sufficient to 'correct' the camshaft timing, a new chain should be obtained and set to the standard (No. 2 mark and dowel hole) timing.

The No. 1 hole and timing mark are not relevant to L16 or L18 engines.

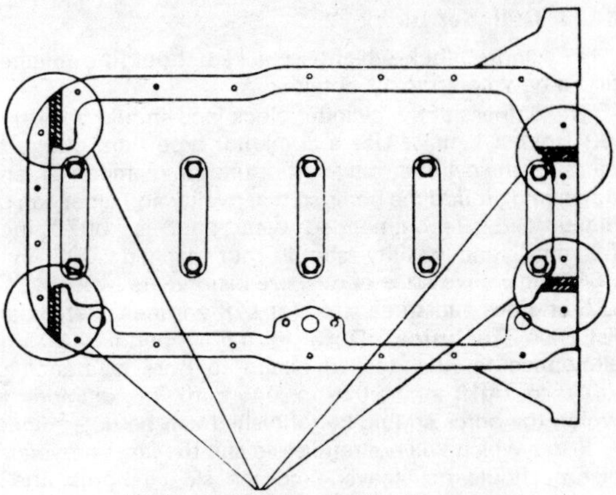

FIG 1:37 Jointing compound application points

1:15 Distributor drive

A skew gear at the forward end of the crankshaft drives the oil pump and distributor. Removal and fitment of the distributor drive is covered in **Section 1:3**.

1:16 Oil sump and strainer

The sump is retained to the crankcase/cylinder block by set bolts. A gasket is fitted between the joint faces. The oil pump draws oil from the sump through a suction pipe and gauze strainer unit which is retained to the crankcase/cylinder block by two bolts (see **FIG 1:1**). The sump is provided with an oil drain plug which should be tightened to a torque of 14 to 22 lb ft (2 to 3 kgm). The engine oil changing procedure is described in **Section 1:2**.

Use a brush and petrol to clean the strainer (cloth may contaminate the gauze). Remove old gasket material and jointing compound from the sump and crankcase faces. When refitting, use a new gasket, refer to **FIG 1:37** and ensure particularly that jointing compound is applied to the four stepped points in the joint face. Tighten the retaining bolts crosswise starting at the centre and working to the front and rear. Finally torque tighten the bolts to 4.3 to 6.3 lb ft (.6 to .9 kgm).

FIG 1:38 The engine/transmission mountings

Key to Fig 1:38 Top Front mountings Bottom Rear mounting and crossmember

1:17 Cylinder block

A cylinder block which is cracked should be rejected and a new component obtained.

The flatness of the cylinder block face should be within .004 inch (.1 mm). Use a comaritor type bore guage to measure the cylinder bores. Measure the diameter up and down and around the bores so that ovality and taper can be determined. Recommended wear limit is .0078 inch (.2 mm) and ovality should not exceed .006 inch (.015 mm). Five sizes of oversize pistons are available for L16 engines and three sizes for L18 engines. Details are listed in **Technical Data** in the Appendix. Making allowance for the desired piston to bore clearance of .0010 to .0018 inch (.025 to .045 mm), the diameter to which the bores should be refinished can be determined.

Bores which will not refinish to suit the largest oversize piston should be sleeved and the sleeve bores finally honed to suit standard pistons. Three sizes of sleeves are available and details are given in **Technical Data.** Fit sleeves with an interference of .0031 to .0035 inch (.08 to .09 mm).

Remove all traces of old gasket material and jointing compound from the front cover face and from the oil sump face. Ensure that all oil passages are clear and clean. Probe and flush the coolant passages.

1:18 Assembling the engine

Assembly instructions are given in the text of each relevant Section. These are largely the dismantling procedures in reverse but, as this may not always be so, the point should be checked against the text. It is then simply a matter of tackling the work in the correct sequence, of applying normal automobile engineering practice, fitting only Datsun replacement parts, using new gaskets and ensuring that joints are well made as it may not easily be possible to rectify an oil leak which is not discovered until assembly and installation of the engine has been completed. For this reason also, scrutinize carefully the condition of oil seals and recognize that it will usually be prudent to fit new.

If the engine has been completely dismantled, the assembly sequence will be the reverse of that described in **Section 1:8**. If the engine has been only partially dismantled, reverse the sequence which was followed when dismantling.

Assemble working parts wetted with engine oil and use oil resistant sealing compound where called for in the text. Refer to sectional texts and to **Technical Data** for torque tightening figures, clearances and end play figures. At each stage of assembly, check where relevant the free rotation of the assembly or component. Ensure that all nuts and bolts are correctly tightened and, where applicable, properly locked. Time the ignition as described in **Chapter 3, Section 3:6**.

1:19 Installing the engine

Refitting the engine and transmission into the vehicle is basically the reverse of the removal sequence described in **Section 1:7**. The quantities of engine oil, transmission oil and antifreeze solution which will be required are given in **Technical Data** in the Appendix under Capacities.

When the installation has been completed and all systems made serviceable, run the engine up to normal temperature and adjust the carburetter(s) as described in **Chapter 2, Section 2:6** or **Section 2:7.** Check over and correct any leaks from pipe or hose connections.

600 miles (1000 km) after reassembling and installing the engine, retighten the cylinder head holding down bolts as described in **Section 1:5**. Check the valve clearances as described in **Section 1:4**.

1:20 Engine mountings

The engine and transmission assembly is carried on three flexible mountings. The two forward mountings are bracketed to the crankcase/cylinder block. The rear mounting is at the transmission rear extension housing and is supported by a crossmember which is itself attached to the chassis by two flexible mountings. The front mountings, the rear mounting, the crossmember and its mountings are shown in **FIG 1:38**. The following procedures relate to operation 11 of the engine removal sequence described in **Section 1:7**.

Rear mounting, removal and fitment:

Support the transmission with a jack, remove the two bolts from the rear mounting at the transmission, remove the two bolts from each side which attach the crossmember to the chassis and detach the mounting assembly.

Fitment is the reverse of this sequence. Ensure that the **F** mark on the rubber of the rear mounting faces the front of the vehicle.

Front mountings, removal and fitment:

With the engine weight supported on suitable lifting tackle, remove the two bolts which attach each mounting to the suspension member. Following removal of the engine, remove the nut which attaches each mounting unit to its engine bracket and dismount the units.

Fitment is this sequence in reverse. Ensure that the single notch in the rubber is towards the front of the vehicle (the two notches will be towards the rear).

1:21 Emission control system

Emission control is fitted only to models which are exported to countries in which emission control requirements are mandatory.

This Section covers the closed breather system and the air injection system. Further aspects of emission control (carburation and ignition) are covered in **Chapter 2, Section 2:9** and **Chapter 3, Section 3:8.** It must be stressed that the effectiveness of the emission control systems is dependent upon proper maintenance.

Closed breather system:

When operating efficiently, this system precludes the escape of noxious engine fumes (blow-by gases and oil fumes) from the engine by ensuring that they are either prevented from leaking from the engine or are ducted into the engine intake and consumed by the engine. The system is illustrated in **FIG 1:39**.

Blow-by gas is ducted via the variable orifice valve 1 to the intake manifold from the crankcase. At partial openings of the throttle, the intake manifold depression

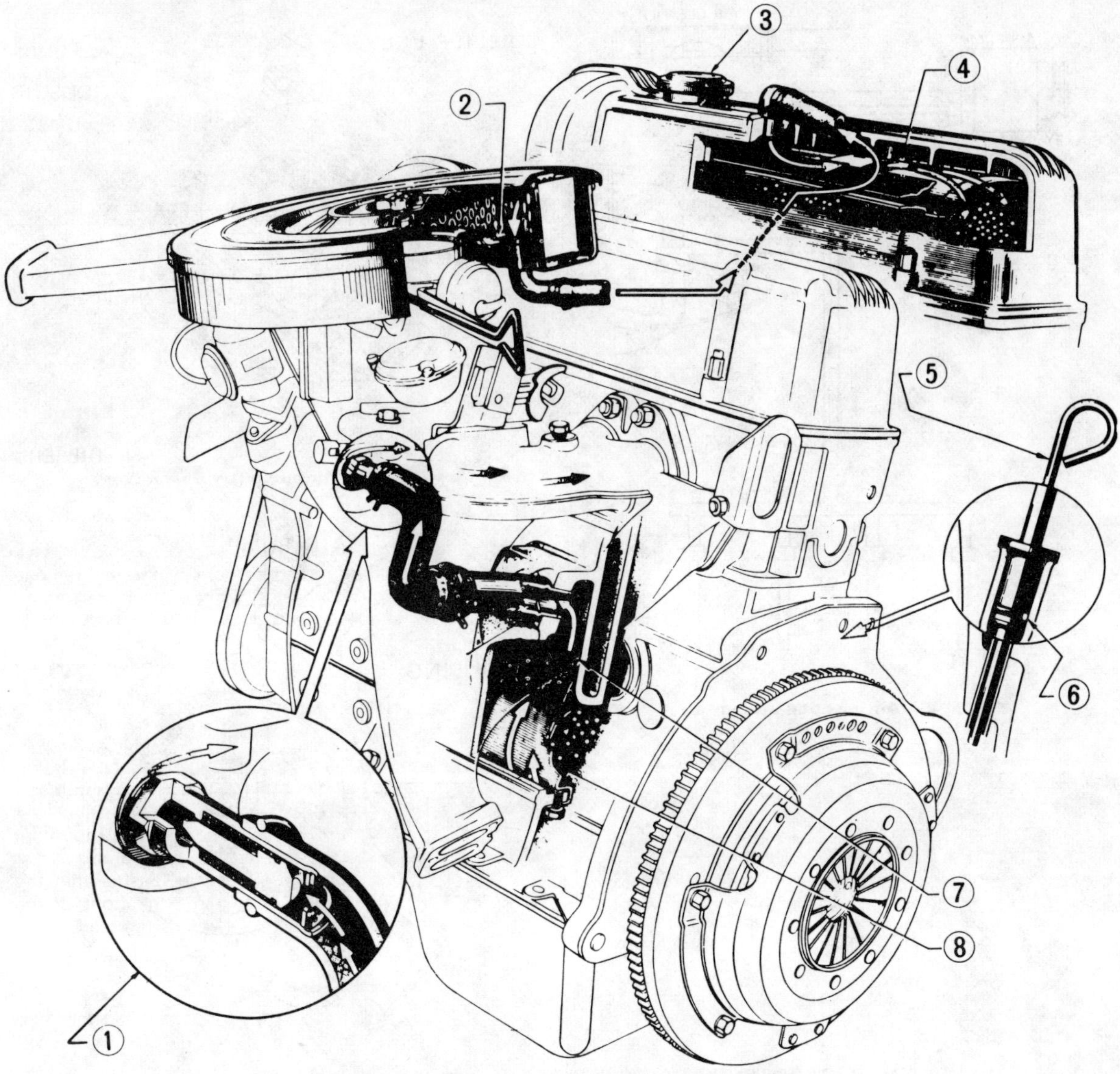

FIG 1 : 39 The closed crankcase breather system

Key to Fig 1 : 39 1 Ventilation control valve 2 Flame trap 3 Filler cap (sealed type) 4 Baffle plate 5 Dipstick 6 'O' ring (dipstick seal) 7 Oil separator 8 Baffle plate

draws the gases through this valve. The capacity of the valve under these conditions is normally adequate to deal with blow-by gas plus some ventilation air which is drawn from the clean side of the air cleaner via the flame trap 2 into the valve gear cover, past the baffle plate 4 and into the crankcase. Under full throttle conditions, however, the manifold depression is insufficient to draw the gases through the valve 1 and the gas flow is reversed and reaches the intake manifold through the valve gear cover, the flame trap 2 and the clean side of the air cleaner.

To preclude blow-by gas from leaving the engine other than via the hose to valve 1 or the hose to the flame trap 2, the oil filler cap 3 is a sealed type and the dipstick is sealed by the 'O' ring 6. Engine oil is prevented from being drawn into the intake manifold or into the cleaner by baffle plates 4 and 8 and oil separator 7.

Servicing the closed breather system:

Once a year or every 12,000 miles (18,000 km), remove the two hoses, blow them through with compressed air and check their condition. If a hose cannot be unblocked or if its condition has deteriorated, discard it and fit a new replacement. The ventilation control valve cannot be overhauled or repaired by an owner and if it is defective (the testing procedure is given later), fit a new assembly.

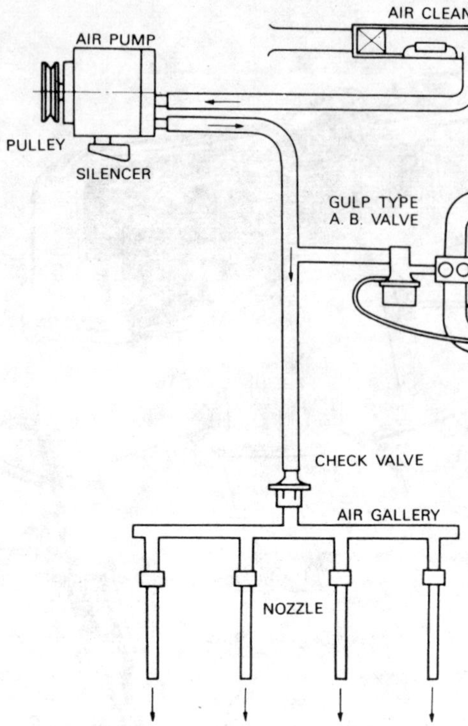

FIG 1:40 Air injection system

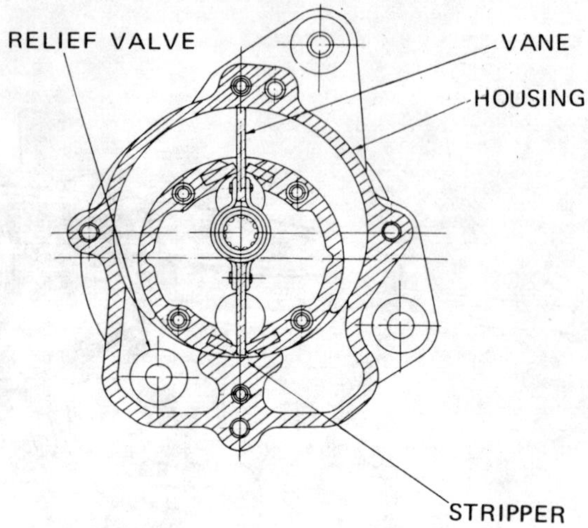

FIG 1:42 Air pump (two-vane type)

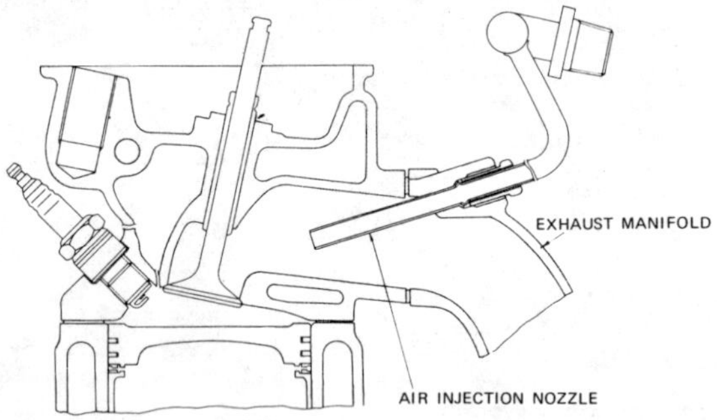

FIG 1:41 Cross-section through cylinder head and exhaust manifold showing positioning of air nozzles

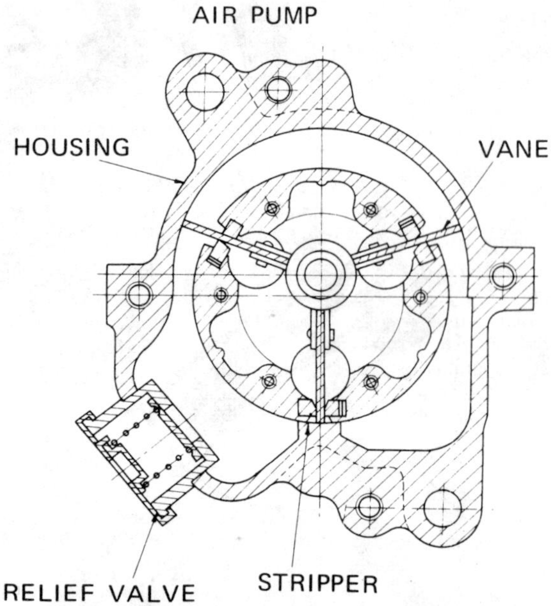

FIG 1:43 Air pump (three-vane type)

Ventilation control valve testing:

With the engine running at idling speed, remove the hose from the ventilation control valve. If the valve is operating, the hissing noise of ambient air passing into the valve will be heard and, when a finger is placed over the valve inlet, a strong vacuum will be felt.

A defective valve cannot be repaired by an owner.

Air injection system:

By injecting air into the incandescent exhaust gases immediately after they leave the cylinders, further combustion of unburned hydrocarbons is encouraged and the final exhaust gases when they leave the exhaust pipe contain less carbon monoxide (but more of the less noxious carbon dioxide) than would be the case with untreated gases.

The system is illustrated diagrammatically in **FIG 1:40**. The air pump, which may be either a two-vane or a three-vane type, draws clean air from the air cleaner and delivers it at a pressure of approximately 5 lb/sq inch (.35 kg/sq cm) to nozzles adjacent to the exhaust valves. The positioning of these nozzles is shown in **FIG 1:41**. To preclude reverse flow of exhaust gases (this can occur if the pump should become defective; if its belt drive should fail or if the pump relief valve should become inoperative), a check valve (a non-return valve) is fitted immediately before the air gallery. When the throttle is closed suddenly, an unburned (excessively rich) petrol/air mixture may be exhausted from the cylinders and, by being diluted by air from the nozzles, will become a combustible mixture. On subsequent opening of the throttle, it will be ignited by the hot exhaust gases and a backfire will result. To minimize the risk of this occurring, the intake manifold is provided with a connection to the pressure air via a gulp type anti-backfire valve. This valve opens when the throttle is suddenly closed (actuated by the sudden increase in depression in the intake manifold) and admits air from the compressor to the intake manifold. The resulting weakening of the petrol/air mixture burns more readily in the cylinders and is expelled as normal exhaust gas.

Air pump:

Every 3000 miles (5000 km), check and adjust if necessary the tension of the air pump drive belt. The tensioning procedure is similar to that described in **Chapter 12, Section 12:4** for tensioning the alternator/cooling fan belt drive.

A vertical cross-section through a two-vane type pump is shown in **FIG 1:42** and a vertical cross-section through a three-vane type pump is shown in **FIG 1:43**. These positive displacement pumps are permanently lubricated and require no routine maintenance. Neither type of pump can be overhauled or repaired by an owner and a defective pump should be exchanged for a new unit.

Check (non-return) valve:

This non-return valve will become inoperative if the spring should fail or if the seal should deteriorate. The valve cannot be overhauled or repaired by an owner and a defective unit must be exchanged for a new unit. The serviceability of the valve should be checked at intervals of 12,000 miles (20,000 km).

Anti-backfire valve:

The operation of the valve is actuated by depression in the intake manifold via a small bore pipe. The condition and air tightness of this pipe and its connections is important.

A defective anti-backfire valve cannot be overhauled or repaired by an owner and must be exchanged for a new unit.

Air injection nozzles:

Every 12,000 miles (20,000 km), check the tightness of the air nozzle retaining nuts by torque tightening them to 36 to 43 lb ft (5 to 6 kgm). Also check the tightness of the pipe connections.

To avoid possible damage to the nozzles, withdraw them from the exhaust manifold before removing the manifolds when decarbonizing or dismantling the engine. When decarbonizing the cylinder head, check the nozzles for cracking or burning and renew as necessary. Clean carbon deposits from the nozzles and check that they are unobstructed and that their seats in the exhaust manifold are clean and clear of carbon.

General:

Check the condition of the hoses and pipelines every 12,000 miles (20,000 km), tighten all connections and renew any pipes or hoses which may have deteriorated.

Since emission control standards are strict in those countries in which the requirements are mandatory, any actual or suspected malfunctioning which the owner cannot readily and effectively correct himself should be referred to an Agent who is equipped to diagnoze and rectify faults and able to supply any replacement parts which may be required.

If pistons, rings or cylinder bores are worn and in need of overhaul, the closed circuit breather system should not be expected to deal with the excessive blow-by gases which will be passing the pistons.

1:22 Fault diagnosis

(a) Engine will not start

1 Defective coil
2 Faulty distributor capacitor
3 Dirty, pitted or incorrectly set contact breaker points
4 Ignition leads loose or insulation faulty
5 Water on sparking plug leads
6 Battery discharged, corrosion of terminals
7 Faulty or jammed starter motor
8 Sparking plug leads wrongly connected
9 Vapour lock in fuel line
10 Defective fuel pump
11 Defective carburetter choke control
12 Blocked fuel filter or carburetter jet(s)
13 Valves leaking or sticking
14 Camshaft or ignition timing incorrect

(b) Engine stalls

1 Check 1, 2, 3, 4, 5, 10, 12 and 13 in (a)
2 Sparking plugs defective or gaps incorrect
3 Excessively retarded ignition
4 Mixture too weak
5 Water in fuel system
6 Fuel tank air vent blocked
7 Incorrect valve clearances

(c) Engine idles badly

1 Check 2 and 7 in (b)
2 Air leak at manifold joint
3 Carburetter adjustment incorrect
4 Air leak at carburetter joint
5 Mixture too rich
6 Worn piston rings
7 Worn valve stems or guides
8 Weak exhaust valve springs
9 Anti-backfire valve defective (emission control models)

(d) Engine misfires

1 Check 1, 2, 3, 4, 5, 8, 10, 12, 13 and 14 in (a)
2 Weak or broken valve springs

(e) Engine overheats (see **Chapter 4**)

(f) Compression low

1 Check 13 in (a); 6 and 7 in (c) and 2 in (d)
2 Worn piston ring grooves
3 Scored or worn cylinder bores

(g) Engine lacks power

1 Check 3, 10, 13 and 14 in (a); 2, 3, 4 and 7 in (b); 6 and 7 in (c); 2 in (d) and check (f)
2 Leaking joint gasket
3 Dirty sparking plugs
4 Automatic advance defective

(h) Burnt valves or seats

1 Check 13 in (a)
2 Excessive carbon deposits round valve seats

(j) Sticking valves

1 Check 2 in (d)
2 Bent valve stem
3 Scored valve stem or guide
4 Incorrect valve clearance

(k) Excessive cylinder wear

1 Check 11 in (a)
2 Lack of oil
3 Dirty oil
4 Piston rings gummed up or broken
5 Connecting rod bent

(l) Excessive oil consumption

1 Check 6 and 7 in (c); 3 in (f) and check (k)
2 Ring gaps over limit
3 Oil return holes in pistons choked
4 Oil level too high
5 External oil leaks

(m) Main or big-end bearing failure

1 Check 2, 3 and 5 in (k)
2 Restricted oilways
3 Worn main journal or crankpin
4 Loose bearing cap(s)
5 Extremely low oil pressure

(n) Internal water leakage

1 Failed cylinder head gasket
2 Cracked cylinder head
3 Cracked cylinder block

(o) Poor coolant circulation (see **Chapter 4**)

(p) High fuel consumption (see **Chapter 2**)

(q) Engine vibration

1 Loose alternator
2 Engine mountings loose or defective
3 Cooling fan out of balance
4 Misfiring due to mixture, ignition or mechanical fault
5 Air cleaner loose
6 Air pump loose (emission control models)

CHAPTER 2

THE FUEL SYSTEM

2:1 **Description**
2:2 **Maintenance**
2:3 **Filter**
2:4 **Pump**
2:5 **Controls**
2:6 **Single (twin venturi) carburetter**
2:7 **Twin (SU type) carburetters**
2:8 **Air cleaner**
2:9 **Emission control system**
2:10 **Fault diagnosis**

2:1 Description

The mechanical diaphragm type fuel pump is mounted at the righthand side of the cylinder head and is operated by an eccentric at the forward end of the camshaft. This eccentric is in direct contact with the pump rocker arm.

Fuel is drawn from the 12 gallons ($11\frac{1}{2}$ gallons on estate car models) capacity tank through a disposable element type filter. The fuel tank is provided with a float and arm type of contents transmitter which operates electrically in conjunction with a fuel gauge which is mounted in the instrument panel and operates only when the ignition is switched on.

A single (Zenith/Stromberg type) downdraught carburetter is fitted to engines have a compression ratio of 8.5:1. The carburetters differ between L16 and L18 engines and also between models which have manual and automatic transmissions. The series numbering and the relevant differences between these four series of carburetters are quoted in **Technical Data** in the Appendix. The difference between the carburetter fitted to manual transmission models and that fitted to automatic transmission models is that the latter is provided with a dashpot which is interlocked with the primary throttle valve through a link mechanism. This device prevents the engine from stalling when the accelerator is suddenly released and, from a predetermined throttle position, allows the primary throttle to close very gradually.

Twin (SU type) variable venturi carburetters are fitted to engines which have a compression ratio of 9.5:1. These are sidedraught carburetters in which the venturi is varied by a piston which moves vertically in a suction chamber. A taper profiled needle is attached to the base of the upper surface of the venturi and, by rising and falling with the venturi control within a fixed jet, meters the fuel flow. The throttles of the twin carburetters are adjustable in relation to each other so that synchronization of the carburetters can be achieved.

Either a viscous paper or a dry type element may be fitted to the air cleaner canister. The air cleaner fitted to single carburetter models incorporates a thermostatically controlled supplementary air valve which controls excessively rich idling mixture at high under bonnet temperatures.

Models for export to countries in which emission control is mandatory are provided with appropriate special equipment which is covered in **Section 2:9**.

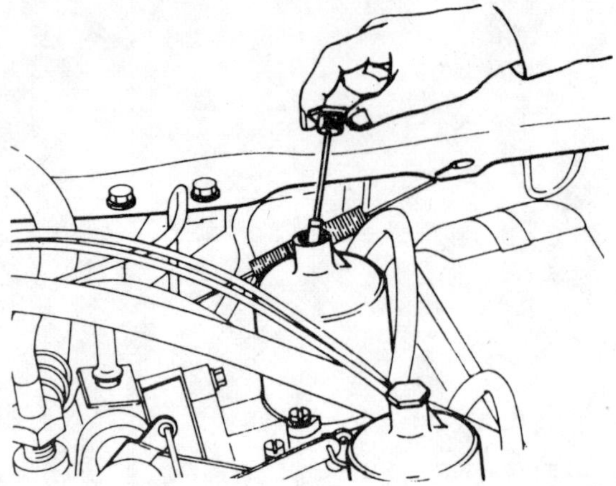

FIG 2:1 Removing the cap nut and plunger (SU type carburetter)

2:2 Maintenance

Fuel lines and connections:

At regular intervals of, say, 3000 miles (5000 km), check the fuel lines and ensure that there are no leaks at the filter, pump or carburetter connections.

Air cleaner:

The maintenance interval differs between models fitted with a 'dry' element and those fitted with a viscous paper type element.

FIG 2:2 Fuel filter

Key to Fig 2:2 1 Filter body 2 Element 3 Cover

Dry type element:

Every 3000 miles (5000 km) or more frequently in dusty terrain, remove the element and clean it off with compressed air. Clean all dust from the canister before refitting the element. Every 24,000 miles (40,000 km), discard the element and fit a new replacement.

Viscous paper type element:

Every 24,000 miles (40,000 km) or more frequently in dusty terrain, renew a viscous paper type element. This type of element cannot be cleaned. Clean all dust from the canister before fitting the new element.

Piston damper (SU type carburetters):

Every 3000 miles (5000 km), refer to **FIG 2:1**, remove the cap nut and plunger and check that the oil level is between the two grooves on the plunger rod. Top up if necessary using a 10W-30 oil. Refit the rod assembly and tighten the cap nut firmly by hand.

Controls:

Every 6000 miles (10,000 km), refer to **Section 2:5** and lubricate the accelerator and choke controls.

Idling speed:

Every 6000 miles (10,000 km) or every 3000 miles (5000 km) in the case of models fitted with emission control equipment, check and adjust the idling speed as described in **Section 2:6, Section 2:7** or **Section 2:9.**

Before carrying out the adjustments, check that valve clearances are correct (see **Chapter 1, Section 1:4**), check that the distributor points gap is correct (see **Chapter 3, Section 3:2** or, in the case of models fitted with emission control equipment, **Section 3:8**), check the ignition timing (see **Chapter 3, Section 3:6**) and set the idling speed with the engine at normal operating temperature.

Model		*Idling speed*	
		Manual	*Autumatic*
Single carburetter	..	600 rev/min	650 rev/min
Twin carburetters	..	650 rev/min	700 rev/min
Emission control	..	700 rev/min	720 rev/min

Fuel filter:

Every 12,000 miles (20,000 km), renew the fuel filter element as described in **Section 2:3**.

2:3 Filter

A cross-section through the fuel filter is shown in **FIG 2:2**. The disposable filter element is a fibre 'mat' and, since the filter body is made of nylon, the element can be viewed and its condition assessed without dismantling the unit.

Renew the element at 12,000 mile (20,000 km) intervals or more frequently if an external examination indicates renewal to be necessary.

Element renewal:

Dismount the filter unit and disconnect the inlet and the outlet pipes. Have a container ready to receive any fuel which may drain from the pipes. Unscrew the top from the body, remove and discard the element. Fit a new element, refit the filter top, reconnect the pipes and fit the unit back into place.

2:4 Pump

The components of the fuel pump are shown in **FIG 2:3**. The pump is mounted on the cylinder head. It is a mechanically operated diaphragm type and is actuated by an eccentric (see **FIGS 1:1** and **1:32**) attached to the front of the camshaft. The spring 13 keeps the outer end of the rocker arm 14 in contact with the camshaft eccentric. The rocker pivots on pin 15. The inner end of the rocker arm engages the rod 8 which is integral with the diaphragm assembly 6 and, when actuated, draws down the diaphragm assembly against the pressure of spring 7. This movement of the flexible diaphragm draws fuel through the inlet pipe 11 and, via the inlet valve, into the pump chamber. The pumping stroke is performed by spring 7 acting upon the lower side of the diaphragm assembly and fuel is forced through the outlet valve and delivered to the carburetter via the outlet pipe 12.

Fuel delivery pressure depends solely upon the load applied by spring 7 and this load is not adjustable. The diaphragm stroke depends upon the amount of undelivered fuel in the pump chamber. If the chamber is full, the rocker will reciprocate idly and the inner end of the arm will not actuate the diaphragm assembly rod. As fuel is used, the diaphragm and rod will rise until again pulled down by the rocker arm. Seal 10 and seal washer 9 prevents oil from reaching the lower side of the diaphragm. The spacer 17 insulates the pump from heat transfer from the cylinder head and gaskets 16 form an oil tight joint between the cylinder head, the spacer and the pump body. The pump upper body is attached to the lower body by six setscrews and the periphery of the diaphragm is retained between the faces of the upper and lower bodies.

Testing:

Low fuel pump pressure and low capacity or high fuel pump pressure can account for faults ranging from weak mixture to carburetter flooding and high fuel consumption. Testing is performed with the pump installed and with the engine at normal operating temperature and running at a speed slightly higher than idling. It is important, before carrying out tests on the pump, to confirm that the fuel pipes are not restricted and that the fuel filter is not limiting fuel flow because of a dirty element.

To carry out pressure and capacity tests, a T-piece must be fitted in the line between the pump outlet pipe and the carburetter(s). Connect a pressure gauge to the T-piece. With the engine running at 1000 rev/min, the fuel pressure should be within the range of 2.6 to 3.4 lb/sq inch (.18 to .24 kg/sq cm). Increase the engine speed. The pressure should remain within this range.

To check capacity, remove the pressure gauge from the T-piece and, in its place, run a tube to a calibrated container. With the engine running at 1000 rev/min, the pump should (in addition to supplying the carburetter(s)) deliver 1¾ pints (1000 cc) in 60 seconds or less.

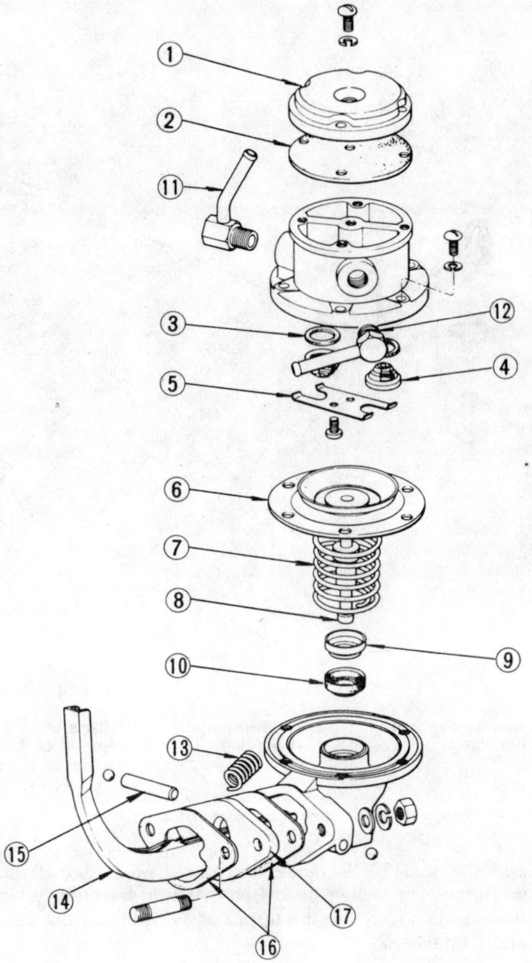

FIG 2:3 Components of the fuel pump

Key to Fig 2:3 1 Cover 2 Gasket 3 Washer 4 Valve 5 Valve retainer 6 Diaphragm assembly 7 Spring 8 Diaphragm rod 9 Seal washer 10 Seal 11 Fuel inlet 12 Fuel outlet 13 Rocker arm spring 14 Rocker arm 15 Pivot pin 16 Gaskets 17 Spacer

Pump removal and fitment:

Disconnect the inlet and outlet pipes. Remove the retaining nuts and washers, dismount the pump and collect the spacer and the gaskets.

Fitment is the reverse of this sequence. Unless gaskets 16 are in perfect condition, use new.

Dismantling:

Remove the six setscrews, collect their washers and separate the upper body from the lower body. Remove the two retaining screws from the valve retainer 5, lift out the valves and collect the washers 3. Press down the diaphragm assembly 6 against the load of spring 7, tilt the diaphragm assembly and disengage the diaphragm rod 8 from the inner end of the rocker arm 14. Remove the diaphragm assembly, the spring and the seal washer 9

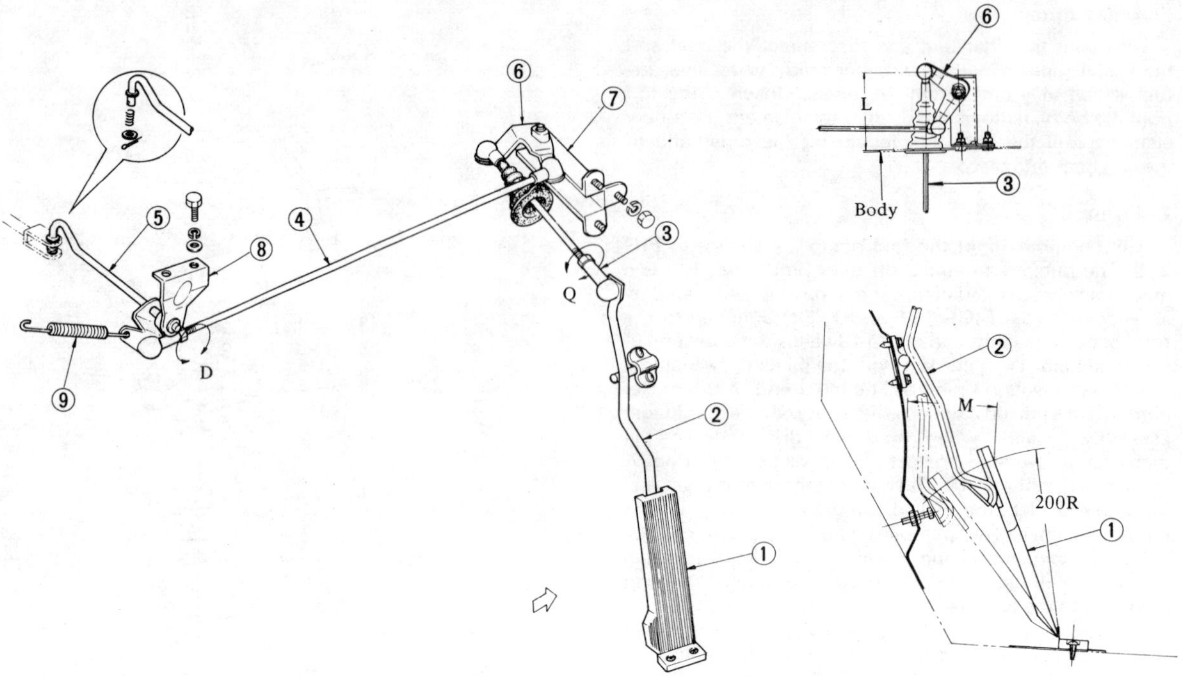

FIG 2:4 Accelerator control linkage

Key to Fig 2:4 1 Accelerator pedal 2 Pedal arm 3 Ball joint assembly 4 Rod 5 Torsion shaft 6 Lever 7 Lever bracket 8 Torsion shaft bracket 9 Spring **D, L, M** and **Q** See text

and the seal 10. Remove the rocker pivot pin 15 and withdraw the rocker arm. Remove the setscrew which retains the cover 1 to the upper body. Remove the cover and its gasket 2.

Inspection:

Check the diaphragm assembly for hardening, cracks and wear. If the vehicle has covered a considerable mileage, it will be prudent to fit a new diaphragm assembly irrespective of its apparent condition. The valves cannot be serviced and, if a spring is weak or broken, if a valve plate is not seating fully or if it or the seat is worn, fit new assemblies. Check the rocker arm for wear at both ends and at its pivot point. Check the pivot pin for wear. Check the pivot pin locations in the lower body. Wear at these points will result in oil leakage. Unless broken, springs 7 and 13 should be serviceable but, if the pump test pressure or delivery was low, renew the diaphragm spring 7.

Assembly:

Assembly of the pump is the reverse of the dismantling sequence. Use new gaskets and sealing washers. Lubricate the rocker arm and pin pivot points and the end of the diaphragm assembly rod which is in contact with the rocker arm. Ensure that the inlet and outlet valves are each fitted the correct way up. Do not use jointing compound on the diaphragm or on the faces of the upper or lower bodies.

Functional test:

Before fitting the pump, check that it has been correctly reassembled. Connect the pump inlet to the fuel feed line. Hold the pump as high as the piping will allow and operate the rocker arm by hand. Fuel should be drawn up and delivered from the outlet pipe.

2:5 Controls

Accelerator control:

The components and layout of the accelerator control are shown in **FIG 2:4**. If the linkage has been dismantled, note, on reassembly, the following points:

1 Adjustment is made at **D** (for length of rod 4) and at **Q** (ball joint 3). These ball joints should initially be screwed .51 inch (13 mm) onto their rods and, after adjustments have been completed, their locknuts must be securely tightened.
2 Dimension **L** should be adjusted to 3.228 inch (82 mm). Dimension **M** should be adjusted at **Q** to 3.701 inch (94 mm).
3 Maintain **L** at 3.228 inch (82 mm) and adjust **D** until the carburetter throttle shaft is in the fully closed throttle position. Check that full throttle can be obtained.
4 With the carburetter throttle shaft in the fully open throttle position, set the pedal arm stop until it just touches the arm and then back it off by one full turn. Tighten the locknut.

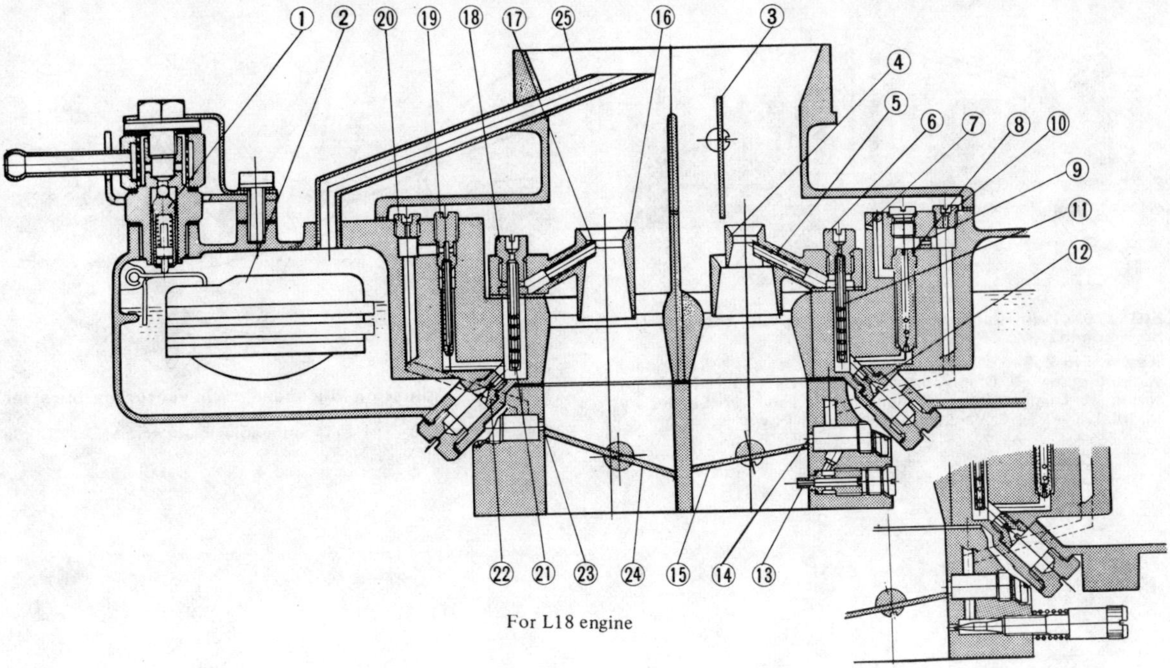

FIG 2:5 Twin venturi carburetter

Key to Fig 2:5 1 Float valve 2 Float 3 Choke valve 4 Primary small venturi 5 Primary main nozzle 6 Primary main air bleed 7 First slow air bleed 8 Slow running jet 9 Slow running economizer jet 10 Second slow air bleed 11 Primary emulsion tube 12 Primary main jet 13 Idling nozzle **L18** engines (see inset for **L16** engine version of this nozzle) 14 Bypass orifice 15 Primary throttle valve 16 Secondary small venturi 17 Secondary main nozzle 18 Secondary main air bleed 19 Step jet 20 Step air bleed 21 Secondary emulsion tube 22 Secondary main jet 23 Step orifice 24 Secondary throttle valve 25 Air vent pipe

Kickdown switch adjustment:

Adjustment is described in **Chapter 7, Section 7:4**.

Dashpot adjustment:

Adjustment is described in **Chapter 7, Section 7:4**.

Choke control:

To remove the Bowden-type cable choke control, disconnect the cable from the carburetter, loosen the locknut and remove the control knob, remove the locknut and withdraw the cables as an assembly. Note that, with the control knob fully in, the inner cable must, after reconnection to the carburetter, be slightly slack.

Lubrication:

The bearing in bracket 8 is made from polyacetal resin and is oil wetted. Use multi-purpose grease at pivots and on the inner cable of the choke control.

2:6 Single (twin venturi) carburetter

Cross-sections through a twin venturi carburetter are shown in **FIGS 2:5** and **2:6** and a cross-section through the accelerator pump is shown in **FIG 2:7**. Note that **FIG 2:6** shows fuel and air flow at maximum engine output (full throttle, high speed). This illustration also shows the vacuum diaphragm which actuates the secondary throttle valve. The carburetter primary system includes starting, idling, the primary main fuel supply and the accelerator pump system. The secondary side provides the step system and the secondary main fuel supply. The single float chamber serves both the primary and the secondary systems. Note that the throttle interlock arrangement prevents the secondary throttle from starting to open until the primary throttle opening exceeds 50 deg.

Removal and fitment:

1 Remove the air clear as described in **Section 2:8**.
2 Disconnect the accelerator and choke controls from the carburetter (see **Section 2:5**). Disconnect the fuel and vacuum pipes.
3 Remove the four nuts and washers which retain the carburetter to the intake manifold. Lift off the carburetter. Remove and discard the gasket which was fitted between the carburetter and the manifold.

Before refitting the carburetter, check, and adjust if necessary, the fast idling interlock and the primary/secondary throttle valve interlock setting as described later in this Section.

Fitment is the reverse of the removal sequence. Use a new gasket at the manifold joint. Do not use jointing compound. On completion of the installation, check the accelerator and choke control settings as described in **Section 2:5** and adjust the idling speed to that specified in **Section 2:2** for the relevant model.

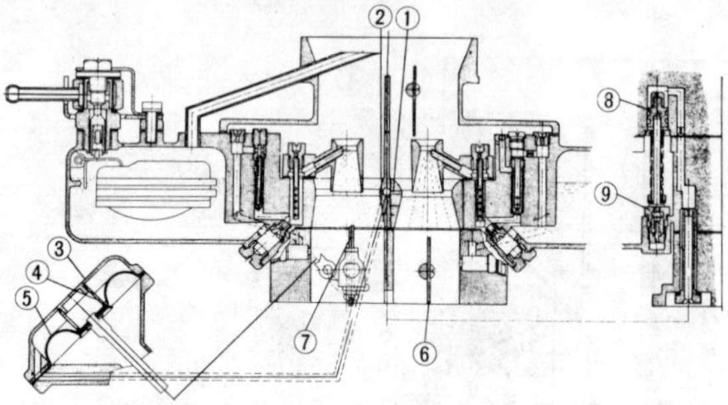

FIG 2:6 Twin venturi carburetter at full throttle (at high speed)

Key to Fig 2:6 1 Primary vacuum port 2 Secondary vacuum port 3 Diaphragm chamber cover 4 Diaphragm spring 5 Diaphragm 6 Primary throttle valve 7 Secondary throttle valve 8 Vacuum piston 9 Power jet

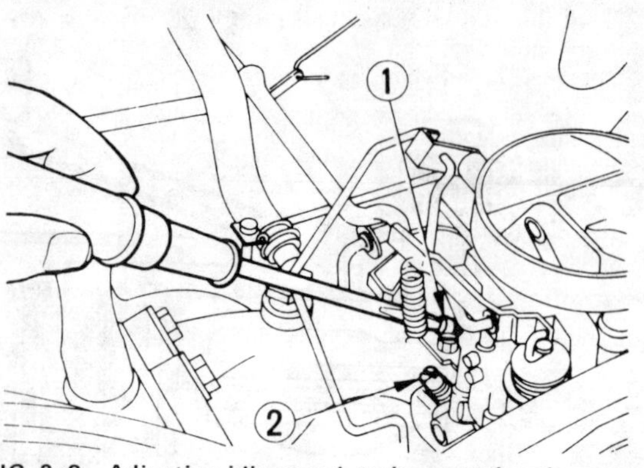

FIG 2:8 Adjusting idle speed, twin venturi carburetter

Key to Fig 2:8 1 Throttle adjustment screw 2 Idle adjustment screw

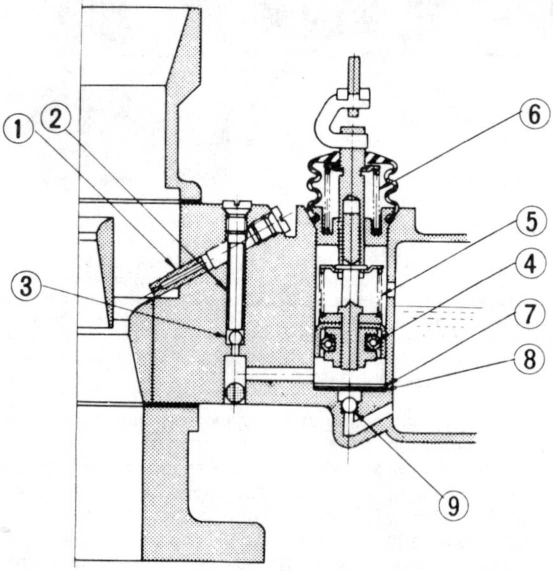

FIG 2:7 Accelerator pump

Key to Fig 2:7 1 Pump injector 2 Cylindrical weight 3 Outlet valve (loaded by 2) 4 Piston 5 Damper spring 6 Piston return spring 7 Clip 8 Gauze strainer 9 Inlet valve

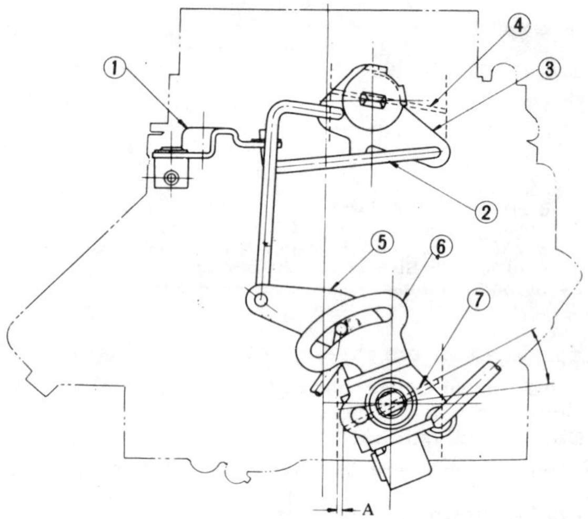

FIG 2:9 Fast idling interlock linkage

Key to Fig 2:9 1 Choke lever 2 Cranked rod 3 Choke arm 4 Choke valve 5 Lever 6 Throttle arm (primary throttle valve) 7 Primary throttle valve **A** See text

Dismantling and reassembly:

Jets and bleeds are accessible without dismantling the carburetter and may be identified by reference to **FIGS 2:5, 2:6** and **2:7**. Be careful when dismantling the interlocks not to disturb their settings by bending them.

The choke chamber may be separated after removing the connecting rod, pump rod, return spring, stop pin and three setscrews. The emulsion tubes may be dismantled by removing the respective air bleeds. The throttle chamber is detached from the float chamber by removing the rod linking the diaphragm assembly with the secondary throttle valve and the three retaing screws. The diaphragm unit is dismantled by removing the three screws which retain the cover.

Wash all parts in petrol. Flush all passages but **do not probe them, the jets or the bleeds.** Dry off all parts with compressed air.

Reassembly is the reverse of the dismantling sequence. Use new gaskets and, on completion, check the settings of the interlocks as described later in this Section.

Idling speed adjustment:

The correct idling speed for all models is tabulated in **Section 2:2**. The setting procedure is as follows:

1 Refer to **FIG 2:8** and, before starting the engine, turn out the idle adjustment screw 2 by $2\frac{1}{4}$ turns in the case of L16 engines and by $1\frac{1}{2}$ turns in the case of L18 engines.

2 Turn the throttle adjustment screw 1 by two or three turns and start the engine. Turn screw 1 until the specified idling speed is approximately obtained.
3 Turn screw 2 in or out until the highest smooth engine running is obtained.
4 Adjust screw 1 to give the specified idling speed.
5 Repeat operations 3 and 4 until both smooth running and the specified idling speed are achieved.

Fast idling interlock:

When the choke control is operated, the choke valve 3 in **FIG 2:5** turns to the closed position as shown at 4 in **FIG 2:9**. The linkage automatically opens the primary throttle valve 7 to the optimum angle for starting the engine from cold and the gap (**A** in **FIG 2:9**) between the throttle valve and the carburetter body should then be .051 inch (1.3 mm) in the case of L16 engines and .061 inch (1.55 mm) in the case of L18 engines. These dimensions apply to both manual and automatic transmission models and correspond to primary throttle valve openings of 19 deg. (L16 engines) and 18 deg. (L18 engines).

Adjustment of the gap **A** is made by bending the choke connecting rod which connects arm 3 with lever 5 in **FIG 2:9**. Measurement of the gap should be made using wire of appropriate diameter. The carburetter must be removed to enable this adjustment to be made.

Primary/secondary throttle valve interlock:

The interlock arrangement shown in **FIG 2:10** prevents the secondary throttle valve from starting to open until the primary throttle valve is open by more than 50 deg.

When the primary throttle valve is 50 deg. open, the connecting link 2 comes into contact at **A** with the end of the groove in the primary throttle arm. When the primary valve opens beyond this point, the locking arm 4 disengages from the secondary throttle arm 5 and allows initiation of the secondary throttle valve opening sequence.

The 50 deg. primary throttle valve opening corresponds to gap **G** between the primary throttle valve and the body.

Adjustment is made by bending the connecting link 2. Measurement of the gap should be made using wire of appropriate diameter. Access requires removal of the carburetter. **G**, for L16 engines should be .291 inch (7.4 mm) or, for L18 engines, .248 inch (6.3 mm).

Fuel level:

Use fuel level gauge ST19200000 to check the fuel level with the engine running at idling speed and, if necessary, adjust by bending the float arm 4 in **FIG 2:11**. The required effective stroke **H** of the needle valve is .04 inch (1 mm) and adjustment is made by bending the float stop 5.

Jets:

Use only petrol and compressed air to clean jets. Do not attempt to clean them by probing the orifices as this will ruin their calibration. If a vehicle is to operate continuously at higher altitudes, smaller than standard jets should be fitted. If fuel economy (but with sacrifice of performance) is required, smaller jets and/or larger bleeds may be fitted and vice versa. Tuning the carburetter to achieve either improved fuel consumption or improved performance is a matter of trial and error and compromise. The assistance of an experienced tuner is desirable.

Dashpot:

This device is fitted only to automatic transmission models and its setting is described in **Chapter 7, Section 7:4**.

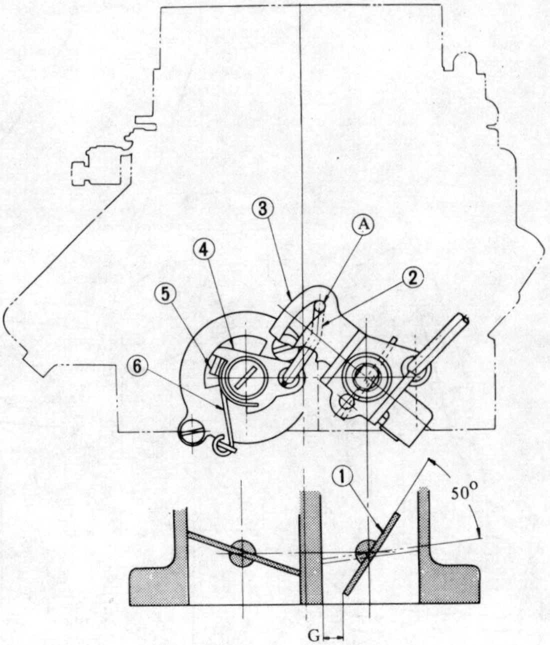

FIG 2:10 Primary/secondary throttle valve interlock

Key to Fig 2:10 1 Primary throttle valve 2 Connecting link 3 Throttle arm (primary) 4 Locking arm 5 Throttle arm (secondary) 6 Locking arm return spring **A** See text

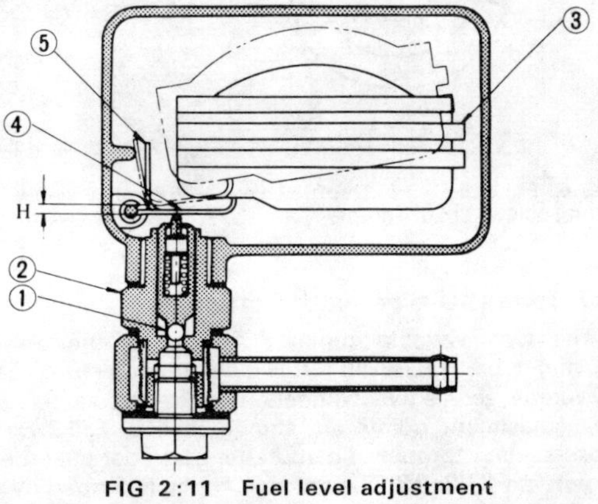

FIG 2:11 Fuel level adjustment

Key to Fig 2:11 1 Ball valve 2 Valve seat 3 Float 4 Float arm 5 Float stop **H** See text

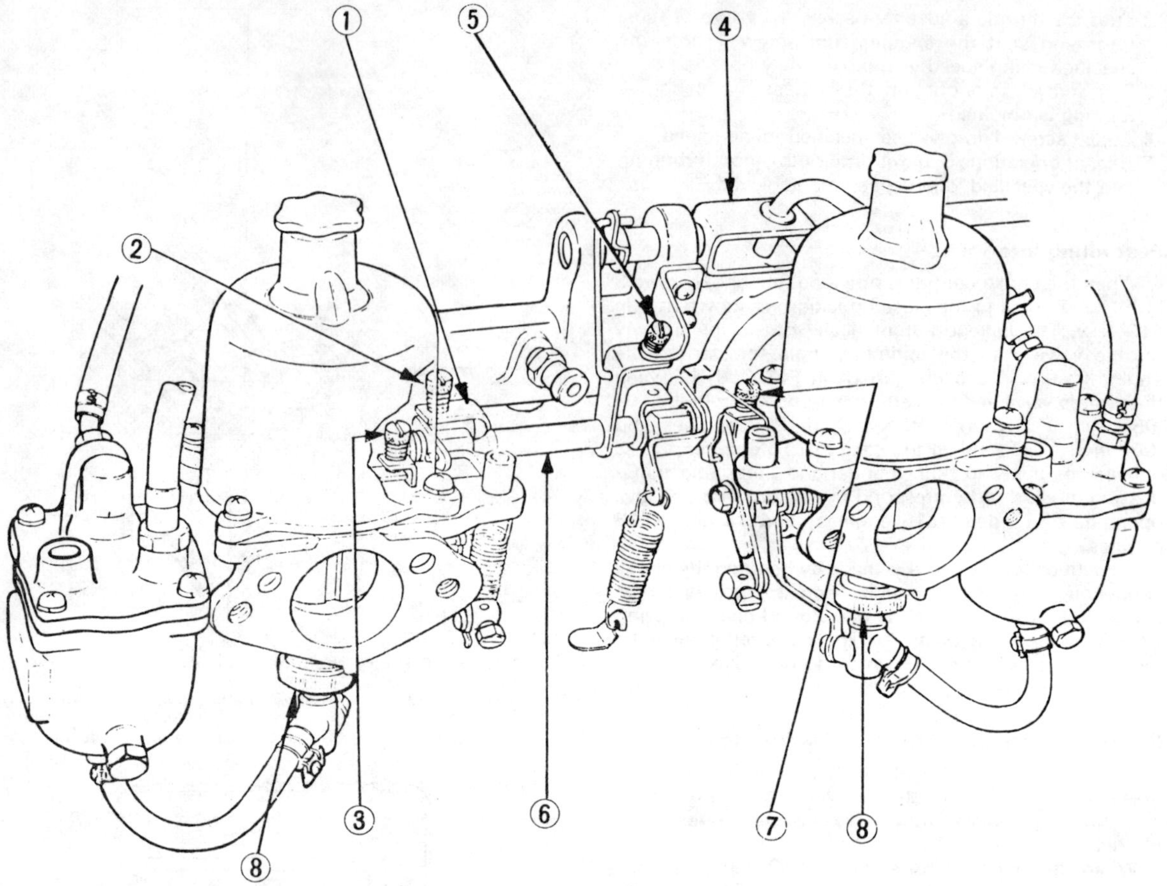

FIG 2:12 Twin (SU type) carburetters

Key to Fig 2:12 1 Throttle lever 2 Balance screw 3 Throttle adjustment screw (front) 4 Auxiliary shaft 5 Fast idle setting screw 6 Throttle shaft 7 Throttle adjustment screw (rear) 8 Idle adjustment nuts

2:7 Twin (SU type) carburetters

The twin variable choke SU type carburetters are 38 mm type HJL38W6 of Hitachi manufacture. Each carburetter serves two cylinders. The controls are ganged. The adjustment points are shown in **FIG 2:12** and a cross-section through a carburetter and float chamber is shown in **FIG 2:13**. The variable choke is formed by the lower (smaller diameter) part of the stepped piston assembly 20 rising and falling automatically depending upon the depression in the intake system as dictated by the opening of throttle valve 9 and the engine load. To maintain the correct fuel mixture in the varying volume of intake air, a tapered needle attached to the piston assembly is raised or lowered in the aperture of jet 21. The smallest diameter of the needle is in the jet orifice when the piston assembly is at the top of its travel and the flow of fuel is then a maximum. Rapid fluctuations of the piston assembly are prevented by the hydraulic damper 19, oil being contained in the well of the hollow piston rod 7. This oil level must be topped up periodically as described in **Section 2:2**. Spring 2 assists gravity to return the piston assembly to its lowest point.

Cold starting enrichment is provided by the choke mechanism pulling the jet 21 downwards to a predetermined lower position so that the effective orifice diameter of the jet is increased for a given position of the jet needle. At the same time, the throttle valves are opened by the choke linkage to approximately $6\frac{1}{2}$ deg.

Removal and fitment:

1 Remove the air cleaner as described in **Section 2:8**.
2 Disconnect the accelerator and choke controls (see **Section 2:5**). Disconnect the fuel feed piping.
3 Remove the nuts and washers which retain each carburetter to the intake manifold. Lift off the carburetters. Remove and discard the gaskets fitted between the manifold and the carburetters.
Before refitting the carburetters, check, and adjust if necessary, the starting interlock as described later in this Section.

Fitment is the reverse of the removal sequence. Use new gaskets. Do not use jointing compound. After reconnecting the controls, resynchronize the carburetters and set the idling speed as described later in this Section.

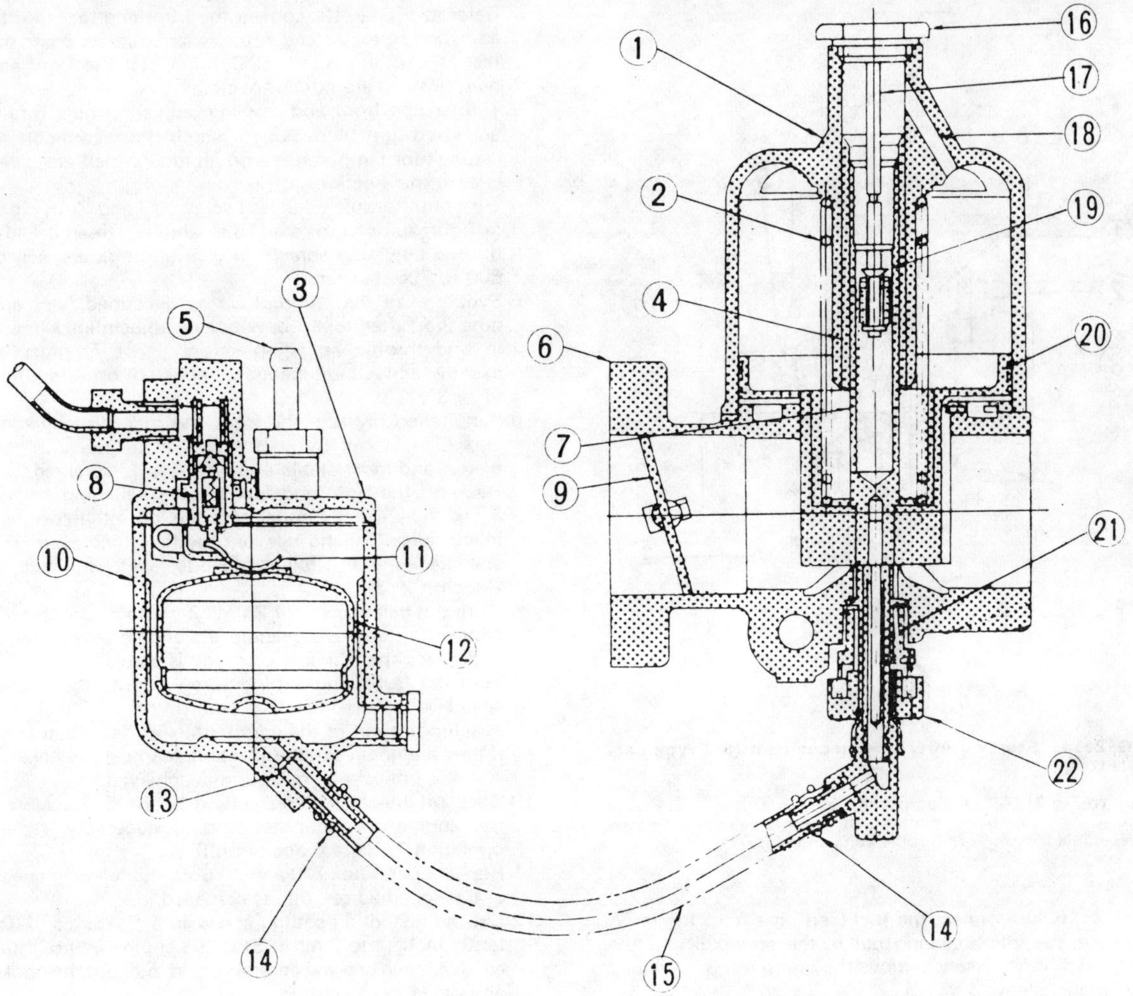

FIG 2:13 Cross-section through one SU type carburetter and its float chamber

Key to Fig 2:13 1 Suction chamber 2 Spring 3 Float chamber cover 4 Guide 5 Connector 6 Throttle chamber 7 Piston rod 8 Needle valve assembly 9 Throttle valve 10 Float chamber 11 Float lever 12 Float 13 Connector 14 Clip 15 Fuel pipe 16 Cap nut 17 Rod 18 Balance passage 19 Damper 20 Suction piston assembly 21 Jet 22 Idle mixture adjustment nut

Dismantling and reassembly:

Except for the suction chamber/piston assembly and, possibly, the jet assembly, dismantling of the carburetters will not normally be required and, unless absolutely essential, should not be attempted.

Suction chamber/piston dismantling:

Refer to **FIG 2:13**. Remove the cap nut 16 and withdraw the damper assembly 19. Remove the four setscrews and washers which retain the suction chamber 1 to the throttle chamber 6 and lift off the suction chamber. Remove the spring 2, nylon packing and, taking great care not to bend the jet needle, lift out the suction piston and jet assembly. Empty the oil from the well of the suction piston rod.

Wash all components in petrol and dry off with compressed air. If the jet needle has been rubbing against the bore of the jet, it and the jet should be renewed.

Suction chamber/piston reassembly:

Assembly is the reverse of the dismantling sequence. The inside of the suction chamber 1 and **the grooved periphery of the large diameter of the suction piston 20 must be assembled dry**. Light oil should, however, be applied sparingly to outer diameter of the piston rod 7. Refill the damper well with oil as described in **Section 2:2**.

Jet assembly dismantling:

Refer to **FIG 2:14.** Remove the retaining screw and uncouple the connecting plate from the jet. Refer to

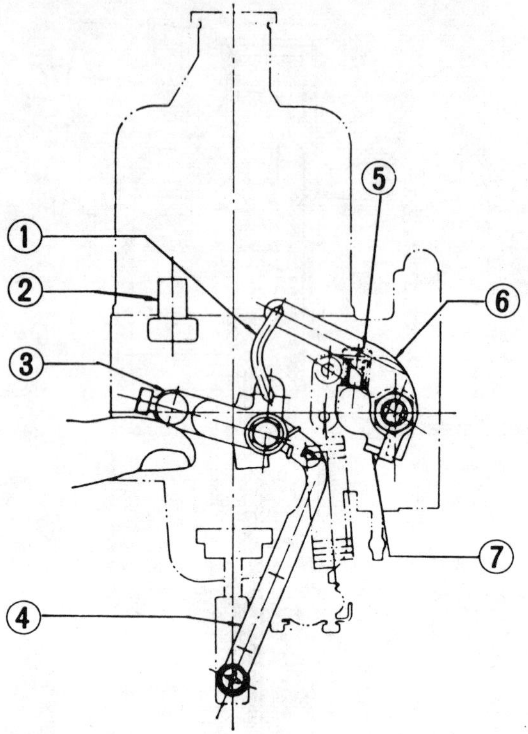

FIG 2:14 Starting interlock mechanism (SU type carburetter)

Key to Fig 2:14 1 Connecting rod 2 Guard 3 Choke lever 4 Connecting plate 5 Throttle adjustment screw 6 Fast idle lever 7 Throttle adjusting plate

FIG 2:15. Disconnect the fuel feed pipe from the jet 7. Remove the idle adjusting nut 6, the spring 5 and the shim(s) 4. If necessary, remove the union nut 3, washer 2 and the jet sleeve 1.

Wash all parts in petrol and dry off with compressed air. If the jet needle has been rubbing against the bore of the jet, it and the jet should be renewed.

Reassembling the jet assembly:

Assembly is the reverse of the dismantling sequence. Ensure that the jet is correctly centred before finally tightening the jet sleeve union. Check by lifting the suction piston assembly by means of the lifting pin and allowing it to drop. If the piston assembly does not drop with a clear sharp click, the jet and jet needle combination is not correctly centred. Adjustment is made by turning the jet sleeve to its optimum position. If this adjustment is not successful, suspect that the jet needle is bent.

Idling speed adjustment:

Adjustment must be made with the engine at normal operating temperature. The procedure is as follows:

1 Remove the air cleaner as described in **Section 2:8**. Run the engine up to normal operating temperature. Check that the choke is released and fully out of operation.

2 Refer to **FIG 2:12**. Loosen the front and rear throttle adjusting screws 3 and 7, the balance screw 2 and the fast idle setting screw 5. Confirm that the front and rear throttles are not connected.

3 Tighten the front and rear idle adjusting nuts 8 fully and then turn them out to match the recommended settings for temperature and altitude which are given later in this Section.

4 Turn both throttle adjusting screws (3 and 7) by three or four turns and start the engine. Readjust the throttle adjusting screws to give an engine speed of 600 to 700 rev/min.

5 Synchronize the carburetters as described later and note that, after doing so, whatever adjustment is made to one throttle adjusting screw (3 or 7) must be exactly and simultaneously repeated on the other (7 or 3).

6 Simultaneously turn the front and rear idle adjusting nuts 8 in or out by $\frac{1}{8}$ of a turn at a time until the fastest and most stable engine speed is obtained.

7 Back off the front and rear throttle adjusting screws 3 and 7 by exactly equal amounts until the specified idling speed for the relevant model is achieved. The specified engine idling speeds are tabulated in **Section 2:2**.

8 Turn the balance screw 2 until it contacts the throttle connecting lever. Accelerate the engine several times and check that the idling setting is stable.

9 Turn the fast idling setting screw 5 until the engine speed is approximately 1500 rev/min. Check the synchronization of the carburetters as described later. If they are not in synchronization, readjust the balance screw 2 until synchronization is achieved.

10 Back off the fast idling setting screw 5. Accelerate the engine several times and, if necessary, repeat operation 7. Repeat operation 9.

11 Repeat operations 7, 9 and 10 until stable idling speed at the specified rev/min is achieved.

12 Set the fast idling setting screw to a clearance of .04 to .08 inch (1 to 2 mm). Stop the engine and refit the air cleaner. When the engine is cold, pull out the choke and check cold starting.

Starting interlock adjustments:

Adjustment of the starting interlock requires the carburetters to be removed to allow measurement of the throttle valve opening.

Refer to **FIG 2:14**. With the choke lever 3 held (press upwards) in the starting position as shown in the illustration, the throttle valve should be open to the extent that the gap between the valve and the carburetter body is .024 inch (.6 mm). Adjustment is made by bending the connecting rod 1. The throttle valve opening is increased by 'straightening' the rod and vice versa.

After refitting the carburetters and recoupling the controls, check that the choke control operates fully. The idling setting and the synchronization of the carburetters should also be checked and adjusted if necessary.

Synchronizing the carburetters:

Carburetters are in synchronization when both are passing precisely the same amount of air. Synchronization should ideally be checked by means of a flowmeter. If access to a flowmeter (tool EG16700000) is not possible, judgement of the suction of each carburetter is made by placing one end of a length of rubber or plastic tubing (of, say, $\frac{1}{2}$ inch (12.5 mm) diameter) to the ear and the other end just inside each carburetter intake in turn. The carburetters are in synchronization when the level of suction noise is judged to be equal. With experience, this procedure can approximate closely to the precise measurement which is achieved when using a flowmeter.

Altitude and temperature adjustment:

In climates where the ambient temperature is consistently higher or lower than normal, the basic setting of the idle adjustment nuts 8 in **FIG 2:12**, 22 in **FIG 2:13** (for normal temperature these will be backed off by about two full turns from the fully tightened position) should be backed off (richened) by a further half a turn per 10°C (18°F) below normal of 20°C (68°F) or turned in (weakened) by half a turn per 10°C (18°F) above this temperature.

Adjustment for altitude should be made by turning in (weakened) the idle adjusting nuts from the basic setting by quarter of a turn per 3250 feet (1000 m) above sea level.

Fuel level:

Use float level gauge ST19200000 to check the fuel level with the engine running at idling speed. The gauge is marked with the standard fuel level which should be .866 to .945 inch (22 to 24 mm) below the float chamber joint face. Adjustment is made by bending the float lever 1 in **FIG 2:16** (bend at point 2) to give dimension **H** of .433 to .472 inch (11 to 12 mm).

Piston damper:

The procedure for topping up the oil level is described in **Section 2:2**.

2:8 Air cleaner

The air cleaner element may be either a 'dry' or a viscous paper type. Maintenance differs between the two types and is described in **Section 2:2**

Element renewal:

Remove the cover from the canister and withdraw the element. Clean all dust from inside the canister and, in doing so, ensure that dust does not enter the carburetter(s). Fit the new element and refit the cover.

Removal and fitment:

In the case of the cleaner fitted to single carburetter models, disconnect the piping of the thermostatic idle compensator, remove the bolts which attach the support strut and lift off the canister.

In the case of the cleaner fitted to twin carburetter models, remove the cover, lift out the element, remove the bolts which attach the canister to the carburetter flanges and dismount the canister.

Refitment is, in each case, the reverse of the removal sequence.

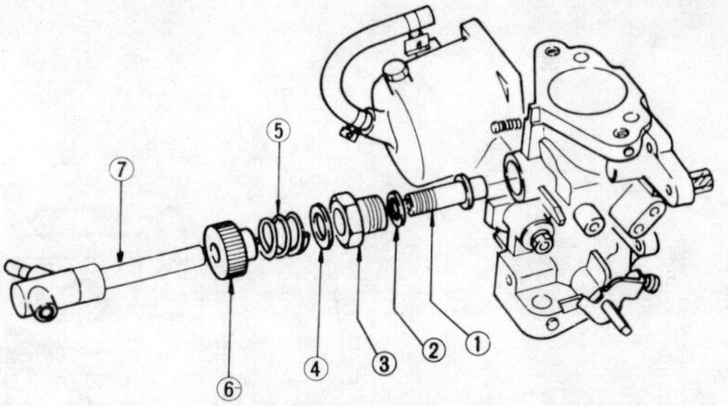

FIG 2:15 Jet assembly (SU type carburetter)

Key to Fig 2:15 1 Jet sleeve 2 Washer 3 Jet sleeve union 4 Adjusting shim 5 Idle mixture adjustment nut spring 6 Idle mixture adjustment nut 7 Jet

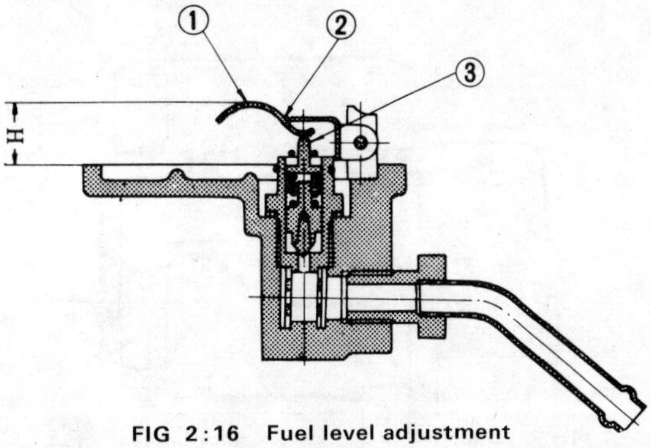

FIG 2:16 Fuel level adjustment

Key to Fig 2:16 1 Float lever 2 Bend here to adjust dimension **H** 3 Valve stem **H** See text

Thermostatic valve:

This valve, which compensates for excess idling richness when the under bonnet air temperature is high, is fitted only to single carburetter models. The valve partially opens at 55°C (131°F) and opens fully at 65°C (149°F). The thermostatic unit cannot be repaired by an owner and, if defective, should be replaced by a new unit.

2:9 Emission control

Fuel vapour:

To preclude emission of fuel vapour, the fuel tank is sealed, a vapour/liquid separator is incorporated and is vented to the intake manifold. The arrangement of the system is shown in **FIG 2:17**. The vapour vent line is connected with the closed crankcase breather system (see **Chapter 1, Section 1:21**) by a flow guide valve. This valve only allows vapour to pass when its pressure exceeds .4 inch Hg. It precludes blow-by gases, oil fumes, etc., from passing to the vapour separator or fuel tank. As fuel is consumed, depression in the tank and vapour line draws clean air from the air cleaner and substantially atmospheric pressure is maintained in the fuel tank.

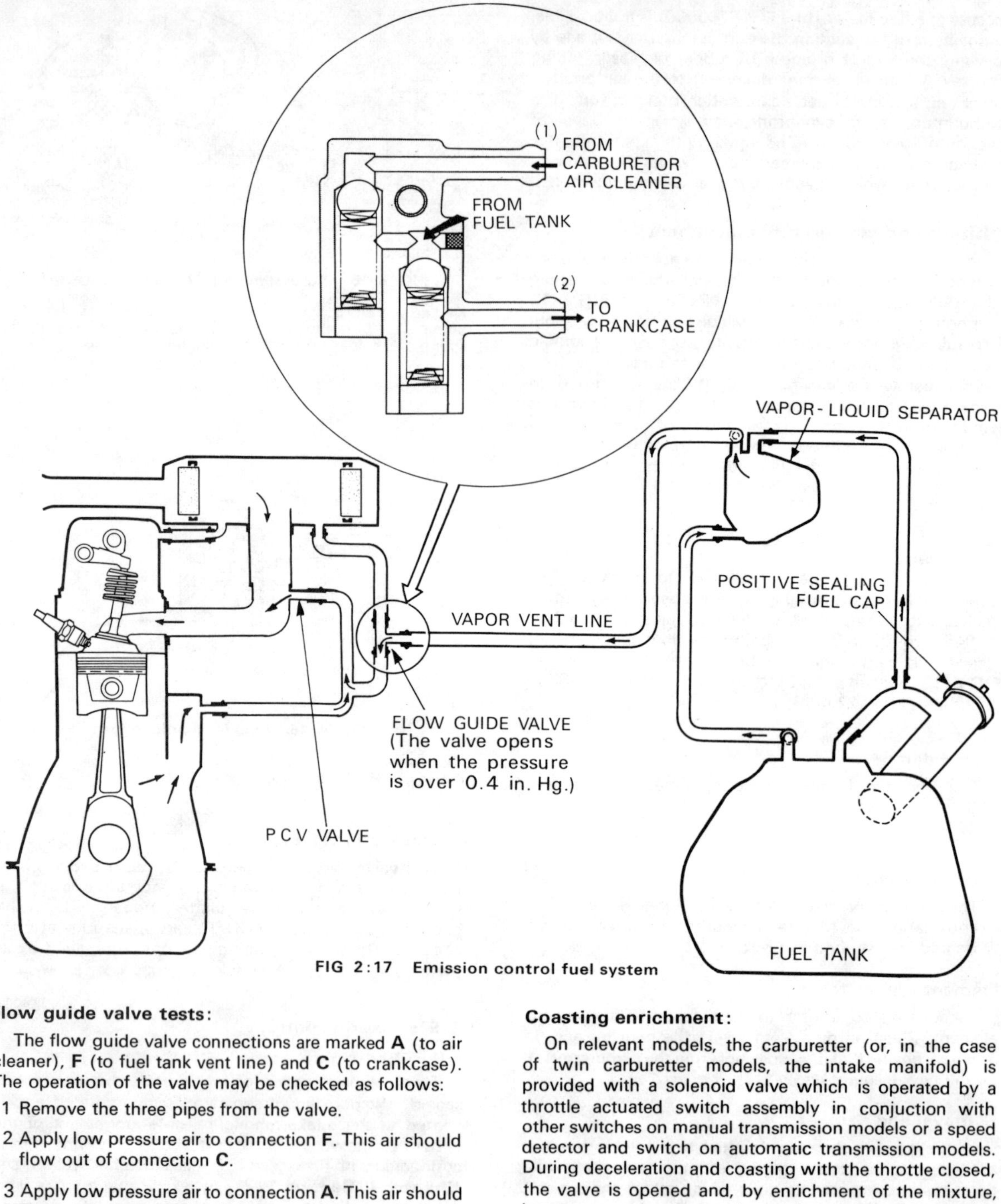

FIG 2:17 Emission control fuel system

Flow guide valve tests:

The flow guide valve connections are marked **A** (to air cleaner), **F** (to fuel tank vent line) and **C** (to crankcase). The operation of the valve may be checked as follows:

1 Remove the three pipes from the valve.

2 Apply low pressure air to connection **F**. This air should flow out of connection **C**.

3 Apply low pressure air to connection **A**. This air should flow out of connection **F**.

4 Apply suction to connection **F**. Air should flow in at connection **A** and be sucked out at connection **F**. No air should flow in at connection **C**.

A defective flow guide valve cannot be repaired by an owner and must be replaced by a new unit.

Coasting enrichment:

On relevant models, the carburetter (or, in the case of twin carburetter models, the intake manifold) is provided with a solenoid valve which is operated by a throttle actuated switch assembly in conjuction with other switches on manual transmission models or a speed detector and switch on automatic transmission models. During deceleration and coasting with the throttle closed, the valve is opened and, by enrichment of the mixture, improves combustion and so reduces carbon monoxide emission.

The arrangement is included schematically in **FIGS 3:10** and **3:11** in **Chapter 3** together with emission control features which are incorporated in the ignition system. If the serviceability of the solenoid valve is suspect, carry out the relevant test procedure.

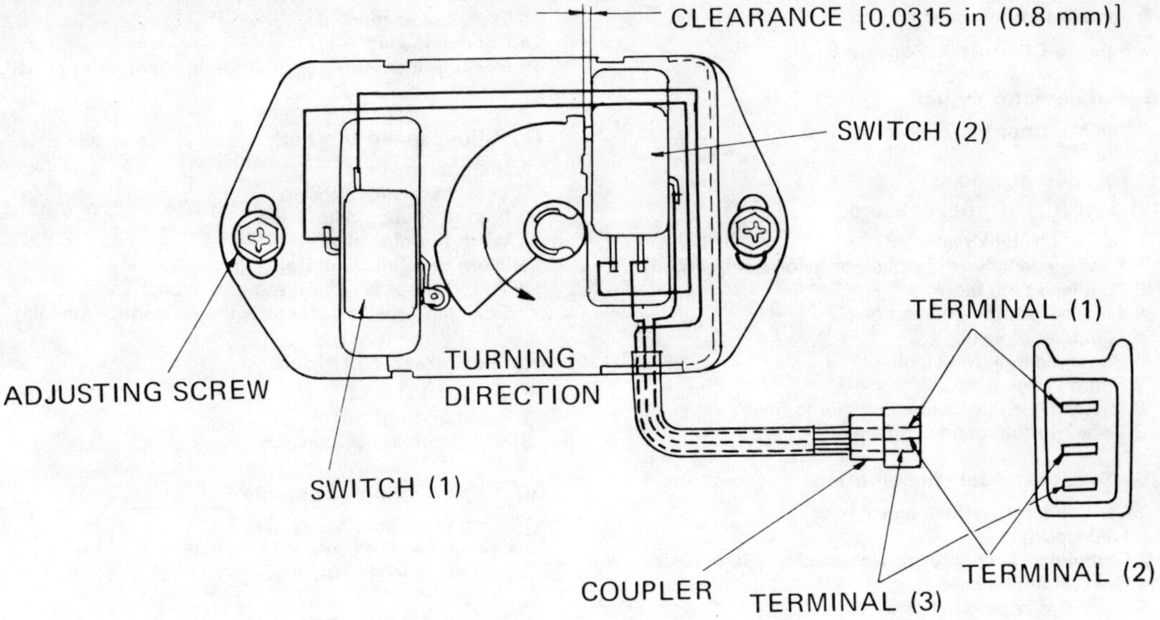

FIG 2:18 Emission control throttle switch

Solenoid valve, manual transmission models:

FIG 3:10 is relevant. **Test 1.** Disconnect the black (earth) lead from the solenoid and connect an ammeter between earth and the solenoid earth terminal. Engage any gear **other than neutral** and switch on the ignition. The ammeter should read approximately .4 amp. **with the throttle closed.** The ammeter reading should be zero when either the throttle is opened (even slightly) or the clutch pedal is depressed or the gearchange lever is shifted to the neutral position. **Test 2.** If test 1 is satisfactory, disconnect the ammeter and reconnect the black lead to the solenoid. Start the engine and, by means of a jump wire, connect the other terminal of the solenoid direct to the battery positive. The engine speed should increase to approximately 1100 rev/min. If this increase in speed does not occur, remove the solenoid and fit a new replacement.

If, at the specified conditions of test 1, the ammeter does not read the specified current, check the wiring and switches before proceeding to test 2.

Solenoid valve, automatic transmission models:

FIG 3:11 is relevant. **Test 1.** Disconnect the black (earth) lead from the solenoid and connect an ammeter between earth and the solenoid earth terminal. The ammeter must be positioned so that it can be read while driving the vehicle. Drive the vehicle and check that, when the road speed is in excess of 13 mile/hr, the ammeter reads approximately .4 amp. **when the throttle is closed.** For all other drive conditions (throttle open, road speed under 13 mile/hr), the ammeter reading should be zero. If, at the specified conditions, the ammeter does not read the specified current, check the wiring, switches and speed detector before proceeding to test 2. **Test 2.** This test is as described earlier for test 2 of the manual transmission test procedure.

Throttle switch:

The switch connections are show diagrammatically in **FIGS 3:10** and **3:11** in **Chapter 3** for manual and automatic transmission models respectively. The switch arrangement is shown in **FIG 2:18**. Switch 1 detects the closed throttle position. Switch 2 detects the throttle open position.

Adjustment of throttle switch:

Ensure that the accelerator control (see **Section 2:5**) is operating correctly over its full range. The clearance between the cam and the body of switch 1 should be .0315 inch (.8 mm). Adjustment, if necessary, is made by loosening the adjusting screws (see **FIG 2:18**) and turning the body of the switch assembly. Ensure that these screws are correctly retightened after adjustment is made.

Electrical checks on throttle switch:

Disconnect the cable coupler. Refer to **FIG 2:18** and connect an ohmeter across coupler terminals 1 and 2. The reading should be zero with the throttle closed and infinity when the accelerator pedal is depressed even slightly. If this check is not as specified, renew switch 2. Connect the ohmeter across terminals 1 and 3. The reading should be infinity when the throttle is closed and zero when the accelerator pedal is partially depressed. If this check is not as specified, renew switch 1.

Clutch switch:

Refer to **Chapter 5, Section 5:2.**

Neutral gear switch:

Refer to **Chapter 6, Section 6:2.**

Transmission switch:

Refer to **Chapter 6, Section 6:2.**

Speed detector switch:

Refer to **Chapter 7, Section 7:3.**

2:10 Fault diagnosis

(a) Insufficient fuel delivered

1 Air vent to tank restricted
2 Flow guide valve defective (emission control models)
3 Fuel feed pipe blocked
4 Air leaks at pipe connections
5 Fuel filter blocked
6 Pump diaphragm defective
7 Pump valves defective
8 Fuel vapourizing in pipeline due to heat
9 Defective fuel gauge (tank empty)

(b) Excessive fuel consumption

1 Carburetter(s) require adjustment
2 Fuel leakage
3 Carburetter suction piston(s) sticking (SU types)
4 Dirty air filter element
5 Excessive engine temperature
6 Air bleed(s) blocked (twin venturi carburetter)
7 Choke not releasing fully
8 Starting interlock not correctly adjusted
9 Idling speed too high
10 High pump pressure
11 High float level
12 Brakes binding
13 Tyres under-inflated
14 Car overloaded
15 Mixture incorrect for altitude or temperature (SU types)

(c) Idling speed too high

1 Rich fuel mixture
2 Throttle control sticking
3 Incorrect idling adjustment
4 Worn throttle valve(s)
5 Worn throttle spindle(s)
6 Throttles not synchronized (SU types)
7 Solenoid valve defective (emission control models)

(d) Carburetter(s) flooding

1 Check 10 and 11 in (b)
2 Punctured float
3 Sticking float needle valve

(e) Engine idling not stable

1 Idling not correctly adjusted
2 Low oil level in damper (SU types)
3 Jet needle loose (SU types)

(f) No fuel delivery

1 Check 1 to 9 in (a) and 3 in (d)
2 Fractured fuel feed line
3 Punctured fuel tank (no fuel)
4 Pump rocker arm pivot pin missing
5 Pump diaphragm spring broken
6 Pump actuating eccentric not fitted

CHAPTER 3

THE IGNITION SYSTEM

3:1 Description
3:2 Maintenance
3:3 Ignition faults
3:4 Distributor
3:5 Coil
3:6 Timing the ignition
3:7 Sparking plugs
3:8 Emission control system
3:9 Fault diagnosis

3:1 Description

The complete ignition circuit diagram is shown in **FIG 3:1**. To improve ignition component life, running voltage is reduced by the resistor inserted between the coil and the battery (via the ignition switch). To promote easy starting, however, the resistor is shortcircuited when the ignition switch is in the start position.

The dismantled components of the Hitachi distributor are shown in **FIG 3:2** and a cross-section through an assembled distributor is shown in **FIG 3:3**. The distributor incorporates variable timing which is controlled centrifugually and also by a vacuum operated advance/retard unit. As engine speed increases, the centrifugal action of rotating weights pivoting against the tension of small springs, advances the contact breaker cam relative to the distributor drive shaft and progressively advances the ignition timing. The vacuum control unit is connected with the intake depression by small-bore piping. At high degrees of depression it advances the ignition but, under load, at reduced degrees of depression the unit progressively retards the ignition timing.

Exhaust emission control models are fitted with a modified type of distributor (see **Section 3:8**) which is provided with an extra set of contact breaker points. This extra set of points is positioned to operate on the opposite face of the distributor cam and is phased to lag in opening by approximately 5 distributor degrees behind the 'standard' set of points. This corresponds to 10 crankshaft degrees. The retarded set of points are brought into circuit automatically by an electrical relay under the following circumstances.

In the case of manual transmission models, the relay is energized only when the vehicle is cruising or accelerating in third gear with the throttle partially open. In the case of automatic transmission models, the relay is only energized when the vehicle is cruising or accelerating at over 13 miles/hr with the throttle partially open. The relevant electrical circuits are shown in **Section 3:8**.

The firing order is 1, 3, 4, 2 for all models covered by this manual.

3:2 Maintenance

Distributor breaker points:

Every 3000 miles (5000 km), check and adjust, if necessary, the distributor points gap as described later. If the points are badly burnt, worn or if excessive transfer of metal has taken place, a new set of points should be fitted as described in **Section 3:4**.

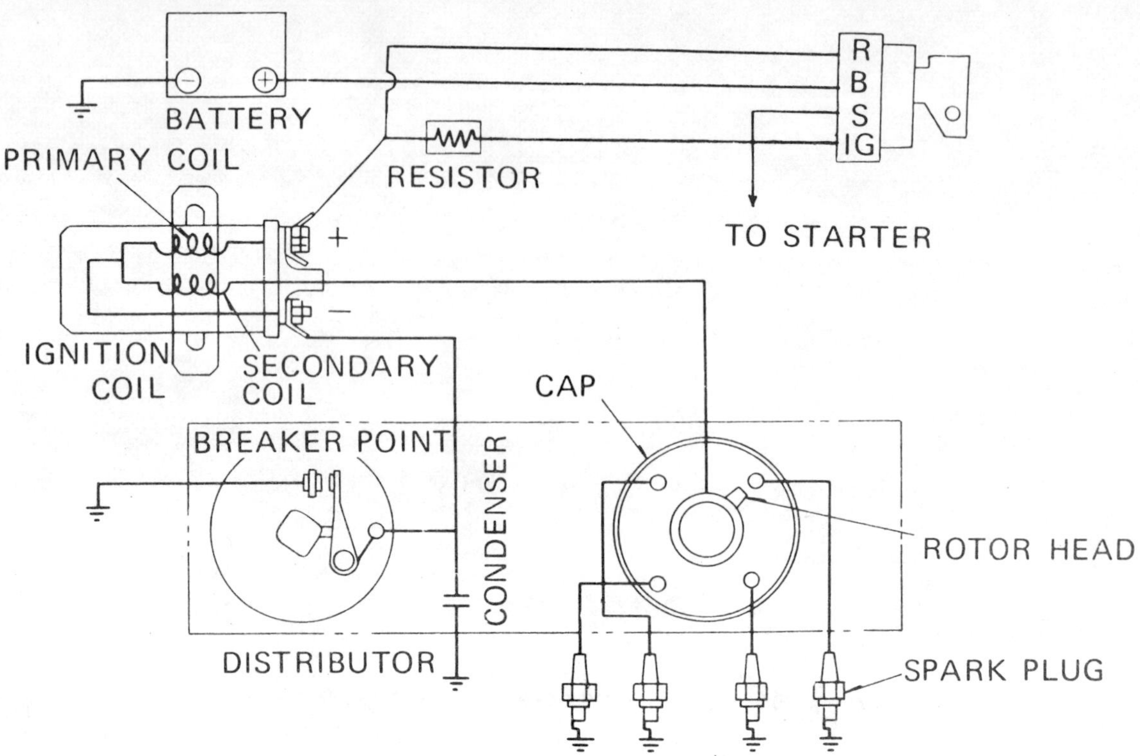

FIG 3:1 Ignition electrical circuit

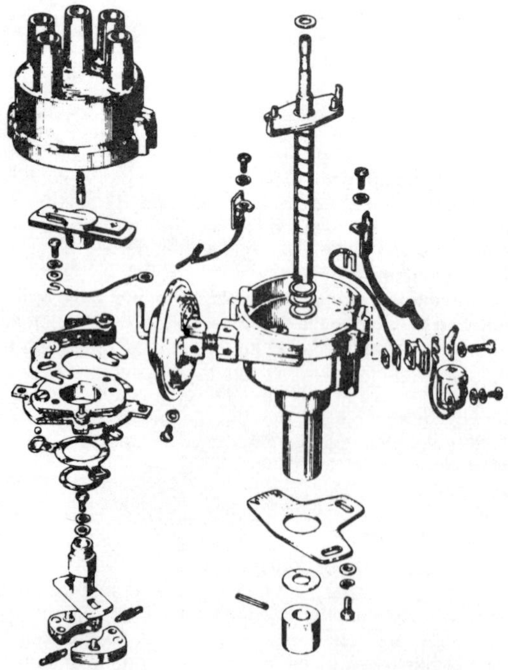

FIG 3:2 Components of the distributor

Points gap setting:

Remove the distributor cap and turn the engine until the points are fully open. Refer to **FIG 3:4**, loosen the setscrews 5, turn the adjuster screw 2 and, using feeler gauges as shown in **FIG 3:5**, set the points gap to .018 to .022 inch (.45 to .55 mm). Retighten the setscrews 5.

Distributor lubrication:

Every 6000 miles (10,000 km), remove the distributor cap and pull off the rotor arm. Fill the cavity in the shaft with multi-purpose grease and apply a film of grease to the lobes of the cam. Refit the rotor and the cap.

Ignition timing:

Every 6000 miles (10,000 km), have the ignition timing checked stroboscopically and adjusted if necessary. The procedure is described in **Section 3:6** and timing data is given in that Section and also in **Technical Data** in the Appendix.

Sparking plugs:

Every 6000 miles (10,000 km), remove the sparking plugs, clean them and reset the gaps as described in **Section 3:7**.

Every 12,000 miles (20,000 km), discard the plugs and fit a new set. Recommended types of sparking plugs are listed in **Technical Data** in the Appendix and also in **Section 3:7**.

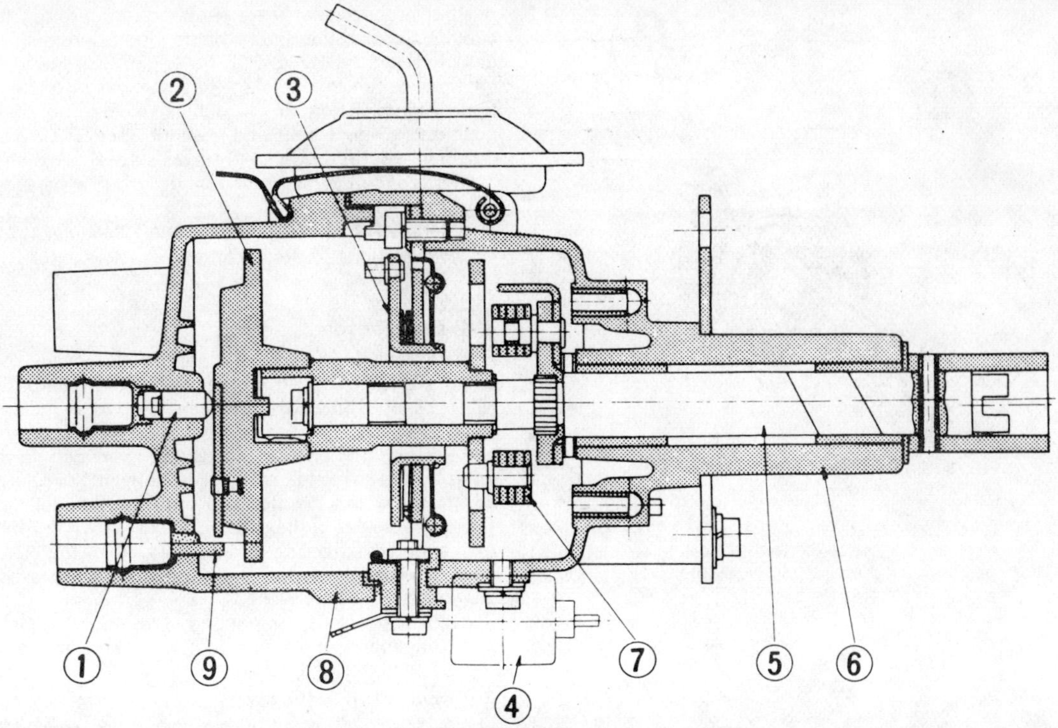

FIG 3:3 Cross-section through the distributor

Key to Fig 3:3 1 Carbon brush 2 Rotor arm 3 Contact breaker plate 4 Capacitor 5 Shaft 6 Body 7 Centrifugal weight 8 Cap 9 HT cable connector

3:3 Ignition faults

If the engine runs unevenly, set it to idle at about 1000 rev/min and disconnect and reconnect each high tension cable from its sparking plug in turn. Doing this to a plug which is firing properly will accentuate the uneven running but it will make no difference if the plug is not firing. Locate the faulty plug and, taking care not to touch any metal part of the lead while the engine is running, remove the insulator. With the engine running, hold this lead so that the conductor is about $\frac{1}{8}$ inch (3 mm) away from the cylinder head. A strong, regular spark will confirm that the fault lies with the sparking plug which should be cleaned or renewed. If, on the other hand, there is no spark, suspect the cable or its connection at the distributor cap.

If the spark is weak and irregular, check the condition of the cable and, if it is perished or cracked, renew it. If no improvement results, check the distributor cap. It must be clean and dry. Check that good contact is being made between the centre carbon contact brush and the rotor arm and that there is no 'tracking' which will show as a thin black line between the electrodes or to a metal part in contact with the cap. 'Tracking' cannot be rectified except by fitting a new cap.

If the contact breaker points are serviceable and the gap is correctly set but there is no spark, refer to **FIG 3:1** and to the wiring diagram in the Appendix, use a 0-20 range voltmeter with its negative connected to a good earth and, with the ignition switched on (in the 'run'

FIG 3:4 Distributor with cap removed

Key to Fig 3:4 1 Setscrew 2 Adjuster screw 3 Primary lead terminal (retaining) 4 Earth wire 5 Setscrew

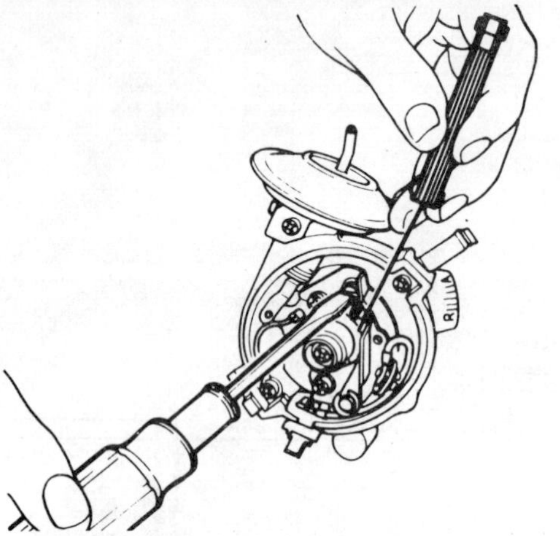

FIG 3:5 Setting the points gap

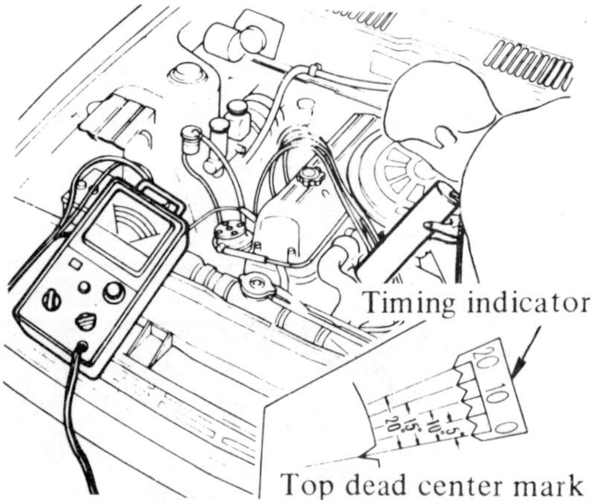

FIG 3:6 Timing marks on crankshaft pulley and front cover. A dwell meter is shown

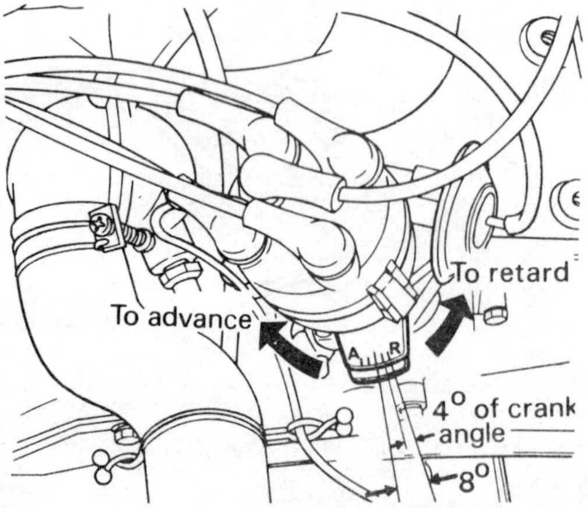

FIG 3:7 Adjusting the timing

position), check that there is voltage throughout the LT circuit. Correct the faulty cable, loose connection or defective ignition switch. If the engine will fire with the ignition switch in the 'start' position but does not continue to run when the switch is released to the 'run' position, suspect that the resistor (see **FIG 3:1**) is defective and fit a new one. Its resistance is 1.6 ohm.

If the circuit is in order but the trouble persists, the coil or capacitor must be suspect. These are best checked by substituting components which are known to be serviceable.

3:4 Distributor

Hitachi D411-58K distributors are fitted to engines which are provided with single (twin venturi) carburetters. Hitachi D 409-54K distributors are fitted to engines which have twin (SU type) carburetters. Both the centrifugal and vacuum unit characteristics differ between these two types but, as they are mechanically similar, the operations described in this Section are applicable to all models. The components of the distributor are shown in **FIG 3:2**. Access to a test bench is necessary when the advance/retard performance of a suspect or a reassembled distributor is to be checked.

Adjustment of the points gap is described in **Section 3:2**. Renewal of the set of points is described later.

Removal of distributor:

Remove the sparking plugs, refer to **FIG 3:6** and turn the engine until No. 1 piston is on TDC of its compression stroke (both valves closed and with the rotor arm aligned with the No. 1 sparking plug lead segment). Unclip and disconnect the leads from the sparking plugs and from the coil. Note the position of the graduations on the attachment plate (refer to **FIG 3:7**), remove the bolt which secures this plate to the cylinder block and dismount the distributor. Refer to **Chapter 1, Section 1:15** and note that the distributor drive shaft dog is positioned as shown in **FIG 1:5**. If the same distributor is being refitted, do not disturb the bolt which attaches the graduated plate to the distributor body.

Refitment of distributor:

Refer to **FIG 3:6** and, with the sparking plugs removed, turn the engine until No. 1 piston is on TDC of its compression stroke (both valves closed). Check that the distributor driving dog is positioned as shown in **FIG 1:5**. Fit the distributor and, with the rotor arm aligned with the No. 1 sparking plug lead segment, loosely fit the bolt which retains the graduated plate to the cylinder block. Turn the engine until the position of the graduations on the attachment plate is exactly as noted on removal. Tighten the plate retaining bolt. Have the timing checked as described in **Section 3:6**.

Fitment of a new distributor:

If a new distributor is being fitted, follow the procedure described earlier and refer to **FIG 3:7**. Set the graduated plate to approximately the middle of the A and R graduations and have the timing checked and accurately adjusted stroboscopically as described in the relevant part of **Section 3:6**.

Dismantling:

1 Remove the distributor as described earlier. Remove the cap and the rotor arm. Remove the vacuum unit.
2 Remove the contact breaker set as described later in this Section. Be careful not to lose the balls from between the breaker spring and the plate.
3 Punch out the pin which retains the driving collar to the shaft. Withdraw the shaft complete with the rotating parts.
4 Mark the cam and shaft so that they be reassembled in their original relative position. Remove the setscrew which retains the cam and pull off the cam.
5 Take careful note of how the centrifugal weights and springs are fitted and, being careful not to deform the springs, disconnect them from the weights. Remove the capacitor by withdrawing the single retaining screw.

Assembly:

Assembly is the reverse of the dismantling sequence. Refer to **FIG 3:8** when reassembling the centrifugal weights and springs. The breaker spring tension should be 1.1 to 1.4 lb (.5 to .65 kg) when measured with a tension gauge operating at right angles to the breaker arm. On completion of assembly, the unit should preferably be check tested on a distributor test bench and the advance/retard characteristics compared with those of the relevant distributor type.

Breaker points renewal:

Refer to **FIG 3:4**. Back off setscrew 1 by $1\frac{1}{2}$ to 2 turns and withdraw the primary lead. Remove the setscrews 5, withdraw the earth lead 4 and, while holding the contact arm aside, slide out the fixed contact point assembly after raising it slightly. Be careful not to lose the balls from between the breaker spring and the plate. Remove the contact breaker arm.

Fitment of the new set of points is the reverse of the removal sequence. Set the points gap as described in **Section 3:2**.

3:5 Coil

The oil insulated coil is of Hitachi manufacture and is a 6R-200 type. No maintenance is required and, should its performance be suspect, it is best checked by substitution.

An unserviceable coil cannot be repaired by an owner and must be replaced by a new component.

3:6 Timing the ignition

The timing marks are shown in **FIG 3:6**. The distributor attachment plate (refer to **FIG 3:7**) is provided with graduations which, as shown in **FIG 3:7**, form a scale for fine adjustment of the timing.

Maintenance timing check:

Every 6000 miles (10,000 km), have the ignition timing checked stroboscopically. Disconnect the pipe from the distributor vacuum unit, run the engine at idling rev/min and, under the light of a stroboscopic lamp triggered by connecting to No. 1 or No. 4 sparking plug, note the timing on the scale shown in **FIG 3:6**. For single carburetter

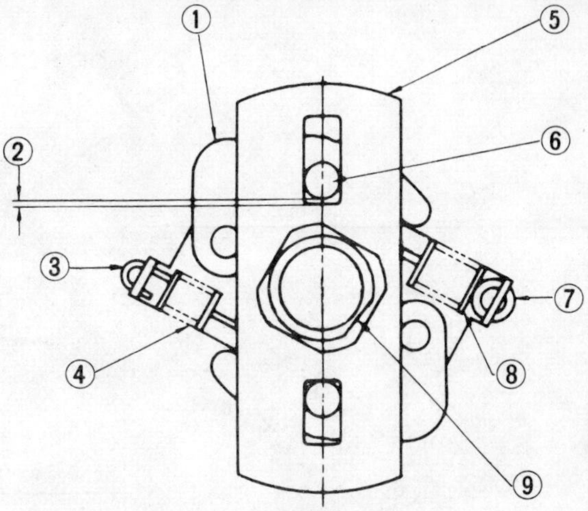

FIG 3:8 Centrifugal governor

Key to Fig 3:8 1 Centrifugal weight 2 Clearance 3 Hook 4 Spring 5 Cam plate 6 Pin 7 Hook 8 Spring 9 Flat for rotor arm drive

models the timing should be 10 deg. BTDC and for twin carburetter models, 14 deg. BTDC. Adjust, if necessary, as described later. Refit the pipe to the vacuum unit.

Adjustment:

Refer to **FIG 3:7**. Adjustment to the timing is made by loosening the bolt which locks the graduated plate to the cylinder block and rotating the complete distributor in the advance or retard direction as appropriate. Retighten the bolt and recheck the timing.

Reassembly timing:

Fit the distributor as described in **Section 3:4** and, on completion of the installation, have the timing checked and accurately set stroboscopically as described earlier in the current Section.

3:7 Sparking plugs

Recommended types:

Sparking plugs with 14 mm diameter threads are used. Plugs of NGK manufacture are officially recommended. BP-5ES type plugs are recommended for single carburetter engines and BP-6ES type plugs for twin carburetter engines. British, American or Continental equivalents which have a reach of 19 mm may be fitted. The electrode gap should be .031 to .035 inch (.8 to .9 mm).

Cleaning and testing:

At least every 6000 miles (10,000 km), have the plugs cleaned on an abrasive-blasting machine and tested under pressure with the gaps correctly set.

Prior to setting the gaps on used plugs, the electrodes should be filed until they are bright and parallel. The gaps must always be adjusted by bending the earth electrode. **Do not attempt to bend the centre electrode or the insulation will be damaged.**

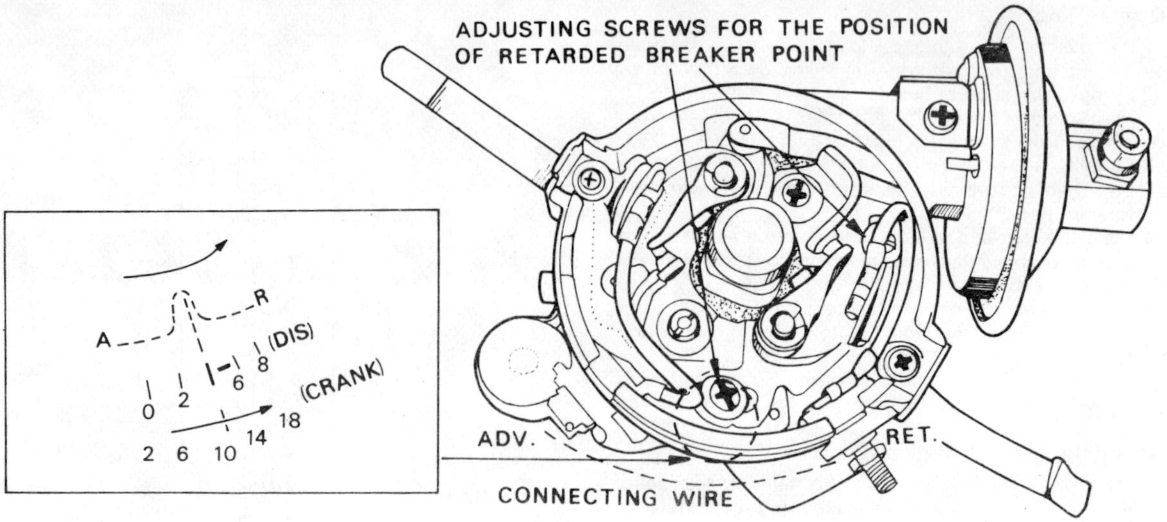

FIG 3:9 Emission control (dual contact breaker) distributor with cap removed

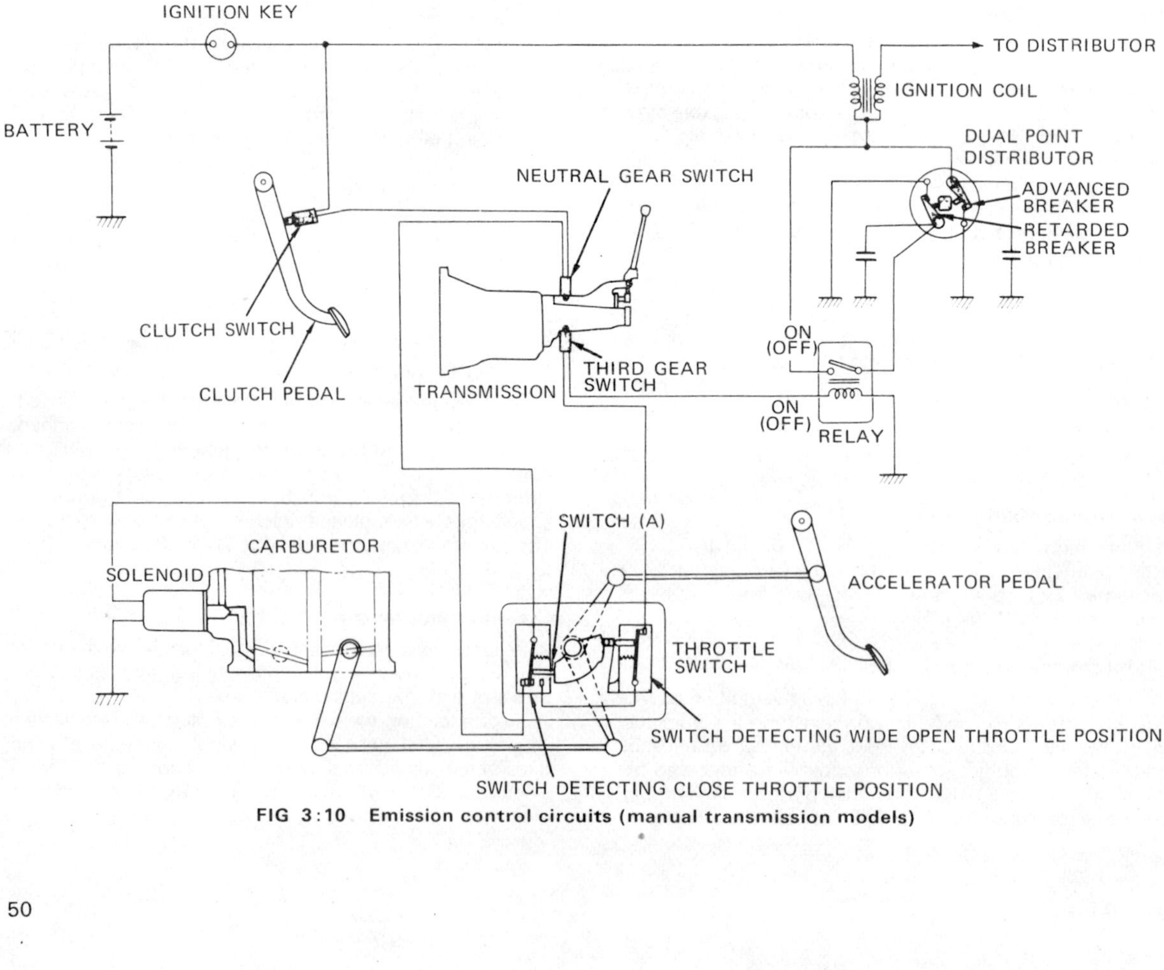

FIG 3:10 Emission control circuits (manual transmission models)

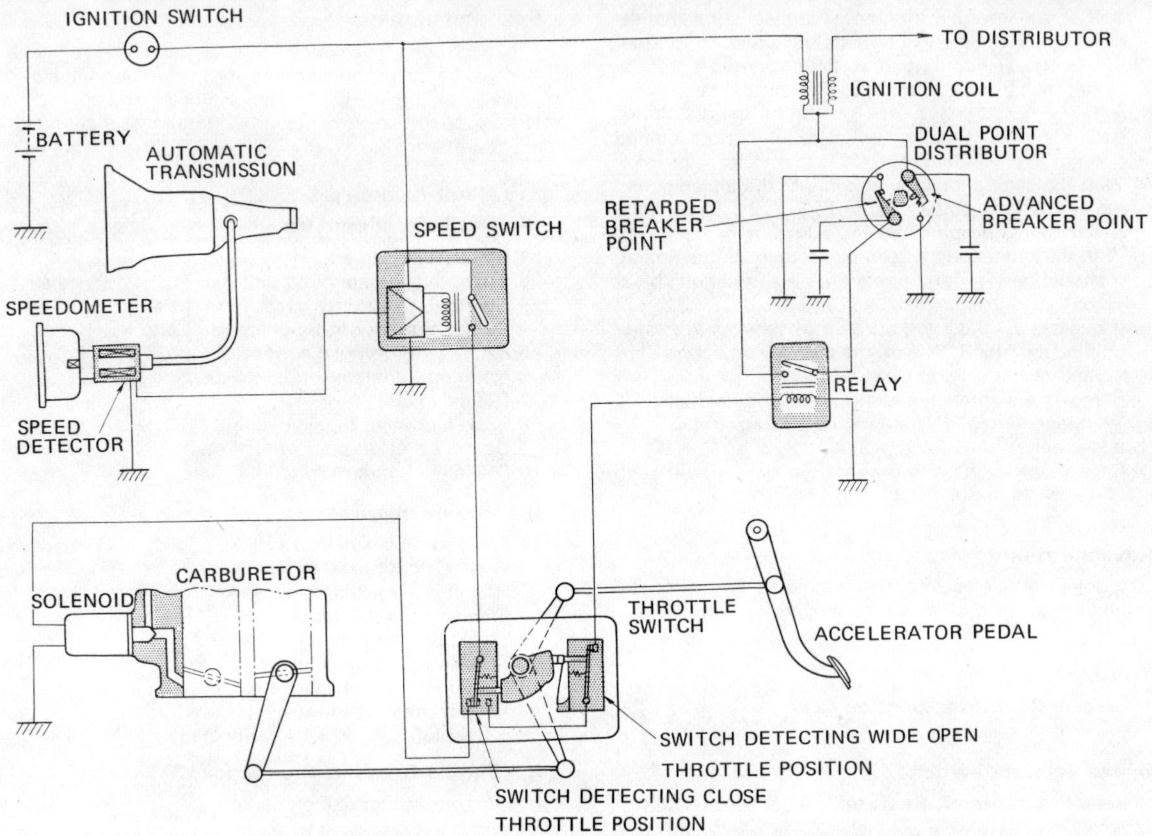

FIG 3:11 Emission control circuits (automatic transmission models)

Plugs as tuning guide:

Inspection of the deposits on electrodes can be a helpful guide when tuning. Normally, from mixed periods of high and low speed driving, the deposits should be powdery and range in colour from brown to greyish tan. There will also be some slight wear of the electrodes. Long periods of fairly constant speed driving or low speed city driving will produce white or yellowish deposits. Dry, black fluffy deposits are due to incomplete combustion and indicate running with a rich mixture, excessive idling and possibly defective ignition. Overheated plugs have a white or light grey look round the centre electrode and the electrodes themselves will appear bluish and burnt. This may be due to weak mixture, poor cooling, incorrect ignition or sustained high speed running with a heavily loaded vehicle.

Black, wet deposits result from oil in the combustion chamber from worn pistons, rings, valve stems or guides or from worn and scored cylinder bores. Spark plugs which run hotter may alleviate this problem but the cure is in an engine overhaul.

3:8 Emission control system

As described in **Section 3:1**, the distributor which is fitted to models equipped for emission control, is provided with two sets of contact breaker points and the relevant part of the distributor (with the cap removed) is shown in **FIG 3:9**. The retard set of points are brought into circuit when an electrical relay is energized. The circuit is included in **FIGS 3:10** and **3:11**.

The manual transmission model circuit is shown in **FIG 3:10**. The relay is energized only when the transmission is in third gear and the throttle is partially open.

The automatic transmission model circuit is shown in **FIG 3:11**. In this case the relay is only energized when the vehicle road speed is in excess of 13 miles/hr with the throttle partially open.

Maintenance:

Follow the recommendation given in **Section 3:2** but check the ignition timing every 3000 miles (5000 km), clean the sparking plugs at this same mileage interval and renew the contact breaker points every 12,000 miles (20,000 km).

Ignition timing check:

1 Check, and adjust if necessary, both sets of points before proceeding with the ignition timing checks. Both breaker gaps should be set to .018 to .022 inch (.45 to .55 mm).
2 Ensure that the idling speed is correctly set (as described in **Chapter 2, Section 2:6** or **Section**

2:7 at 700 rev/min for manual transmission models or at 720 rev/min for automatic transmission models.

3 Check the 'standard' ignition timing stroboscopically as described in **Section 3:6**. This should be 10 deg. BTDC. Adjust as necessary by rotating the distributor body and tighten the bolt which retains the graduated plate to the cylinder block.

4 With the engine idling, interconnect the advance and the retard (see dotted line in **FIG 3:9**). The engine speed should drop by 100 to 150 rev/min.

5 With the connecting wire in place, recheck the timing. It should now (with the retard points in circuit) be at TDC.

6 If necessary, adjust the position of the retard breaker points (see **FIG 3:9**) with the engine stationary. Start up and recheck. Readjust if necessary.

7 Remove the interconnecting wire and recheck the 'standard' timing. This should be 10 deg. BTDC.

8 If it is not, readjust by repeating operation 3.

9 Repeat operations 4 to 8 until both timing points are correctly set and are stable.

Advance/retard relay:

A defective relay cannot be repaired by an owner and should be replaced by a new assembly.

Third gear switch:

Refer to **Chapter 6, Section 6:2**.

Speed detector switch:

Refer to **Chapter 7, Section 7:3**.

Sparking plugs:

NGK type BP-6E sparking plugs are officially recommended for fitment to emission control models. Equivalent plugs with threads of 14 mm diameter and a reach of 19 mm of British, American or Continental manufacture may be fitted.

3:9 Fault daignosis:

(a) Engine will not fire

1 Battery discharged
2 Distributor points dirty, pitted or out of adjustment
3 Distributor cap dirty, cracked or 'tracking'
4 Centre contact not touching rotor arm
5 Faulty wire or loose connection in LT circuit
6 Rotor arm defective
7 Defective coil
8 Broken contact breaker spring
9 Contact breaker points stuck open
10 Defective ignition switch

(b) Engine misfires

1 Check 2, 3, 5 and 7 in (a)
2 Weak contact breaker spring
3 HT cables cracked or perished
4 Sparking plug(s) loose
5 Sparking plug insulation cracked
6 Sparking plug gaps incorrectly set
7 Ignition timing too far advanced
8 Fouled sparking plug(s)
9 HT cable(s) incorrectly connected

(c) Engine fires but then stops

1 Ignition resistor defective

CHAPTER 4

THE COOLING SYSTEM

4:1 Description
4:2 Maintenance
4:3 The radiator
4:4 The fan and water pump
4:5 The thermostat
4:6 Frost precautions
4:7 Fault diagnosis

4:1 Description

The coolant flow path is indicated in the partially cutaway radiator, cylinder block and cylinder head illustration shown in **FIG 4:1**.

The system is thermostatically controlled and is pressurized. The relief valve which is incorporated in the radiator filler cap, limits the maximum pressure to approximately 13 lb/sq inch (.9 kg/sq cm). Coolant circulation is assisted by a centrifugal pump which is incorporated in the engine front cover and is belt driven from a pulley on the crankshaft together with the cooling fan and the alternator. The pump receives coolant from the bottom of the radiator and passes it to the cylinder block from which it rises to the passages of the cylinder head. At normal operating temperatures, coolant returns from the cylinder head to the top of the radiator through a thermostatically controlled valve in the coolant outlet elbow at the cylinder head. At lower coolant temperatures, this valve remains closed and coolant by-passes the radiator until it has warmed up and the valve opens. This arrangement provides a rapid warm-up of the coolant.

On models which are equipped with air conditioning, a fluid coupling is incorporated into the fan drive. This limits the fan speed to 3000 rev/min and reduces fan noise and the power taken to drive the fan at high engine speeds.

4:2 Maintenance

Check the coolant level regularly. If the engine is hot, to avoid the danger of being scalded and to prevent loss of coolant, place a cloth over the filler cap and release the pressure before removing the cap.

If antifreeze solution (see **Section 4:6**) is not in use, the system should be drained and flushed to remove sediment every 6000 miles (10,000 km). If antifreeze solution is being used, it should be inspected every 12,000 miles (20,000 km) or every 12 months and, if it is dirty or has a rusty appearance, flush the system and refill with fresh solution. The antifreeze solution should, in any case, be discarded after every two winters or after 24,000 miles (40,000 km). It is preferable that this maintenance is carried out immediately before the start of winter.

Draining:

Open the radiator and cylinder block drains, remove the filler cap and allow the system to drain completely.

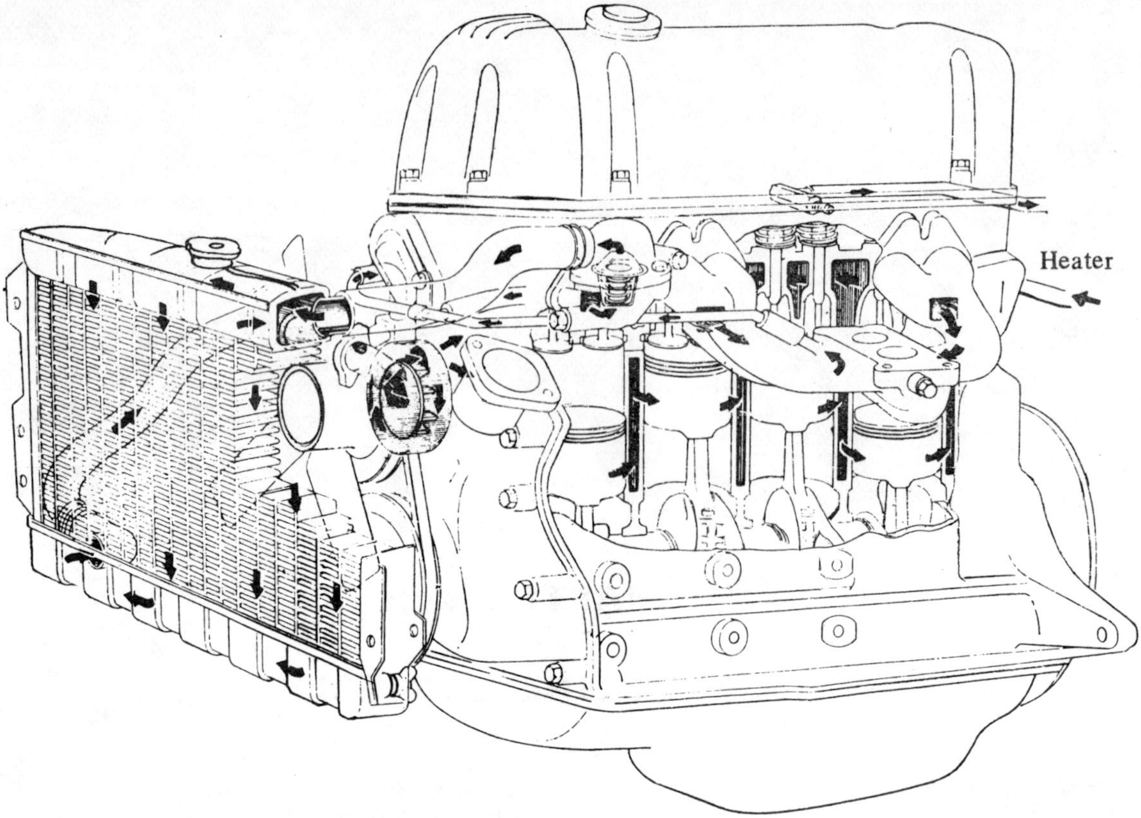

FIG 4:1 The cooling system

Certain operations (removal of the thermostat, for example) do not require the system to be fully drained and, in these cases, the drain taps should be closed when the level has fallen sufficiently.

Flushing:

Drain the system. Remove the thermostat as described in **Section 4:5** and temporarily refit the outlet elbow.

Use a water hose and allow water to run into the radiator filler orifice. Adjust the rate of flow to balance the rate of drainage and, with the header tank full, run the engine at about 1000 rev/min to assist circulation until the drainage water runs clear. Remove the outlet elbow and refit the thermostat as described in **Section 4:5**.

Filling:

Close the drain taps. Prepare the correct solution of antifreeze as described in **Section 4:6** and fill the system. Fit the filler cap and run the engine up to normal operating temperature. When the coolant is cold, check the level of the radiator and top up as necessary.

The capacity of the cooling system inclusive of the heater is approximately 11 pints (6.5 litres).

4:3 The radiator

Radiators fitted to automatic transmission models incorporate a transmission fluid cooler in the bottom tank.

Removal:

1 Drain the coolant as described in **Section 4:2**. If antifreeze is in use and its condition is serviceable, collect it for re-use.
2 Remove the front grille as described in **Chapter 13, Section 13:3.**
3 Disconnect the upper and lower hoses.
4 In the case of automatic transmission models, disconnect the cooler inlet and outlet pipes from the bottom tank of the radiator and blank off the pipe and radiator connections to preclude entry of foreign matters.
5 Remove the bolts which attach the radiator to the side supports and withdraw the radiator upwards.

Keep the radiator in an upright position so that any scale or sediement in the bottom tank will not pass into the matrix and cause a blockage.

A radiator in which the matrix is leaking or which has a defective top or bottom tank should be passed to a specialist for repair. A radiator which is severely corroded or which has suffered serious damage should be rejected and replaced by a new unit.

In the case of an automatic transmission model radiator, a leaking transmission fluid cooler will allow fluid to enter the cooling system and evidence of this will show in the contaminated coolant.

Refitting:

The installation of the radiator is the reverse of the removal sequence. Fit new hoses if their condition is doubtful. Fill the radiator as described in **Section 4:2** and, for preference, use antifreeze. Run the engine up to normal operating temperature and check that there are no leaks from the hose connections. After driving the car, check automatic transmission models for leaks at the cooler connections.

Restricted flow:

If poor flow through the radiator matrix is suspected, a proprietary radiator cleaning chemical may be used. Flush the system as described in **Section 4:2**, refill with the cleaning solution and, after the prescribed period of running, drain the system and repeat the flushing procedure. Use only a reputable cleaning chemical and adhere to the makers' instructions rigidly.

4:4 Fan and water pump

The belt drive pulley and the fan are attached to the flange of the water pump spindle by the same bolts. The belt also drives the alternator and the procedures for tensioning the belt and renewing it when necessary are described in **Chapter 12, Section 12:4**.

It is important to maintain correct belt tension. A belt that is too tightly tensioned will strain the alternator and water pump bearings while a belt that is loose will slip. This will result in inefficient operation of the fan and alternator and may, while slipping, emit squealing noise.

Fan removal:

Remove the drive belt as described in **Chapter 12, Section 12:4**. Remove the bolts which retain the fan and pulley to the water pump flange and dismount the fan and the pulley.

Fan fitment:

This is the reverse of the removal sequence. Fit the belt and tension it as described in **Chapter 12, Section 12:4**.

Fluid fan drive:

On models which are equipped with air conditioning equipment, the fan and water pump are provided with a fluid couping drive. Silicon oil of 700 CTS viscosity number is used in the unit. The refill capacity is .7 cub. inch (11.5 cc) precisely. A veterinary type syringe is required to inject the oil into the coupling as shown in **FIG 4:2**.

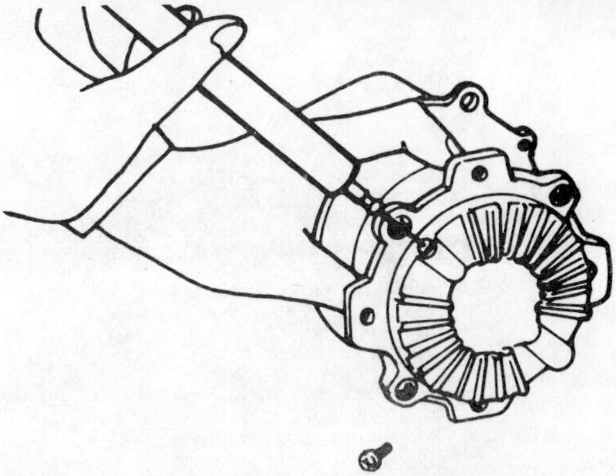

FIG 4:2 Refilling the fluid fan drive (air conditioned models)

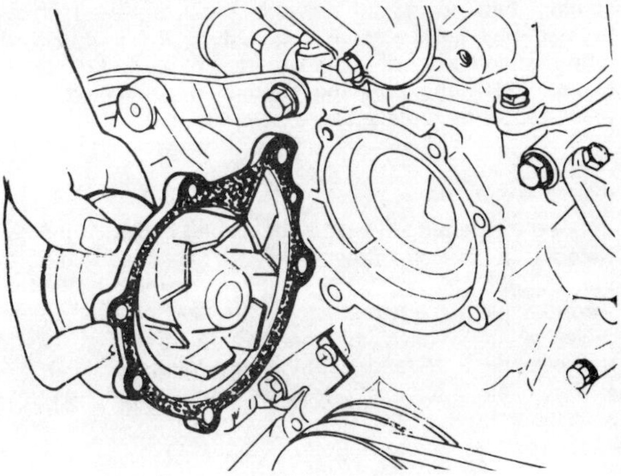

FIG 4:3 Removing the pump

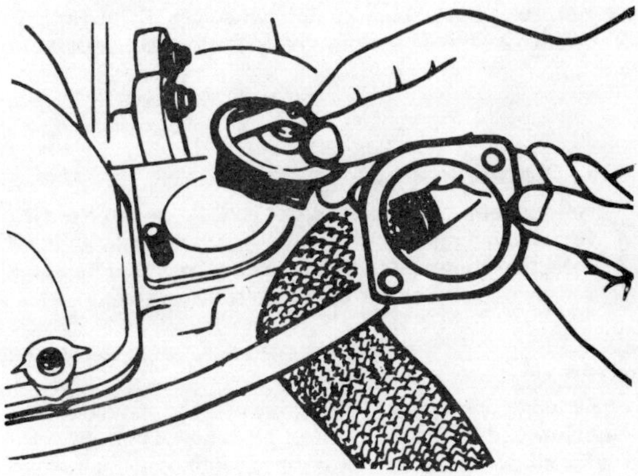

FIG 4:4 Removing the thermostat valve

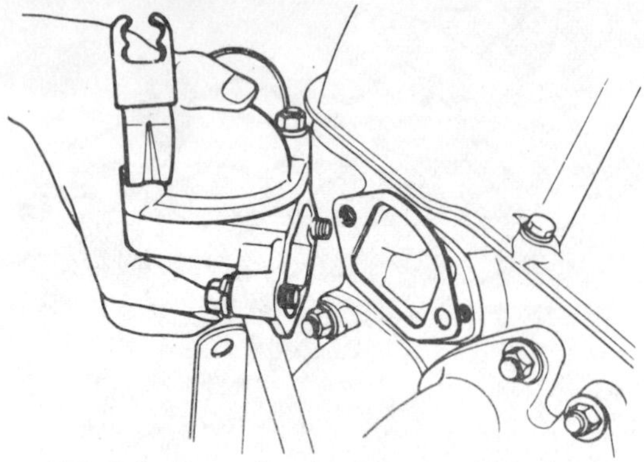

FIG 4:5 Removing the thermostat housing

Water pump:

The pump is a centrifugal impeller type in which coolant is drawn into the eye of an impeller and discharged to a volute which is integral with the front cover. The pump spindle runs in a double row ballbearing which is permanently lubricated and sealed to prevent loss of lubricant and entry of water or dirt. The pump cannot be overhauled by an owner and, should it become unserviceable, it must be replaced by a new assembly.

Pump removal:

Drain the cooling system as described in **Section 4:2**. Remove the fan and drive pulley as described earlier. If the radiator has not been removed, dismount the fan shroud which is retained by four bolts. Removal of the drive belt is covered in **Chapter 12, Section 12:4**. Remove five bolts and withdraw the pump (**FIG 4:3**). Remove all traces of gasket material and jointing compound from the front cover face and, if the same pump is being refitted, from the pump joint face.

Pump fitment:

Fitment is the reverse of the removal sequence. Use a new gasket and tighten the retaining bolts evenly. Refill the cooling system as described in **Section 4:2**. Fit and tension the drive belt as described in **Chapter 12, Section 12:4**. Run the engine up to normal temperature and check for coolant leaks.

4:5 The thermostat

The function of the thermostat is described in **Section 4:1**. It is located in coolant outlet from the cylinder head. A defective thermostat must be removed and replaced by a new unit. It cannot be repaired by an owner.

Removal:

Partially drain the cooling system as described in **Section 4:2**. Disconnect the upper radiator hose from the outlet elbow at the cylinder head. Remove the coolant outlet and, as shown in **FIG 4:4**, remove the thermostat. **FIG 4:5** shows the thermostat housing complete with coolant outlet (and thermostat) being removed from the cylinder head.

Fitting:

Use a new gasket. Insert the thermostat, fit the outlet connection and recouple the hose. Top up the level of the coolant. Run the engine up to normal operating temperature and check for coolant leaks.

Testing a thermostat:

Remove the thermostat as described earlier. Clean it off and ensure that no scale or sediment is interfering with its operation. Immerse it in a container of cold water together with a 0° to 100°C (32° to 212°F) thermometer. Heat the water and, keeping it stirred, observe if the thermostat begins to open at the specified temperature and opens by .315 inch (8 mm) at the specified full open temperature. There are three types of thermostats to suit different climatic conditions. The temperatures at which each begins to open and at which each is fully open are given in **Technical Data** in the Appendix.

4:6 Frost precautions

The use of antifreeze at all times is recommended since, apart from it providing protection from frost, the correct solution will inhibit corrosion in the cooling system. Use only an ethylene-glycol type antifreeze of reputable make. The recommended proportions of water and the antifreeze chemical should be measured into a separate container and the cooling system filled from this and not by adding the chemical directly into the radiator.

The proportions of antifreeze for different degrees of frost protection are generally as follows but the manufacturer's recommendations may differ slightly.

Per cent of antifreeze	*Starts freezing at*	*Absolute safe limit*
20%	—19°C	—9°C
25%	—26°C	—13°C
30%	—33°C	—16°C
40%	—40°C	—19°C

A 30% solution will normally be satisfactory. If antifreeze is not used, it must be remembered that the action of the thermostat will delay circulation of warm coolant to the radiator which may consequently freeze after the engine has started.

After two winters use, discard the antifreeze and, after flushing the system as described in **Section 4:2**, refill with fresh solution. This maintenance should preferably be carried out immediately before winter.

4:7 Fault diagnosis

(a) Internal coolant leakage

1 Cracked cylinder block
2 Loose cylinder head bolts
3 Cracked cylinder head
4 Faulty head gasket

(b) Poor circulation

1 Radiator matrix blocked
2 Coolant passages restricted
3 Low coolant level
4 Fan belt loose
5 Defective pump
6 Defective thermostat valve
7 Perished or collapsed hose(s)
8 Defective fluid fan drive (air conditioned models)

(c) Corrosion

1 Impurities in the coolant
2 Infrequent draining and flushing

(d) Overheating

1 Check (b)
2 Sludge in crankcase
3 Low oil level in sump
4 Tight engine
5 Faulty ignition timing
6 Retarded ignition
7 Incorrect valve timing
8 Mixture too weak
9 Choked exhaust system
10 Binding brakes
11 Slipping clutch
12 Slipping fluid fan drive (air conditioned models)

NOTES

CHAPTER 5

THE CLUTCH

5:1 Description
5:2 Maintenance
5:3 Removing and refitting the clutch
5:4 Servicing the clutch
5:5 The release mechanism
5:6 Fault diagnosis

5:1 Description

The assembly is a single dry-plate clutch which operates directly against the rear face of the flywheel onto which the clutch cover assembly is bolted. The operational pressure is provided by a diaphragm type spring acting through a pressure plate. The components are shown partly dismantled in **FIG 5:1**.

When the clutch is engaged, the driven plate which is splined to the gearbox primary shaft and is nipped between the pressure plate and the flywheel by the diaphragm spring, is caused to rotate with the flywheel and transmits torque to the gearbox. The clutch is released (disengaged) when the pressure plate is withdrawn from the driven plate by hydraulically connected leverage between the clutch pedal and the clutch release bearing. The driven plate then ceases to transmit torque. The hydraulic release system is covered in **Section 5:5**.

The complete clutch assembly can be removed from the vehicle without removing the engine but the propeller shaft and the manual transmission gearbox must first be dismounted.

On manual transmission models equipped with exhaust emission control, the clutch switch (see **Chapter 3, FIG 3:10**) is actuated by the clutch pedal and adjustment of this switch is described in **Section 5:2**.

5:2 Maintenance

Fluid level:

Check the level in the master cylinder reservoir every 3000 miles (5000 km) and top up as necessary. Use the same approved fluid as that already in the system. This should be heavy duty brake fluid of reputable manufacture to SAEJ170a specification.

Free play adjustment:

Every 6000 miles (10,000 km), check the pedal free play as described in **Section 5:5** and adjust as necessary.

Pedal height adjustment:

Every 12,000 miles (20,000 km), check and, if necessary, adjust the clutch pedal height. The procedure is described in **Section 5:5**. Lubricate the clutch pedal pivot and the master cylinder clevis pin. These points are marked MG in **FIG 5:2**. Use multi-purpose grease.

Clutch switch adjustment:

This adjustment is only applicable to models which are equipped with exhaust emission control. It should be carried out at the same time as adjustment of the clutch pedal height as referred to earlier.

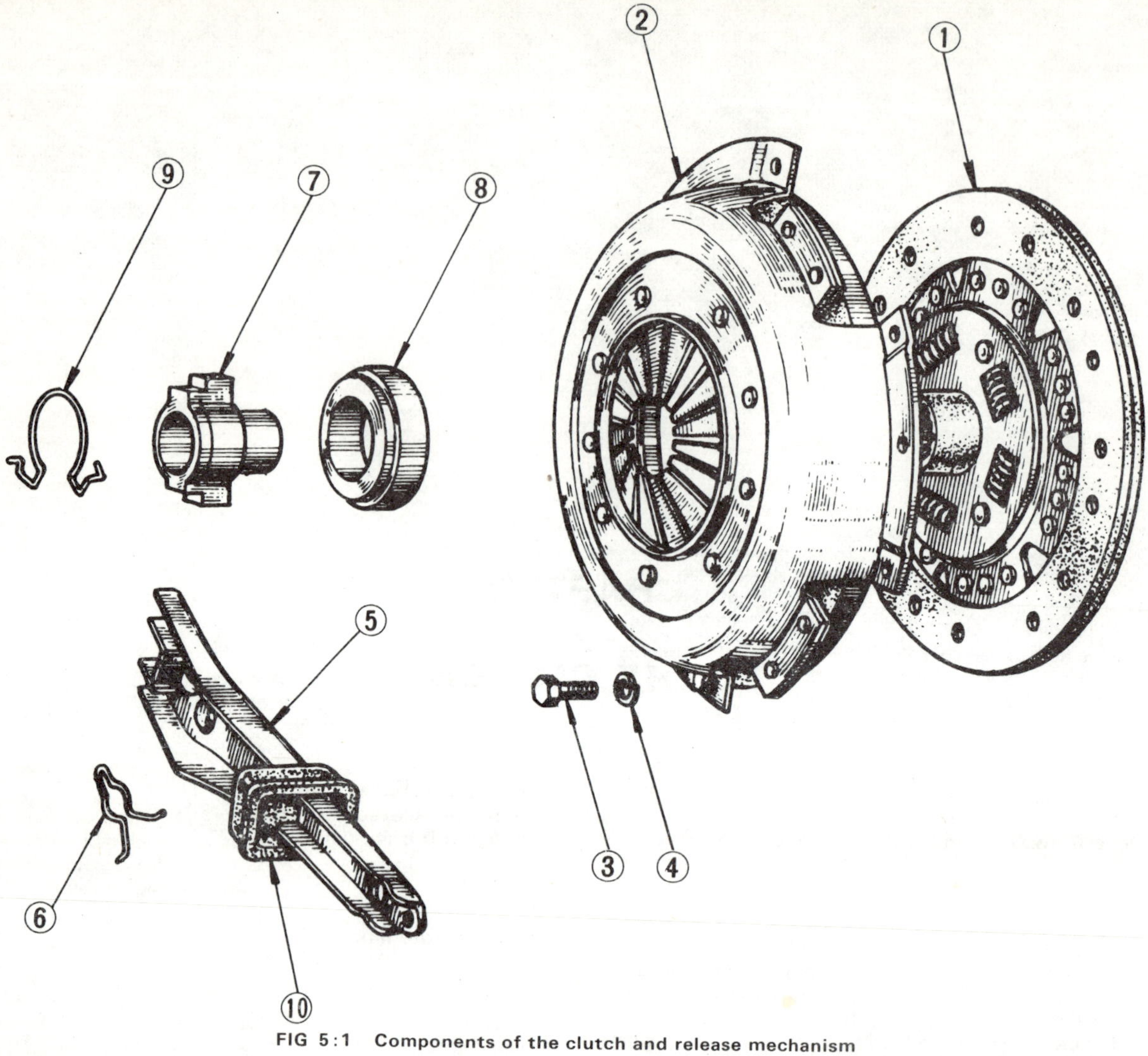

FIG 5:1 **Components of the clutch and release mechanism**

Key to Fig 5:1 1 Driven plate 2 Clutch cover/pressure plate assembly 3 Bolt 4 Washer 5 Release lever 6 Spring 7 Release sleeve 8 Release bearing 9 Spring 10 Rubber boot

The switch circuitry is included in **FIG 3:10** and the switch itself is shown in **FIG 5:3**. The switch is 'off' when the clutch pedal is depressed and, at other times, it is 'on'.

Remove the two wires from the switch. Rig a battery and test lamp to the two connections and adjust the switch mounting so that the test lamp goes out when the clutch pedal is depressed but is on when the pedal is in the clutch engaged position. After adjustment, disconnect the battery and test lamp and reconnect the switch wiring.

5:3 Removing and fitting the clutch

The following procedure for removing the clutch applies in its entirety when the engine and transmission unit has not been removed from the vehicle. If the engine and transmission unit has been removed as described in **Chapter 1, Section 1:7,** operation 1 will not be relevant nor will the earlier stages of operation 2.

Removal with the engine in the vehicle:

1 With the vehicle on a hoist or over a pit, remove the clutch release actuating cylinder as described in **Section 5:5**. Remove the propeller shaft as described in **Chapter 8, Section 8:2**.
2 Remove the transmission gearbox as described in **Chapter 6, Section 6:3**.
3 Refer to **FIG 5:4** and fit a clutch aligning bar ST20600000 through the hub of the driven plate and into the pilot bearing in the crankshaft. It is important

to support the weight of the driven plate while removing the clutch cover and pressure plate assembly.

4 Working diagonally and evenly, loosen the bolts (3 in **FIG 5 : 1**) which retain the assembly to the flywheel by one turn at a time until the diaphragm spring load has been released.

5 Support the cover assembly, remove the bolts and collect the washers. Dismount the cover assembly.

6 Support the driven plate, remove the aligning bar and dismount the driven plate. Do not allow oil or grease to contaminate the friction linings.

Fitment:

After servicing the clutch or obtaining new parts as described in **Section 5 : 4**, fitment of the driven plate and the clutch cover/pressure plate assembly is basically the removal sequence in reverse.

Ensure that the flywheel face is clean and free from grease and oil and that the three dowels which locate the clutch cover are clean and free of burrs. Slight surface roughness of the flywheel face may be smoothed with fine emery cloth. Check that the pilot bush in the tail end of the crankshaft is serviceable and, if it is not, refer to the relevant part of **Chapter 1, Section 1 : 13**. Proceed then as follows and ensure that no oil or grease is allowed to contaminate the flywheel face, the pressure plate face or the driven plate friction linings.

1 Apply a light coating of molybdenum disulphide grease to the splines of the gearbox main drive shaft. Slide the driven plate onto and off these splines several times and then wipe off excess grease from the faces of the plate hub.

2 Position the plate onto the flywheel and support it in position by fitting the aligning bar ST20600000 as at operation 3 of the removal procedure.

3 Confirm that the faces of the pressure plate and clutch cover are clean, fit the assembly to locate with the three dowels and fit the retaining washers and bolts.

4 Working diagonally and evenly, tighten the retaining bolts one turn at a time and finally torque tighten then to 12 to 16 lb ft (1.6 to 2.2 kgm).

5 Withdraw the aligning bar. **Do not operate the clutch release lever until after the gearbox has been fitted** or the driven plate will slip out of alignment.

6 The remaining operations are the reverse of removal operations 1 and 2.

5 : 4 Servicing the clutch

Remove the clutch cover assembly and the driven plate as described in **Section 5 : 3**. Dismantle the clutch release lever, release bearing sleeve and the release bearing as described in **Section 5 : 5**.

Clutch cover assembly:

Wash off the clutch cover assembly in paraffin and dry thoroughly. Note that any oil on or in the assembly is indicative of a defective crankshaft or transmission gearbox seal.

The clutch cover/pressure plate/diaphragm spring assembly is a rivetted and factory balanced unit. It cannot be dismantled for fitment or new parts and, if the assembly is unserviceable in any of the following respects, a new replacement assembly will be required.

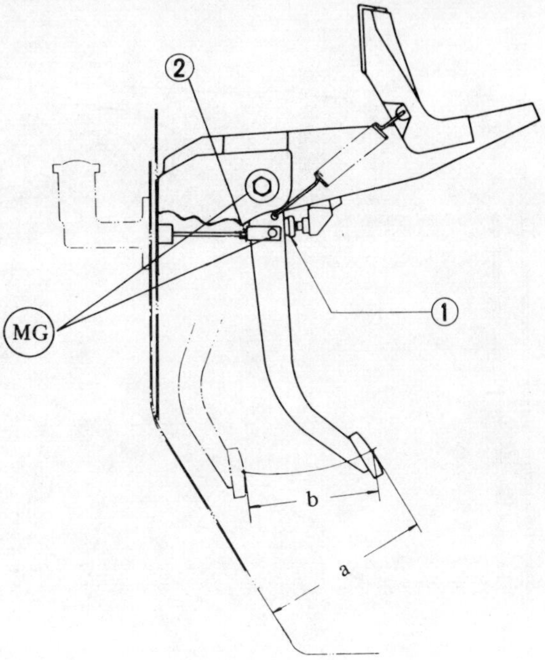

FIG 5 : 2 Clutch pedal

Key to Fig 5 : 2 1 Pedal stop locknut 2 Pushrod locknut

Pressure plate:

Examine the surface of the pressure plate. Slight roughness may be removed with emergy paper (as also may the surface of the flywheel be so treated). The face should be flat to within .004 inch (.1 mm). The allowable refacing limit is also .004 inch (.1 mm). If the surface is deeply scored or grooved, a new assembly will be required.

Diaphragm spring:

Check that none of the diaphragm spring fingers is broken or excessively worn at the inner end. If a finger is broken or if wear is excessive, a new assembly will be required.

Diaphragm spring height:

Measure the height of the diaphragm spring as shown in **FIG 5 : 5**. The clutch cover and pressure plate assembly is bolted down onto base plate ST20500010 with distance piece ST20500100 positioned under the pressure plate. The dimension **A** must be within the range of 1.693 to 1.772 inch (43 to 45 mm). If the dimension **A** is outside this range, adjust the spring height using diaphragm spring adjusting tool ST 20500240 as shown in **FIG 5 : 6**. Variation in the height of individual spring fingers should not exceed .002 inch (.5 mm). If the diaphragm spring height cannot be brought within this specification, a new assembly will be required.

Thrust rings:

The thrust rings cannot be inspected visually. Shake the cover assembly up and down and listen for the noise of loose rivets, etc. A new assembly will be required if the rivets or thrust rings are loose or cracked.

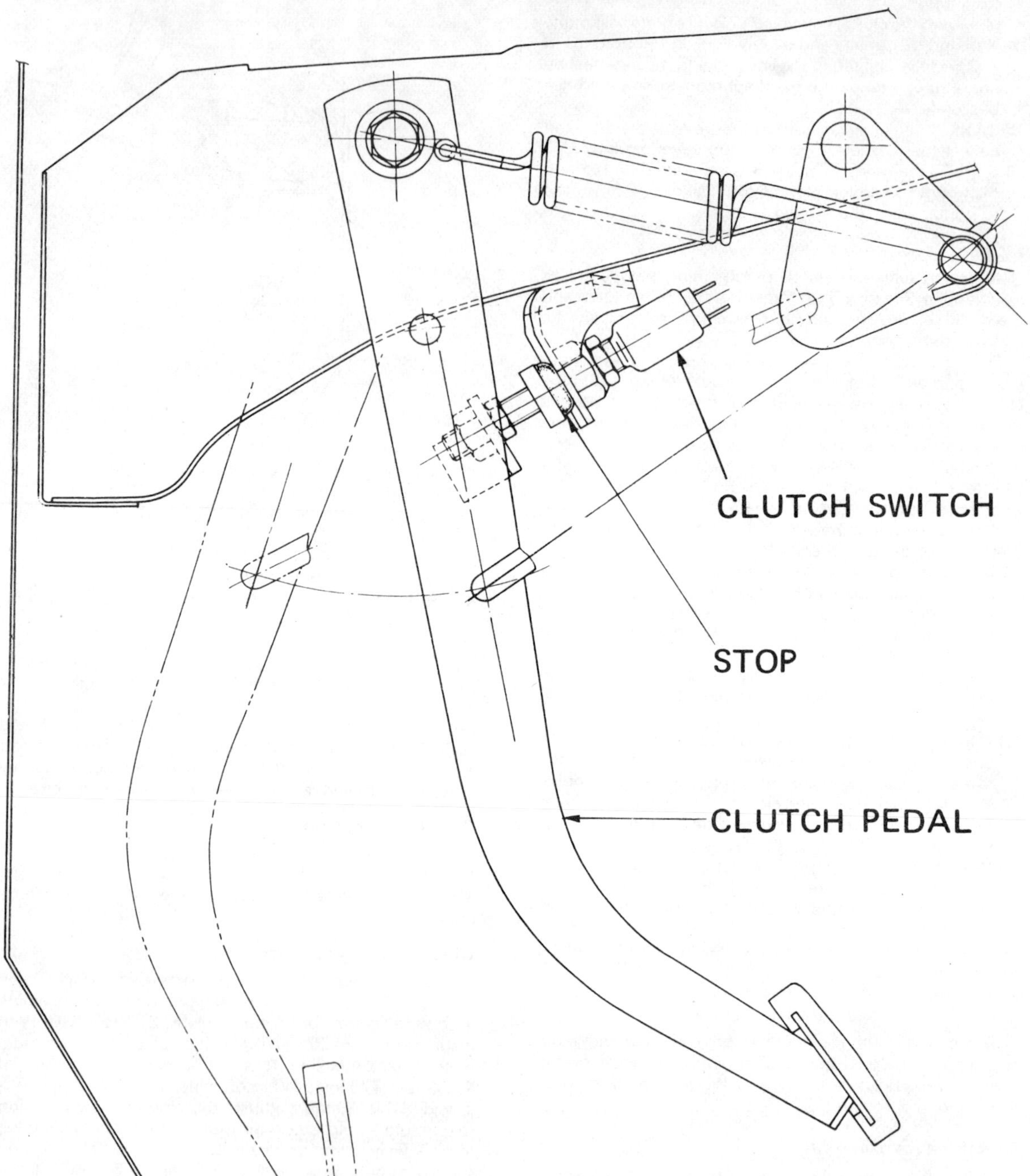

FIG 5:3 Clutch switch (emission control models)

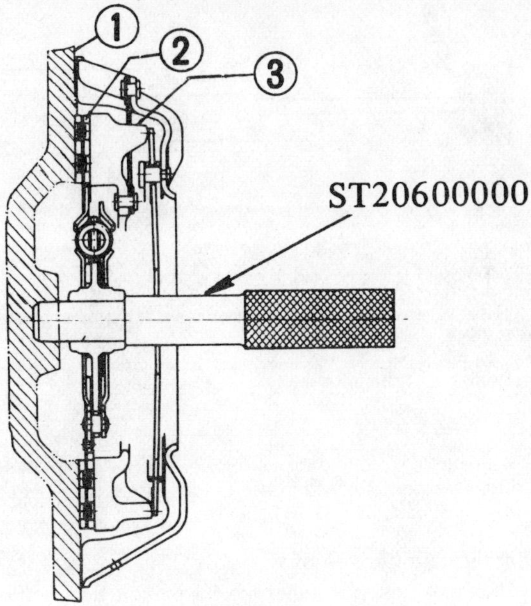

FIG 5:4 Alignment bar in position

Key to Fig 5:4 1 Flywheel 2 Driven plate 3 Pressure plate

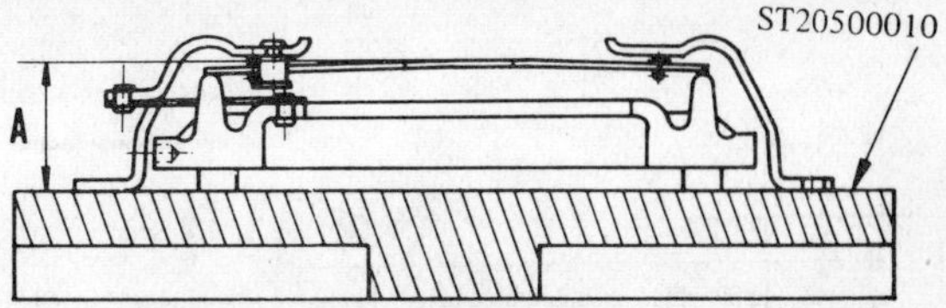

FIG 5:5 Measuring the spring height

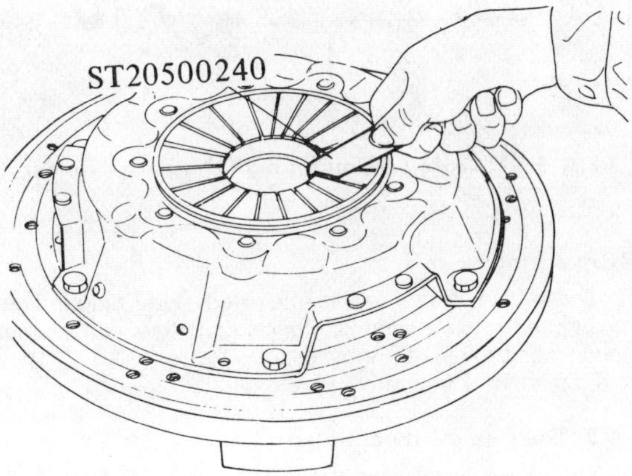

FIG 5:6 Adjusting the spring height

Clutch driven plate:

Clean the hub and splines. This should be done 'dry' to preclude the possibility of cleaning solvent contaminating the friction linings. If the linings are found to be contaminated with oil or grease, reject the plate and obtain a new replacement. Note that any oil on the component is indicative of a defective oil seal in the gearbox or crankshaft.

Friction linings:

Using a depth gauge as shown in **FIG 5:7**, measure the thickness of friction lining remaining above the rivets. Reject the plate if the lining thickness on either side is worn below .012 inch (.3 mm).

Hub splines:

Check the hub/main drive shaft spline combination for wear. Backlash, measured at the periphery of the driven plate, should not exceed .016 inch (.4 mm). If it exceeds this figure, recheck with a new plate and/or new drive shaft and renew whichever part(s) may then be then indicated.

Driven plate runout:

The runout, measured at a radius of 3.740 inch (95 mm), should not exceed .02 inch (.5 mm).

Driven plate thickness:

The free thickness of a new plate is .338 to .354 inch (8.6 to 9.0 mm). The compressed thickness is .301 to .313 inch (7.65 to 7.95 mm).

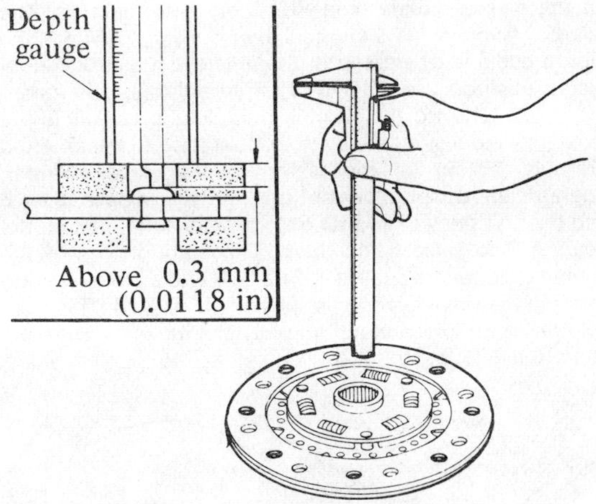

FIG 5:7 Measuring lining thickness

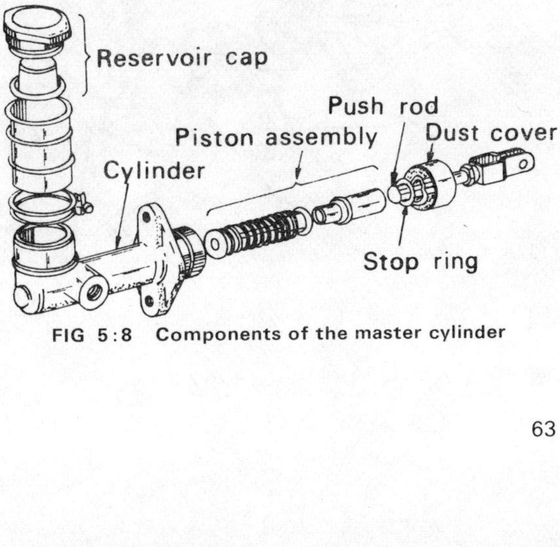

FIG 5:8 Components of the master cylinder

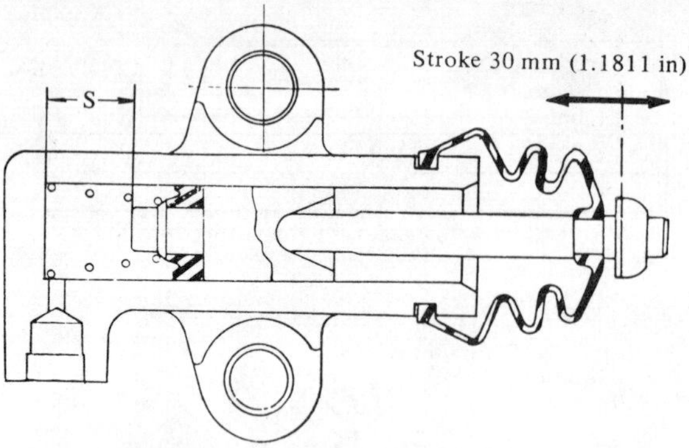

FIG 5:9 **Cross-section through the slave cylinder**

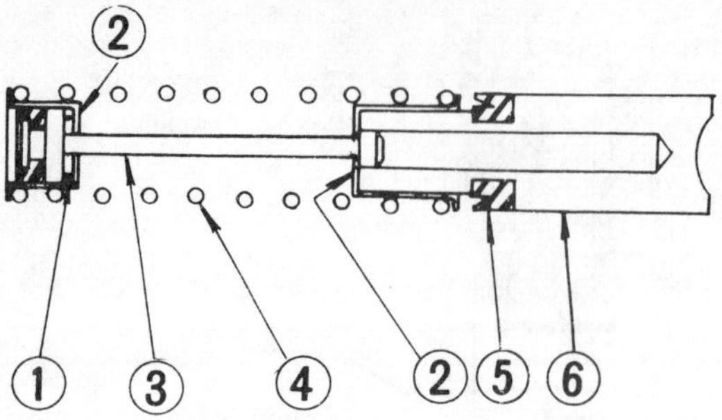

FIG 5:11 **Cross-section through master cylinder piston assembly**

Key to Fig 5:11 1 Valve spring 2 Spring seal 3 Valve assembly 4 Return spring 5 Piston cup 6 Piston

Hub springs:

The driven plate hub is provided with tangentially positioned torsion springs. Check that these are neither loose nor broken. Springs cannot be renewed. If they are defective, a new driven plate will be required.

5:5 The release mechanism

The clutch is released when the release bearing 8 in **FIG 5:1** is levered forwards against the diaphragm spring fingers and the spring load on the peripheral projection on the pressure plate (see **FIG 5:4**) is withdrawn. The release leverage is actuated hydraulically. When the clutch pedal is depressed it operates the master cylinder piston pushrod (see **FIG 5:2**). Hydraulic fluid is forced by the piston into the flexible pipe which connects the master cylinder with the slave or operating cylinder. Fluid pressure, acting on the piston in the slave cylinder, operates the pushrod which, through the release lever 5 and bearing sleeve 7 in **FIG 5:1**, provides the load on the bearing 8 to release the drive. The components of the master cylinder are shown in **FIG 5:8** and a cross-section through the slave cylinder is shown in **FIG 5:9**. The slave cylinder and its connection with the release lever are shown in **FIG 5:10**.

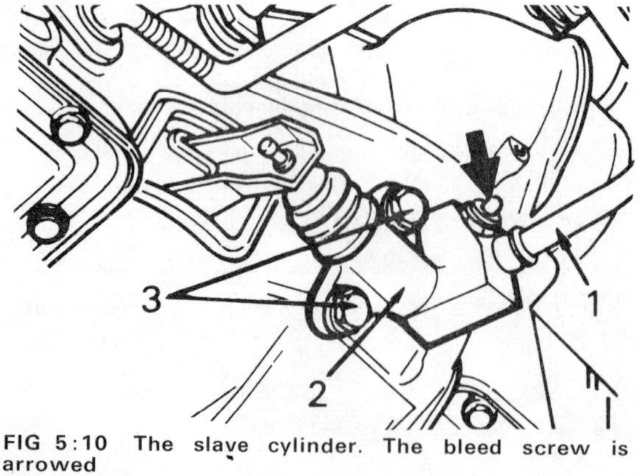

FIG 5:10 **The slave cylinder. The bleed screw is arrowed**

Key to Fig 5:10 1 Flexible pipe 2 Slave cylinder 3 Retaining bolts

Adjustment to compensate for wear of the driven plate linings is automatic within the range of the slave piston end clearance **S** in **FIG 5:9**.

Master cylinder removal:

Uncouple the pushrod from the clutch pedal. Disconnect the flexible pipe, drain the fluid and blank off the open orifices. Remove the bolts which attach the cylinder to the bulkhead and dismount the cylinder assembly.

Master cylinder overhaul:

Refer to **FIG 5:8**. Remove the stop ring from the cylinder body and withdraw the pushrod. Withdraw the piston assembly. Refer to **FIG 5:11**. Dismantle the piston assembly by straightening the 'tooth' of the spring seat 2. Use fresh hydraulic fluid to clean the internal parts. Discard the piston cup 5. Piston to cylinder bore clearance should not exceed .006 inch (.15 mm).

Assembly is the reverse of the dismantling sequence. Fit a new piston cup 5 and assemble internal parts wetted with fresh hydraulic fluid. Renew the dust cover if it is cracked, perished or torn.

Master cylinder fitment:

This is the reverse of the removal sequence. Torque tighten the retaining bolts to 5.7 to 8 lb ft (.79 to 1.07 kgm). Torque tighen the pipe connection to 11 to 13 lb ft (1.5 to 1.8 kgm). Use a new splitpin to retain the clevis pin. Adjust the pedal height and free play as described later. Fill the reservoir with fresh fluid and bleed the system as described later.

Slave cylinder removal:

Refer to **FIG 5:10**. Disconnect the flexible pipe 1 and drain the fluid. Blank off the pipe and cylinder orifices. Remove the retaining bolts 3 and, withdrawing the pushrod from the eye of the release lever, dismount the slave cylinder assembly.

Slave cylinder overhaul:

Refer to **FIG 5:9**. Disengage the convoluted boot and withdraw the pushrod. Remove the piston assembly and spring. If necessary, remove the bleed screw. Remove and discard the piston cup.

Assembly is the reverse of this sequence. Fit a new piston cup and assemble the internal parts wetted with fresh fluid. Renew the boot if it is cracked, perished or torn.

Slave cylinder fitment:

This is the reverse of the removal sequence. Lubricate the pushrod ball seat with multi-purpose grease. Torque tighten the retaining bolts to 18 to 22 lb ft (2.5 to 3 kgm). Torque tighten the pipe connection to 11 to 13 lb ft (1.5 to 1.8 kgm). Fill the master cylinder reservoir and bleed the system as described later.

Pedal height adjustment:

Refer to **FIG 5:2**. Loosen locknut 1. Adjust the pedal stop to bring dimension **a** to 6.89 inch (175 mm). Tighten locknut 1 to a torque of 5.7 to 8 lb ft (.79 to 1.07 kgm).

Free play adjustment:

Set the pedal height as described earlier. Refer to **FIG 5:2** and loosen locknut 2. Turn the master cylinder pushrod in or out until a play of .04 to .20 inch (1 to 5 mm) is achieved. Tighten locknut 2 to a torque of 5.7 to 8 lb ft (.79 to 1.07 kgm).

Release lever/bearing overhaul:

Remove the gearbox and bellhousing assembly. Refer to **FIG 5:1** and remove the dust cover 10. Remove the release lever 5, unclip the retaining spring 6 and withdraw the bearing sleeve and spring (items 8, 7 and 9) as an assembly. Remove the spring. A suitable puller will be required to separate a defective bearing or a worn sleeve.

Access to a hydraulic press will be necessary to assemble the bearing and sleeve if either was renewed. Assembly will then be the dismantling sequence in reverse. Using multi-purpose grease sparingly, lubricate the inner recess of the release bearing sleeve as shown in **FIG 5:12** and the contact surfaces of the release lever and sleeve. **An excess of grease** may, in service, contaminate the clutch working surfaces. Renew the dust cover if it is cracked, perished or torn.

Bleeding the system:

Two operators are required for this procedure which is necessary whever air has entered the system after a dismantling and assembly operation or if the fluid level in the master cylinder reservoir has been allowed to fall so low that air has entered the system.

Fill the master cylinder reservoir with fresh fluid and, during the procedure, **keep the level topped up**.

Remove the dust cap from the bleed screw (arrowed in **FIG 5:10**) and attach a length of tubing to it. Immerse the other end of the tubing into a clean container partially filled with hydraulic fluid. Open the bleed screw by approximately one turn. Depress the clutch pedal quickly and close the bleed screw. Gradually return the pedal to the free position. Open the bleed screw and repeat the sequence until no further air bubbles emerge from the tubing. Remove the tubing, torque tighten the bleed screw to 5.1 to 6.5 lb ft (.7 to .9 kgm) and refit the dust cap.

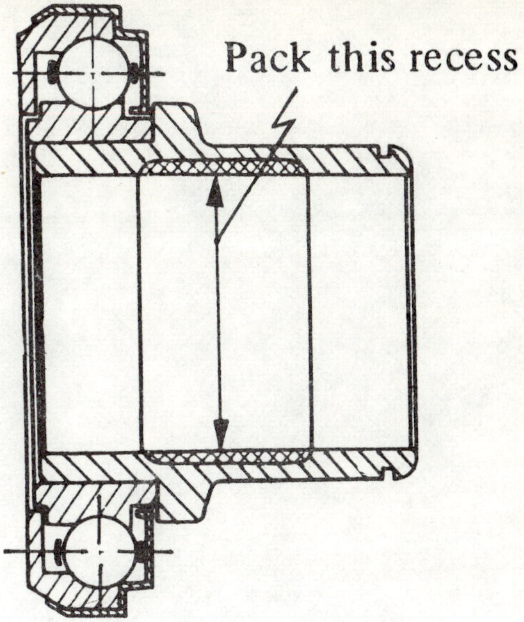

FIG 5:12 Release bearing and sleeve

5:6 Fault diagnosis

(a) Drag or spin

1 Oil or grease on driven plate linings
2 Fluid leak in hydraulic system
3 Driven plate hub splines binding
4 Distorted driven plate
5 Distorted pressure plate or clutch cover
6 Broken driven plate linings
7 Air in hydraulic system
8 Incorrectly adjusted free play or pedal height

(b) Fierceness or snatch

1 Check 1 and 2 in (a)
2 Excessively worn driven plate linings

(c) Slip

1 Check 1 and 8 in (a); 2 in (b)
2 Weak or broken diaphragm spring
3 Seized piston in slave cylinder

(d) Judder

1 Check 1 in (a)
2 Contact area of driven plate linings not evenly distributed
3 Badly worn splines in driven plate hub
4 Buckled driven plate

(e) Rattles

1 Check 2 in (c); 3 in (d)
2 Broken springs in driven plate hub
3 Worn release lever, sleeve or bearing

NOTES

CHAPTER 6

THE GEARBOX

6:1 Description
6:2 Maintenance
6:3 Removing and fitting the gearbox
6:4 Dismantling the gearbox
6:5 Reassembling the gearbox
6:6 Gearchange control
6:7 Fault diagnosis

6:1 Description

The manual control gearbox fitted to models covered by this manual may have either three forward gears and reverse or four forward gears and reverse. In both types of gearbox, synchromesh engagement is incorporated in all forward gears. Reverse gear is engaged by means of an idler gear interposed between the mainshaft and the layshaft. Gear ratios of both transmissions are quoted in **Technical Data** in the Appendix.

The bellhousing, within which the flywheel and clutch are accommodated, is integral with the gearbox casting and this, with the rear extension housing, completes the gearbox casings. The main drive shaft extends forwards and is splined to take the drive from the clutch driven plate. It is supported at its extreme forward end in a pilot bush bearing in the rear end of the crankshaft. Splines on the gearbox output shaft engage with internal splines in the sleeve yoke of the propeller shaft assembly. This arrangement of splines accommodates axial movement of the propeller shaft/rear axle combination.

The gear engagement synchronization mechanism in 4-speed gearboxes may be either Warner or Servo type. In the case of the Warner type, the baulk rings synchronize the coupling sleeves with the relevant mainshaft gear while, in the case of the Servo type gearbox, this is accomplished by synchro-rings. The Warner and Servo type gearboxes differ only in this respect and, except where procedures are stated to differ specifically, the dismantling, inspection and assembly of the two types are identical. Where relevant, notes of the differences are given in **Sections 6:4** and **6:5**.

The gearchange synchronizing mechanism in 3-speed gearboxes is by baulk rings which synchronize the coupling sleeves with the relevant mainshaft gear.

Gearchange in the case of 4-speed gearboxes is by means of a floor level control lever. 3-speed gearbox gearchange is by linkage from a steering column mounted control lever.

Both the 3-speed and the 4-speed gearbox can be dismounted from the vehicle without removing the engine but, if the engine is to be removed, the engine and gearbox should, as described in **Chapter 1, Section 1:7**, be removed together as a unit.

Emission control models:

On 4-speed gearbox models which are equipped with emission control, the neutral gear switch and the third speed gear switch are fitted to the gearbox. The servicing

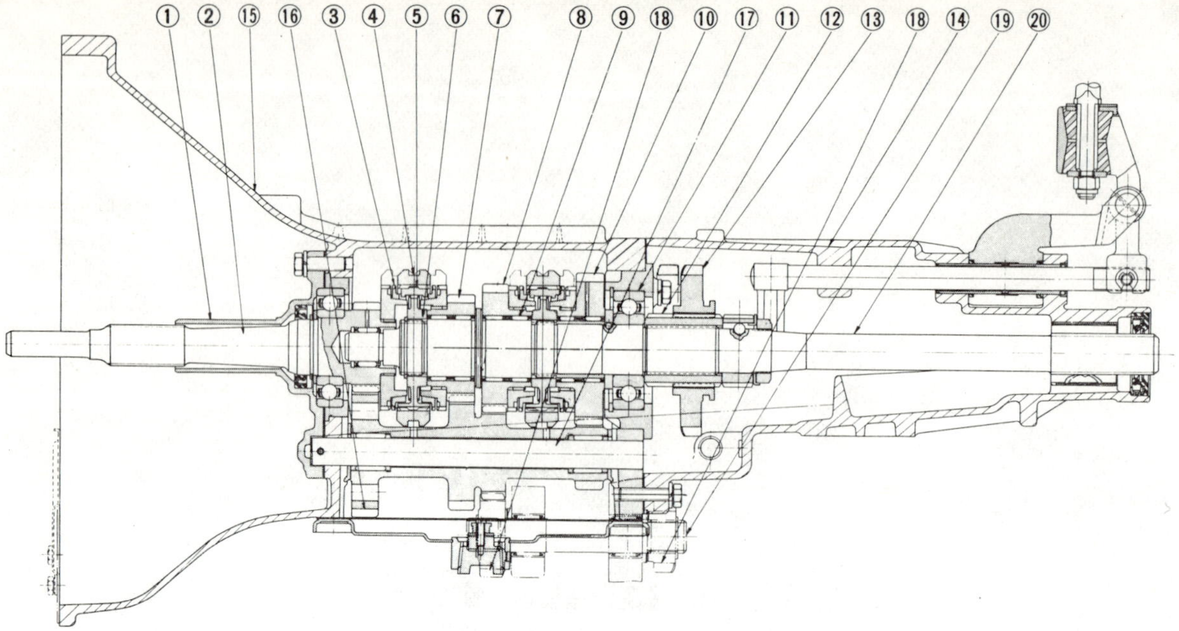

FIG 6:1 Cross-section through a 4-speed gearbox (F4W63)

Key to Fig 6:1 1 Front cover 2 Main drive (primary) shaft 3 Baulk ring 4 Coupling sleeve 5 Insert 6 Synchro hub 7 Third speed gear (mainshaft) 8 Second speed gear (mainshaft) 9 Needle bearing 10 First speed gear (mainshaft) 11 Mainshaft bearing 12 Reverse gear hub 13 Reverse gear 14 Rear extension casing 15 Gearbox (and bellhousing) casing 16 Countershaft assembly 17 Countershaft 18 Reverse idler gear 19 Reverse idler shaft 20 Mainshaft

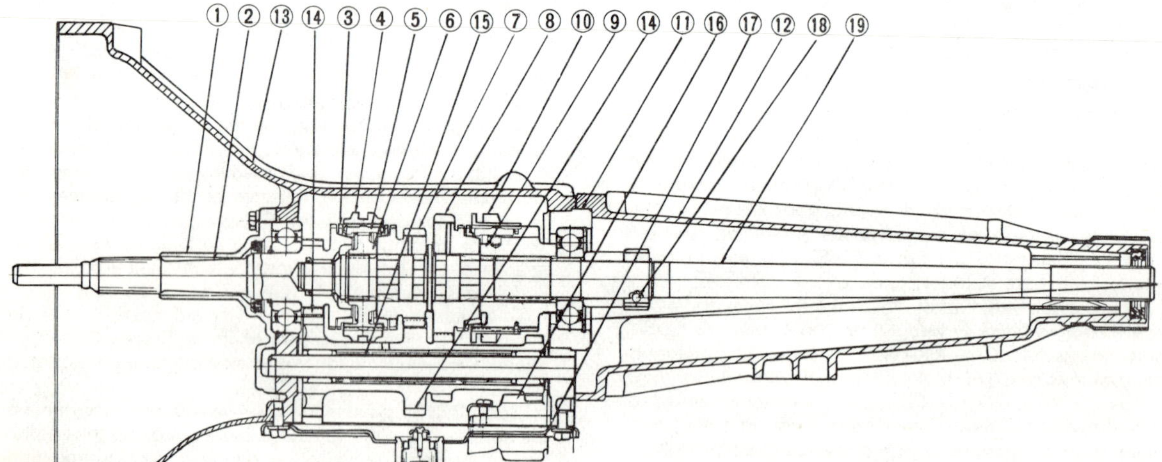

FIG 6:2 Cross-section through a 3-speed gearbox (R3W65)

Key to Fig 6:2 1 Front cover 2 Main drive shaft 3 Baulk ring 4 Coupling sleeve 5 Insert 6 Synchro hub 7 Second speed gear (mainshaft) 8 First speed gear (mainshaft) 9 Synchro hub 10 Reverse gear 11 Bearing retainer 12 Rear extension casing 13 Gearbox (and bellhousing) casing 14 Countershaft assembly 15 Countershaft 16 Reverse idler gear 17 Reverse idler shaft 18 Steel ball 19 Mainshaft of these switches is covered in **Section 6:2** and their circuitry is included in **Chapter 3, FIG 3:10**. The switches are actuated by movement of the striking rod and the fork rod in the gearbox.

6:2 Maintenance

Oil level:

Every 3000 miles (5000 km) check the level of oil in the gearbox. With the vehicle standing on level ground, clean any dirt from the area round the filler plug which is located in the lefthand side of the gearbox casing. Remove the filler plug and, if necessary, add approved oil of the same grade and brand as that already in use until the level is up to the bottom of the filler plug hole. Refit the plug and tighten securely.

Oil grades:

Depending upon the normal range of climatic ambient temperature, use a reputable oil of grade as listed in the following tabulation.

Ambient temperature	*SAE of oil*
30°C (86°F) and downwards ..	80
0° to 40°C (32° to 104°F) ..	90
10°C (50°F) and upwards ..	140

Changing gearbox oil:

Every 30,000 miles (50,000 km), drain the oil from the gearbox and refill with an appropriate grade of reputable brand. Draining should be carried out when the oil is hot after a run. The drain plug is located in the gearbox bottom cover. Clean the areas round the drain and filler plugs and remove both. When the oil has drained completely, fit the drain plug and fill the gearbox to the correct level as described earlier.

Neutral gear switch:

The contacts of this switch should be closed except when the gearchange lever is in the neutral position when the contacts should be open. If the function of the switch is suspect, check that the insulation between the wiring and the switch body is effective. If this is in order, disconnect the wiring and check, either by ohmeter or by battery and test lamp, that the contacts are open with the gearchange lever in neutral and that they are closed in all other gear positions including reverse. A defective switch must be removed and a new replacement fitted.

Third gear switch:

The contacts of this switch should be closed when the gearchange lever is in third gear position and open in all other positions including neutral. If the function of the switch is suspect, check that the insulation between the wiring and the switch body is intact. If this is in order, remove the wiring and check, either by ohmeter or by battery and test lamp, that the contacts are closed when the lever is in third speed position and open in all other posit ons including neutral. A defective switch must be removed and a new replacement fitted.

Reversing light switch:

The contacts in this switch should be closed only when reverse gear is selected. If, with the ignition switched on, the reversing light does not come on when the gearchange lever is moved to the reverse position, check that

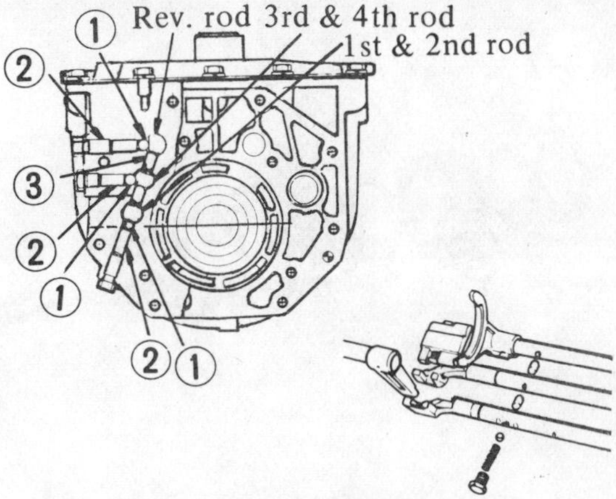

FIG 6:3 Interlocks (4-speed gearbox)

Key to Fig 6:3 1 Balls 2 Springs 3 Plungers

the bulbs have not blown. If these are in order, disconnect the wiring from the switch and, either using an ohmeter or a battery and test lamp, check that the switch contacts are closed with the gearchange lever in the reverse position and open in all other positions. If the switch is serviceable, locate the discontinuity in the wiring. If the switch is defective, fit a new replacement.

6:3 Removing and fitting the gearbox

Removal, all models:

1 Disconnect the negative (earthed) cable from the battery. With the vehicle on a hoist or over a pit, remove the clutch release actuating cylinder as described in **Section 5:5**. Disconnect the speedometer drive from the rear extension housing of the gearbox.
2 Dismount the propeller shaft as described in **Chapter 8, Section 8:2**.
3 Refer to **Chapter 13, Section 13:12** and remove the front exhaust pipe assembly in the case of saloon models. In the case of estate cars, remove the front exhaust pipe and pre-silencer assembly.
4 Disconnect the wiring from the reversing light switch and, from emission control models, disconnect the wiring from the neutral and third gear switches.

3-speed gearbox models:

5 Refer to **Section 6:6** and uncouple the gearchange controls at the gearbox.

4-speed gearbox models:

6 Remove the gearchange control lever as described in **Section 6:6**.

All models:

7 Support the engine by means of a jack positioned under the oil sump. Interpose a suitable block of wood between the jack and the sump to prevent damage to the sump. Note that this support must not be removed until re-installation of the gearbox has been completed.

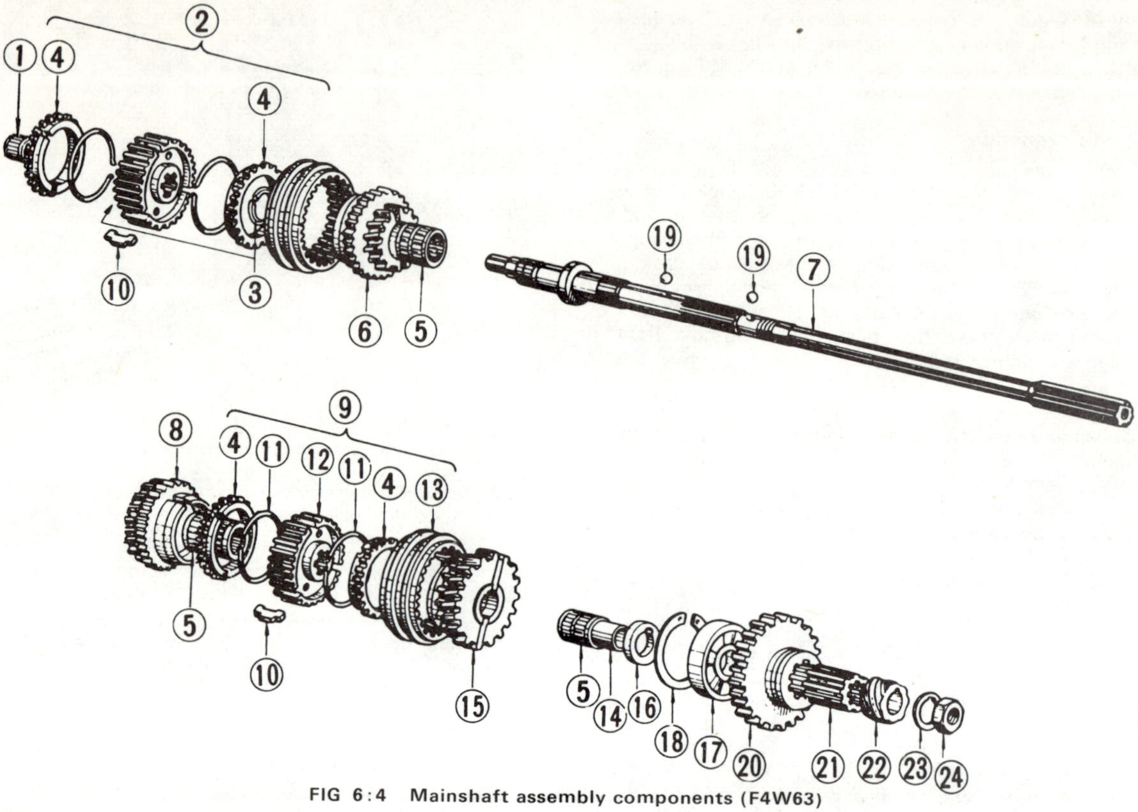

FIG 6:4 Mainshaft assembly components (F4W63)

Key to Fig 6:4 1 Pilot bearing 2 Third/fourth synchromesh assembly 3 Snap ring 4 Baulk ring 5 Needle bearing 6 Third speed gear (mainshaft) 7 Mainshaft 8 Second speed gear (mainshaft) 9 First/second synchro assembly 10 Insert 11 Spread spring 12 Synchro hub 13 Coupling sleeve 14 Bush 15 First speed gear (mainshaft) 16 Thrust washer 17 Mainshaft bearing 18 Snap ring (mainshaft bearing) 19 Steel ball 20 Reverse gear 21 Reverse gear hub 22 Speedometer drive gear 23 Tab washer 24 Mainshaft nut

8 Support the gearbox by means of a jack. Interpose a block of wood between the jack and the gearbox.

9 Refer to **Chapter 1, Section 1:20** and to **FIG 1:38**. Remove the two bolts which attach the gearbox to the mounting, remove the two bolts which attach the crossmember to the chassis at each side and dismount the crossmember and mounting assembly.

10 Remove the starter motor as described in **Chapter 12, Section 12:3**.

11 Remove the bolts which secure the bellhousing to the engine.

12 Taking great care that the main drive shaft does not foul anything, move the gearbox rearwards to disengage the main drive shaft from the clutch driven plate. Lower the supporting jack and withdraw the gearbox.

If the engine and gearbox were removed as a unit (as described in **Chapter 1, Section 1:7**), the gearbox should be separated from the engine by carrying out operation 11. Note the warning given in operation 12.

Fitment, all models:

Fitment of the gearbox is, for each model, the removal sequence in reverse. Apply grease to the clutch release mechanism as described at the end of **Section 6:5**. Torque tighten the bellhousing to engine retaining bolts to 18 to 29 lb ft (2.5 to 4 kgm). On completion of the installation, refill the gearbox with approved oil or, if it was not drained, check the oil level.

6:4 Dismantling the gearbox

The type number of the 4-speed gearbox which is fitted with Warner type synchromesh is F4W63 and that for the gearbox fitted with Servo type synchromesh is F4C63. The type number of the 3-speed gearbox (this has Warner type synchromesh) is R3W65. A cross-section through a type F4W63 gearbox is shown in **FIG 6:1** and a cross-section through a type R3W65 gearbox is shown in **FIG 6:2**.

Backlash:

Check backlash between mating gears after removing the bottom cover (dismantling operation 3). Doing so at this point will avoid the need for trial reassembly and will indicate the possible requirement for new sets of gears at an early stage. Standard backlash is .002 to .0055 inch (.05 to .14 mm). Drive and driven gears must be renewed together and not individually.

End play:

Check the end play before the relevant assembly is removed or dismantled. This will indicate the possible requirement for new parts at an early stage. Standard end play figures are as follows.

Gearbox	*Gear*	*End play*
R3W65	First	.0022 to .0087 inch (.05 to .22 mm)
	Second	.004 to .0087 inch (.1 to .22 mm)
	Counter	.0016 to .0047 inch (.04 to .12 mm)
	Reverse idler	.0079 to .0157 inch (.2 to .4 mm)
F4W63 and F4C63	All gears	.002 to .006 inch (.05 to .15 mm)

End play is adjusted by fitting snap rings and thrust washers of suitable thicknesses as described in **Section 6:5**.

Dismantling, all models:

1 Drain the gearbox if this was not done at an earlier stage. Clean the exterior of the casings as described in Hints on Maintenance and Overhaul in the Appendix.

2 Refer to **Chapter 5, Section 5:5**. Detach the dust cover and remove the clutch release mechanism from the bellhousing.

3 Remove the retaining bolts and detach the front cover (1 in **FIGS 6:1** and **6:2**). Remove and discard the oil seal from the front cover. Remove the retaining bolts and detach the bottom cover. Remove the reversing light switch (collect the two balls in the case of the 3-speed gearbox). Remove the speedometer drive pinion assembly.

4 Select neutral gear position. Remove the rear extension bolts and, by lightly tapping with a soft hammer on the mounting projections, remove the rear extension casing. Remove and discard the oil seal from the rear extension casing.

4-speed gearbox:

5 If necessary, remove the striker rod pin and withdraw the striker rod forwards from the rear extension casing.

6 Refer to **FIG 6:3**. Remove the check ball plugs, the three springs 2 and the check balls 3. Drive out the retaining pins (the official tool is ST23540000) from the fork rods. Withdraw the rods taking care not to lose the two plungers.

7 Lock the mainshaft by engaging two gears, untab the locking washer and loosen the mainshaft nut.

8 Working from the rear of the casing and using dummy countershaft ST23100000, drive out the countershaft (1 in **FIG 6:1**). Lift out the counter gear assembly complete with thrust washers, needle bearings and dummy countershaft (this will be required for reassembly). Remove the pin from the forward end of the countershaft.

9 Remove the reverse idler gear forward snap ring and withdraw the assembly rearwards. Collect the washers.

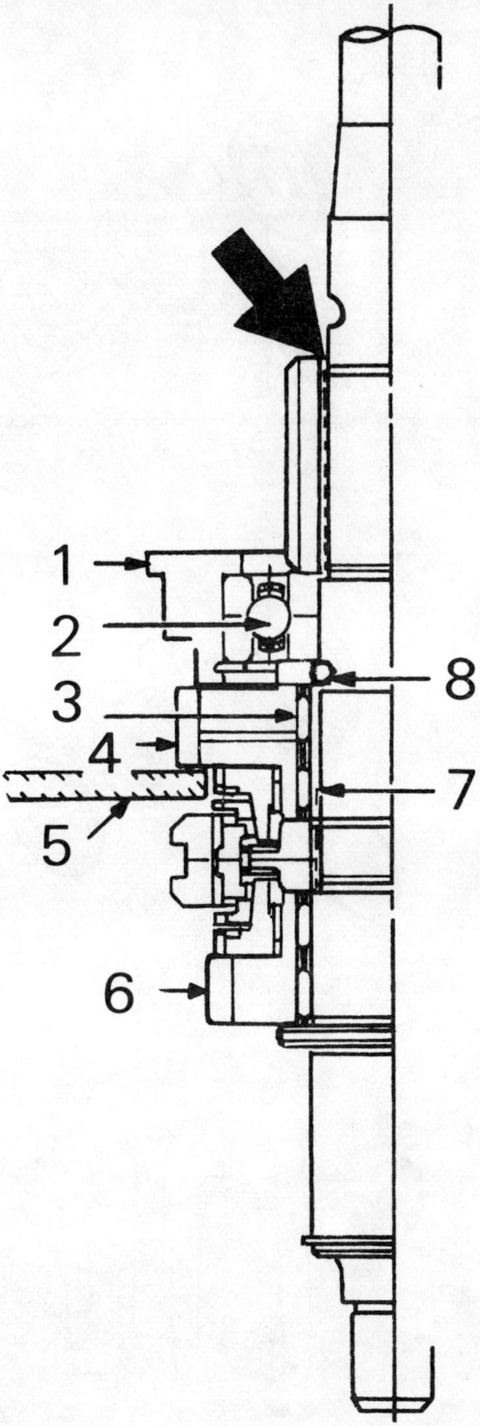

FIG 6:5 Mainshaft bearing and first/second synchro assembly

Key to Fig 6:5 1 Bearing retainer 2 Bearing 3 Needle bearing 4 First speed gear (mainshaft) 5 Dismantling position for puller 6 Second speed gear 7 Bush 8 Steel ball Arrow See text

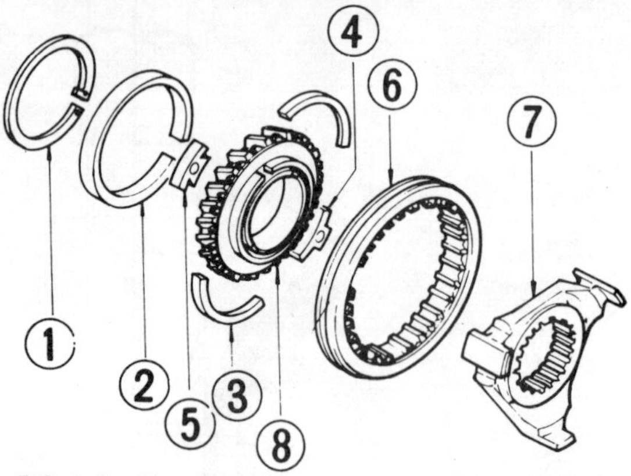

FIG 6:6 Components of the synchromesh (F4C63)

Key to Fig 6:6 1 Circlip 2 Synchro ring 3 Brake band 4 Thrust block 5 Anchor block 6 Coupling sleeve 7 Synchro hub 8 Clutch gear

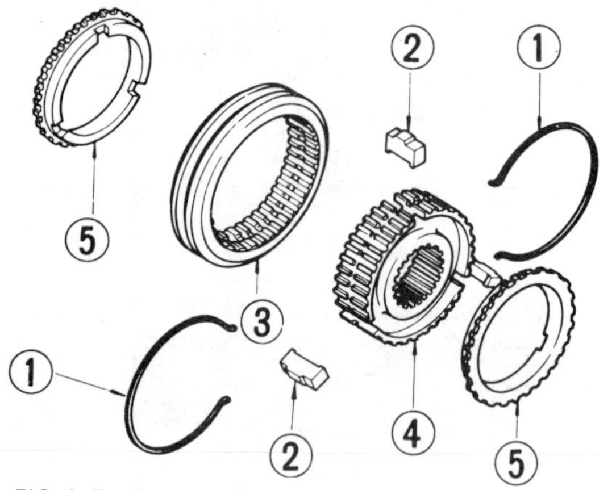

FIG 6:7 Components of the synchromesh (F4W63)

Key to Fig 6:7 1 Spring ring 2 Inserts 3 Coupling sleeve 4 Synchro hub 5 Baulk ring

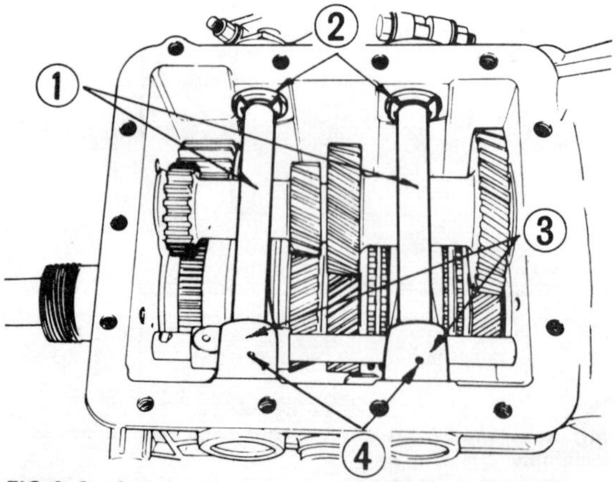

FIG 6:8 3-speed gearbox with bottom cover removed

Key to Fig 6:8 1 Cross-shafts 2 Washers 3 Levers 4 Pins

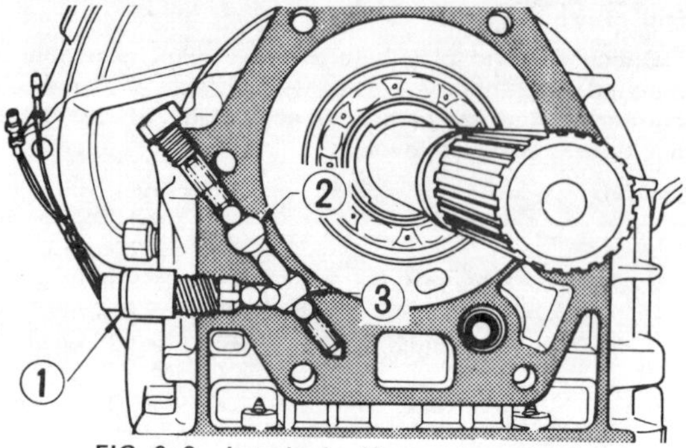

FIG 6:9 Interlocks (3-speed gearbox)

Key to Fig 6:9 1 Reverse light switch 2 Second/third rod 3 First/reverse rod

10 Remove the bolts which secure the mainshaft bearing retainer. Withdraw the mainshaft assembly rearwards. Remove the pilot bearing from between the mainshaft and the main drive shaft. Using the wooden handle of a hammer, knock the main drive shaft forwards and out of the casing.

Mainshaft, 4-speed gearbox:

11 Refer to **FIGS 6:1** and **6:4**. Remove the snap ring from the forward end of the mainshaft and withdraw the third/fourth gear synchromesh assembly (2 in **FIG 6:4**) followed by the third speed gear (7 in **FIG 6:1**, 6 in **FIG 6:4**). Remove the nut (24 in **FIG 6:4**) from the rear of the mainshaft (loosened at operation 7).

12 Remove the tabwasher, the speedometer drive gear (collect the ball key), the reverse gear 13 and the reverse hub 12 (items 23, 22, 20 and 21 in **FIG 6:4**).

13 Refer to **FIG 6:5**. Using a suitable puller behind the first speed gear (5 in the illustration), remove the gear 4 and the bearing and retainer assembly 1 and 2. If necessary, the bearing may be removed from the retainer after removing the internal circlip.

14 Pull off the second speed gear 6 together with the first speed gear bearings 3 and the first/second speed synchromesh assembly.

Main drive (primary) shaft, 4-speed gearbox:

15 Remove the snap ring and spacer from the front side of the bearing. Under a press, or with suitable puller, remove the primary shaft bearing.

Synchromesh, Servo type:

16 This operation is relevant only to the F4C63 type gearbox. Refer to **FIG 6:6**. Remove circlip 1, synchro ring 2, brake bands 3, thrust block 4, anchor block 5, sleeve 6, hub 7 and gear 8.

Synchromesh, Warner type:

17 This operation is only relevant to F4W63 type gearboxes. Refer to **FIG 6:7**. Remove the spread rings 1, the inserts 2 and separate the coupling sleeve 3 from the hub 4 and baulk ring 5.

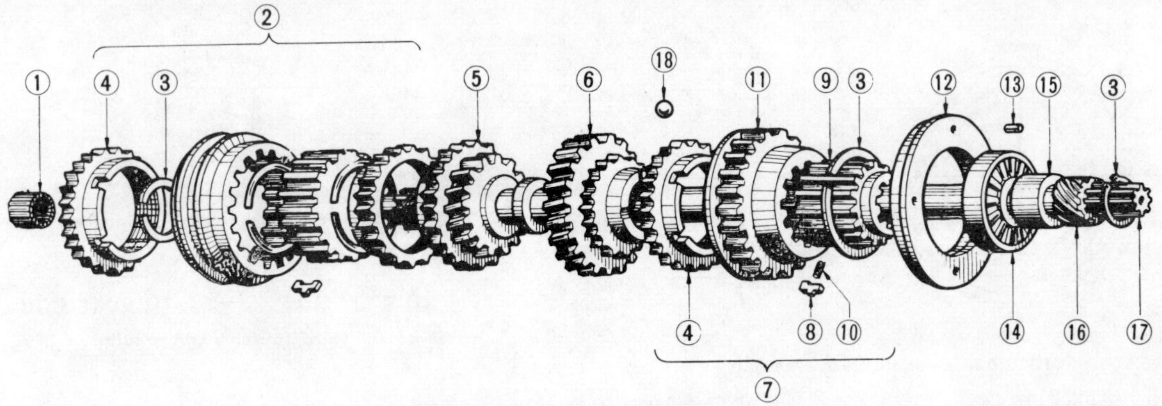

FIG 6:10 Mainshaft assembly components (F3W65)

Key to Fig 6:10 1 Pilot bearing 2 Second/third synchromesh assembly 3 Snap ring 4 Baulk ring 5 Second speed gear (mainshaft) 6 First speed gear (mainshaft) 7 First speed synchromesh assembly 8 Insert 9 Synchro hub 10 Spring 11 Reverse gear 12 Bearing retainer 13 Peg 14 Mainshaft bearing 15 Distance piece 16 Speedometer drive gear 17 Mainshaft 18 Steel ball

3-speed gearbox:

18 With the bottom cover removed, the gearbox interior will be as shown in **FIG 6:8**. Drive out the pins which retain the cross-shafts to the operating levers (the official tool is ST23550000). Remove the retaining rings on the gearchange lever side and withdraw the cross-shafts and levers.

19 Refer to **FIG 6:9**. Remove the reversing light switch if this was not done earlier (collect two balls). Remove the check ball plug and withdraw the second/third and first/reverse check balls 2 and 3.

20 Refer to operation 8 and drive out the countershaft. Remove the setscrew from the reverse idler shaft (see **FIG 6:2**), withdraw the reverse idler shaft and the gear.

21 The components of the mainshaft assembly are shown in **FIG 6:10**. It may be dismantled after removing the two snap rings 3. The components of the synchromesh assemblies are shown at 2 and 7 in **FIG 6:10**, in **FIG 6:11** and in cross-section in **FIG 6:2**.

Inspection:

Wash all parts in paraffin and dry off with compressed air or lint free rag. Brush clean gearbox oil over all bearings and steel parts. Reject gears which are chipped, cracked or which have excessive backlash. Check shafts for straightness. Bent shafts cannot be salvaged. Check all splines and particularly those on the main drive shaft. Reject front and rear oil seals even if they appear to be serviceable. Check the covers and casings for cracks (see Hints on Maintenance and Overhaul in the Appendix) and that mating faces are clean and free from burrs.

Renew any baulk rings which may be deformed, cracked or excessively worn. Wear is checked as shown in **FIG 6:12**. The clearance **L** should be between .0472 and .0630 inch (1.2 and 1.6 mm). If the clearance is less than the minimum quoted, renew the baulk ring(s).

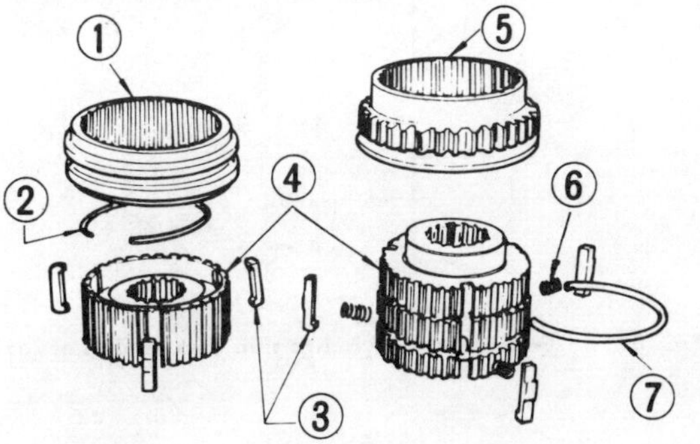

FIG 6:11 Synchromesh components

Key to Fig 6:11 1 Coupling sleeve 2 Spread spring 3 Insert 4 Synchro hub 5 Reverse gear 6 Spring 7 Stop ring

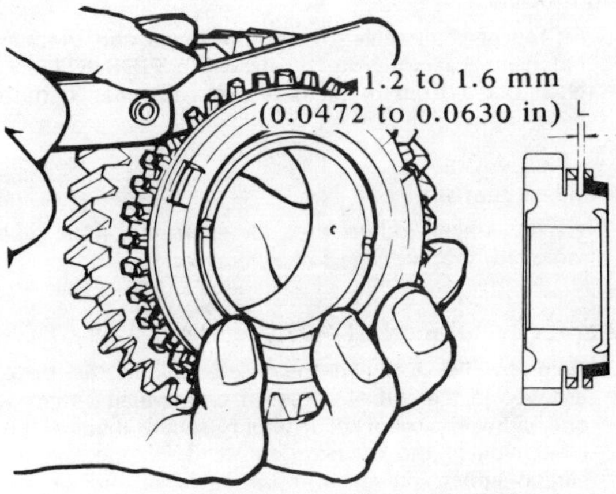

FIG 6:12 Measuring baulk ring clearance

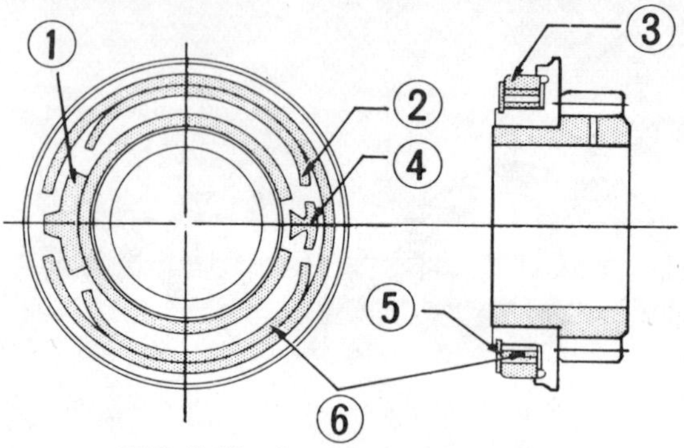

FIG 6:13 Synchromesh assembly

Key to Fig 6:13 1 Thrust block 2 Band brake 3 Synchro ring 4 Anchor block 5 Circlip 6 Band brake

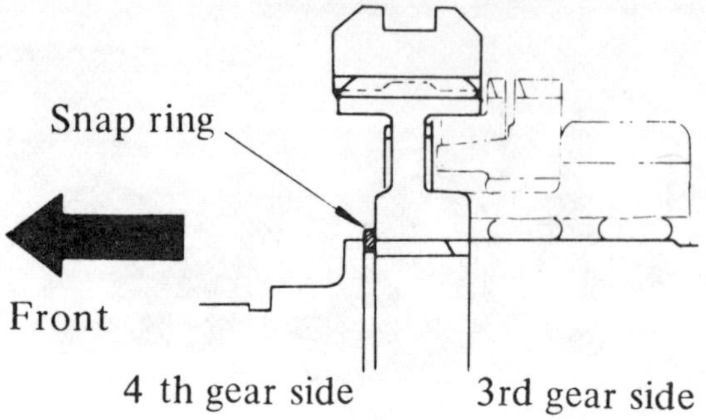

FIG 6:15 Third/fourth synchro hub

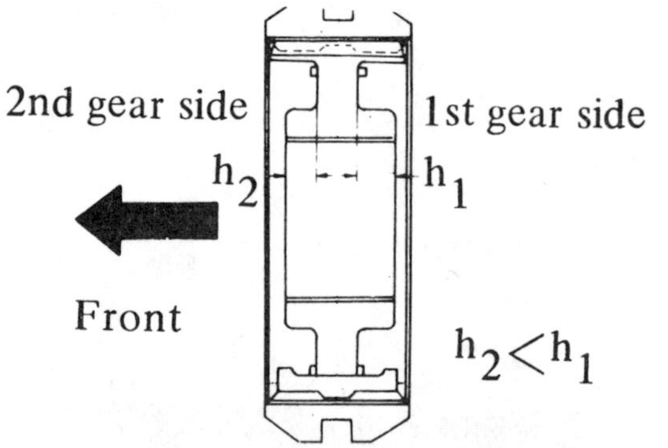

FIG 6:14 First/second synchro hub (4-speed gearbox)

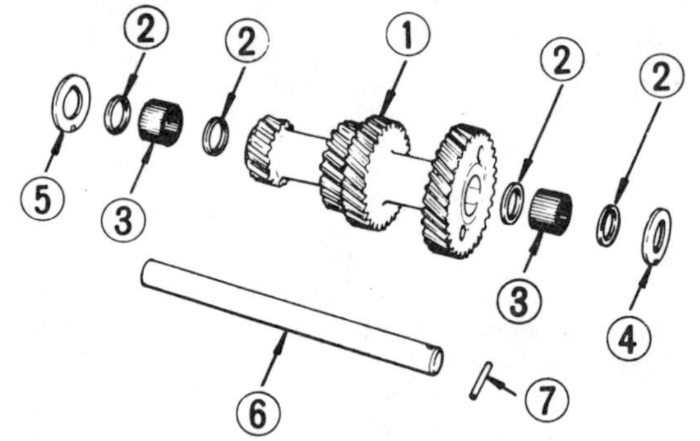

FIG 6:16 Components of the countershaft assembly

Key to Fig 6:16 1 Countershaft gears 2 Washer 3 Needle rollers 4 Thrust washer (front) 5 Thrust washer (rear) 6 Countershaft 7 Pin

6:5 Reassembling the gearbox

All internal parts should be assembled wetted with clean oil of the grade and brand which is to be used (see **Section 6:2**).

All models:

1 Fit the new oil seals to the front cover and the rear extension casing. Note, as shown in **FIGS 6:1** and **6:2**, that the lip of the seal faces inwards in both cases.

4-speed gearbox:

2 Fit the striker rod to the rear extension (if it was removed) and refit the striker rod pin.

Warner sychromesh (F4W63 gearbox):

3 Refer to **FIG 6:7**. Fit the inserts 2 into the three grooves in the hub 4. Position one spread spring 1 on the lower side of the inserts to secure them to the inner side of the coupling sleeve 3. Fit the second spread spring on the opposite side of the sleeve. Ensure that they are opposite to each other.

Servo synchromesh (F4C63 gearbox):

4 Refer to **FIGS 6:6** and **6:13**. Place the clutch gear on a clean, flat surface and fit the synchro ring to the inner side of the gear. Fit the thrust block into place as shown in **FIG 6:13**. Fit the anchor block and brake band. Fit the circlip.

Mainshaft (4-speed gearbox):

5 Assembly is the reverse of the dismantling sequence. Refer to **FIG 6:5**. Apply grease to the steel ball 8 and, using a puller on the face of the reverse gear hub (at the point arrowed in the illustration), fit the main bearing and its retainer and the reverse gear hub. Ensure that the first/second synchro hub is the correct way round as shown in **FIG 6:14**.

6 Proceed with the fitment of the third gear and third/fourth synchromesh assembly (refer to **FIG 6:1**). Ensure that this synchro hub is the correct way round as shown in **FIG 6:15**.

7 Select and fit a snap ring to the groove arrowed in this illustration. Five thicknesses of snap ring are available in .002 inch (.05 mm) steps from .0551 to .0631 inch (1.4 to 1.6 mm). Select a thickness which will give a minimum clearance between the ring and the face of the hub.

8 Fit the mainshaft assembly from the rear of the casing. Fit and torque tighten the bearing retainer securing bolts to 5.8 to 7.2 lb ft (.8 to 1.0 kgm). Fit the reverse gear, the speedometer drive gear, the locking plate and (finger tight at this stage) the mainshaft nut.

Main drive shaft (4-speed gearbox):

9 Refer to **FIG 6:1**. Press the bearing onto the shaft and retain it with the spacer ring and a selected snap ring of thickness which will give a minimum clearance between the ring and the spacer. Seven thicknesses of rings are available as follows:

No.	*Thickness, inch (mm)*
1	.0587 to .0602 (1.49 to 1.53)
2	.0610 to .0642 (1.55 to 1.63)
3	.0642 to .0661 (1.63 to 1.68)
4	.0661 to .0685 (1.68 to 1.74)
5	.0685 to .0709 (1.74 to 1.80)
6	.0709 to .0732 (1.80 to 1.86)
7	.0732 to .0756 (1.86 to 1.92)

Ensure that the pilot bearing is not omitted.

Reverse idler gear assembly (4-speed gearbox):

10 Refer to **FIG 6:1**. Fit a thrust washer (align the grooved side of the washer with the grooved side of the gear) and the spur gear to the rear end of the shaft (this end has the wider snap ring groove). Fit the snap ring. Fit the shaft to the casing.

11 Fit a thrust washer and the helical gear. Select a snap ring for fitment to the forward groove which will limit end play to .002 to .006 inch (.05 to .15 mm). Five thicknesses of snap rings are available in .004 inch (.1 mm) steps from .0433 to .0593 inch (1.1 to 1.5 mm).

Countershaft assembly (4-speed gearbox):

12 Assemble the components of the countershaft which are shown in **FIG 6:16** onto dummy countershaft ST23100000 (used in dismantling operation 8). If necessary, select a new rear thrust washer 5 to limit the end play of the assembly to .002 to .006 inch (.05 to .15 mm). Five thicknesses of washers are available as follows:

No.	*Thickness, inch (mm)*
1	.0925 to .0945 (2.35 to 2.40)
2	.0945 to .0965 (2.40 to 2.45)
3	.0965 to .0984 (2.45 to 2.50)
4	.0984 to .1004 (2.50 to 2.55)
5	.1004 to .1024 (2.55 to 2.60)

13 Working from the front (and with the countershaft retaining pin hole towards the front), drive in the countershaft and displace the dummy shaft. Fit the retaining pin 7.

Final assembly operations (4-speed gearbox):

14 Lock the mainshaft by engaging two gears (as at dismantling operation 7). Torque tighten the mainshaft nut to 65 to 80 lb ft (9 to 11 kgm) and bend up the tabwasher to lock. Disengage the gears.

15 Refer to **FIG 6:17**. Align the first/second fork 1 and the third/fourth fork 2 with the coupling sleeve grooves. Fit the first/second rod 3 and secure with a pin 10. With the first/second rod in neutral, fit interlock

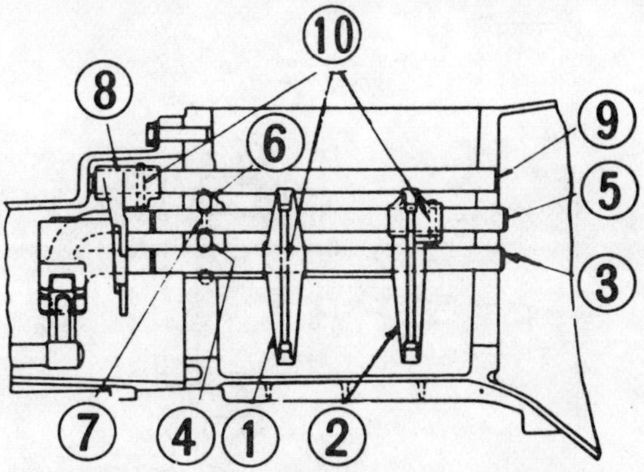

FIG 6:17 Rods and forks (4-speed gearbox)

Key to Fig 6:17 1 First/second fork 2 Third/fourth fork 3 First/second rod 4 Plunger 5 Third/fourth rod 6 Plunger 7 Plunger 8 Reverse fork 9 Reverse rod 10 Pins

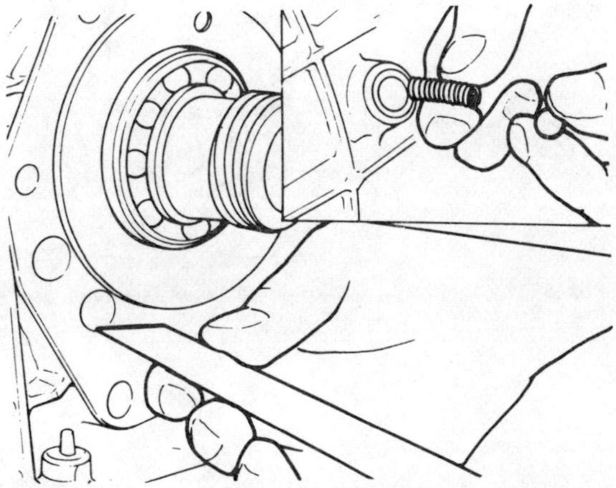

FIG 6:18 Locking spring and ball fitment (3-speed gearbox)

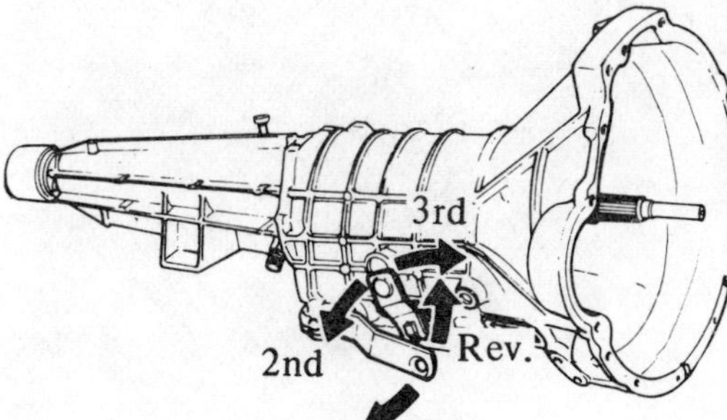

FIG 6:19 Gearchanges on 3-speed gearbox

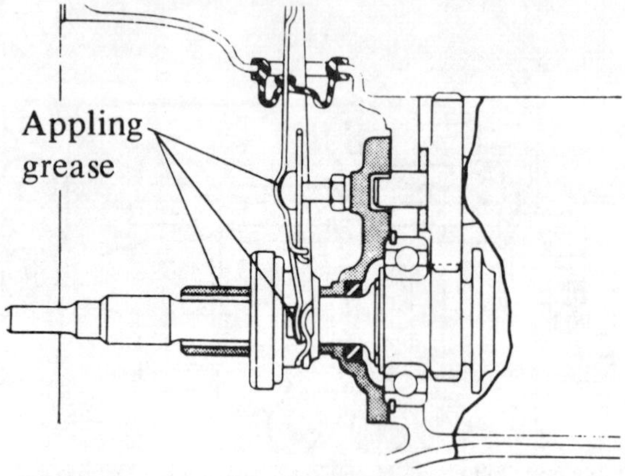

FIG 6:20 Lubrication of clutch release mechanism

FIG 6:21 Removing gearchange lever (4-speed gearbox)

plunger 4 and fit and pin the third/fourth rod securely into position. With the third/fourth rod 5 in neutral, fit the interlock plunger 6. Fit the reverse rod 9 into the reverse fork 8 and secure with a pin 10.

16 Fit the check balls and the locking springs. Apply jointing compound to the plug heads. Fit and tighten the plugs to a torque of 12 to 15 lb ft (1.7 to 2.1 kgm). These parts are shown in **FIG 6:3**. Apply oil to all sliding parts and check that gears mesh smoothly.

17 With the gears in neutral, apply jointing compound to the faces, fit the rear extension and check that the gearchange mechanism operates correctly. Fit the front cover and the bottom cover. Use jointing compound.

3-speed gearbox:

18 Certain assembly operations are similar to those described for assembly of the 4-speed gearbox. Note, however, that, where relevant, snap ring and thrust washer thicknesses are not identical and that 3-speed snap ring and washer thicknesses are quoted later.

Synchromesh (R3W65 gearbox):

19 Reassembly of the first/reverse and the second/third synchromesh assemblies is the reverse of the dismantling sequence. Ensure that the reverse gear is the correct way round. Refer to **FIGS 6:2, 6:10** and **6:11**.

Mainshaft (3-speed gearbox):

20 Assembly is the reverse of the dismantling sequence. Select a snap ring (3 in **FIG 6:10**) for the forward groove which will give a minimum clearance between the synchro hub and the snap ring. Five thicknesses of snap rings are available in .002 inch (.05 mm) steps from a thickness of .063 to .071 inch (1.6 to 1.8 mm).

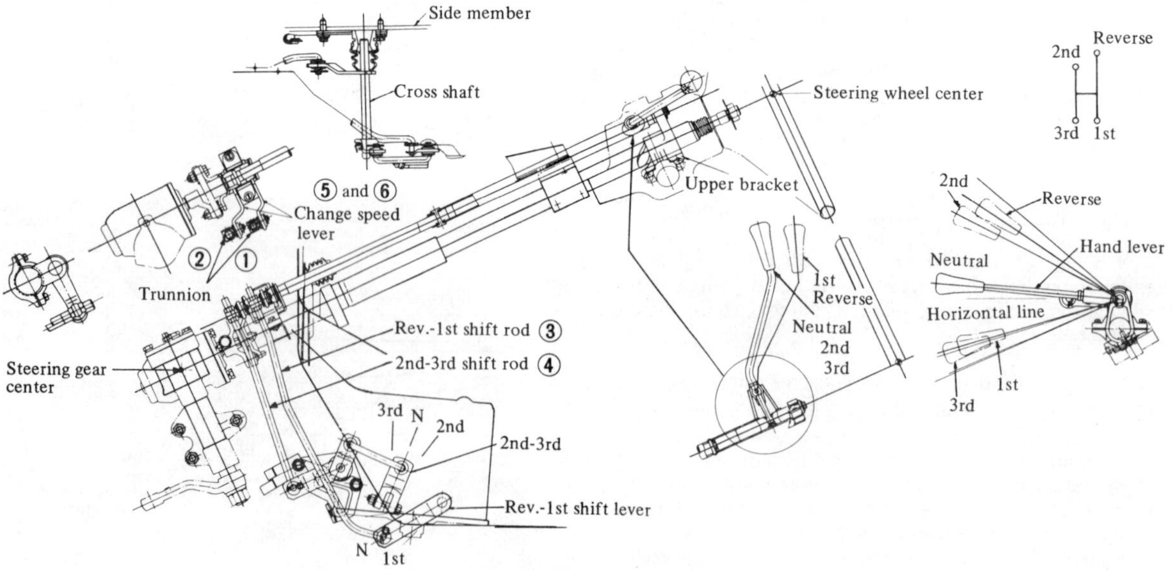

FIG 6:22 Gearchange lever and linkage (3-speed gearbox)

21 Select a snap ring (3 in **FIG 6:10**) for the rear groove which will give a minimum clearance between the ring and the speedometer gear. Eight thicknesses of snap ring are available for this position. Their thicknesses range between .051 and .067 inch (1.3 to 1.7 mm).

22 Fit the mainshaft from the rear of the casing. Fit the main drive shaft from the front of the casing. Do not omit the pilot bearing 1 in **FIG 6:10**.

Reverse idler gear (3-speed gearbox):

23 Align the hole in the shaft with that in the casing. Fit, tighten and lock the setscrew.

Fork rod assembly (3-speed gearbox):

24 Refer to **FIGS 6:9** and **6:18**. Fit the spring and ball into the blind hole. Fit the first/reverse and the second/third forks to each groove in the coupling sleeve. Use guide tool ST23620000 and, while holding the check ball, push the tool inwards until the spring and ball are positioned.

25 Fit the first/reverse fork rod and drive out the guide tool. Align the holes in the fork and fork rod and secure with the retaining pin.
Position the fork rod in neutral. Position the interlock plunger (see **FIG 6:9**), fit the second/third fork rod. Fit the ball and spring. Apply jointing compound to the head of the plug. Fit and tighten the plug. Fit two balls and screw in the reversing light switch.

26 Align the holes in the fork and fork rod and fit the retaining pin securely.

27 Fitment of the countershaft follows the basic procedure described in operations 12 and 13 for the 4-speed gearbox.

28 Note that the larger diameter thrust washer is at the front. Select a rear thrust washer of thickness which will limit the end play of the assembly to .0016 to .0047 inch (.04 to .12 mm). Five thicknesses of rear thrust washer are available as follows:

No.	*Thickness, inch (mm)*
1	.1575 to .1594 (4.00 to 4.05)
2	.1555 to .1575 (3.95 to 4.00)
3	.1535 to .1555 (3.90 to 3.95)
4	.1516 to .1535 (3.85 to 3.90)
5	.1496 to .1516 (3.80 to 3.85)

29 Refer to **FIG 6:8** and fit the cross shafts. Refer to **FIG 6:19** and check the gear selection. Apply jointing compound to the faces and fit the rear extension, the front cover and the bottom cover.

All models, final operations:

30 Refit the clutch release mechanism and lubricate by applying grease at the points shown in **FIG 6:20**.

6:6 Gearchange control

4-speed gearbox:

Removal of the floor level control lever is shown in **FIG 6:21**. Withdraw the rubber boot and remove the retaining nut from the lower end of the lever.

Fitment is the reverse of this sequence. No adjustment is required.

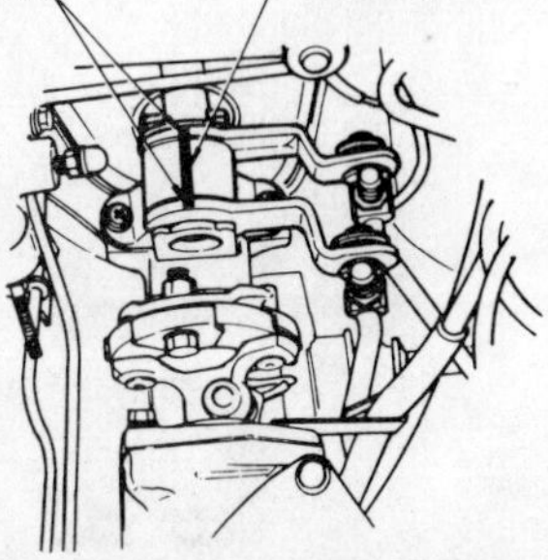

FIG 6:23 Adjusting neutral position (3-speed gearbox)

3-speed gearbox:

The righthand drive steering column mounted gear-change lever and linkage is shown in **FIG 6:22**. The only adjustment which may normally be required is for the position of neutral.

Neutral position adjustment:

If adjustment is required, proceed as follows.

Refer to **FIG 6:22**. Loosen trunions 1 and 2. Position rods 3 and 4 into neutral. Adjust the trunions until the projection on the lower bracket is aligned with the groove in levers 5 and 6 as shown in **FIG 6:23**. Lock the trunions in this position.

6:7 Fault diagnosis

(a) Jumping out of gear

1 Broken detent spring
2 Broken or missing detent ball
3 Weak detent spring
4 Worn synchromesh assembly
5 Worn selector fork
6 Loose fork on rod
7 Linkage requires adjustment (3-speed column gear-change)

(b) Noisy gearbox

1 Oil level low
2 Excessive end play in mainshaft
3 Countershaft thrust washer(s) worn or broken
4 Excessive backlash between gears
5 Worn or damaged bearings

(c) Difficulty in changing gear

1 Clutch not releasing
2 Bent selector rod
3 Distorted linkage (3-speed column gearchange)
4 Broken pin in selector mechanism

(d) Oil leaks

1 Defective front or rear oil seal
2 Loose bottom cover
3 Loose drain or filler plug
4 Loose interlock plug
5 Defective rear extension or front cover joint

NOTES

CHAPTER 7

AUTOMATIC TRANSMISSION

7:1 Description
7:2 Maintenance
7:3 Tests
7:4 Adjustments
7:5 Removing and refitting the transmission
7:6 Fault diagnosis

7:1 Description

The automatic transmission is manufactured by Nissan and is model 3N71 B. This same transmission model is fitted to all vehicle models covered by this manual. As gearchanges occur within specific ranges of transmission, output shaft speeds, due to differing final drive gear ratios and tyre sizes, correspond to differing road speeds on different models. Output shaft speeds are given for normal gearchange points in **Section 7:3**. Conversion to the corresponding road speed for the relevant vehicle model can readily be made.

Three forward speeds and reverse are provided by combinations of multi-disc clutches, a band brake, a multi-disc brake, a one-way clutch and set of epicyclic gearing. Gear ratios are listed in **Technical Data** in the Appendix. A three-element hydraulic torque converter is interposed between the engine and the automatic gearbox.

A cross-section through the complete transmission is shown in **FIG 7:1**, a half cross-section through the clutches and gearing is shown in **FIG 7:2** and a diagramatic cross-section through the torque converter is shown in **FIG 7:3**.

Torque converter:

The impeller 4 in **FIG 7:3** is integral with the converter casing 9 which is driven by the engine. The impeller transmits torque by means of the transmission fluid to the turbine 3 which drives the input shaft. The stator 5 redirects the flow of fluid as it leaves the turbine so that it enters the impeller at the most effective angle.

The maximum torque multiplication through the converter is 2.0. As the turbine picks up speed and the slip between it and the impeller becomes less the torque multiplication reduces progressively until their speeds become substantially equal; whereupon the unit acts as a fluid coupling. In this condition the stator is no longer required to redirect the fluid flow and the one-way clutch 6 permits it to rotate in the same direction as the impeller and turbine.

Fluid cooler:

Transmission fluid is water cooled in a unit which is incorporated in the bottom tank of the engine cooling system radiator. Feed and return pipes connect the transmission with the fluid cooler.

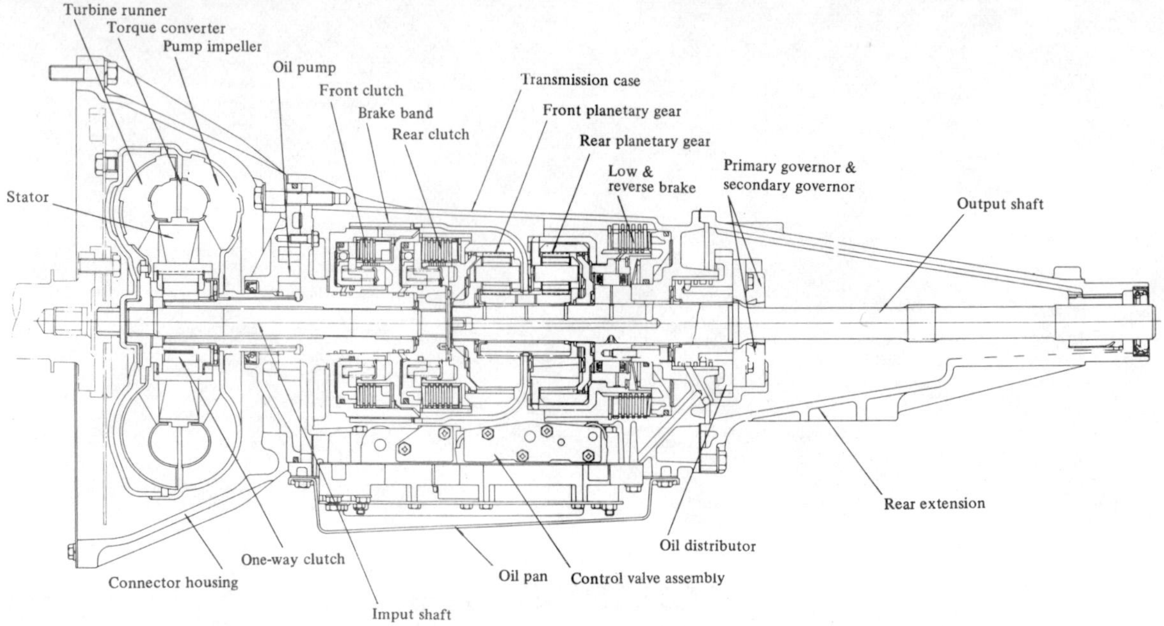

FIG 7:1 Cross-section through the complete automatic transmission unit

Transmission operation:

The hydraulic circuits are shown diagramatically in **FIG 7:4**. The oil pump, which is driven at engine speed via the converter casing (see **FIG 7:3**) provides fluid to the converter and to the gearbox for lubrication and control. The manual valve, through the selector linkage, dictates the driver's requirement. The vacuum control valve indicates through the engine intake manifold depression the 'power' available and the governor valves indicate the output shaft speed (the vehicle road speed). The front and rear clutches and the low/reverse brake (2, 4 and 8 in **FIG 7:2**) are engaged hydraulically and, when the fluid pressure is released, disengaged by spring load. The brake band 3 in **FIG 7:2** is engaged by and positively released by fluid pressure.

The selector is a **P, R, N, D, 2, 1** arrangement. Refer to **FIG 7:2**. With **P** selected, all clutches and the band brake are disengaged but an internal linkage engages the parking pawl which prevents the vehicle from rolling either forwards or rearwards. With **R** selected, the front clutch 2 and the low/reverse brake 8 are applied. With **N** selected, all clutches and the band brake are disengaged. This is as when **P** is selected except that the parking pawl does not engage. With **D** selected, low gear starting is provided and automatic upward and downward gear-changes occur depending upon the engine throttle position and the vehicle speed. In top gear the front and rear clutches are engaged (2 and 4 in **FIG 7:2**). In intermediate gear the rear clutch 4 and the band brake 3 are engaged. In low gear (with **D** engaged) the rear clutch 4 is engaged and the one-way clutch 10 is operative. Full throttle kick-down within certain output shaft speeds is available. This is actuated by the solenoid valve and throttle operated switch and, by initiating a downwards gearchange, provides rapid acceleration when required. With **2** selected, the transmission is locked in the intermediate ratio. The rear clutch 4 is applied and the band brake 3 holds the front clutch drum from rotating. If, when running with **2** selected, the selector lever is moved to **1**, the downward gearchange will not occur until the output shaft speed has dropped to within a specific speed range (see **Section 7:3**) irrespective of the throttle position. When starting with **1** selected, the transmission is locked in the low ratio gear. The rear clutch 4 and the low/reverse brake 8 are engaged. It will be noted that this differs from the drive path when, in low gear, **D** selected.

To prevent the engine from being started with **D, 2, 1** or **R** selected, a starter inhibitor switch is incorporated in the starter motor solenoid circuit. The contacts of this switch (when correctly set) are closed only when **P** or **N** has been selected.

The work which an owner can normally carry out on an automatic transmission is limited to that covered in **Sections 7:2** and **7:4**. Much of the fault diagnosis section is included for information rather than action by an owner. The converter and transmission can be removed from the vehicle without removing the engine and the procedure is described in **Section 7:5**. If the engine is to be removed, the engine and the complete automatic transmission should be removed as a unit as described in **Chapter 1, Section 1:7**.

7:2 Maintenance

Fluid level:

Every 3000 miles (5000 km), check and top up the transmission fluid level as described later. Use the same specification and brand of fluid as that already in use.

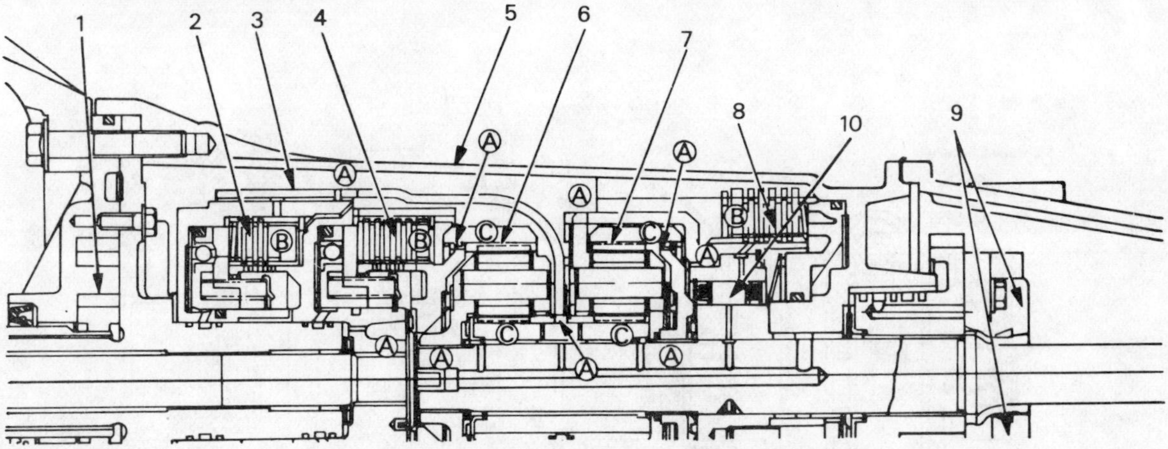

FIG 7:2 Cross-section through the automatic gearbox

Key to Fig 7:2 **A** Spline coupling **B** Clutch coupling **C** Gear coupling 1 Fluid pump 2 Front clutch 3 Brake band 4 Rear clutch 5 Casing 6 Front gearing 7 Rear gearing 8 Low/reverse brake 9 Governors 10 One-way clutch

Check the fluid level with the transmission at a normal operating temperature (50° to 80°C or 120° to 180°F). If the car has not been on the road, run the engine for about ten minutes to raise the fluid temperature.

With the vehicle on level ground, the transmission fluid within the normal operating temperature range and the engine running at the correct idling speed, apply the handbrake and move the selector lever through all driving positions. Return the lever to **P**. With the engine running, remove the dipstick, wipe it clean with lint free cloth, insert it fully and quickly withdraw it again. Add fluid to bring the level up to the F mark. Approximately $\frac{1}{4}$ pint (.4 litre) of fluid is required to raise the level from L to F. Do not overfill.

Approved fluid:

Fluids which are approved for use in the 3N71 B automatic transmission are:

BP	BP Autran DX Dexron
CASTROL	Castrol TQ Dexron
MOBIL	Mobil ATF 220
SHELL	Shell ATF Dexron
TEXACO (and CALEX)	Texamatic Fluid 6673 Dexron

Adjustments:

When necessary, make adjustments to the units and controls which are covered in **Section 7:4**. No specific mileage intervals can be indicated for this maintenance.

7:3 Tests

Before carrying out either stationary or road testing procedures, ensure that the transmission fluid level is up to the F mark on the dipstick. Ensure also that the manual selector lever linkage is correctly adjusted and that the engine idling speed is set at the rev/min specified in **Chapter 2, Section 2:2** for the relevant model.

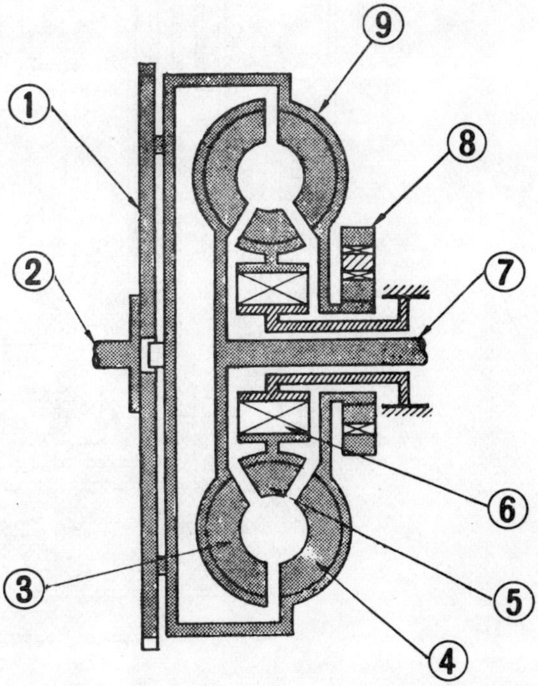

FIG 7:3 Diagrammatic cross-section through the torque coverter

Key to Fig 7:3 1 Drive plate (flywheel) 2 Crankshaft 3 Turbine 4 Impeller 5 Stator 6 One-way clutch 7 Input shaft 8 Fluid pump 9 Casing

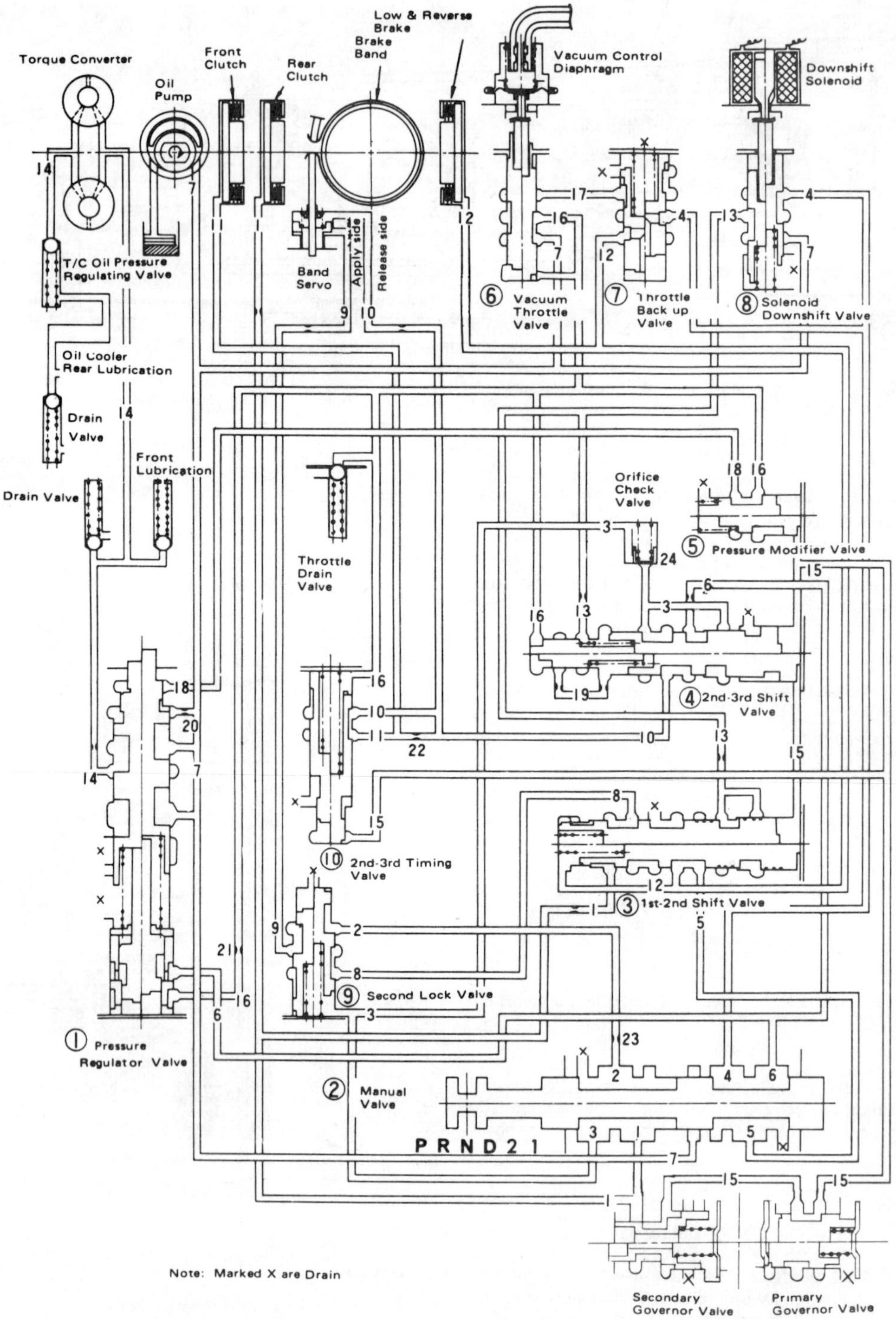

FIG 7:4 Diagrammatic cross-section through the hydraulic control system

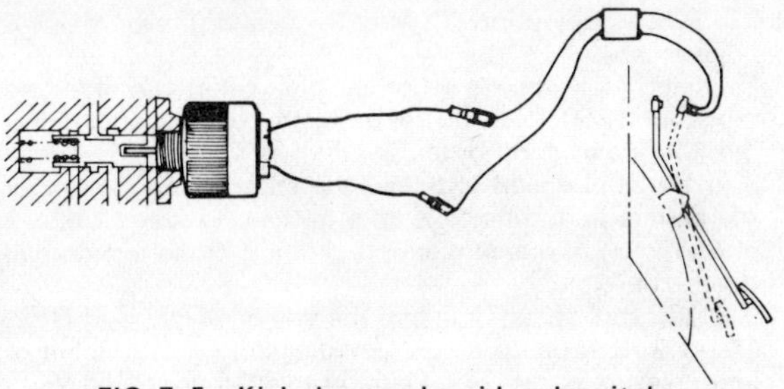

FIG 7:5 Kick-down solenoid and switch

Stationary tests:

The following tests are carried out with the vehicle stationary. An engine operated tachometer is essential for stall speed testing.

Starting inhibitor switch:

1 With the manual selector lever at **P**, confirm that the starter motor will operate when the ignition key is turned fully clockwise to the START position. Confirm this also when **N** is selected.
2 With the selector lever in each drive position, confirm that the starter motor will not operate.
3 With the engine running, confirm that when **R** is selected the reversing lights come on.

If the inhibitor switch does not operate as specified in these tests, refer to the adjustment procedure which is described in **Section 7:4**.

Kick-down switch and solenoid:

The arrangement is shown in **FIG 7:5**. With the engine stationary but with the ignition switched on, depress the accelerator pedal fully. The switch contacts should close and the solenoid should be heard to operate. If the solenoid does not click, either the solenoid, the switch or the wiring continuity is defective. Check the solenoid by using 'jump' wires across the switch. Check the switch by means of an ohmeter or battery and test lamp. Before removing a defective solenoid, lower the level of the transmission fluid by draining off approximately $1\frac{3}{4}$ pints (1 litre) of fluid. The location of the switch is shown in **FIG 7:6**.

Vacuum control valve:

A cross-section through this valve is shown in **FIG 7:7**. Before suspecting that the valve is defective, ensure that there is no air leak in the piping which connects it with the intake manifold.

If the valve is to be removed, lower the level of the transmission fluid level by draining off approximately $1\frac{3}{4}$ pints (1 litre) of fluid. With the valve removed, the possibility of a punctured diaphragm or broken spring can be checked by applying suction and checking that the operating rod moves into the body of the valve and emerges when the suction is released.

Speed detector and switch:

The speed detector and switch are fitted only to models which incorporate emission control equipment. Their function is covered in **Chapter 3, Sections 3:1** and **3:8**.

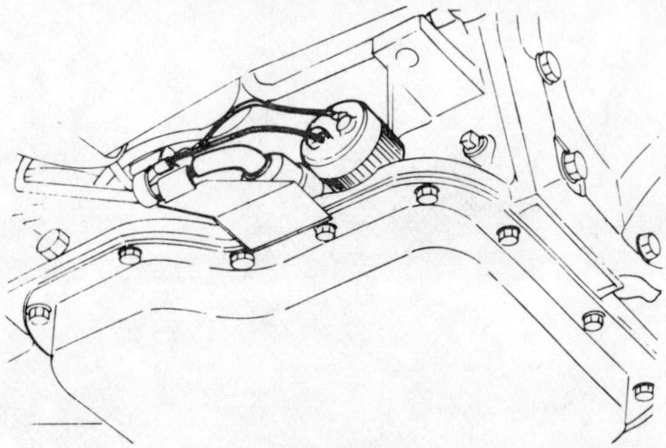

FIG 7:6 Location of kick-down solenoid and vacuum diaphragm valve

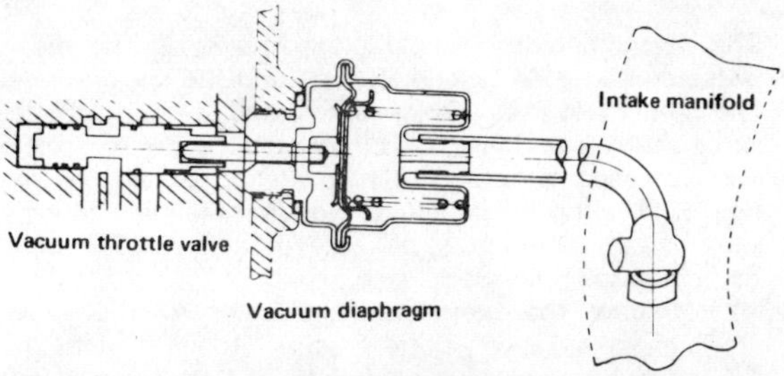

FIG 7:7 Cross-section through the vacuum diaphragm valve

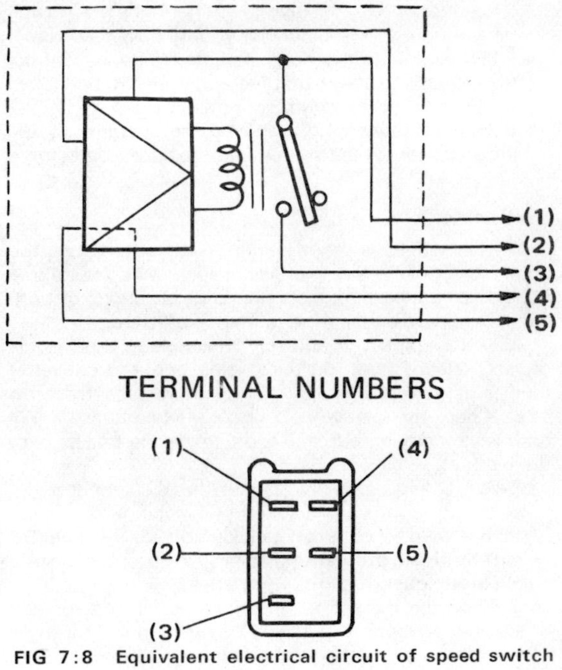

FIG 7:8 Equivalent electrical circuit of speed switch

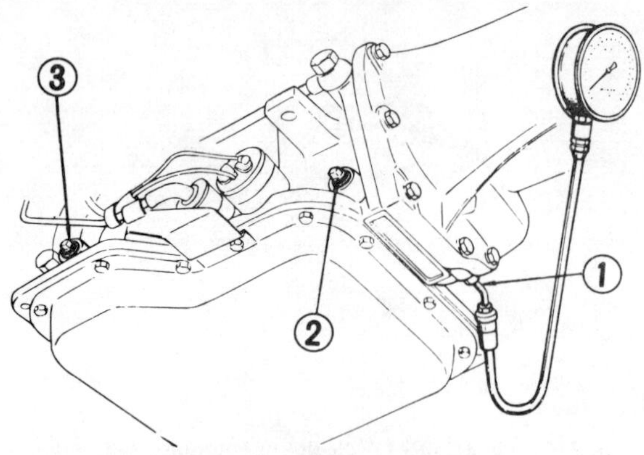

FIG 7:9 **Measuring the line pressure**

Key to Fig 7:9 1 Line pressure 2 Governor feed 3 Servo release pressure

The electric circuitry is included in **FIG 3:11**. The speed detector is located immediately behind the speedometer and is fitted between this instrument and the speedometer drive cable. The speed switch should be off when the vehicle speed is below 13 mile/hr and on above that speed. If either the detector or the switch become unserviceable, both must be renewed as a set. Testing is carried out as follows:

1 Withdraw the connector and refer to **FIG 7:8**. Connect a 12-volt battery across 1 and 5 with the negative terminal connected to 5. Connect a 3-volt battery across 2 and 4 with the negative terminal connected to 4.
2 Connect a suitable voltmeter across 3 and 5. The voltmeter should read 12-volts.
3 Disconnect the positive terminal of the 3-volt battery from 2. The voltmeter should now read zero.
4 If this sequence does not occur, detach the cover from the switch and check that the armature can be moved freely and that the return spring is intact.
5 Repeat operations 1, 2 and 3. If the operation is still incorrect, renew the switch and the speed detector.

Stall tests:

The stall speed is the maximum rev/min at which the engine can drive the converter impeller while the turbine is held stationary. Stall tests provide indications of both engine and transmission performance efficiency.

With the engine oil and the transmission fluid levels correct, select **P** and run the engine until the converter fluid is at normal operating temperature (see **Section 7:2**). Chock the road wheels, apply the handbrake firmly and, while carrying out stall tests, apply the brakes with the left foot.

1 Select **D** and gradually depress the accelerator pedal until full throttle is reached. As soon as a steady engine speed is obtained, quickly note the rev/min. Do **not hold the stall speed for more than 5 seconds without carrying out operation 2.**
2 Release the accelerator pedal, select N and run the engine at approximately 1200 rev/min for some minutes to allow the torque converter to cool.
3 Repeat operation 1 with **2**, **1** and finally with **R** selected.

If the stall speeds recorded are within the standard range of 1800 to 2000 rev/min, the engine and transmission are in good order.

If the stall speed is below the standard range, either the engine performance is poor or the one-way clutch (6 in **FIG 7:3**) in the converter is slipping. Road testing will determine which.

If the stall speed is above the standard range in **D**, **2**, **1** and **R**, low line pressure is indicated. Measurement of line pressure is described later in this Section.

A stall speed which is above the standard range in **D**, **2** and **1** but within the range in **R**, indicates a slipping rear clutch (4 in **FIG 7:2**).

A stall speed which is above the standard range in **D** and **2** but which is within the standard range in **1** indicates that the one-way clutch in the transmission gearbox (10 in **FIG 7:2**) is slipping.

A stall speed which is above the standard range in **R** indicates that either the front clutch 2 or the low/reverse brake 8 in **FIG 7:2** is slipping.

Road tests:

The following tests are carried out with the vehicle in motion.

General performance:

If acceleration is poor up to approximately 30 miles/hr (50 km/hr) but normal above that speed, a slipping one-way clutch in the converter is indicated. If, with an engine of normal performance, the maximum vehicle speed obtainable does not exceed 50 miles/hr (80 km/hr) a seized converter one-way clutch is indicated.

If, while coasting after starting with **1** selected, engine braking is not effective, a slipping low/reverse brake 8 in **FIG 7:2** or a slipping front clutch 2 is indicated.

Slipping of the brake band 3 in **FIG 7:2** is difficult to determine but, if it occurs with **2** selected, the engine speed will increase to the equivalent of low gear.

Stop the car on a gradient and engage **P**. Confirm that the parking pawl holds the car.

With an engine of normal performance, gearchanges should occur at the points given in the following tabulation in which **L** is low gear, **I** is intermediate and **T** is top gear. Manifold depression is given in mm Hg.

Selector position	*Throttle position*	*Manifold depression*	*Gearchange*	*Output shaft rev/min*
D	Full	nil	**L** to **I**	1840 to 2340
			I to **T**	3340 to 3840
	Kick-down		**T** to **I**	3460 to 2960
			I to **L**	1790 to 1290
D	Half	200	**L** to **I**	330 to 830
			I to **T**	1720 to 2220
			T to **I** or **T** to **L**	1350 to 850
			I to **L**	700 maximum
1	Full	nil	**I** to **L**	1860 to 1360
1	Minimum	450	**I** to **L**	1860 to 1360

Output shaft rev/min (R) may be converted to road speed (S) in miles/hr as follows. r is the effective radius of the rear tyres in feet. G is the final gear ratio.

$$S = \frac{Rr}{88G}$$

Line pressure:

FIG 7:9 shows oil pressure tool set ST25050001 fitted to the transmission. Normal line pressures are given in lb/sq inch in the following tabulation. The operation point of the pressure modifier valve is termed the 'cut back' point.

Selector position	*Throttle position*	*At 'cut back' (under 9 miles/hr*)*	*After 'cut back' (over 22 miles/hr*)*
	Full	135 to 156	78 to 92
D	Half	92 to 108	84 to 77
	Minimum	43 to 57	43 to 57
	Full	145 to 168	84 to 78
2	Half	145 to 168	84 to 98
	Minimum	145 to 168	84 to 98
	Full	199 to 228	199 to 228
R	Half	139 to 162	139 to 162
	Minimum	67 to 81	67 to 81

*approximately

Manifold depression at full throttle is nil; at half throttle, 200 mm Hg; and at minimum throttle, 450 mm Hg.

7:4 Adjustments

Throttle dashpot:

The function of this device is stated in **Chapter 2, Section 2:1**. Refer to **FIG 7:10**. Adjustment is correct when, with the primary throttle valve 5 open by 11 deg., the stem of the dashpot just touches the throttle lever 4. The 11 deg. opening of the throttle valve corresponds to a gap of dimension B between the carburetter body. In the case of L16 engines (213282-341 type carburetter), **B** should be .023 inch (.58 mm) and, in the case of L18 engines (213304-421 type carburetter), **B** should be .031 inch (.78 mm).

Adjustment is effected by loosening the locknut 2 and turning the dashpot body 3 in the appropriate direction. Retighten the locknut when adjustment is completed.

Manual selector mechanism:

The floor level selector lever is shown in **FIG 7:11** and the linkage in **FIG 7:12**. The steering column mounted lever and its linkage are shown in **FIGS 7:13** and **7:14**.

Floor level control adjustment:

1 Refer to **FIG 7:11**. Remove two small screws and pull the control handle off the lever. Check that the clearance **A** is .433 to .472 inch (11 to 12 mm). If necessary, adjust the clearance to bring it within this range. Refit the control handle.
2 Confirm that clearance **B** is .0039 to .0433 inch (.1 to 1.1 mm) and that clearance **C** is .039 inch (1 mm).
3 Refer to **FIG 7:12**. The datum for adjustment of the linkage rod is the **N** position. Set the manual selector lever in the **N** position. If the selector lever at the transmission is not also in the **N** position (detent engaged), loosen off the trunnion adjustment screw locknut and turn the adjuster nut to bring the lever to the **N** detent. Retighten the locknut.
4 Check that the floor lever can be moved to all positions without binding and that the transmission selector lever detents and floor lever positions correspond throughout the range.
5 If correct adjustment cannot be achieved, inspect the linkage for worn parts and renew as necessary.

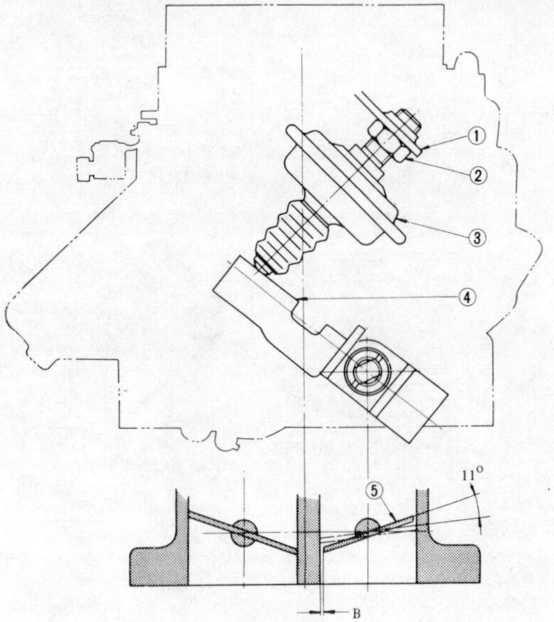

FIG 7:10 Dashpot adjustment

Key to Fig 7:10 1 Bracket 2 Locknut 3 Dashpot body 4 Throttle lever 5 Primary throttle valve **B** See text

Column mounted control, removal:

1 Refer to **FIG 7:13**. Disconnect the upper selector rod from the manual selector lever by removing the cotter pin, plain washer and spring washer at the trunnion.
2 Remove the selector position plate from the lower bracket clamp by removing two bolts. Remove the lower bracket and lower support bracket clamp by removing the attachment bolts.
3 Remove the indicator arm retaining screw and washer. Dismount the indicator arm from the control rod.
4 Remove the bolt, plain washer and C-washer. The control rod can now be removed together with the rod insert, return spring, etc.

Column mounted control, fitment:

Fitment is the reverse of the removal sequence. Coat all sliding and pivoting surfaces sparingly with multipurpose grease and, while refitting, carry out the following adjustment procedure.

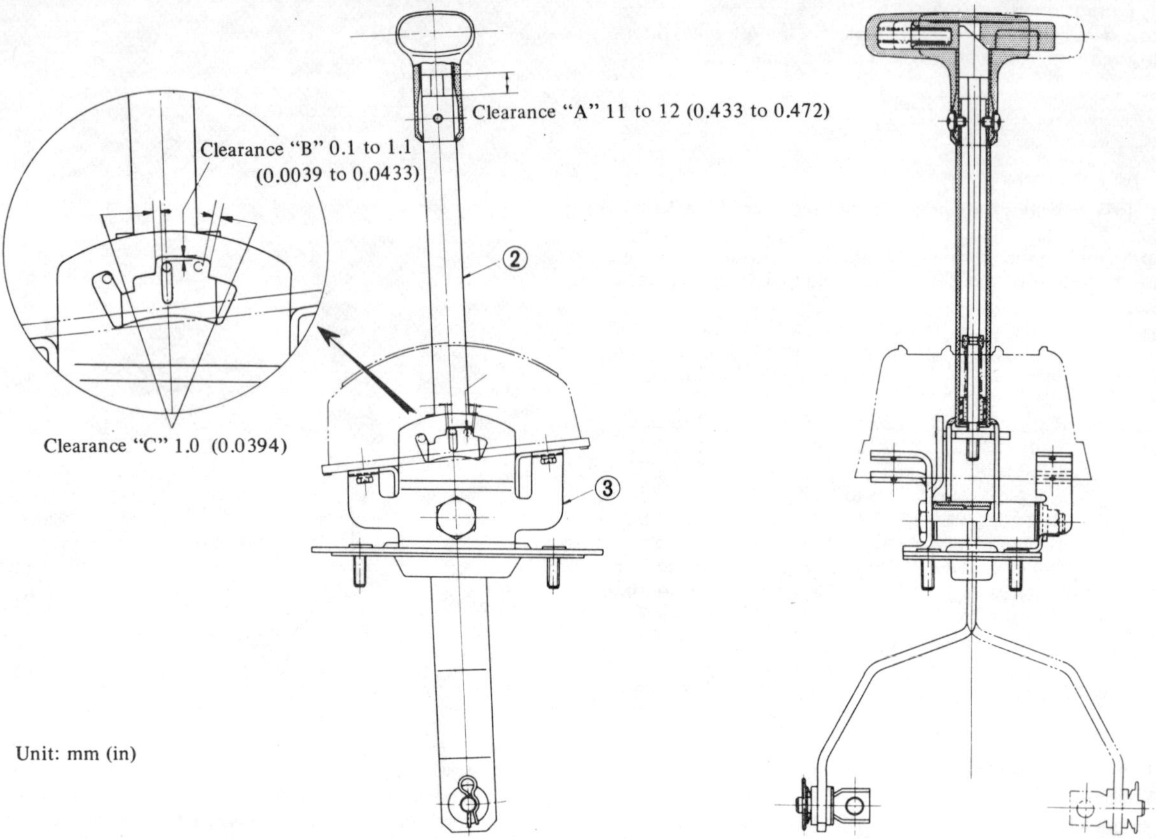

FIG 7:11 Floor mounted control lever

Key to Fig 7:11 2 Control lever 3 Bracket

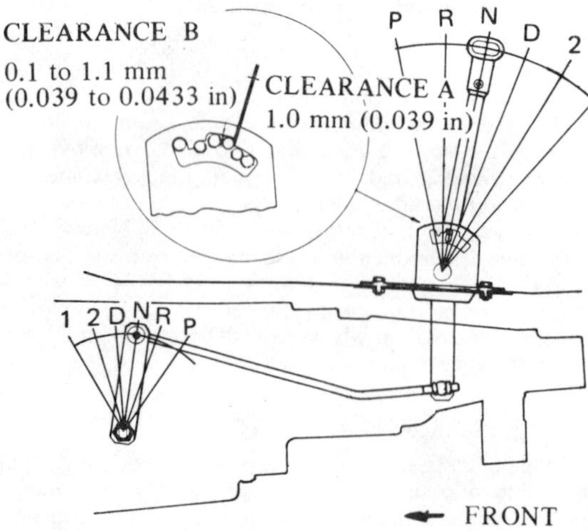

FIG 7:12 Floor mounted control lever linkage

Column mounted control adjustment:

1 Refer to **FIG 7:13**. Set the transmission selector lever 1 to **N**. Fit the upper rod 2 to the control lever 3.
2 Adjust the trunnion nuts so that, while pushing down the upper selector rod 2 slightly, the clearance between the selector lever stop pin 4 and the position plate 5 is .0197 to .0394 inch (.5 to 1 mm) as shown in the insets to **FIGS 7:13** and **7:14**.
3 Check that the linkage operates smoothly in all positions and that all manual lever positions correspond with the transmission detents.
4 If correct adjustment cannot be achieved, inspect the linkage for worn parts and renew as necessary.

Starter inhibitor switch:

The location of the starter inhibitor switch (with which is incorporated the reversing light switch) is shown in **FIG 7:15**. The circuitry is included in **FIG 14:1** in the Appendix.

The purpose of the inhibitor switch is to preclude the starter motor from being operated except when the transmission selector lever 9 in **FIG 7:15** is within an angle of approximately 3 deg. on either side of the **P** or **N** detent positions. The reversing light switch closes when

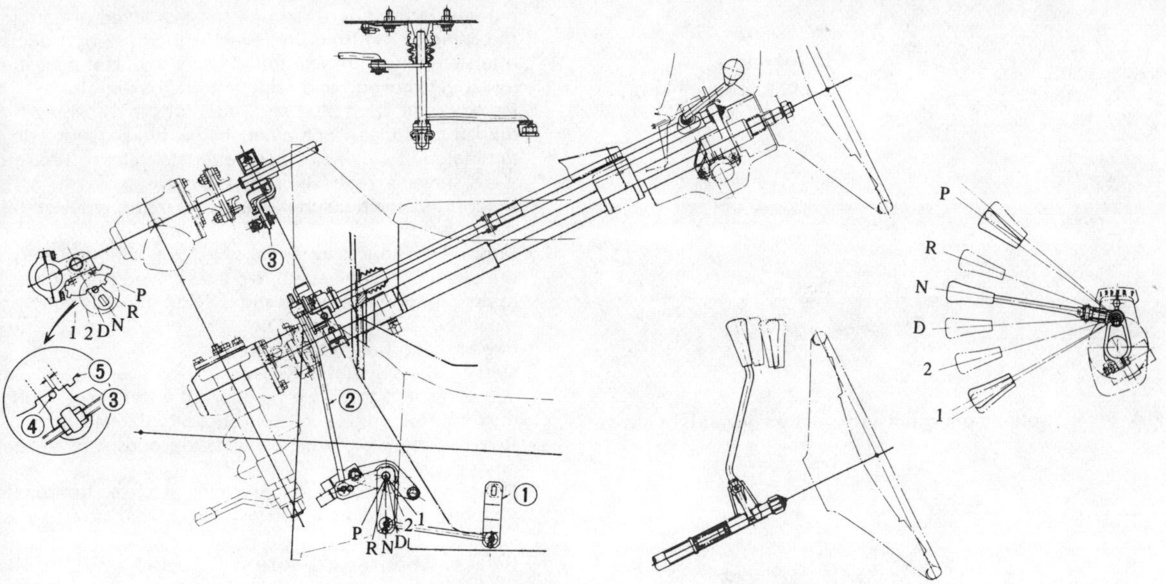

FIG 7:13 **Steering column mounted control and linkage**

Key to Fig 7:13 1 Selector lever 2 Upper selector rod 3 Linkage selector lever 4 Stop pin 5 Plate

the selector lever is in the **R** detent position. Incorrect operation (the testing procedure is described in **Section 7:3**) may be due to incorrect adjustment, a defective switch or to a discontinuity in the wiring.

Adjustment:

1 Ensure that the manual selector mechanism is correctly adjusted as described earlier in this Section. Position the selector lever in the **N** position detent (see **FIG 7:12** or **FIG 7:14**).
2 Remove the nut and washer 6 and 7 in **FIG 7:15** and withdraw the lever 9. Confirm that the **N** detent is engaged (the slot in the shaft will be vertically disposed). Remove the alignment hole access screw from under the switch body.
3 Loosen the two bolts which retain the switch to the casing. Move the switch body as necessary until a pin of .059 inch (1.5 mm) diameter inserted into the switch body aligns with the hole in the switch rotor and the hole in the selector shaft 2.
4 Tighten the switch body retaining bolts to a torque of 2.5 to 3.2 lb ft (.35 to .45 kgm), refit the alignment hole access screw and reassemble the selector lever to its shaft. Torque tighten the retaining nut to 33 to 47 lb ft (4.5 to 6.5 kgm).

If, in spite of correct adjustment, incorrect operation persists, check the switch itself after disconnecting four wires. Using an ohmeter or a battery and test lamp, check that the inhibitor switch contacts (the two black/yellow switch wires) are closed when the **P** or **N** detent is engaged. Similarly check that the reversing light switch contacts (the two red/black switch wires) are closed when the **R** detent is engaged. If the switch is defective, fit a new replacement. If the switch is serviceable, check the wiring continuity (see **FIG 14:1** in the Appendix).

Brake band:

A cross-section through the brake band and its actuating mechanism is shown in **FIG 7:16** and its location at the forward end of the gearbox is shown at 3 in **FIG 7:2**.

Access for adjustment of the band requires removal of the transmission casing sump. Proceed as follows:

1 Drain off the transmission fluid and remove the sump (oil pan). Discard the joint gasket.
2 Refer to **FIG 7:16**. Loosen the piston stem locknut. Torque tighten the piston stem 4 to 8.7 to 10.8 lb ft (1.2 to 1.5 kgm) and then back off the stem by two turns. Retighten the locknut to a torque of 22 to 29 lb ft (3 to 4 kgm).
3 Use a new joint gasket and torque tighten the sump retaining bolts to 2.5 to 3.2 lb ft (.35 to .45 kgm). Refill the transmission and, after running the engine, check the fluid level as described in **Section 7:2**.

7:5 Removing and refitting the transmission

Removal:

1 With the vehicle on a hoist or over a pit, disconnect the battery cables. Uncouple the speedometer drive from the transmission extension casing.
2 Dismount the propeller shaft as described in **Chapter 8, Section 8:2**. Refer to **Chapter 13, Section 13:2** and remove the front exhaust pipe assembly in the case of saloon models. Remove the front exhaust pipe and the pre-silencer assembly in the case of estate cars.
3 Disconnect the starting inhibitor switch. Remove the piping from the vacuum diaphragm control valve and disconnect the wiring from the kick-down solenoid.
4 Disconnect the torsion shaft from the accelerator linkage (see **Chapter 2, Section 2:5**). In the case of

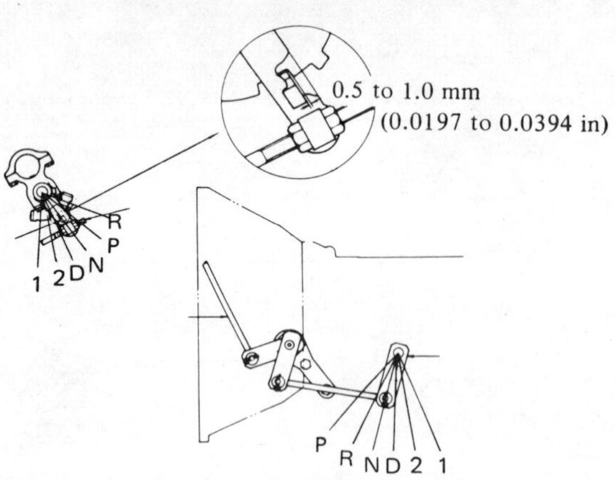

FIG 7:14 Column mounted control linkage adjustment

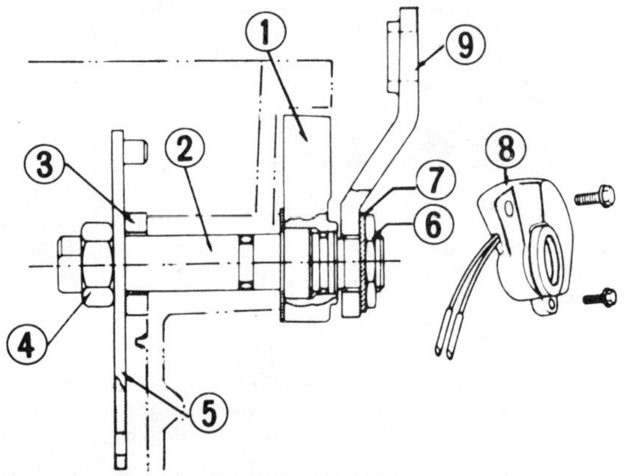

FIG 7:15 Starter inhibitor switch

Key to Fig 7:15 1 Inhibitor switch 2 Selector shaft 3 Washer 4 Nut 5 Plate 6 Nut 7 Washer 8 Inhibitor switch 9 Selector lever

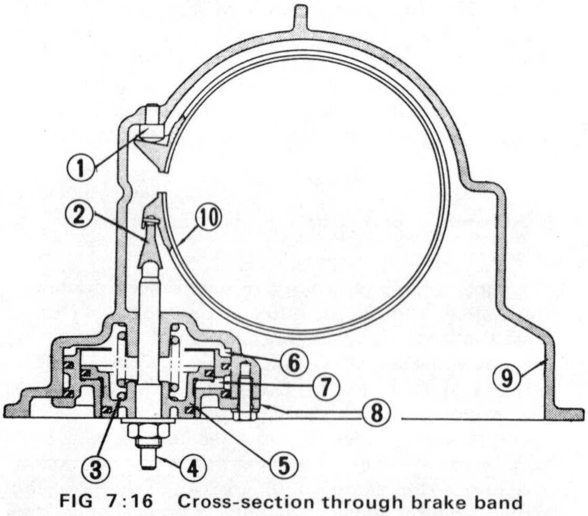

FIG 7:16 Cross-section through brake band

Key to Fig 7:16 1 Anchor pin 2 Band strut 3 Return spring 4 Piston stem 5 Band servo 6 Release side of servo 7 Apply side of servo 8 Piston 9 Casing 10 Brake band

models with a floor mounted selector lever, uncouple the selector rod from the lever. In the case of models fitted with a column mounted linkage, disconnect the lower selector rod and remove the cross-shaft.

5 Remove the drain plug and drain off the transmission fluid into a clean container. If the fluid is not contaminated, it may be re-used after straining it through a 100-mesh screen. Refit the drain plug.

6 Disconnect the fluid cooler feed and return pipes at the transmission.

7 Support the engine by means of a jack positioned under the oil sump with a suitable piece of wood interposed to prevent damage to the sump. Note that this support must not be removed until re-installation of the transmission has been completed.

8 Detach the converter housing dust cover. Mark the converter and the drive plate so that, on reassembly, they may be refitted in their original relative position. Remove the bolts which attach the converter to the drive plate.

9 Support the transmission by means of a jack. Interpose a suitable block of wood to prevent damage to the sump.

10 Refer to **Chapter 1, Section 1:20** and to **FIG 1:38**. Remove the two bolts which attach the transmission to the mounting, remove the two bolts which attach the crossmember to the chassis at each side and dismount the crossmember and mounting assembly.

11 Remove the starter motor as described in **Chapter 12, Section 12:3**. Remove the bolts which attach the bellhousing to the engine.

12 Gradually lower the jack which is supporting the transmission until the unit can be withdrawn from under the vehicle.

Fitment:

Fitment of the automatic transmission unit is the removal sequence in reverse. Ensure that the converter and drive plate marks (see removal operation 8) are re-aligned. Torque tighten the bellhousing to engine bolts and the torque converter to drive plate bolts to 30 to 36 lb ft (4 to 5 kgm). Refill the transmission with approved fluid. Approximately 10 pints (5.5 litre) of fluid will be required. After running the engine and operating the transmission control through all drive positions, check the fluid level as described in **Section 7:2**.

7:6 Fault diagnosis

This section indicates the checks relevant to an extensive list of possible faults. Although the owner will be in a position to deal with only a few of these himself, the list will assist him to consult knowledgeably with the specialist whose services will have to be enlisted to deal with many of these possible faults.

The numbers shown in the tabulation indicate the sequence in which checks should be carried out. Note that the first sixteen columns in the tabulation relate to checks which can be carried out without removing the transmission from the vehicle while the remaining eleven columns relate to checks which require the transmission to fully or partially dismantled after it has been removed from the car as described in **Section 7:5**. The list of checks is given after the tabulation.

Fault	A	B	C	D	E	F	G	H	I	J	K	L	M	N	O	P	m	n	q	r	s	t	u	v	w	x	y
	Transmission in vehicle																*With transmission removed*										
Will not start in **N** or **P**	–	2	3	–	–	–	–	–	–	–	–	–	–	–	1	–	–	–	–	–	–	–	–	–	–	–	–
Starts in other than **N** or **P**	–	1	2	–	–	–	–	–	–	–	–	–	–	–	–	–	–	–	–	–	–	–	–	–	–	–	–
Harsh engagement of **D** from **N**	–	–	–	2	–	1	3	–	–	4	–	–	–	–	–	–	5	–	–	–	–	–	–	–	–	–	–
Drives in **2**, **1** and **R** but not in **D**	–	1	–	–	–	–	2	–	–	3	–	–	–	–	–	–	–	–	–	–	–	–	–	4	–	–	–
Drives in **R** but not in **D**, **1** or **2**. Poor acceleration	1	2	–	–	–	–	4	–	–	5	–	–	6	3	–	7	8	10	–	–	–	9	–	–	–	–	–
Drives in **D**, **1** and **2** but not in **R**. Poor acceleration	1	2	–	–	–	–	3	–	–	5	–	–	6	4	–	–	9	8	–	7	–	10	–	–	–	11	–
No drive in any position	1	2	–	–	–	–	3	–	–	5	–	–	6	4	–	–	–	–	–	–	7	8	–	–	–	9	–
Clutches or brakes slip when starting	1	2	–	6	–	–	3	–	–	5	–	–	7	4	–	–	–	–	–	–	8	9	–	–	–	–	–
Drives in **N**	–	1	–	–	–	–	–	–	–	3	–	–	–	2	–	–	4	–	–	–	–	–	–	–	–	–	–
Poor maximum speed. Poor acceleration	1	2	–	–	–	–	4	5	–	7	–	6	–	3	–	8	11	12	9	10	13	–	–	–	–	–	–
Excessive creep	–	–	–	–	–	1	–	–	–	–	–	–	–	–	–	–	–	–	–	–	–	–	–	–	–	–	–
No creep at all	1	2	–	–	–	3	–	–	–	5	–	–	–	4	–	–	8	9	–	–	6	7	–	–	–	–	–
No speed change from I to T	–	1	–	2	3	–	–	–	–	5	6	8	7	4	–	–	–	–	9	–	–	10	–	–	–	–	–
No speed change from L to I		1	–	2	3	–	–	–	–	5	6	8	7	4	–	–	–	9	–	–	–	10	–	–	11	–	–
L to I and I to T change points high	–	–	–	1	2	–	3	–	–	5	6	–	–	4	–	–	–	–	–	–	–	7	–	–	–	–	–
Speed change from L to T occurs	–	–	–	–	–	–	–	–	–	2	4	–	3	1	–	–	–	–	5	–	–	6	–	–	–	–	–
Harsh L to I change	–	–	–	1	–	–	–	2	–	4	–	5	–	3	–	–	–	–	6	–	–	–	–	–	–	–	–
Harsh I to T change	–	–	–	1	2	–	3	–	–	3	–	5	4	–	–	–	–	6	–	–	–	–	–	–	–	–	–
Clutches slip in change from L to I	1	2	–	3	–	–	4	–	–	6	–	8	7	5	–	–	–	–	9	–	–	10	–	–	–	–	–
Clutches slip in change from I to T engine races	1	2	–	3	–	–	4	–	–	6	–	8	7	5	–	–	–	9	–	–	–	10	–	–	11	–	–
Vehicle braked by change from L to I	–	–	–	–	–	–	–	–	–	2	–	–	–	1	–	–	–	4	–	3	–	–	–	5	–	–	–
Vehicle braked by change from I to T	–	–	–	–	–	–	–	–	–	3	–	2	–	1	–	–	–	–	4	–	–	–	–	–	–	–	–
No speed change T to I	–	–	–	1	–	–	–	–	–	3	4	6	5	2	–	–	–	7	8	–	–	9	–	–	–	–	–
No speed change I to L or T to L	–	–	–	1	–	–	–	–	–	3	4	6	5	2	–	–	–	–	7	–	–	–	–	8	–	–	–
High change point T to I or I to L	–	1	–	2	3	–	4	–	–	5	6	–	–	–	–	–	–	–	–	–	–	7	–	–	–	–	–
Kick-down inoperative within kick-speed range	–	–	–	2	1	–	–	–	–	4	5	–	–	3	–	–	–	–	6	–	–	7	–	–	–	–	–
Kick-down operates or engine over-runs outside kick-down speed range	–	1	–	2	–	–	3	–	–	5	6	–	7	4	–	–	–	8	–	–	–	9	–	–	–	–	–
No change from T to I when **2** selected	–	1	–	–	–	–	2	–	–	4	–	5	–	3	–	–	–	–	6	–	7	–	–	–	–	–	–
Not locked in I with **2** selected	–	1	–	–	–	–	2	–	–	3	–	–	–	–	–	–	–	–	–	–	–	–	–	–	–	–	–
When in **1** no shock or engine races when **2** selected	1	2	–	3	–	4	–	8	–	6	–	–	7	5	–	–	–	–	9	–	10	–	–	–	–	–	–
No change from T to I when **1** selected	–	1	–	–	–	–	2	–	–	4	5	7	6	3	–	–	–	8	9	–	–	10	–	–	–	–	–
No braking effect in **1**	–	1	–	–	–	–	2	–	–	4	–	–	5	3	–	–	–	–	–	6	–	7	–	–	–	–	–
Change from L to I or I to T with **1** selected	–	1	–	–	–	–	–	–	–	2	–	–	–	–	–	–	–	–	–	–	–	3	–	–	–	–	–
No change from I to L in **1**	1	2	–	–	–	–	–	–	–	4	5	6	7	3	–	–	–	–	–	8	–	9	–	–	–	–	–
Harsh change from I to L in **1**	–	–	–	1	–	–	–	2	–	4	–	–	–	3	–	–	–	–	–	5	–	–	–	–	–	–	–
Parking pawl does not engage in **P** or will not disengage	–	1	–	–	–	–	–	–	–	–	–	–	–	–	–	–	–	–	–	–	–	–	–	–	–	2	–
Transmission overheats	1	–	–	–	–	–	3	4	2	6	–	8	7	5	–	–	–	9	10	11	12	13	14	–	–	–	15

Fault	Transmission in vehicle																With transmission removed										
	A	*B*	*C*	*D*	*E*	*F*	*G*	*H*	*I*	*J*	*K*	*L*	*M*	*N*	*O*	*P*	*m*	*n*	*q*	*r*	*s*	*t*	*u*	*v*	*w*	*x*	*y*
Oil ejected, white smoke emitted while running	1	–	–	3	–	–	5	6	2	7	–	–	8	4	–	–	–	9	10	11	12	13	14	–	–	–	15
Offensive smell at oil filler	1	–	–	–	–	–	–	–	–	–	–	–	–	2	–	–	3	4	5	6	7	8	9	–	–	–	10
Transmission noise with **P** or **N** selected	1	–	–	–	–	–	2	–	–	–	–	–	–	–	–	–	–	–	–	–	3	–	–	–	–	–	–
Transmission noise in **D**, **2**, **I** or **R** ..	1	–	–	–	–	–	2	–	–	–	–	–	–	–	–	–	3	–	–	–	4	–	–	5	–	–	6

Key to tabulated checks:

A Oil (fluid) level
B Manual selector linkage
C Starting inhibitor switch and wiring
D Vacuum diaphragm valve and piping
E Kick-down switch, wiring and solenoid
F Idling speed
G Fluid pressure
H Stall rev/min
I Lubrication
J Control valve
K Governor
L Band adjustment and/or band servo
M Transmission air check
N Oil (fluid) quantity
O Ignition switch and starter motor
P Engine performance
m Rear clutch
n Front clutch
q Band brake
r Low/reverse brake
s Oil (fluid) pump
t Internal oil (fluid) leakage
u Converter one-way clutch
v Gearbox one-way clutch
w Front clutch check ball
x Parking pawl linkage
y Planetary gears

CHAPTER 8

THE PROPELLER SHAFT, REAR AXLE AND REAR SUSPENSION

8:1 The propeller shaft
8:2 Shaft removal and fitment
8:3 Shaft dismantling and reassembly
8:4 Rear suspension
8:5 Spring removal and fitment
8:6 Damper removal and fitment
8:7 Hubs and shafts
8:8 Final drive unit (saloon and coupe)
8:9 Differential unit (estate car)
8:10 Fault diagnosis

8:1 The propeller shaft

Two types of open tubular propeller shafts are fitted to the vehicles covered by this manual. Saloon models are provided with a one-piece shaft which has a universal joint and coupling at each end as shown in **FIG 8:1**. Estate car models have a two-piece shaft with a universal joint coupling them and a universal joint and coupling at each end. This type of shaft is shown in **FIG 8:2**. The rear end of the forward shaft is supported in a flexibly mounted ball bearing which is carried in a composite bracket attached to the chassis as shown in **FIG 8:3**.

The forward coupling on both types of shaft is splined to the transmission output shaft to allow for axial movement of the propeller shaft assembly. The transmission rear extension oil seal runs on the outer diameter of this forward coupling.

8:2 Shaft removal and fitment

With the vehicle on a hoist or over a pit, mark the relative position of the rear flange yoke and the drive pinion companion flange and remove the coupling bolts. In the case of estate car models also remove bolts 1 in **FIG 8:3** which retain the bearing support bracket to the chassis. Dismount the rear end of the shaft from the companion flange and carefully withdraw the shaft assembly rearwards and out of engagement with the output shaft splines. Use plastic material retained by rubber bands to blank off the rear extension.

Fitment is the reverse of this sequence. Align the rear coupling marks and torque tighten the bolts to 14.5 to 19.5 lb ft (2 to 2.7 kgm). In the case of estate cars, torque tighten the bearing bracket to chassis bolts to 26 to 34.7 lb ft (3.6 to 4.8 kgm).

8:3 Shaft dismantling and reassembly

Dismantling:

Propeller shafts are factory balanced. If dismantling is essential, mark all relevant parts so that on reassembly their original relative positions can be restored.

Remove the snap rings which retain the bearings and, as shown in **FIG 8:4**, lightly tap the yoke to remove each bearing.

To remove the centre bearing from a two-piece shaft, refer to **FIG 8:2**, mark the position of the flange 8 in relation to the companion flange 5, remove the retaining nuts and bolts and separate the flanges. Use tool

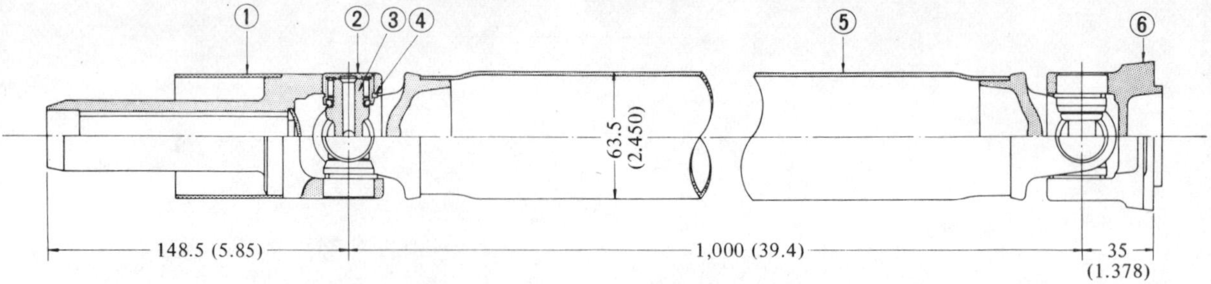

FIG 8:1 Propeller shaft, saloon models

Key to Fig 8:1 1 Sleeve yoke 2 Bearing 3 Spider 4 Snap ring 5 Propeller shaft 6 Flange yoke

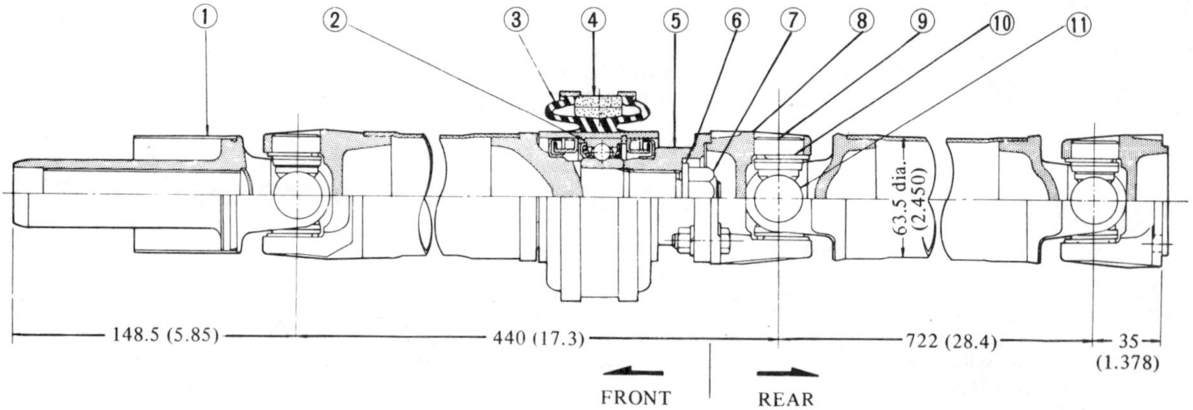

FIG 8:2 Propeller shaft, estate car models

Key to Fig 8:2 1 Sleeve yoke 2 Centre bearing 3 Centre bearing insulator 4 Cushion rubber 5 Flange 6 Plain washer 7 Nut 8 Flange yoke 9 Bearing 10 Snap ring 11 Spider

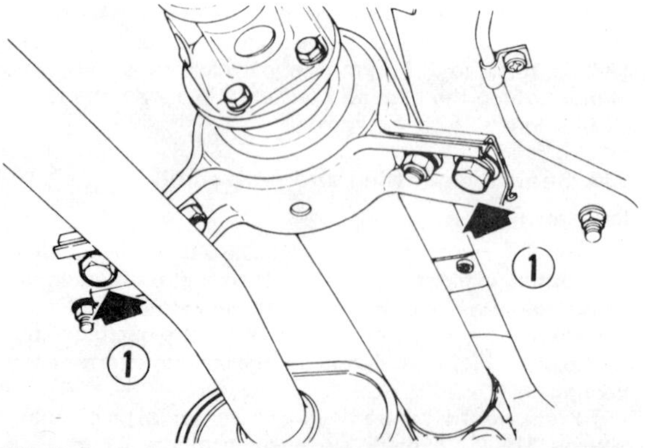

FIG 8:3 Centre bearing bracket, estate car models

Key to Fig 8:3 1 Bracket to chassis attachment bolts

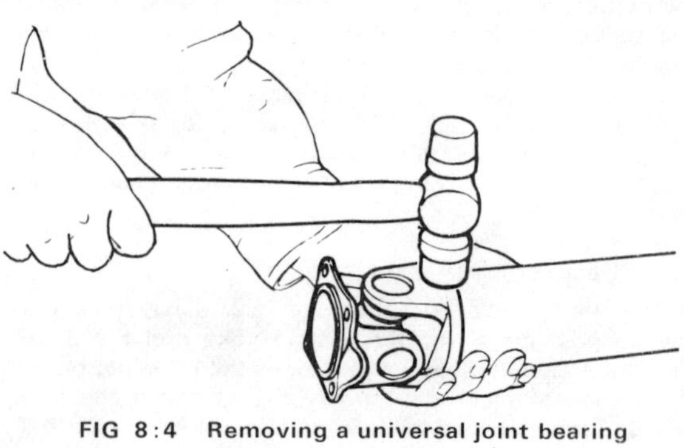

FIG 8:4 Removing a universal joint bearing

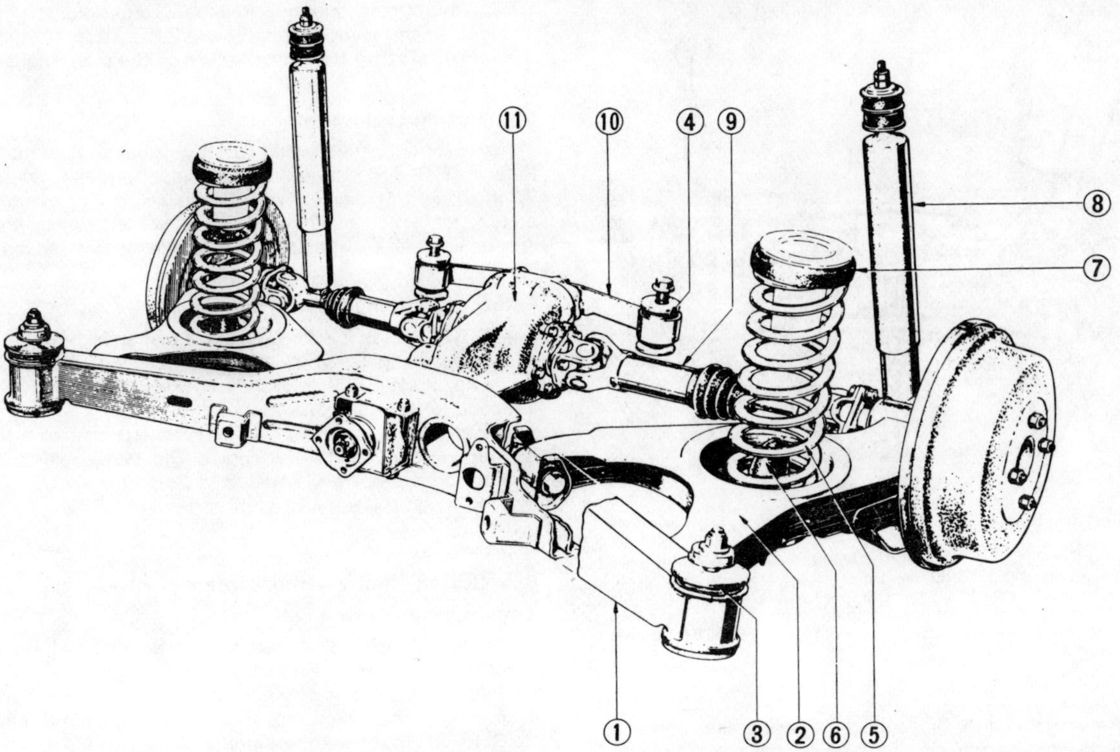

FIG 8:5 Rear suspension and drive shafts, saloon models

Key to Fig 8:5 1 Suspension crossmember 2 Suspension arm 3 Mounting bush 4 Drive unit mounting bush 5 Coil spring 6 Bump stop rubber 7 Spring seat 8 Damper 9 Drive shaft 10 Drive unit mounting member 11 Final drive unit

ST31530000 to hold the companion flange and remove retaining nut 7 and washer 6. Withdraw the centre bearing assembly. Remove the bracket, seals, circlip and bearing.

No attempt should be made to salvage a bent or dented shaft which must be replaced by a new component.

Assembly:

Follow the dismantling sequence in reverse. Grease universal joint bearings but note that a new centre bearing is lubricated for life and does not require to be greased. Universal joint bearing end play should be limited to .0008 inch (.02 mm) by selection of snap rings of appropriate thickness. Seven thicknesses are available as follows.

Thickness	*Colour identification*
.0788 inch (2.00 mm)	White
.0795 inch (2.02 mm)	Yellow
.0803 inch (2.04 mm)	Red
.0811 inch (2.06 mm)	Green
.0819 inch (2.08 mm)	Blue
.0827 inch (2.10 mm)	Light brown
.0835 inch (2.12 mm)	Nil

The out of balance of a one-piece shaft should not exceed .2 oz inch (15 gr cm) and that of a two-piece shaft should not exceed .5 oz inch (35 gr cm).

When fitting the companion flange retaining nut 7 in **FIG 8:2** (estate car models), use tool ST31530000 to hold the flange and torque tighten the nut to 145 to 174 lb ft (20 to 24 kgm). Torque tighten the centre joint yoke flange to companion flange retaining nuts and bolts to 14.5 to 19.5 lb ft (2 to 2.7 kgm). Torque tighten the nuts and bolts which unite the two parts of the centre bearing bracket to 13.7 to 18.8 lb ft (1.9 to 2.6 kgm).

8:4 Rear suspension

The rear suspension and final drive differs between saloon and estate car models.

Saloon models:

FIG 8:5 shows the independent suspension trailing arms, coil road springs, telescopic dampers, final drive unit, universally jointed and extensible drive shafts, and the drum brake hubs which form the rear suspension and drive on saloon models.

Removal (saloon models):

Where removal of the complete suspension is not necessary, refer to the relevant part(s) of the dismantling sequence which is described later.

1 Raise the rear of the vehicle and support it on stands positioned slightly forwards of the suspension crossmember. Remove the rear road wheels.

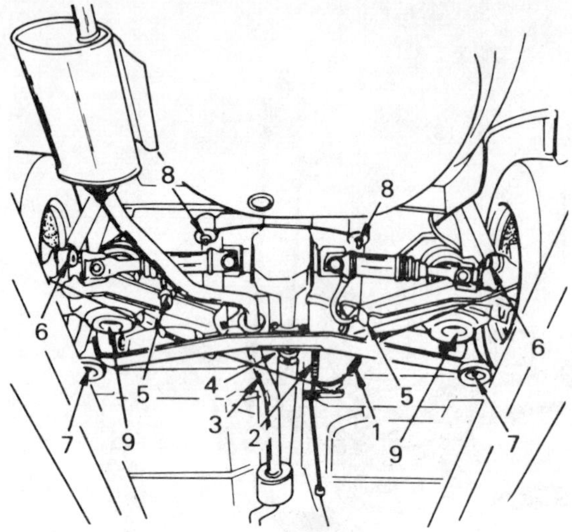

FIG 8:6 **Removing the rear suspension, saloon models**

Key to Fig 8:6 1 Handbrake adjuster 2 Handbrake return spring 3 Exhaust pipe 4 Propeller shaft 5 Brake hoses 6 Damper lower attachment points 7 Suspension crossmember attachment points 8 Drive unit mounting member attachment points 9 Bump stop attachment points

2 Refer to **FIG 8:6**. Disconnect the handbrake cables by removing the adjuster nut at adjuster 1 and the spring 2.
3 Refer to **Chapter 13, Section 13:12** and remove the silencer and exhaust pipe 3. Remove the propeller shaft as described in **Section 8:2**.
4 Uncouple the brake hoses at points 5 and blank off the pipes to preclude ingress of dirt. Uncouple the lower end 6 of each damper (see **Section 8:6**).
5 Support the final drive unit with a jack. Remove nuts 7 and 8 and, holding the suspension assembly so that it does not tilt, carefully lower the jack until the assembly can be withdrawn from beneath the car.

Dismantling (saloon models):

1 Remove the drive shafts as described in **Section 8:7**. Remove the final drive unit as described in **Section 8:8**. Remove the coil springs as described in **Section 8:5**.
2 Disconnect the suspension arms from the cross-member by removing the bolts from the pivot bushes. The bushes may be removed if necessary using tool ST38280000. Removal of the brake assemblies and the hubs is described in **Section 8:7** and **Chapter 11, Section 11:4.**
3 If necessary, use tool ST38290000 to remove the rubber bushes from the crossmember and drift ST33300020 to remove the bushes from the final drive unit rear mounting member.

Assembly (saloon models):

Assembly is the reverse of the dismantling procedure. Use tool ST33300020 under a press to fit new bushes to the drive unit rear mounting member. Torque tighten the suspension arm pivot bolts to 58 to 72 lb ft (8 to 10 kgm) **after completing the installation of the suspension.**

Installation (saloon models):

Installation is the reverse of the removal sequence. Refer to **FIG 8:6**. Torque tighten nuts 7 and 8 to 51 to 72 lb ft (7 to 10 kgm). With the installation completed and the rear wheels taking the vehicle weight, tighten the suspension arm pivot bolts to the torque quoted earlier.

Estate car models:

FIG 8:7 shows the semi-elliptical leaf springs and the telescopic dampers which form the rear suspension of estate car models. Note that the rear axle is conventionally attached to the springs by U-bolts.

Removal and installation of the rear suspension is, after uncoupling the handbrake cables, the brake hydraulic pipes, etc., compositely covered in **Sections 8:2, 8:5, 8:6, 8:7** and the relevant parts of **Section 8:9**.

8:5 Spring removal and fitment

Saloon models, removal:

1 Refer to **Section 8:4** and carry out operations 1 and 2 of the suspension removal procedure.
2 Remove the nuts and bolts which couple the drive shaft flange to the wheel hub. Remove the nut (9 in **FIG 8:6**) which retains the bump stop.
3 Using a jack, raise the suspension arm slightly to relieve the tension on the damper. Refer to **Section 8:6** and disconnect the lower end of the damper.
4 Carefully lower the jack and allow the spring to extend fully. Remove the spring seat, spring and rubber bump stop as shown in **FIG 8:8**

Standard springs have $9\frac{1}{4}$ coils and a spring rate of 367 lb/inch (6.56 kg/mm) when new. Hard suspension springs have $9\frac{1}{2}$ coils and a spring rate of 444 lb/inch (7.93 kg/mm). The wire diameter is .571 inch (14.5 mm) and the coil diameter is 3.54 inch (90mm) in both cases.

Saloon models, fitment:

Spring fitment is the reverse of the removal sequence. Ensure that the spring is the correct way up (flat face at the top). Torque tighten the bump stop nut and the damper lower attachment bolt to 12 to 16 lb ft (1.6 to 2.2 kgm) and the drive shaft bolts to 36 to 43 lb ft (5 to 6 kgm).

Estate cars, removal:

1 Raise the rear of the vehicle and support it on stands. Remove the relevant road wheel.
2 Refer to **FIG 8:9**. Disconnect the damper lower attachment 1. Remove the U-bolt nuts 2.
3 Using a jack under the rear axle casing, raise the axle off the spring. Refer to **FIG 8:10**, remove the two nuts (arrowed) and uncouple the spring shackle.
4 Refer to **FIG 8:11**. Remove the nut (arrowed) which retains the pin in the front bracket. Remove the pin and withdraw the spring.

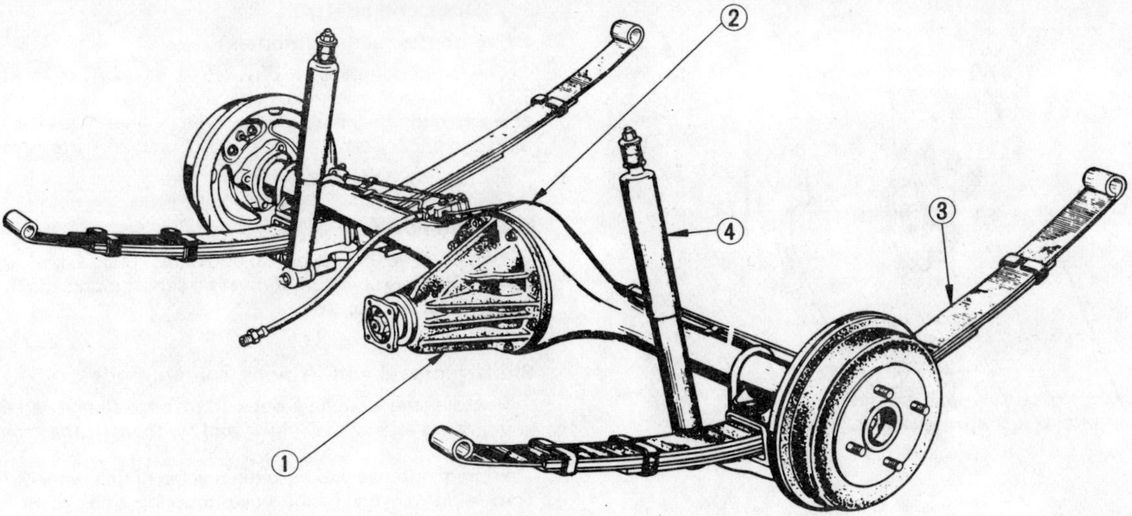

FIG 8:7 Rear suspension and axle, estate car models

Key to Fig 8:7 1 Differential carrier 2 Axle casing 3 Semi-elliptical spring 4 Damper

Estate cars, fitment:

Spring fitment is the reverse of the removal sequence. Coat the front pin, shackle pins and bush with a soap solution before assembly. Torque tighten the U-bolt nuts to 43 to 47 lb ft (6 to 6.5 kgm). Do not fully tighten the front or the shackle pin nuts fully until the weight of the vehicle is on the rear wheels. They should then be torque tightened to this same figure.

8:6 Damper removal and fitment

Removal:

1 Refer to **FIG 8:6** in the case of saloon models and to **FIG 8:9** in the case of estate car models. Disconnect the lower end of the damper.
2 In the case of **estate car models,** remove the two bolts which retain the damper top bracket to the chassis and withdraw the damper.
3 In the case of **saloon models**, work from inside the luggage compartment, remove the trim, remove the locknut and the retaining nut from the top of the damper. Collect the washers and withdraw the damper downwards.

Dampers are not identical for all models and, if a replacement is required, ensure that the new damper is the same type as that removed.

Fitment:

Fitment is the reverse of the removal sequence. **Do not finally tighten the damper lower attachment until the vehicle weight is on the rear wheels.** Torque tightening figures are 12 to 16 lb ft (1.6 to 2.2 kgm) for both ends of the dampers fitted to saloon models. In the case of estate cars the upper bracket retaining bolts should be tightened to a torque of 6.5 to 8.7 lb ft (.9 to 1.2 kgm) and the lower attachment to a torque of 25 to 33 lb ft (3.5 to 4.5 kgm).

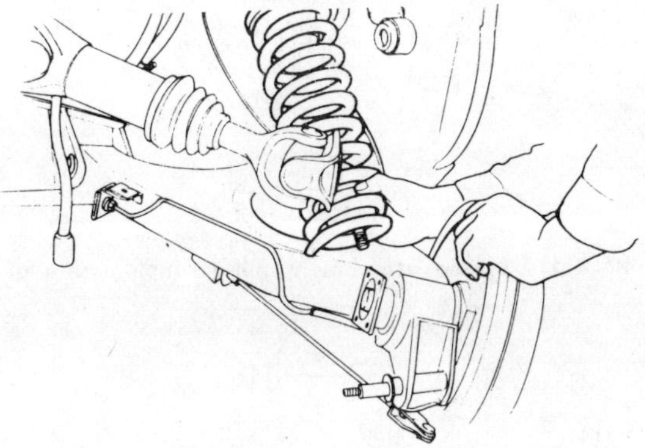

FIG 8:8 Removing a spring, saloon models

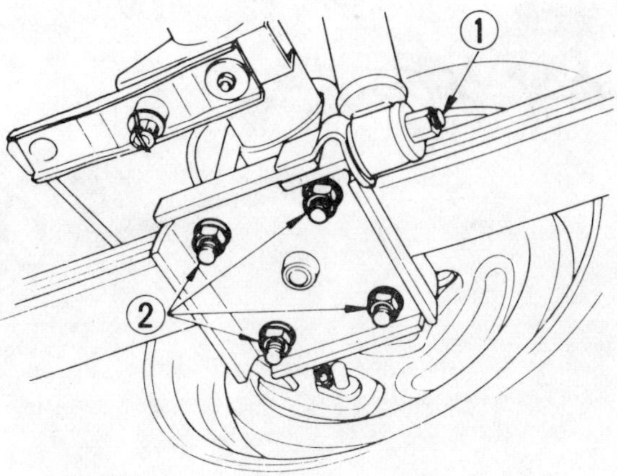

FIG 8:9 Removing a spring, estate car models

Key to Fig 8:9 1 Damper lower attachment point 2 U-bolt nuts

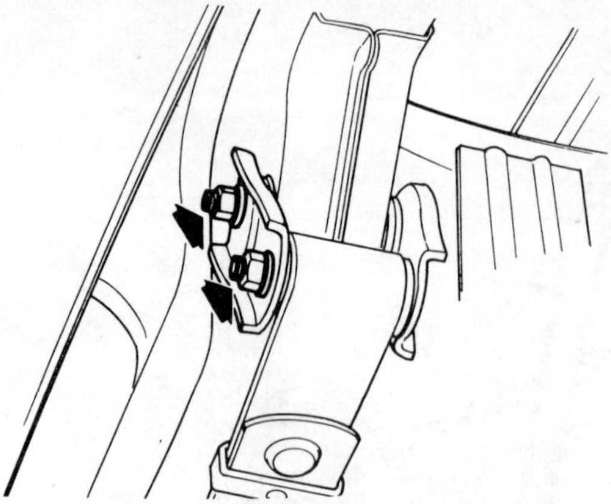

FIG 8:10 Spring shackle, estate car models

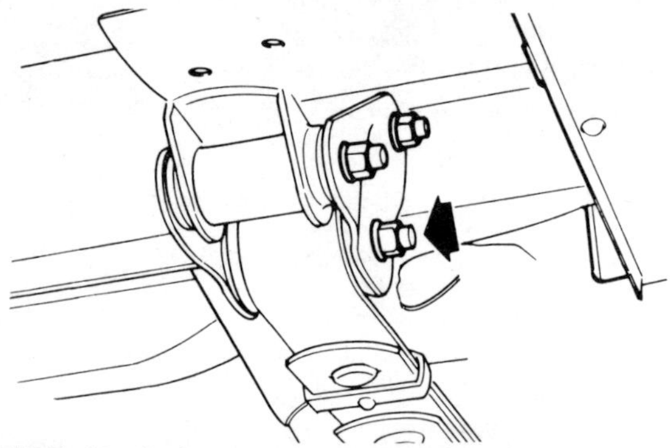

FIG 8:11 Spring attachment pin (front), estate car models

8:7 Hubs and shafts

Drive shafts, saloon models:

The components of a drive shaft are shown in **FIG 8:12**. The open two-piece shafts are universally jointed at each end. Ball and groove type splines allow axial movement between the final drive unit and the wheel axle.

Maintenance:

Every two years or every 30,000 miles (50,000 km), the ball and groove spline joint must be serviced and the hub bearings regreased.

Shaft removal and fitment, saloon models:

Remove the coupling bolts from both flange yokes, compress the shaft slightly and withdraw the shaft assembly.

Fitment, after servicing, is the reverse of this procedure. Torque tighten the flange yoke coupling bolts to 36 to 43 lb ft (5 to 6 kgm).

Servicing the drive shafts, saloon models:

1 Remove the shafts as described earlier. Dismantle the inner universal joints. The procedure is as described for the propeller shaft in **Section 8:3**.
2 Refer to **FIG 8:12**. Remove snap ring 7 and plug 9. Compress the shaft and, using snap ring pliers ST38300000, remove the drive shaft stop 4.
3 Disconnect the rubber boot and, taking care to collect the balls 2 and spacers 3 (three of each from each groove), separate the sleeve yoke 8 from the shaft 1.
4 Clean off old grease from the grooves, balls and spacers and check the condition of the components.

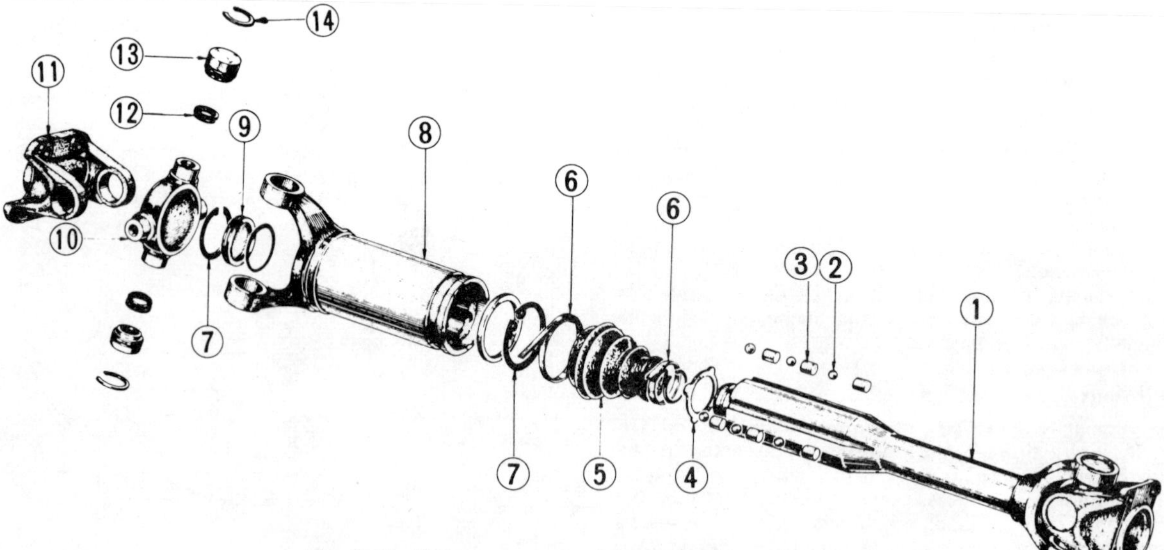

FIG 8:12 Components of a drive shaft, saloon models

Key to Fig 8:12 1 Drive shaft 2 Spline ball 3 Spacer 4 Drive shaft stop 5 Rubber boot 6 Boot retaining band 7 Snap ring 8 Sleeve yoke 9 Plug 10 Spider 11 Flange yoke 12 Seal 13 Bearing 14 Snap ring

5 Apply approximately .35 oz (10 gr) of multi-purpose grease to the grooves (internal and external), balls and spacers. Assemble the shaft, fit stop 4 and secure the rubber boot.
6 Apply approximately 1.23 oz (35 gr) of grease in the space shown in **FIG 8:13**. Fit the sleeve yoke plug and snap ring 7.
7 Reassemble the universal joint. Bearing end play which must not exceed .0008 inch (.02 mm) is controlled by the thickness of snap rings 14. Four thicknesses are available in steps of .012 inch (.03 mm) from .0586 to .0622 inch (1.49 to 1.58 mm).

Hub maintenance, saloon models:

A cross-section through a saloon model hub is shown in **FIG 8:14**. Every 30,000 miles (50,000 km) the hub bearing grease must be renewed. Proceed as follows:

1 Raise the rear of the vehicle and remove the road wheels. Remove the brake drums as described in **Chapter 11, Section 11:4**. Uncouple the drive shafts as described earlier.
2 Using ST38060001 as shown in **FIG 8:15**, remove and **discard the retaining nut and the seal** (4 and 1 in **FIG 8:14**). Using ST07640000 and sliding hammer ST36230000 withdraw the axle shaft 5 as shown in **FIG 8:16**.
3 Pack the bearings with multi-purpose grease. Use drift ST37710000 to fit a new seal and grease its lip. Fit the shaft and flange. Use a new retaining nut torque tightened to 180 to 240 lb ft (25 to 33 kgm).

Hub bearing renewal, saloon models:

Carry out operations 1 and 2 of the hub maintenance procedure described earlier. Use drift ST37750000 to remove the inner bearing. Use a suitable puller to withdraw the outer bearing. **Bearings which have been extracted must not be re-used.** When fitting the new bearings, ensure that the closed sides face outwards as shown in **FIG 8:14**. If a new suspension arm is being installed, refer to **FIG 8:17**, measure **L1** and select a distance piece (3 in **FIG 8:14**) of length **L2** which is nominally .002 inch (.05 mm) shorter than **L1**. Three lengths of distance piece are available and are listed in the following tabulation. Dimensions are in inches with mm equivalents in brackets.

Mark	*L1*	*L2*
A	2.325 to 2.329	2.324 to 2.320
	(59.05 to 59.15)	(59.02 to 59.08)
B	2.321 to 2.325	2.320 to 2.322
	(58.59 to 59.05)	(58.92 to 58.98)
C	2.317 to 2.321	2.316 to 2.318
	(58.85 to 58.95)	(58.82 to 58.88)

Assembly is the reverse of the dismantling sequence. Apply multi-purpose grease as shown in **FIG 8:14** and carry out operation 3 of the hub maintenance procedure.

Shaft end play must not exceed .006 inch (.15 mm) and is controlled by **L1**/**L2** (see FIG 8:17).

Shaft removal and fitment, estate car models:

1 Raise the rear of the car and remove the road wheels.
2 Uncouple the handbrake control and the hydraulic pipe at each backplate. Refer to **Chapter 11, Section 11:4** and remove the brake drums.

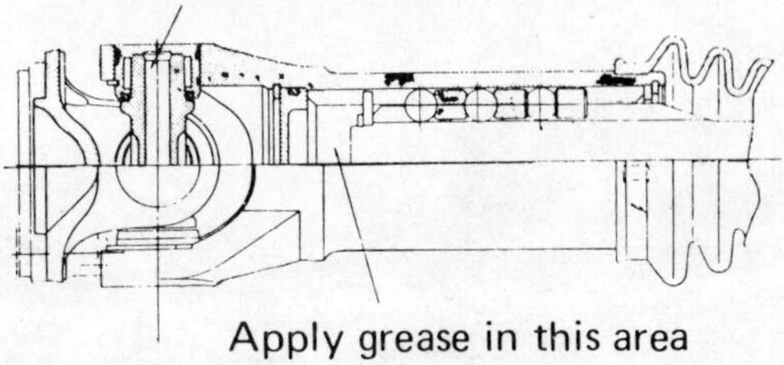

FIG 8:13 Cross-section through drive shaft splined joint

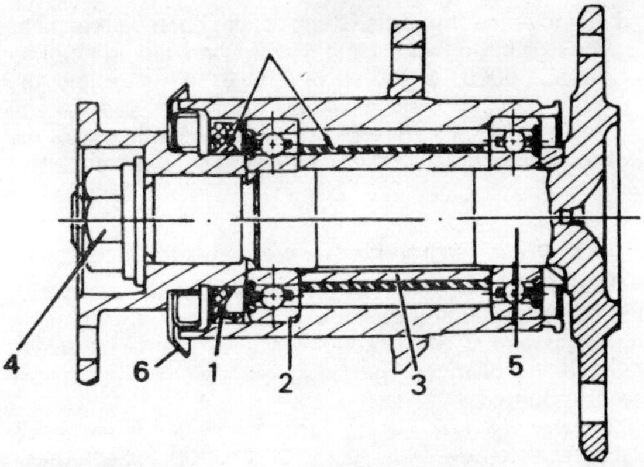

FIG 8:14 Cross-section through a rear wheel hub, saloon models

Key to Fig 8:14 1 Seal 2 Inner bearing 3 Distance piece 4 Nut 5 Axle shaft 6 Thrower

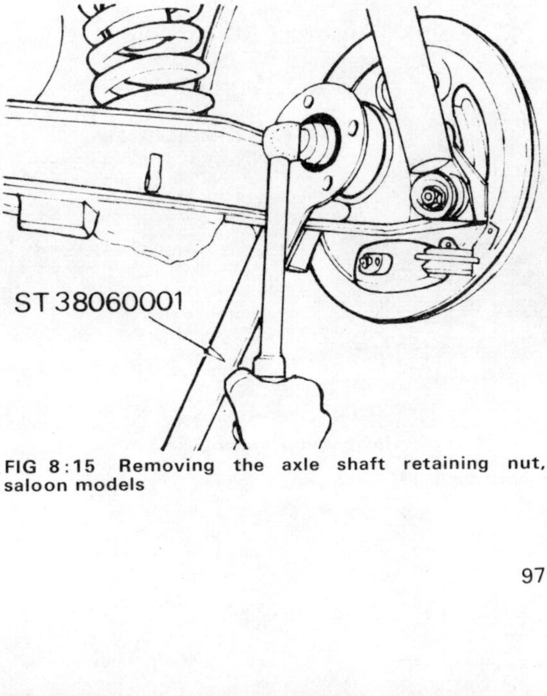

FIG 8:15 Removing the axle shaft retaining nut, saloon models

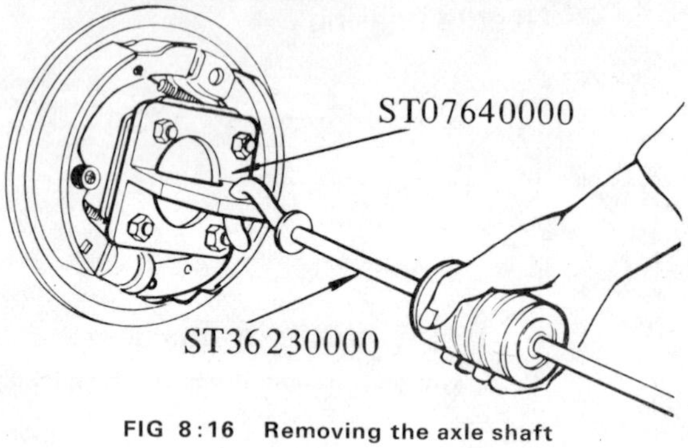

FIG 8:16 Removing the axle shaft

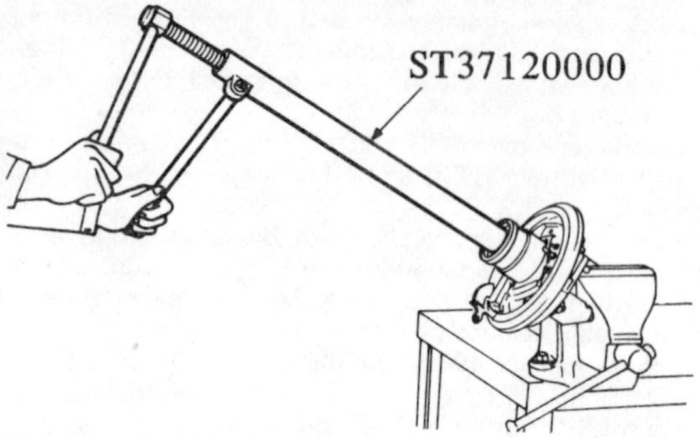

FIG 8:18 Removing a hub bearing, estate car models

3 Remove the four nuts which secure each backplate to the axle casing and, using ST0764 and sliding hammer ST36230000 as shown in **FIG 8:16**, withdraw the axle shaft and brake assembly from each side.

Fitment is the reverse of this sequence. Torque tighten the backplate retaining nuts to 16 to 20 lb ft (2.2 to 2.7 kgm).

Hub bearing renewal, estate car models:

Withdraw the axle shaft(s) as described earlier. Cut the bearing retaining collar with a cold chisel and, using puller assembly ST37120001 as shown in **FIG 8:18**, remove the bearing. The backplate assembly can now be dismounted.

Fitment of a new bearing is the reverse of this sequence. To press on a new collar, use ST38210000 under a press. A load of 3 to 5 tons will be required. Refer to **FIG 8:19** and adjust gap **C** between the bearing and the axle casing to .004 inch (.1 mm) by means of the thickness of the adjusting shims. Use a new seal and lubricate the bearing with multi-purpose grease. Axial play of the shaft should not exceed .004 inch (.1 mm).

8:8 Final drive unit (saloon and coupe)

Maintenance:

Use only SAE 80 or SAE 90 gear oil of reputable brand. A drain plug and filler plug are provided in the rear of the unit. The level is correct when filled to the bottom of the filler plug orifice.

Removal and fitment:

1 Refer to **Section 8:4** and carry out operations 1, 2 and 3 of the suspension removal sequence. Remove the drive shafts as described in **Section 8:7**.

2 Support the drive unit on a jack. Refer to **FIG 8:6** and remove the nuts 8 which attach the mounting member to the chassis. Remove four bolts which retain the forward end of the unit to the suspension crossmember.

3 Simultaneously lower the jack and remove the drive unit rearwards. Withdraw the unit. Collect spacers.

Fitment is the reverse of this sequence. Torque tighten the four bolts to 36 to 51 lb ft (5 to 7 kgm) and nuts 8 to 51 to 72 lb ft (7 to 10 kgm).

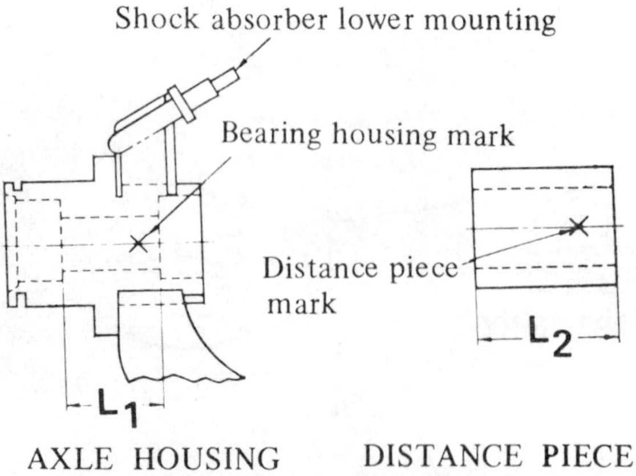

FIG 8:17 Hub bearing housing, saloon models

Key to Fig 8:17 L1 and L2 See text

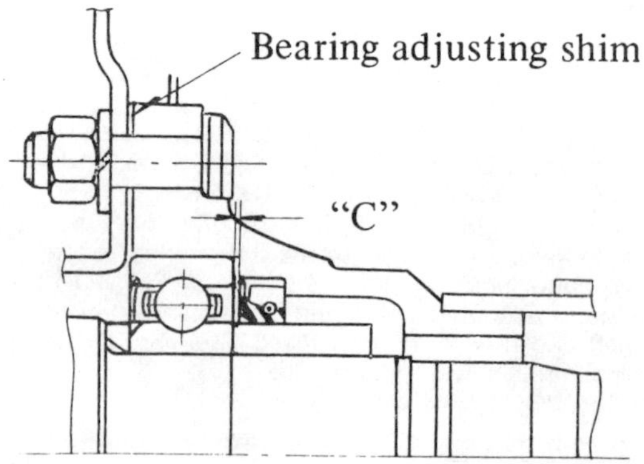

FIG 8:19 Cross-section through a rear hub, estate car models

Key to Fig 8:19 C Gap to be adjusted to .004 inch (.1 mm)

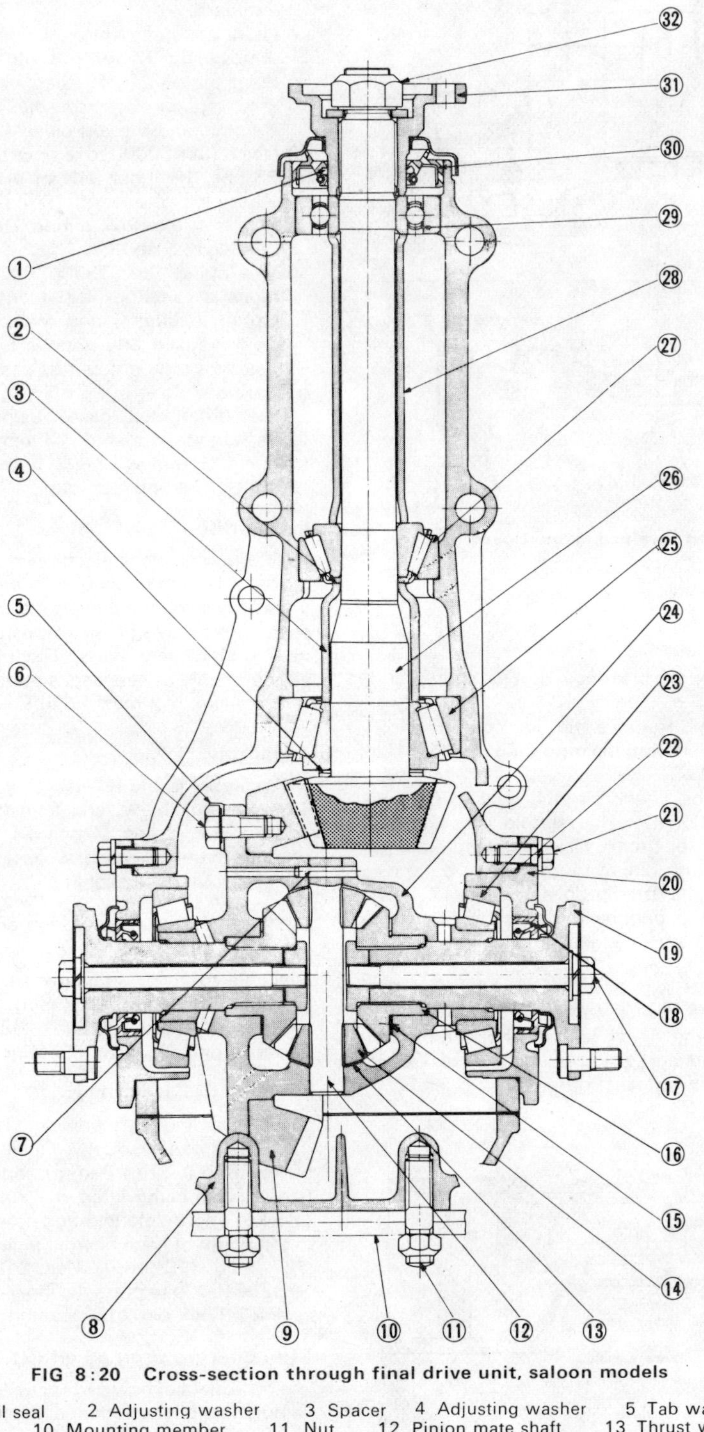

FIG 8:20 Cross-section through final drive unit, saloon models

Key to Fig 8:20 1 Oil seal 2 Adjusting washer 3 Spacer 4 Adjusting washer 5 Tab washer 6 Bolt 7 Pin 8 Cover 9 Ring gear 10 Mounting member 11 Nut 12 Pinion mate shaft 13 Thrust washer 14 Mate gears 15 Thrust washer 16 Side gear 17 Bolt 18 Oil seal 19 Side flange 20 Side retainer 21 Bolt 22 Side retainer shims 23 Side bearing 24 Differential case 25 Pinion rear bearing 26 Drive pinion 27 Pinion front bearing 28 Bearing spacer 29 Bearing 30 Oil seal 31 Companion flange 32 Nut

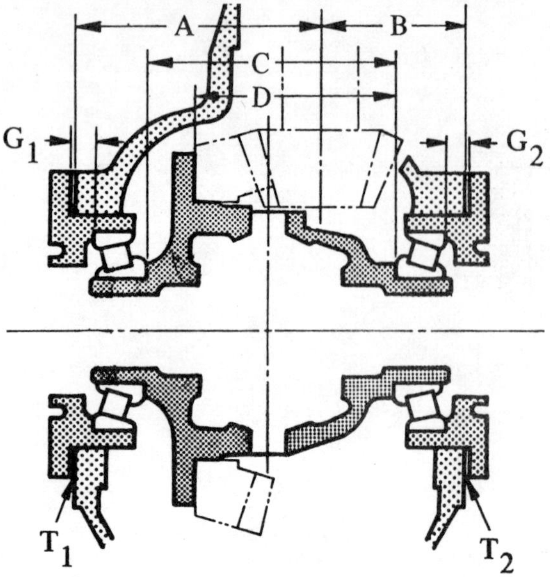

FIG 8:21 Side bearing preload adjustment (saloon models)

Key to Fig 8:21 See text

Dismantling:

A cross-section through the drive unit is shown in **FIG 8:20**.

1 Drain off the gear oil. Remove the rear cover 8 and, if necessary, separate it from the mounting member 10 by removing nuts 11.
2 Using a dial indicator, check the ring gear to pinion backlash at several points. This should not exceed .004 to .008 inch (.1 to .2 mm). Using marking raddle, check the ring gear and pinion tooth contact pattern. Check that the ring gear runout does not exceed .002 inch (.05 mm) at the periphery. These checks will indicate whether a new ring gear and pinion set is required.
3 Remove bolts 17 and withdraw the side flanges 19. Identify the side retainers 20 (note the arrow which aligns with one of the bolts) left and right, remove the bolts and washers and, using puller ST33710000, withdraw them. Lift out the differential assembly.

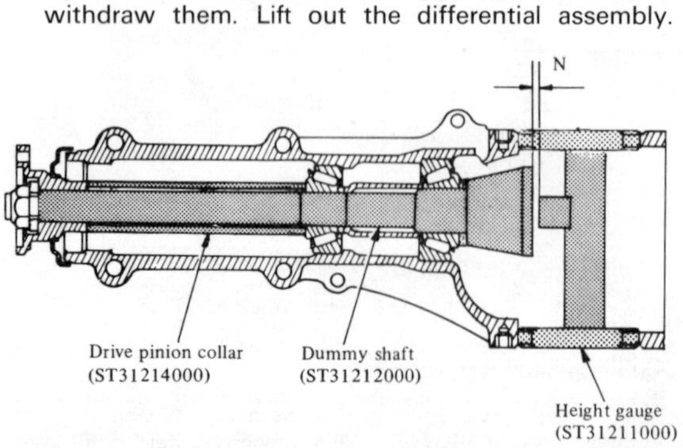

FIG 8:22 Pinion height adjustment (saloon models)

Key to Fig 8:22 See text

If the side bearings 23 are to be renewed, use puller ST 33290001 to withdraw the outer races from the side retainers.

4 Hold the companion flange 31 with ST31530000, remove nut 32 and pull off the flange. Press out the drive pinion 26 together with the rear bearing inner race, spacer 3 and adjusting washers 2 and 4. Remove and discard oil seal 30.
5 Use ST30650000 to remove bearing 29. Lift out spacer 28 and the inner race of bearing 27. To remove the inner race of bearing 25, hold it in ST30031000 and press out the drive pinion. Drift out the outer races of bearings 25 and 27.
6 Use puller set ST3306S000 to withdraw the inner races of bearings 23. Identify them left and right. Untab locking 5 and, working diagonally, progressively loosen and remove bolts 6. Separate the ring gear from the differential case.
7 Carefully drive out pin 7 (note locking by peening of the differential case) using punch ST23510000, withdraw mate shaft 12, remove mate gears 14, side gears 16 and washers 15. Identify relevant parts left, right, front and rear, etc.

Inspection:

Thoroughly clean all components and, applying normal automobile engineering standards, inspect for distortion, wear, scoring, cracking and corrosion. Discard all oil seals irrespective of their apparent condition and obtain new replacement parts. The ring gear and pinion are supplied only as sets and, should either be unserviceable, a new paired set must be obtained.

Assembly:

Assembly is the reverse of the dismantling sequence. The relevant checks and adjustments are applied at the appropriate stages. Assemble with all internal components wetted with new gear oil. Apply grease in the cavity between oil seal lips.

Differential gear backlash adjustment:

Three thicknesses of side gear thrust washer 15 are available to allow adjustment of the end play to within .004 to .008 inch (.1 to .2 mm). Thicknesses are .0295 to .0315 inch (.75 to .80 mm), .0315 to .0335 inch (.80 to .85 mm) and .0335 to .0355 inch (.85 to .90 mm).

Differential assembly:

Use new lock washers 5 and tighten the ring gear bolts diagonally and gradually. Finally torque tighten them to 50 to 58 lb ft (7 to 8 kgm) and tab to lock. If new side bearings are being fitted, measure (under a load of 5.5 lb (2.5 kg) approximately) and note the difference (E and F) in the width of each bearing against the standard width of .787 inch (20 mm). Use ST33230000 and adaptor ST330610000 to press the inner races onto the differential case 24. Lock pin 7 by peening.

Side bearing preload adjustment:

The fitment of new parts or new bearings will necessitate calculation of the required thicknesses of shims 22 (T1 and T2). Refer to **FIG 8:21** and apply the following:

$$T1 = (A+C+G1 - D+H^{1}) \times .01 + .76 - E$$
$$T2 = (B + D + G2 - H^{1}) \times .01 + .76 - F$$

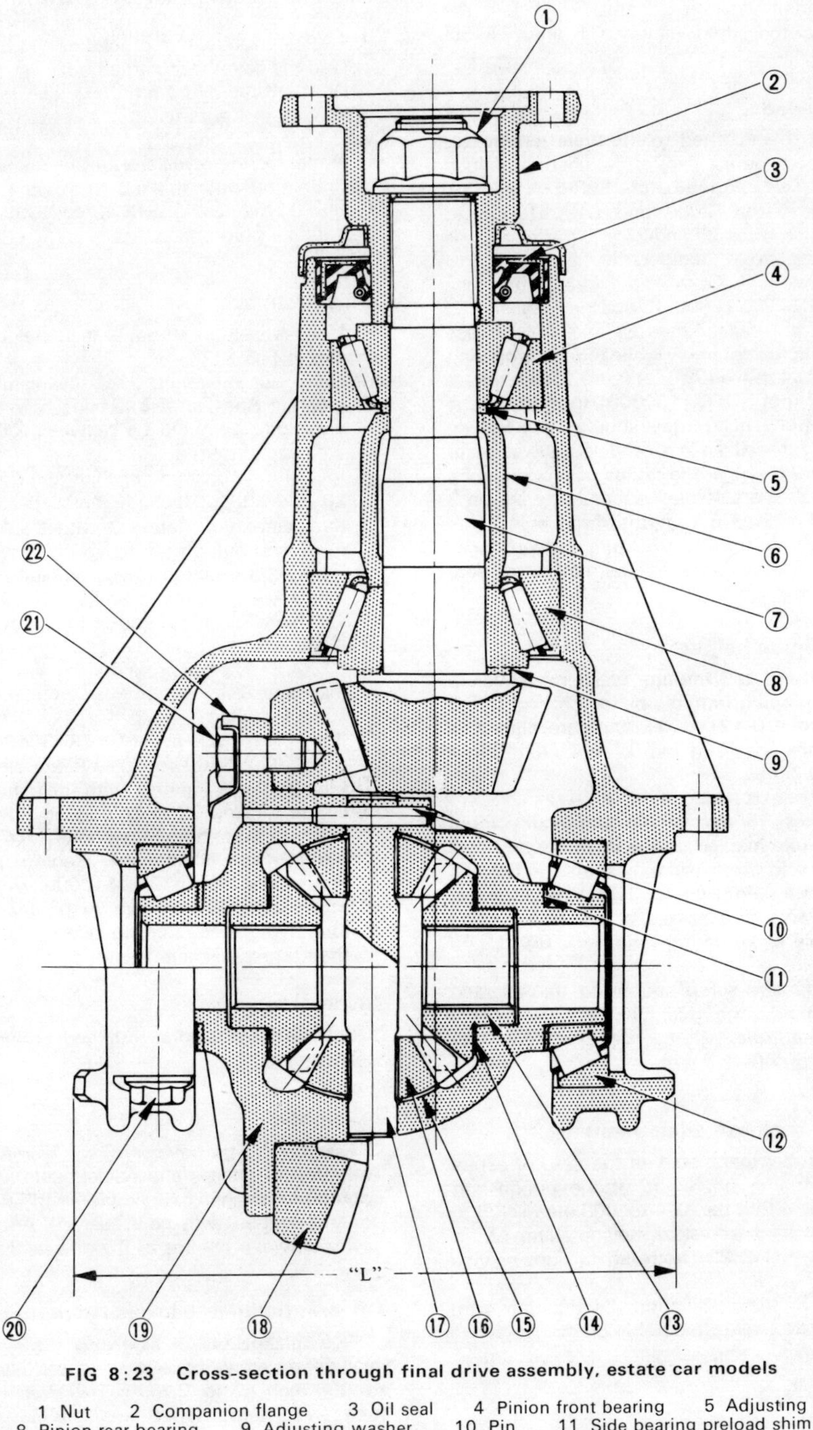

FIG 8:23 Cross-section through final drive assembly, estate car models

Key to Fig 8:23 1 Nut 2 Companion flange 3 Oil seal 4 Pinion front bearing 5 Adjusting washer 6 Spacer 7 Drive pinion 8 Pinion rear bearing 9 Adjusting washer 10 Pin 11 Side bearing preload shim 12 Side bearing 13 Side gear 14 Thrust washer 15 Thrust washer 16 Mate gear 17 Mate shaft 18 Ring gear 19 Differential case 20 Bolt 21 Bolt 22 Tab washer

All dimensions other than T1 and T2 (which are in mm) are differences from standard dimensions in .01 mm units. A and B are marked on the main casing. C and D are marked on the differential case. E and F were, if the bearings are new, measured earlier. G1 and G2 are marked on the ring gear.

Drive pinion preload:

If new parts are being fitted to the drive pinion and main casing assembly, adjustment of the bearing preload will be necessary. This is done before fitting oil seal 30. Use ST30611000, ST30612000 and ST30613000 to press fit bearing outer races 25 and 27 into the casing. As an arbitrary starting point, temporarily fit the original height adjusting washer 4. Fit the rear bearing inner race onto dummy shaft ST31212000, fit spacer 3, washer 2, dummy collar ST31214000, flange 31 and nut 32. Use ST31213000 to hold the assembly while torque tightening the nut to 123 to 144 lb ft (17 to 20 kgm). Use a torque gauge (the official tool is ST31190000) to measure the shaft rotation torque. This torque should be between 6 and 9 lb inch (7 to 10 kg/cm) and is equivalent to 4.4 to 6.4 lb (2 to 2.9 kg) at the radius of a companion flange bolt hole. Select a suitable washer 2 and spacer 3 to give the required preload. Six lengths of spacer in .2 mm steps are available from 56.2 to 57.2 mm. Fifteen thicknesses of washer are available in .02 mm steps from 2.31 to 2.59 mm.

Adjustment of pinion height:

Pinion height is adjusted through washer 4. Refer to **FIG 8:22** and, continuing from the pinion preload setup, install height gauge ST312110000. Measure clearance N in mm. The thickness T in mm of the final height adjusting washer will be:

$$T = W + N - (H - D^1 - S) \times .01 - .2$$

W is the thickness in mm of the temporarily fitted washer. H is the figure marked on the drive pinion head. D^1 is the figure marked on the dummy shaft and S is the figure marked on the height gauge. H, D^1 and S are in .01 mm units. Twenty thicknesses of height adjusting washer are available in .03 mm steps from 3.09 to 3.66 mm.

Dismantle the dummy setup and using the selected adjusting parts complete the assembly. With the oil seal fitted, the preload torque will be approximately 7 to 9.5 inch (8 to 11 kg/cm).

Pinion/ring gear backlash adjustment:

Repeat operation 2 (operation 1 in the case of estate cars) of the dismantling procedure. If the pinion/ring gear backlash is not within the .004 to .008 inch (.005 to .007 for estate cars) limit, adjust by moving shims (22 in **FIG 8:20** or 11 in **FIG 8:23**) from left to right or vice versa.

On completion of the installation, fill the unit with SAE 80 or SAE 90 gear oil of reputable brand.

8:9 Rear axle (estate car)

Maintenance:

Refer to this heading in **Section 8:8**.

Removal and fitment:

Removal of the differential can be effected after removing the drive shaft as described in **Section 8:2** and withdrawing both axle shafts as described in **Section 8:7**. The following procedure assumes that these operations have been carried out.

Drain off the oil from the axle casing, remove the nuts which retain the differential assembly in the casing and withdraw the assembly.

Fitment is the reverse of this sequence. Torque tighten the retaining nuts to 14.5 to 18 lb ft (2 to 2.5 kgm). Finally fill the casing with approved gear oil to the level of the filler plug orifice.

Dismantling:

A cross-section through the final drive assembly is shown in **FIG 8:23**.

1 Carry out operation 2 of the dismantling sequence given in **Section 8:8**. Backlash, in the case of estate car models, should be between .005 and .007 inch (.13 to .18 mm).
2 Identify the bearing caps left and right. Remove bolts 20 and lift out the differential case assembly. Hold the companion flange 2 with ST31530000, remove nut 1 and pull off the flange.
3 Remove the pinion drive complete with rear bearing inner race 8, spacer 6 and washer 5. Tapping with a soft hammer on the end of the shaft will be required.
4 If necessary, hold the rear bearing inner race in ST30031000 and press out the pinion drive. Front and rear races may be removed from the casing using a suitable puller.
5 If necessary, use puller set ST3305S000 with adaptor set ST3306S000 to pull off the side bearing races. Identify these together with their shims 11.
6 Untab locking 22 and, working diagonally, progressively loosen and remove bolts 21. Carefully drive out pin 10 (note locking by peening of the differential case) using punch ST23510000, withdraw the pinion mate shaft 17, remove mate gears 16 and, after identifying them, remove side gears 13 together with their thrust washers 14.

Inspection:

Follow the procedure outlined under this heading in **Section 8:8**.

Assembly:

Assembly is the reverse of the dismantling sequence. The relevant checks and adjustments are applied at the appropriate stages. Assemble with all internal components wetted with new gear oil. Apply grease in the cavity between the lips of the oil seal 3.

Differential gear backlash adjustment:

Five thicknesses of side gear thrust washers 14 are available to allow adjustment of end play to within .004 to .008 inch (.1 to .2 mm). Their thicknesses are .0309 inch (.785 mm), .0329 inch (.835 mm), .0348 inch (.885 mm), .0408 inch (1.035 mm) and .0467 inch (1.185 mm).

Differential assembly:

Use new lock washers 22 and tighten the ring gear bolts diagonally and gradually. Finally torque tighten them to 50 to 58 lb ft (7 to 8 kgm) and tab to lock. If new side bearings 12 are being fitted, measure (under a load of 5.5 lb (2.5 kg) approximately) and note the difference in width (E and F) of each bearing against the standard width of .728 inch (18.50 mm). The fitment of new components or new bearings will necessitate adjustment of the bearing preload. Calculate the thickness of shims 11 (T1 and T2) as follows:

$$T1 = (A - C + D - H^1) \times .01 + .200 + E$$
$$T2 = (B - D + H^1) \times .01 + .090 + F$$

All dimensions, other than T1 and T2 (which are in mm), are differences from standard dimensions in .01 mm units. The locations of A, B, C and D are shown in **FIG 8:25**. E and F were measured earlier. H^1 is marked on the ring gear. Use ST33210000 and adaptor ST33052000 to press the inner races onto the differential case 19. Lock pin 10 by peening. Instal the assembled differential case into the main casing by tapping with a soft hammer. Check the bearing cap identifications, fit the cap retaining bolts and torque tighten to 36 to 43 lb ft (5 to 6 kgm). Measure dimension L (see **FIGS 8:23** and **8:24**) between the edges of the bearing caps. L should be within 6.8201 and 6.8224 inch (173.23 to 173.29 mm).

Adjustment of pinion height:

Refer to **FIG 8:25** and position dummy shaft ST31942000 and height gauge ST31141000. Measure the clearance N. The thickness of the drive pinion height adjusting washer 9 in **FIG 8:23** must be T mm and is calculated from:

$$T = N - (H - D^1 - S) \times .01 + .28.$$

H is the figure marked on the head of the drive pinion. D^1 is the figure marked on the height gauge. H, D^1 and S are in .01 mm units. Five thicknesses of height adjusting washers are available.

Drive pinion preload:

If new parts are being fitted, adjustment of the pinion drive preload will be necessary. This is carried out before fitting the oil seal 3 in **FIG 8:23**. As an arbitrary starting point, temporarily fit the original washer 5 and spacer 6. Lubricate the bearings, complete the pinion drive assembly (except for the oil seal) and torque tighten nut 1 to 101 to 130 lb ft (14 to 17 kgm). Use a torque gauge (the official tool is ST31190000) to measure the shaft rotation torque. This torque should be between 6 and 9 lb inch (7 to 10 kg/cm) and is equivalent to 4.4 to 6.4 lb (2 to 2.9 kg) at the radius of a companion flange bolt hole. Select washer 5 and spacer 6 which give the required preload. Fifteen thicknesses of washer are available in .02 mm steps from 2.31 to 2.59 mm. Four lengths of spacer in .2 mm steps are available ranging from 48.4 to 49.0 mm. On completion of the preload adjustment, fit the oil seal. Preload will now be about 7 to 9.5 lb inch (8 to 11 kg/cm).

Pinion/ring gear backlash adjustment:

Refer to this heading in **Section 8:8**.

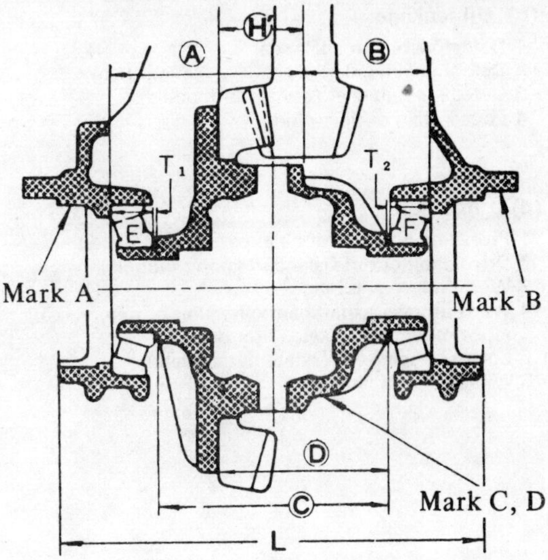

FIG 8:24 **Side bearing preload adjustment, estate car models**

Key to Fig 8:24 See text

8:10 Fault diagnosis

(a) Noisy transmission

1 Insufficient or incorrect gear oil
2 Worn bearings
3 Worn gears
4 Broken or damaged differential teeth
5 Damaged balls in drive shaft (saloon models)

(b) Excessive backlash

1 Check 2, 3 and 5 in (a)
2 Worn side gear splines
3 Worn drive shaft universal joints (saloon models)
4 Worn propeller shaft universal joints
5 Worn yoke sliding joint

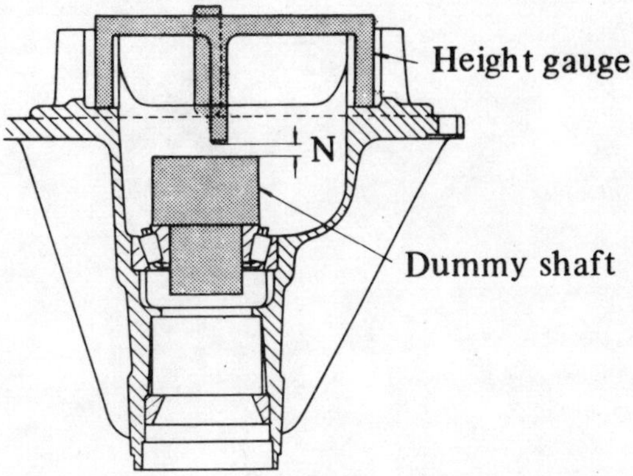

FIG 8:25 **Pinion height adjustment (estate car models)**

Key to Fig 8:25 See text

(c) Oil leakage

1 Defective pinion shaft seal
2 Defective drive flange seal (saloon models)
3 Defective hub seal (estate car models)
4 Loose drain or filler plug

(d) Vibration

1 Propeller shaft out of balance
2 Drive shaft out of balance (saloon models)
3 Worn universal joint
4 Worn propeller shaft centre bearing or defective or loose mounting (estate car models)
5 Loose U-bolt nuts (estate car models)
6 Wheels out of balance

(e) Rattles

1 Suspension arm pivots worn (saloon models)
2 Worn shackles (estate car models)
3 Worn damper attachment
4 Broken road spring
5 Defective or loose damper

(f) 'Settling'

1 Weak or broken road spring
2 Loose or broken damper mounting

(g) 'Bottoming' of suspension

1 Check 1 in (f)
2 Worn or missing bump stop (saloon models)
3 Ineffective damper
4 Vehicle overloaded

CHAPTER 9

FRONT SUSPENSION AND HUBS

9:1 Description
9:2 Maintenance
9:3 Hubs
9:4 Spring and damper strut assemblies
9:5 Tension rods
9:6 Anti-roll bar
9:7 Suspension arms
9:8 Camber and castor angles
9:9 Fault diagnosis

9:1 Description

FIG 9:1 shows the layout of the front suspension system. Integral with cross-member 8 onto which the engine front mountings are bolted, are brackets at each side which carry the pivots of the suspension arms 5. A tension rod 6 provides each arm with fore and aft control and each end of an anti-roll bar 7 which is bracketed to the cross-member is attached to a suspension arm. Each strut assembly 4 incorporates a telescopic hydraulic damper and, at its upper end, the suspension coil spring and a bump stop.

Integral with the lower end of each strut is the wheel stub axle. A ball joint between the lower end of each strut and each suspension arm and a ballbearing which is flexibly mounted to the body at the upper end of each strut spindle allow pivoting of the complete strut assembly, stub axle and wheel to accommodate steering geometry. There is no kingpin as such and the angle of the axis of the strut assembly is, in effect, the 'kingpin' inclination and incorporates the camber and castor angles. A steering arm is attached to each hub.

Hubs may carry either drum or disc brakes. A cross-section through a disc type hub is shown in **FIG 9:2**.

The dampers are not sealed assemblies and may be dismantled for servicing and overhaul.

9:2 Maintenance

Wheels and tyres:

Regularly check and re-inflate tyres to the pressures recommended in **Technical Data** in the Appendix. Every 6000 miles (10,000 km), interchange the wheels to even out tyre wear. A scheme for this interchange is given in **FIG 9:3**. At this same milage interval, have the wheel balance checked and adjusted as necessary.

Suspension:

Every 6000 miles (10,000 km), check over the suspension generally and confirm that all nuts and bolts are tight.

Dampers:

Every 12,000 miles (20,000 km), check the dampers for indications of wear or fluid leakage. Damper/strut assembly servicing is described in **Section 9:4**.

Ball joints:

Every 30,000 miles (50,000 km), check the ball joints as described in **Section 9:7** and, if they are serviceable, repack them with multi-purpose grease.

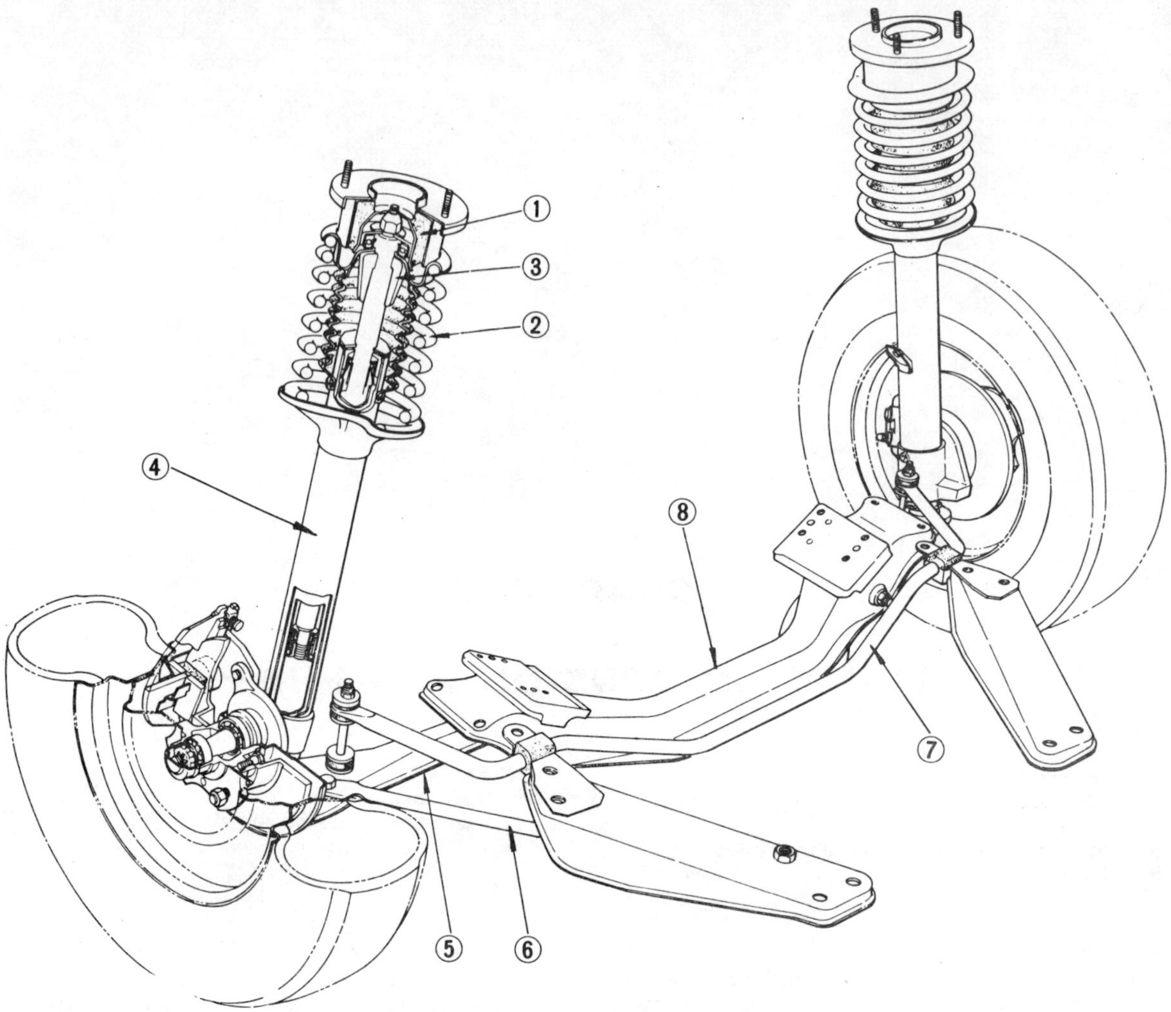

FIG 9:1 The front suspension system

Key to Fig 9:1 1 Insulator 2 Coil spring 3 Bump stop rubber 4 Strut assembly 5 Suspension arm 7 Anti-roll bar 8 Suspension crossmember

Hub bearings:

Every 30,000 miles (50,000 km), repack the hub bearings with multi-purpose grease as described in **Section 9:3**.

9:3 Hubs

Hub removal:

1 Raise the front of the vehicle until the wheels are fully down. Position stands under the crossmember and remove the relevant road wheel.

2 In the case of models fitted with drum brakes, remove the brake drum as described in **Chapter 11, Section 11:3**.

3 In the case of models fitted with disc brakes, remove the brake caliper as described in **Chapter 11, Section 11:5**.

4 Using a thin bladed screwdriver and taking care not to damage the O-ring seal, ease off the hub cap. Remove the splitpin and the adjusting cap. Remove the retaining nut. Withdraw the hub complete, in the case of models fitted with disc brakes, with the brake disc.

Hub fitment:

1 Pack the hub cavities (see shaded areas in **FIG 9:4**) and the bearing inner races and rollers with multi-purpose grease. Apply grease to the lips of the seal.

2 Install the hub, fit the outer bearing inner race and apply grease sparingly to the washer, the threads of the stub axle and to the retaining nut. Fit the hub.

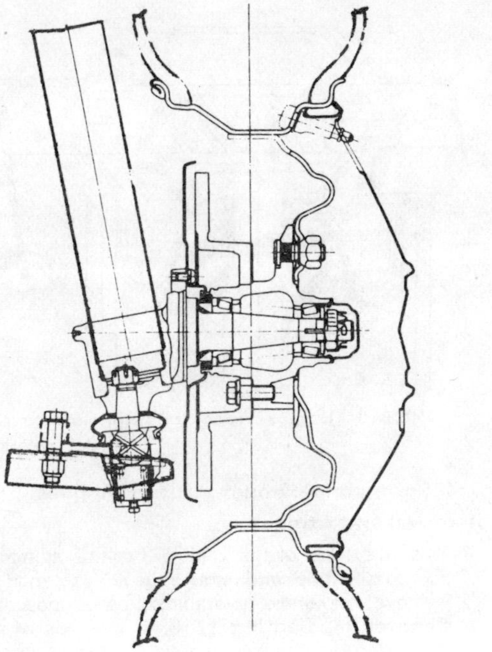

FIG 9:2 Cross-section through a disc brake type hub

3 Torque tighten the retaining nut to 22 to 25 lb ft (3 to 3.5 kgm).
4 Turn the hub in both directions several times to set the bearings.
5 Repeat operation 3.
6 Tighten the retaining nut by a further $\frac{1}{4}$ turn. Fit the adjusting cap (tighten still further if necessary by not more than by 15 deg.).
7 Repeat operation 4 and, as shown in **FIG 9:5**, use a spring balance to measure the preload rotational torque. With the original bearings, the required preload is a spring balance load of $1\frac{1}{2}$ lb (.7 kg) or, with new bearings, $2\frac{3}{4}$ lb (1.22 kg) maximum.
8 Repeat operation 6 until the required preload torque is achieved. Use a new splitpin to lock the retaining nut. Reassemble the brake components and, where the hydraulic system has been reconnected, bleed the system as described in **Section 11:7**.

Bearing renewal:

Remove the hub as described earlier. Use a soft drift in the hub grooves to remove the bearing outer races. Fit the new races using tool set ST35325000 or a soft drift. Ensure that the races are fully bottomed against the hub shoulders. Refit the hub as described earlier.

Hub renewal:

Remove the hub and withdraw the bearings as described earlier. Refer to **Chapter 11**, **Section 11:3** or **Section 11:5** and dismantle the brake components from the hub. Reassemble the brake components to the new hub, fit new bearings and install the new assembly as described earlier in this Section.

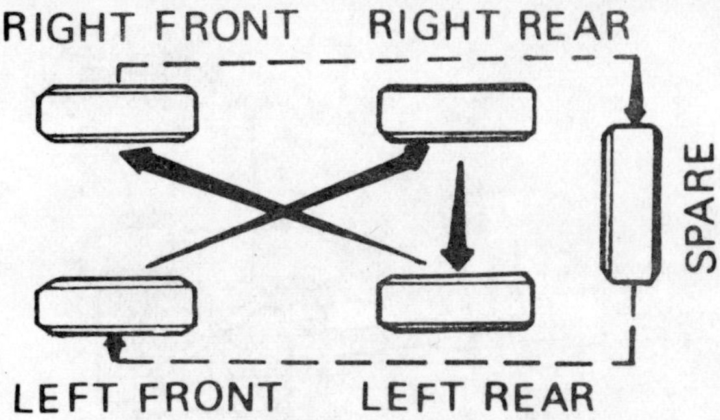

FIG 9:3 Wheel interchange scheme

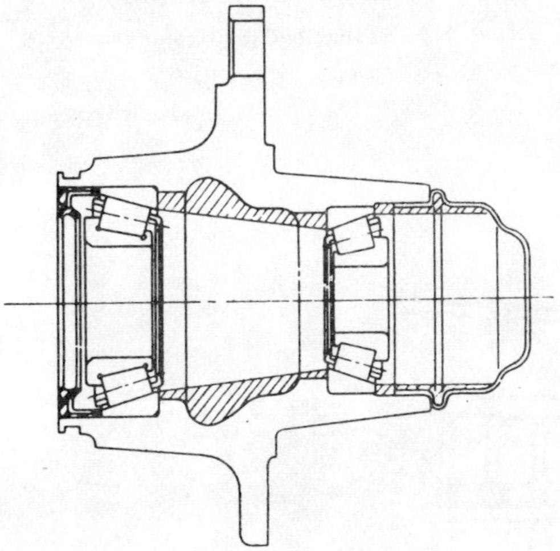

FIG 9:4 Hub lubrication

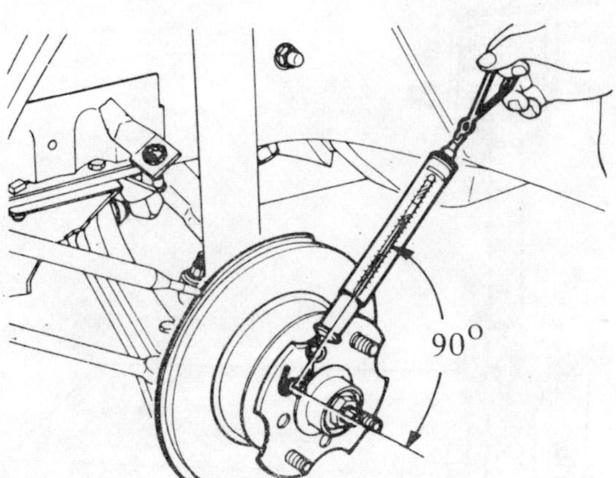

FIG 9:5 Measuring preload torque

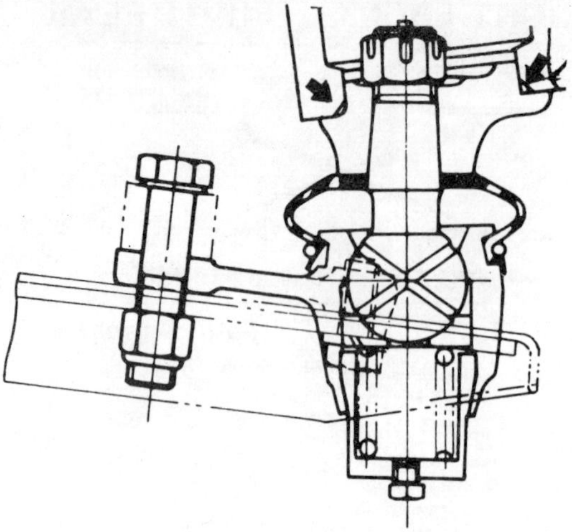

FIG 9:6 Sealing ball joint counterbore

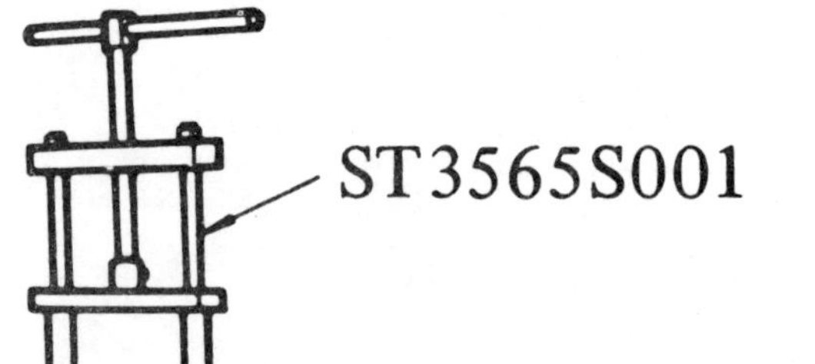

FIG 9:7 Compressing a coil spring

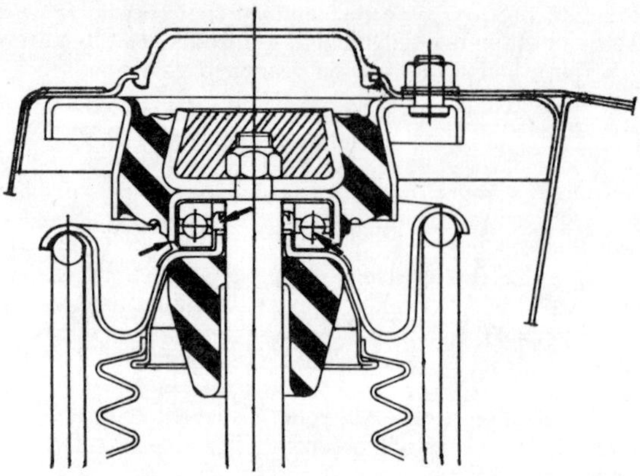

FIG 9:8 Damper upper mounting and bearing

9:4 Spring and damper strut assemblies

Removal and fitment:

1 Raise the front of the vehicle. Position stands under the crossmember and remove the relevant road wheel.
2 Remove the brake hydraulic pipe as described in **Chapter 11, Section 11:8**. In the case of models fitted with disc brakes, remove the caliper assembly.
3 Unbolt the strut from the steering arm and, using leverage, separate the arm from the bottom of the strut.
4 Support the strut assembly on a jack. From inside the engine compartment, remove the three nuts which attach the strut upper mounting to the body. While holding the strut, slowly lower the jack and dismount the strut assembly.

Fitment is the reverse of this sequence. Use new self-locking nuts. Refer to **FIG 9:6** and apply jointing compound to the arrowed counterbore. Torque tighten the upper mounting to body nuts to 18 to 25 lb ft (2.5 to 3.5 kgm) and the steering arm to strut bolts to 53 to 72 lb ft (7.3 to 9.9 kgm).

Spring removal:

Dismount the strut assembly as described earlier. Remove the snap ring from the dust cover. Using tool set ST3565S001 as shown in **FIG 9:7**, compress the spring until the mounting insulator (1 in **FIG 9:1**) can be turned by hand. Refer to **FIG 9:8** and remove the self-locking nut, the bearing, the spring upper seat and the bump stop rubber. Lift off the spring with the compressing tool still attached.

The type of springs fitted depends upon the vehicle model and whether the suspension is hard or standard. The spring ends are colour coded as follows: red/orange, lefthand side of estate car; yellow/orange, righthand side of estate car and both sides of saloon models; yellow, hard suspension both sides.

Spring fitment:

If replacement springs are being fitted, ensure that those obtained are of the correct colour coding. Bleed the damper as described later. Fit the spring compressing tool and proceed with the removal sequence in reverse. Torque tighten the self-locking nut to 43 to 54 lb ft (6 to 7.5 kgm). Install the strut as described earlier.

Strut servicing:

Dismount the strut and remove the coil spring as described earlier. Thoroughly clean off all external dirt. A cross-section through a strut and damper is shown in **FIG 9:9**.

Compress the assembly until the piston bottoms and, using ST35500001, remove and discard the gland packing. Remove the O-ring and withdraw the piston rod and damper cylinder assembly from the strut casing. **Do not, under any circumstance, withdraw the piston assembly from the damper cylinder**. Drain off and discard the damper fluid completely from the cylinder and from the strut casing.

Refit the piston rod and damper cylinder assembly into the strut casing. Use only Nissen Shock Absorber Oil A-2 (or an approved equivalent) to refill the damper. **Precisely** 325 cc of fluid are required for the AMPCO (ATSUGI) unit or **precisely** 332 cc for the K. Y. A. (KAYABA) unit. Lubricate the sealing lip(s) where asterisked in **FIG 9:10** with multi-purpose grease and, using guide ST35530000, fit the new gland packing. Torque tighten to 51 to 94 lb ft (7 to 13 kgm). After bleeding the damper assembly as described later, the unit is ready for fitment of the coil spring and installation to the vehicle. Lubricate the bearing with multi-purpose grease at the points arrowed in **FIG 9:8**.

Bleeding a damper:

Before fitting the coil spring, bleed air from the unit as follows:

1 With the strut the correct way up, pull out the piston rod to the limit of its stroke.
2 Turn the strut upside down and push the piston rod fully inwards until the piston bottoms.
3 Repeat operations 1 and 2 until equal pressure is felt when compressing or extending the unit.

9:5 Tension rods

The tension rods are shown at 6 in **FIG 9:1**. Each rod is connected between a suspension arm and a bracket which is attached to the chassis and provides lateral stability to the suspension arm.

Removal:

With the front of the vehicle raised and supported on stands, remove the relevant road wheel. Refer to **FIG 9:11**. Remove nuts and bolts 2 which attach the rod to the suspension arm and the nut 3 which attaches the rod to its bracket. Withdraw the rod. If necessary, the bracket may be dismounted after removing the four retaining bolts.

Fitment:

Fitment is the reverse of the removal sequence. Torque tighten the bracket bolts (if this was removed) to 37 to 50 lb ft (5.1 to 6.9 kgm), the rod to bracket nut to 33 to 40 lb ft (4.5 to 5.5 kgm) and the rod to suspension arm attachments to 35 to 46 lb ft (4.9 to 6.3 kgm).

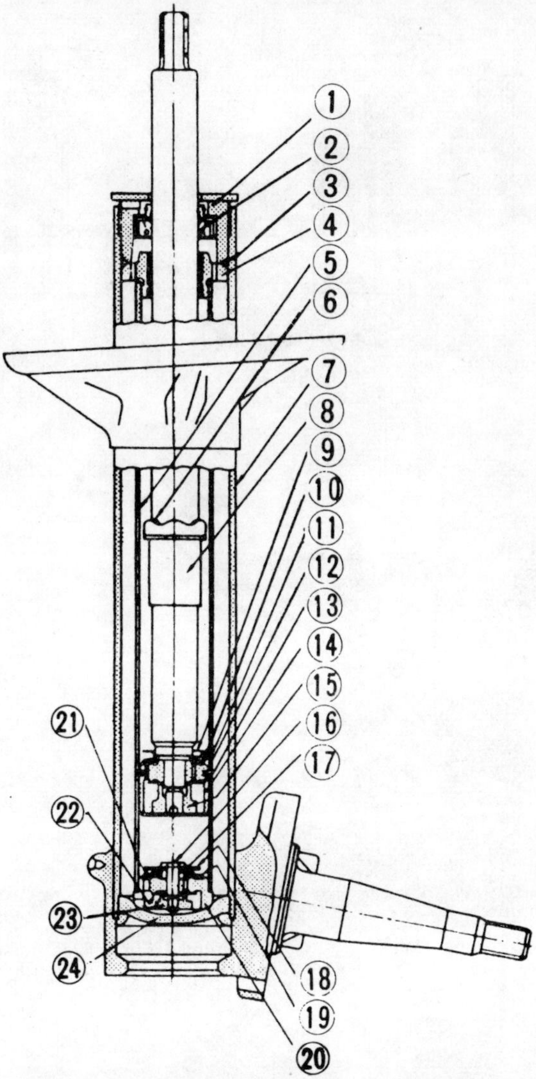

FIG 9:9 Cross-section through a damper and strut

Key to Fig 9:9 1 Gland packing 2 Seal 3 'O' ring 4 Piston guide assembly 5 Cylinder 6 Rebound stop 7 Strut casing 8 Piston rod 9 Check valve spring retainer 10 Check valve spring 11 Check valve plate 12 Piston ring 13 Valve plate 14 Piston body 15 Nut 16 Bolt 17 Distance collar 18 Spring retainer 19 Check valve spring 20 Bottom valve body 21 Check valve plate 22 Valve plate 23 Nut 24 Bottom plate

9:6 Anti-roll bar

The anti-roll bar is shown at 7 in **FIG 9:1**. The bar is carried in two flexible mountings and each end is connected with a suspension arm through a pillar attachment.

Removal:

Remove nut 1 in **FIG 9:11** from each suspension arm. Remove the bolt which secures each anti-roll bar bracket to the chassis. Dismount the anti-roll bar. Renew the rubber bushes if they are worn, cracked or perished.

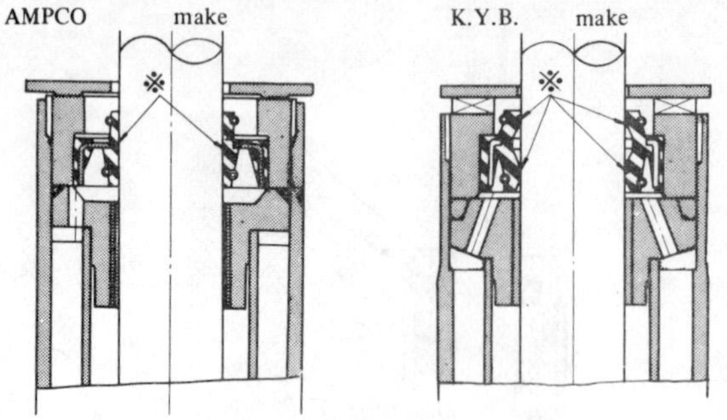

FIG 9:10 Seal lubrication

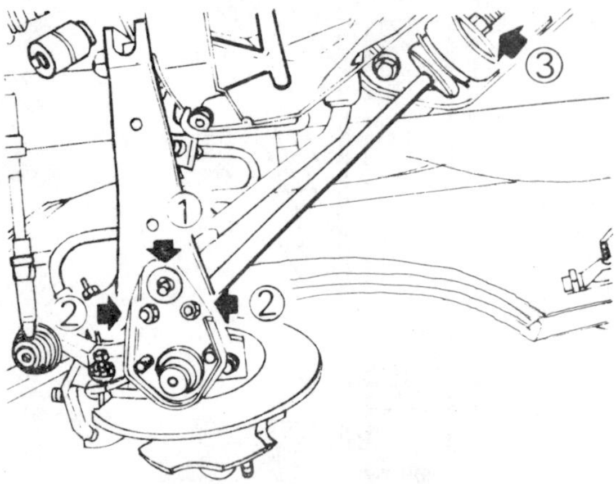

FIG 9:11 Tension rod and anti-roll bar attachment points

Key to Fig 9:11 1 Anti-roll bar pillar attachment 2 Tension rod to suspension arm attachment bolts 3 Tension rod to bracket attachment nut

FIG 9:12 Removing a suspension arm. The pivot bolt is arrowed

Fitment:

Fitment is the reverse of the removal sequence. Torque tighten each bracket bolt to 10 to 13 lb ft (1.4 to 1.8 kgm) and each suspension arm attachment to 8.7 to 12 lb ft (1.2 to 1.7 kgm). Check that the clearance between the anti-roll bar and each tension rod is substantially equal.

9:7 Suspension arms

Each suspension arm 5 in **FIG 9:1** is pivoted in a rubber bush to the suspension crossmember 8 and to a strut assembly 4 through a ball joint (see **FIG 9:6**).

Ball joint maintenance:

Every 30,000 miles (50,000 km), check that the rubber dust cover is in good condition and that the vertical play in the joint does not exceed .004 inch (.1 mm). Ball joints cannot be dismantled or repaired and, if unserviceable, must be replaced by a new assembly. If the joint is in good condition, remove the hexagonal headed plug, fit a grease nipple temporarily and lubricate with multi-purpose grease. Remove the nipple and refit the plug.

Arm removal:

1 Disconnect the tension and the anti-roll bar from the suspension arm as described in **Sections 9:5** and **9:6**.
2 Disconnect the lower end of the strut assembly as described in **Section 9:4** (up to and including operation 3 of the strut removal procedure).
3 The arm will now be only attached to the crossmember at the pivot as shown in **FIG 9:12**. Loosen off and remove the pivot bolt. Dismount the suspension arm.

Arm fitment:

Fitment of the arm is the reverse of the removal sequence. Tighten the tension rod to arm attachment bolts before tightening the arm pivot bolt. Do not fully tighten the pivot bolt until the vehicle weight is on the road wheels; then torque the pivot bolt to 65 to 72 lb ft (9 to 10 kgm).

Ball joint removal:

Remove the split pin from the castellated nut. Remove the nut and, using a suitable extractor, remove the steering arm from the ball joint stud. Remove the attachment nuts and dismount the joint from the suspension arm.

Fitment of a new ball joint is the reverse of this sequence. Torque tighten the castellated nut to 40 to 55 lb ft (5.5 to 7.6 kgm) and fit a new splitpin. Torque tighten the ball joint to arm nuts to 14 to 18 lb ft (1.9 to 2.5 kgm). Check the lubrication of the new joint as described earlier in this Section.

Suspension arm bush:

Tool ST36700000, used under a press, is required to remove an unserviceable bush. Note carefully which way round the original bush is fitted and ensure that the new bush is pressed in to match.

9:8 Camber and castor angles

Neither the camber nor the castor angle require attention. They are preset and cannot be adjusted. Should accident damage occur which might affect the suspension geometry, have appropriate checks carried out by a main agent. If camber and castor angles have been disturbed, the agent will advise regarding the replacement components required to effect corrections.

Wheel alignment is adjustable and is covered in **Chapter 10, Section 10:6**.

9:9 Fault diagnosis

(a) Wheel wobble

1 Worn hub bearings
2 Broken or weak front springs
3 Uneven tyre wear
4 Worn suspension arm pivot
5 Loose or broken tension rod
6 Loose hub nut
7 Loose wheel nuts

(b) 'Bottoming' of suspension

1 Check 2 in (a)
2 Bump rubber worn or missing
3 Damper(s) inoperative

(c) Heavy steering

1 Neglected ball joint lubrication
2 Tyre pressures too low
3 Distorted suspension geometry (see also **Chapter 10**)

(d) Rattles

1 Check 2, 4 and 5 in (a)
2 Damper upper mounting(s) loose
3 Anti-roll bar loose or bushes worn
4 Damper top bearing defective

(e) Excessive rolling

1 Check 2 in (a); 3 in (b) and 3 in (d)
2 Anti-roll bar broken

(f) Vehicle sways on corners

1 Check 4 and 5 in (a); 3 in (b) and 3 in (c)

(g) Excessive tyre wear

1 Check 4 and 5 in (a); 3 in (b) and 3 in (c)
2 Incorrect tyre pressures
3 Incorrect wheel alignment

NOTES

CHAPTER 10

THE STEERING GEAR

10:1 Description
10:2 Maintenance
10:3 Removing and fitting the steering unit
10:4 Servicing the steering unit
10:5 The steering linkage
10:6 Wheel alignment
10:7 Steering angles
10:8 The steering column
10:9 Fault diagnosis

10:1 Description

Cross-sections through the steering unit are shown in **FIG 10:1**. This is a nut and worm type of gearbox in which the longitudinal motion of the nut 2 (with which the short section of rack is integral) is produced from the rotation of the worm shaft by the recirculating balls. The rack gear teeth engage with the quadrant of gear teeth which are integral with the sector shaft 8. A steering arm is fitted to the bottom of the sector shaft. Serrations provide a positive drive between the sector shaft and the arm. The steering unit is filled with gear oil; a filler plug 15 is provided in the top cover. Servicing of the steering unit is covered in **Section 10:4**.

The steering linkage is covered in **Section 10:5**. A cross rod which is actuated by the steering unit arm operates between this arm and the arm of an idler unit. Side rods which are adjustable for length engage each end of the cross rod and transfer steering motion to the wheel hubs through the steering arms which are attached to them. All linkage pivots are ball jointed.

The steering column is not adjustable either for rake or for fore and aft position. It may be either a rigid or a collabsable type. Either a two or a three spoke steering wheel is fitted. The horn is operated on both types by the central horn pad. Certain models are provided with column mounted manual gearchange linkage or column mounted automatic transmission selector linkage. These linkages are covered in **Chapter 6**, **Section 6:6** and **Chapter 7**, **Section 7:4** respectively.

10:2 Maintenance

Steering unit oil level:

Every 6000 miles (10,000 km), check the level of the oil in the steering unit. The filler plug is 15 in **FIG 10:1**. Top up if necessary with the same brand of oil as that already in use (an EP 80, 90 or 140 oil of reputable brand).

Steering linkage:

Every 6000 miles (10,000 km), check over the steering linkage generally and ensure that all joints are secure and that none of the steering unit or idler unit securing bolts are loose.

Wheel alignment:

Every 12,000 miles (20,000 km), check and adjust if necessary the wheel alignment as described in **Section 10:6**.

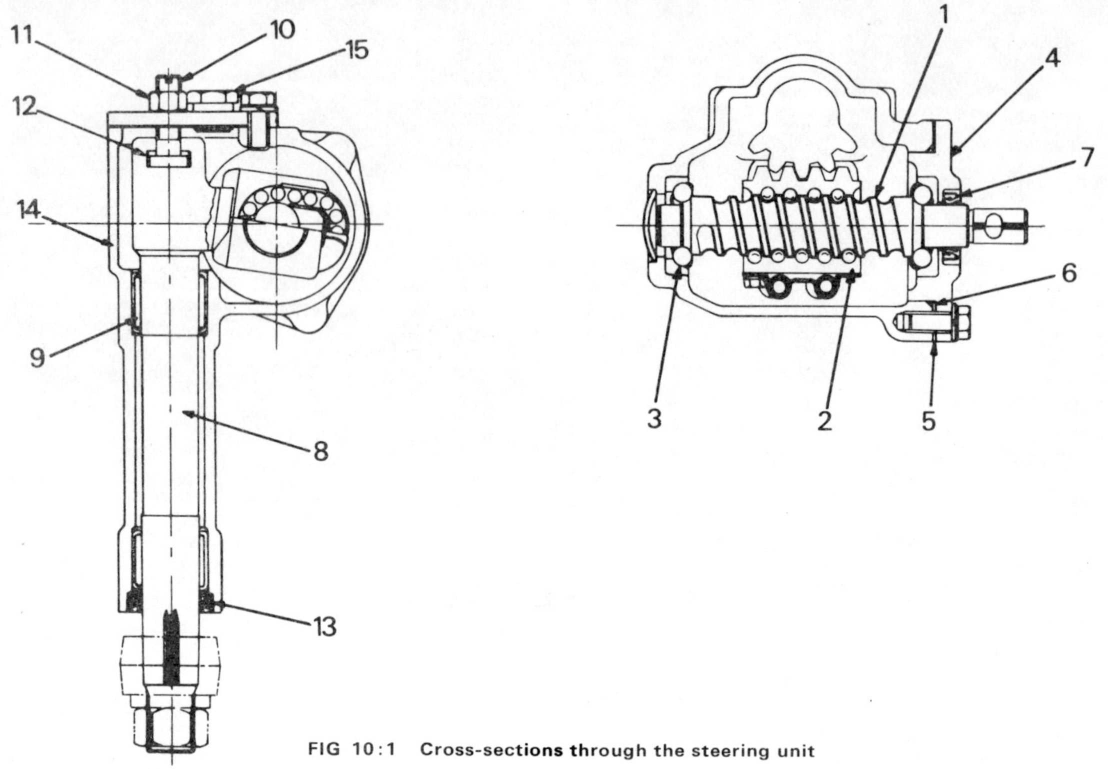

FIG 10:1 Cross-sections through the steering unit

Key to Fig 10:1 1 Worm shaft 2 Ball nut assembly 3 Worm shaft bearing 4 Cover 5 Shims 6 'O' ring 7 Oil seal 8 Sector shaft 9 Sector shaft bearing 10 Adjusting screw 11 Locknut 12 Shim 13 Oil seal 14 Steering unit housing 15 Filler plug

Steering angles:

Every 12,000 miles (20,000 km), check the wheel turning angles and adjust if necessary as described in **Section 10:7**.

Ball joints:

Every 30,000 miles (50,000 km), refer to **Section 10:5** and check that the play in the ball joints is not excessive. Check that the dust covers are not cracked, torn or perished. Renew joints which are no longer serviceable and grease those (the greasing procedure and milage intervals are the same as the suspension ball joints (see **Chapter 9**, **Section 9:7**) and it will be found convenient to deal with these at the same time) which are serviceable.

10:3 Removing and fitting the steering unit

Removal:

1 Refer to **FIG 10:2** and remove the bolt **A** which clamps the coupling to the steering unit worm shaft.
2 Remove nut **F** which retains the steering arm to the sector shaft. Mark the relative position of the arm and sector shaft. Using a suitable puller (the official tool is ST27140000), withdraw the arm from the shaft.
3 Remove the three nuts and bolts which secure the unit to the body side member and dismount the unit.

Fitment:

Installation of the steering unit is the removal sequence in reverse. Align the arm and shaft to their original relative position. Torque tighten the three securing nuts and bolts to 44 to 57 lb ft (6 to 8 kgm), the steering arm retaining nut **F** to 100 lb ft (14 kgm) and the coupling clamp bolt **A** to 29 to 36 lb ft (4 to 5 kgm).

10:4 Servicing the steering unit

The steering unit is shown in cross-section in **FIG 10:1**. The following procedures cover the dismantling, inspection, reassembly and adjustment of the unit.

Dismantling:

1 Remove the unit as described in **Section 10:3**. Remove the filler plug 15 and drain off the gear oil.
2 Loosen locknut 11, remove the three setbolts which retain the sector shaft cover, turn the adjuster screw 10 several turns in a clockwise direction, remove the cover and withdraw the sector shaft 8.
3 Remove three bolts and detach cover 4. Withdraw the shims 5 and the worm shaft assembly 1. Remove and discard oil seals 7 and 13. Discard O-ring 6.
4 Do not attempt to remove the sector shaft bearing 9. If this bearing is unserviceable a new housing will be required. Do not attempt to dismantle the nut and ball assembly 2. If this assembly is unserviceable, a new replacement will be required. Wash off all parts.

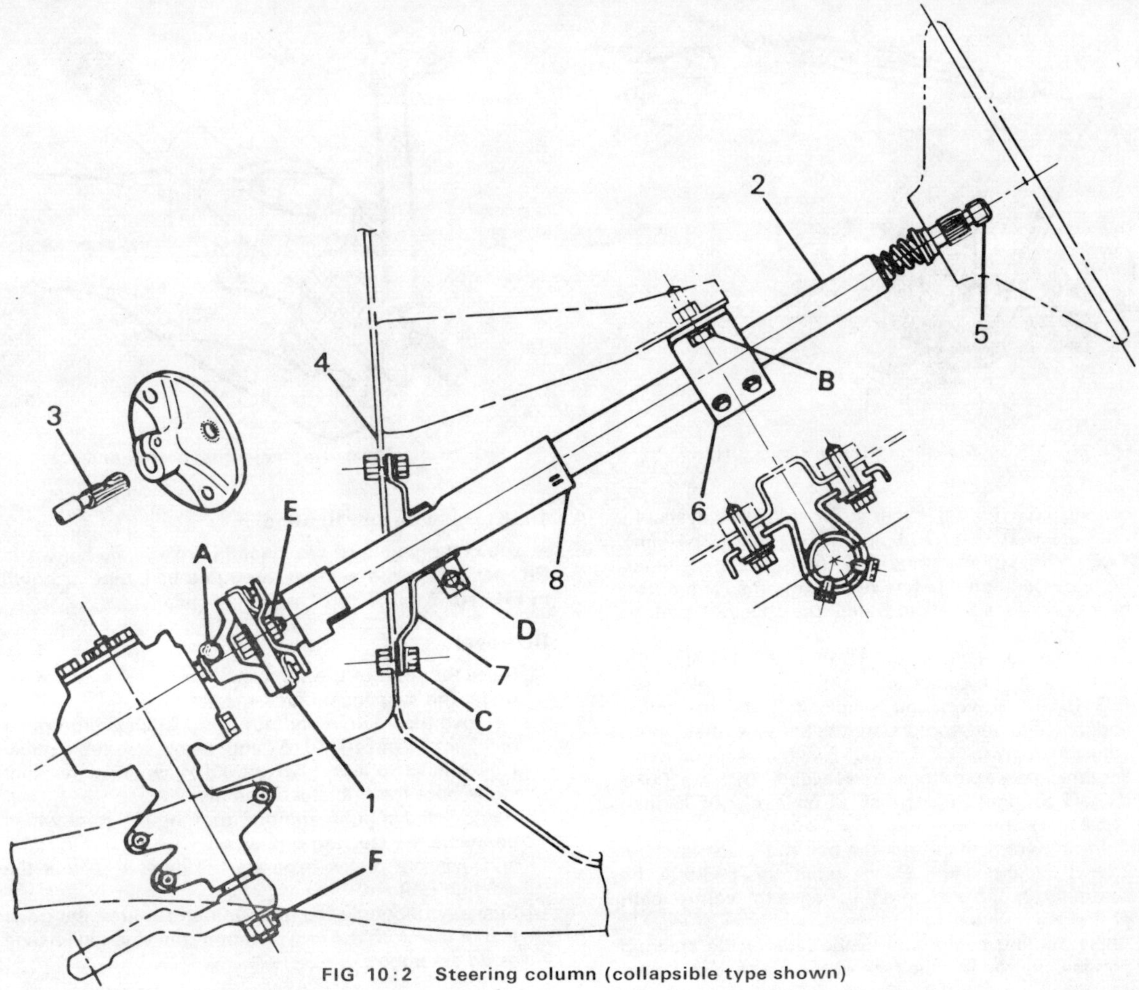

FIG 10:2 Steering column (collapsible type shown)

Key to Fig 10:2 1 Coupling 2 Column assembly 3 Steering unit worm shaft 4 Dash panel 5 Column shaft 6 Column clamp 7 Column flange 8 Upper end of lower jacket **A** Coupling retaining bolt **B** Clamp bolts **C** Flange to panel attachment **D** Flange to lower jacket clamp bolt **E** Coupling nut and bolt **F** Steering unit arm retaining nut

Inspection:

If the sector shaft bearing is unserviceable, the complete steering unit housing 14 must be renewed. The nut assembly 2 should (when lubricated) move down the worm shaft under its own weight in both directions. Check that the nut rack and the sector gear teeth are free of pitting, excessive wear and cracks. Renew the worm shaft, ball nut assembly, sector shaft, housing or bearing as necessary. Obtain new oil seals irrespective of the apparent condition of those removed. Clean off old jointing compound and gasket material from the housing and its cover.

Assembly and adjustment:

Assemble all internal parts thoroughly wetted with fresh gear oil.

1 Apply multi-purpose grease to the lips of the new oil seals before pressing them into position.

2 Fit the new O-ring 6 and, as a starting datum, the original shims 5 (the thickest shim should preferably be outwards) to the cover 4. The thickness of shims 5 may have to be adjusted as described later. If the original shims are not available, fit shims of .060 inch (1.5 mm) thickness to provide a starting point.

3 Install the worm shaft and ball nut assembly. Fit the cover and torque tighten the retaining bolts to 11 to 18 lb ft (1.5 to 2.5 kgm). Turn the worn shaft in both directions a number of times to settle the bearings.

4 Using a spring balance and lever as shown in **FIG 10:3**, measure the torque required to initiate rotation of the worm shaft. If the original bearings were refitted, a torque of between 28 and 56 oz inch (2 to 4 kg/cm) is acceptable. If, however, new bearings were fitted, a torque of between 56 and 83 oz inch (4 to 6 kg/cm) must be achieved.

5 If the torque is too low, increase the thickness of the shims 5. If the torque is too high, reduce the thickness

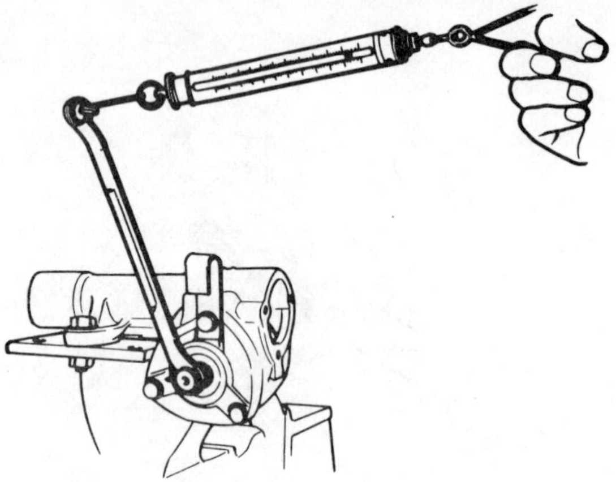

FIG 10:3 Measuring the preload torque

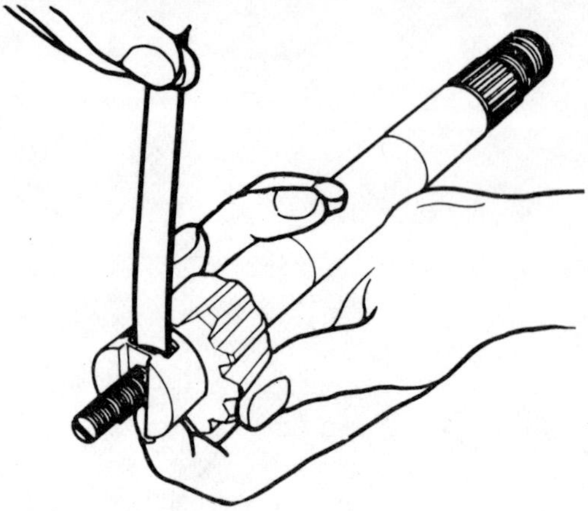

FIG 10:4 Measuring adjusting screw end play

of the shims. Four thicknesses of shims are available. They are .030 inch (.762 mm), .0100 inch (.254 mm), .005 inch (.127 mm) and .002 inch (.050 mm).

6 Repeat operation 3 before rechecking the torque. Repeat operations 3, 4 and 5 until the specified preload is achieved.

7 Insert the adjusting screw 10 in **FIG 10:1** into the T-groove in the sector shaft. Measure the play (see **FIG 10:4**) between the sector shaft and the screw and, by selecting appropriate thicknesses of shim 12, adjust the play to .0004 to .0012 inch (.01 to .03 mm). Four thicknesses of shims are available. They are .0618 inch (1.57 mm), .0610 inch (1.55 mm), .0598 inch (1.52 mm) and .0591 inch (1.50 mm).

8 Turn the worm shaft until the ball nut assembly is in its mid-travel position. Fit the sector shaft so that the centre tooth of the quadrant engages the centre teeth of the rack.

9 Apply jointing compound to the face of the steering unit housing and to the face of the cover. Use a new gasket. By turning the adjusting screw anticlockwise, attach the sector shaft cover to the housing and secure it temporarily.

10 By turning the adjusting screw anticlockwise, pull the sector shaft approximately .08 to .12 inch (2 to 3 mm) towards the cover and tighten the cover retaining bolts to 11 to 18 lb ft (1.5 to 2.5 kgm).

11 Push the sector shaft against the ball nut rack by gradually turning the adjusting screw until the sector shaft gear lightly meshes with the rack and temporarily secure the adjusting screw with its locknut.

12 Fit the steering arm to the sector shaft and operate the assembly a number of times to confirm that it turns smoothly. Adjust the backlash at the mid-travel position by turning the adjusting screw clockwise or anticlockwise until the play measured at the end of the steering arm is less than .004 inch (.1 mm).

13 From this position turn the adjusting screw clockwise by $\frac{1}{8}$ to $\frac{1}{6}$ of a turn, move the steering arm backwards and forwards a number of times and tighten the adjusting screw locknut to a torque of 14.5 to 18 lb ft (2 to 2.5 kgm).

14 Fill the unit with approved gear oil. Fit the filler plug. Install the unit as described in **Section 10:3**.

10:5 The steering linkage

The components of the steering linkage are shown in **FIG 10:5**. A cross-section through a ball joint is shown in **FIG 10:7**.

Removal:

1 Raise the front of the vehicle and support it on stands under the suspension crossmember.

2 Remove the splitpin and nut from each side rod outer ball joint (4 in **FIG 10:5**) and, using a suitable puller (the official tool is ST27850000), separate the joint studs from the hub steering arms.

3 Remove the splitpin and nut from the ball joint which connects the steering unit arm 1 with the cross rod 2 and, using a puller, separate the cross rod from the steering unit arm.

4 Similarly uncouple the idler unit arm 6 from the other end of the cross rod and dismount the steering linkage as an assembly.

Dismantling:

The side rods 3 may be separated from the cross rod by removing each ball joint stud splitpin and nut. The outer and inner sockets 4 and 5 may be removed from a side rod by loosening the locknuts and unscrewing the sockets from the side rod (note lefthand and righthand threads). Ball joints cannot be dismantled.

Idler unit:

The idler unit may be dismounted after uncoupling the ball joint from the cross rod. Remove the two retaining bolts. Check the cross rod joint nylon bush and the idler arm rubber bush and renew if wear or play is excessive.

Inspection:

Do not attempt to salvage any part of the steering linkage which may have sustained accident damage but fit new replacement parts. Ball joints which are worn and have excessive play should be replaced by new assemblies. Refer to **FIG 10:7**. End play should not exceed .0197 inch (.5 mm). The 'swing' torque of a serviceable ball joint should be better than 3.6 lb ft (.5 kgm).

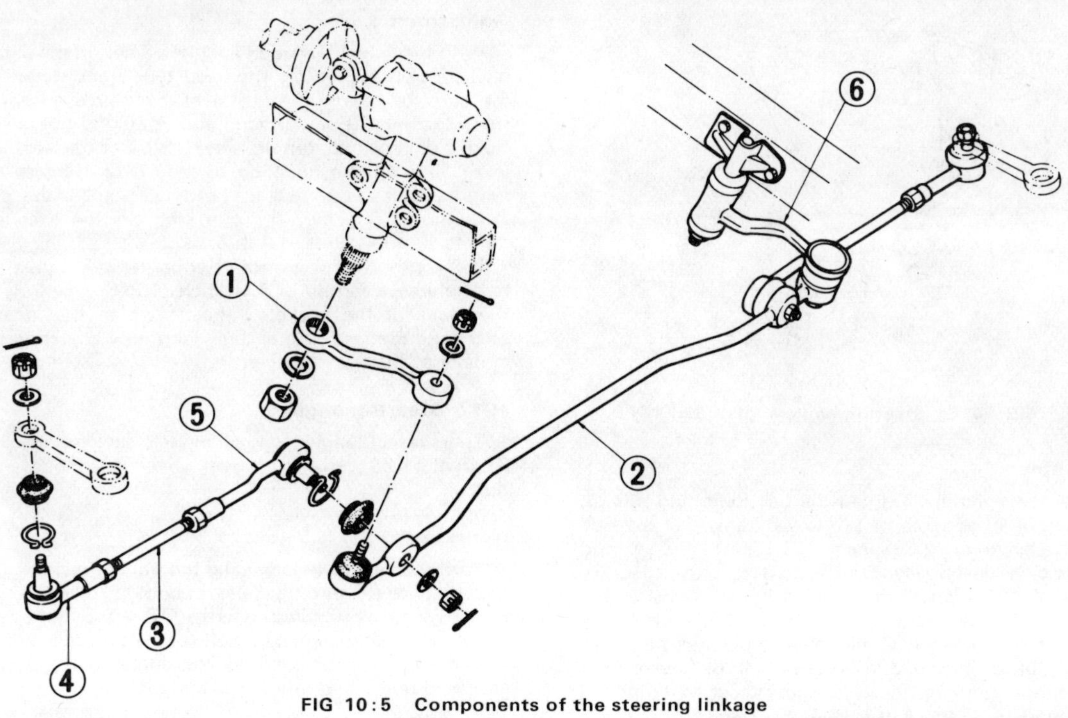

FIG 10:5 Components of the steering linkage

Key to Fig 10:5 1 Steering unit arm 2 Cross rod 3 Side rod 4 Side rod outer socket 5 Side rod inner socket 6 Idler unit arm

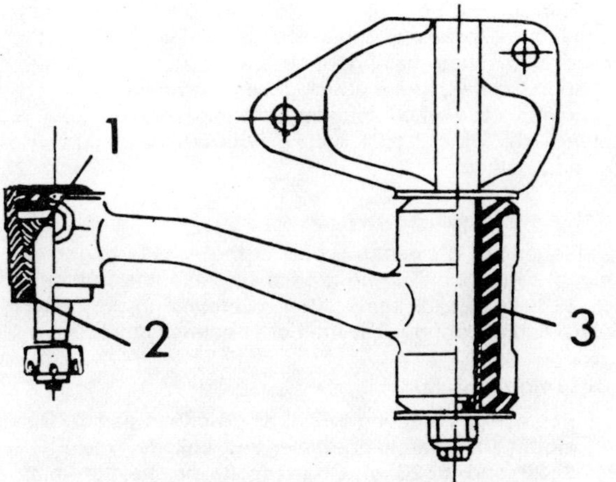

FIG 10:6 Components of the idler unit

Key to Fig 10:6 1 Nylon bush 2 Dust cover 3 Rubber bush

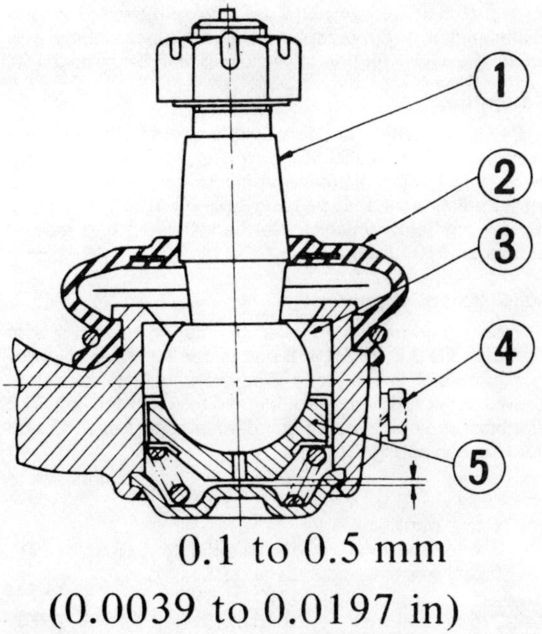

FIG 10:7 Cross-section through a steering linkage ball joint

Key to Fig 10:7 1 Ball joint stud 2 Dust cover 3 Ball seat 4 Plug 5 Spring seat

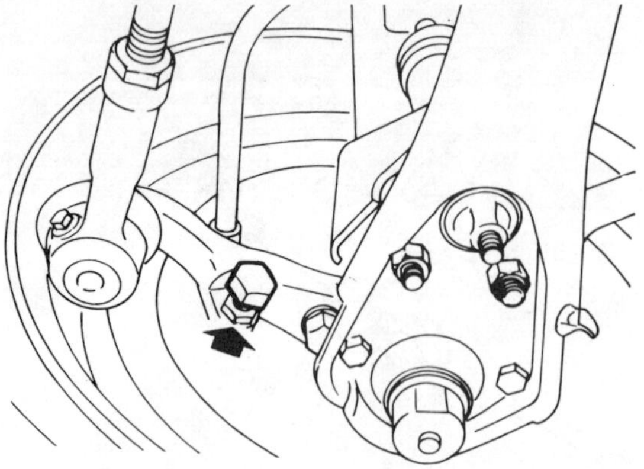

FIG 10:8 Steering angle adjustment

Assembly:

Use new splitpins. Tighten the ball joint stud nuts to a torque of 40 to 55 lb ft (5.5 to 7.6 kgm). Set the side rods to a length of 12.331 inch (313.2 mm) between stud centres or, as described in **Section 10:6**, to the reference length of 4.15 inch (105.5 mm) between faces of the sockets. Side rod socket locknuts need not be finally tightened until the wheel alignment procedure has been carried out as described in **Section 10:6**. After setting the wheel alignment, these locknuts must be tightened to a torque of 32 to 44 lb ft (4.4 to 6.1 kgm).

Fitment:

Fitment of the linkage assembly is the removal sequence in reverse. Torque tighten the ball joint stud nuts to 40 to 55 lb ft (5.5 to 7.6 kgm) and use new splitpins to lock the castellated nuts. On completion of the fitment, check and adjust the wheel alignment as described in **Section 10:6**.

Ball joints:

Ball joints which are serviceable should be regreased every 30,000 miles (50,000 km). Refer to **FIG 10:7**, remove plug 4 and fit a grease nipple. Use a grease gun and, on completion of the greasing operation, refit the plug. Renew any joint which is worn and has an end play in excess of .0197 inch (.5 mm).

10:6 Wheel alignment

Wheel alignment is adjusted by altering the lengths of the side rods 3 in **FIG 10:5** and is correct when the toe-in dimensions is that for the relevant vehicle model as shown in the following tabulation. Note that toe-in is not identical for vehicles with standard suspension (SS) and hard suspension (HS).

Toe-in	*Saloon*	*Estate car*
.197 to .315 inch (5 to 8 mm)	LHD (HS)*	
.236 to .354 inch (6 to 9 mm)	RHD (HS) LHD (HS) LHD (SS)*	RHD (SS)
.276 to .394 inch (7 to 10 mm)	RHD (SS) LHD (SS)	RHD (HS) LHD (HS)
.315 to .433 inch (8 to 11 mm)		LHD (SS)

*USA and Canada

Adjustment:

With the vehicle unladen and the wheels in the straight ahead position, use an approved type track gauge and measure the toe-in. If adjustment is required, loosen off **both** locknuts (note lefthand and righthand threads) on **both** side rods and turn the side rods **by equal amounts** in the appropriate direction to reduce or increase their lengths until the correct toe-in dimension for the particular model is achieved. Torque tighten the four locknuts to 32 to 44 lb ft (4.4 to 6.1 kgm).

If the side rods were not of equal length, adjust both to a reference length of 4.15 inch (105.5 mm) between the faces of the sockets (against which the locknuts bear) and proceed to their final length by adjusting both equally as described earlier.

10:7 Steering angles

The correct angles on all models are: inner wheel, 37 deg. to 38 deg. and, outer wheel, 30¾ deg. to 32¾ deg.

Adjustment:

With the vehicle unladen and the front wheels on turntables, check the turning angles in both full lock positions. If adjustment is required, refer to **FIG 10:8**, remove the nylon cap from the adjuster bolt (arrowed) on both hubs, turn the bolts in or out until the angles are within the specified range and refit the nylon caps.

10:8 The steering column

Either a rigid or a collapsible type column may be fitted. Removal of a steering column will normally only be required following accident damage to the front end of the vehicle. **No attempt should be made to salvage a compressed collapsible type column**. It must be replaced by a new assembly.

Steering wheel removal:

Disconnect the battery earth cable. Disconnect the horn operating pad wiring.

Pull out the horn pad in the cases of wheels having either two spokes or three spokes marked N/P. In the case of a wheel having three spokes but no marking, push in the pad, turn it anticlockwise and then pull it out.

Remove the wheel retaining nut and, using a suitable puller (the official tool is ST27180000), withdraw the steering wheel.

Steering wheel fitment:

Fitment of a steering wheel is the reverse of the removal sequence. Torque tighten the retaining nut to 29 to 36 lb ft (4 to 5 kgm). After reconnecting the battery earth cable, confirm that the horn operates correctly.

Column removal:

1 Remove the steering wheel as described earlier. Dismount the gearchange lever and linkage (see **FIGS 6:22** and **6:23** in **Chapter 6**) or the automatic transmission lever and linkage (see **FIG 7:13** in **Chapter 7**) if relevant to the model.

2 Refer to **FIG 10:2** and remove bolt **A** which retains the column coupling to the steering unit.

3 Remove four screws and dismount the shell covers from the column. Remove two screws and dismount the direction indicator switch.

4 Remove the parcel tray. Remove four bolts **C** which retain the column flange 7 to the dash panel 4. Remove two bolts **B** which retain the column clamp 6. The column can now be withdrawn.

Column fitment:

Fitment is the reverse of the removal sequence. Do not finally tighten the clamp bolts **B** and **D** until the dimension between 6 and 8 measured along the axis of the column has been set to 7.237 inch (183.8 mm). Torque tighten the coupling bolt **A** to 29 to 36 lb ft (4 to 5 kgm).

10:9 Fault diagnosis

(a) Wheel wobble (see **Chapter 9**)

1 Excessive play
2 Slack front wheel bearings
3 Worn ball joints
4 Steering unit mounting loose
5 Steering unit adjustment incorrect
6 Worn steering unit

(b) Heavy steering

1 Low tyre pressure
2 Seized shaft in steering unit or idler unit
3 Low oil level in steering unit
4 Seized ball joint
5 Seized damper mounting top bearing

(c) Wander

1 Check tyre wear and tyre pressures
2 Excessive play in steering unit
3 Worn steering linkage
4 Worn column to steering unit flexible coupling
5 Worn suspension (see **Chapter 9**)
6 Wheel alignment incorrect

(d) Excessive tyre wear

1 Check (a); check 5 and 6 in (c)
2 Lock limits incorrect (see **Section 10:7**)

(e) Rattles

1 Check 2 and 3 in (b); check 3, 4 and 5 in (c)
2 Column bracket loose
3 Column gearchange/selector linkage worn (relevant models)

NOTES

CHAPTER 11

THE BRAKING SYSTEM

11 :1 Description
11 :2 Maintenance
11 :3 Drum brakes, front
11 :4 Drum brakes, rear
11 :5 Disc brakes
11 :6 The hydraulic system
11 :7 Bleeding the hydraulic system
11 :8 Removing and fitting a flexible pipe
11 :9 The vacuum servo unit
11 :10 The handbrake
11 :11 Fault diagnosis

11 :1 General

The brakes are hydraulically operated. The rear brakes on all models are drum type. The front brakes may, depending upon the vehicle model, be either drum or disc type. Dual line hydraulic systems are incorporated but the type of tandem master cylinder differs between models fitted with disc and drum type front brakes. Vehicles fitted with disc front brakes have vacuum assisted brake application, a proportioning valve and either a fluid level or a differential pressure warning light. The brake application warning lights circuit is operated by a switch which is actuated when the foot brake pedal is depressed. The handbrake, which operates on the shoes of the rear brakes only, is mechanically applied. A warning light in the instrument panel lights up when the handbrake is in the applied position and the ignition is switched on.

Front drum brakes:

The components of a front drum brake assembly are shown in **FIG 11 :1**. Two leading shoes operate on the internal diameter of a brake drum which is located on the wheel hub by the road wheel mounting studs and retained by the road wheel. Each brake shoe is actuated by a separate single piston wheel cylinder. A flexible hydraulic feed pipe accommodates suspension and steering movement of the wheel assembly. The two wheel cylinders are hydraulically linked by a rigid pipe.

Routine adjustment is required to compensate for wear of the shoe friction linings and each shoe must be separately adjusted.

Front disc brakes:

The components of a disc brake floating cliper are shown in **FIG 11 :2** and a cross-section through a disc brake hub assembly is shown in **FIG 9 :2**. A wedge shaped friction pad is located on each side of the brake disc. The single piston in the caliper acts directly upon one pad and indirectly by reaction from the caliper unit upon the second pad. No routine adjustment is required to compensate for pad friction lining wear as this is accommodated automatically through the elasticity of the piston hydraulic seal. The caliper carrier must be removed before the wheel hub and brake disc can be withdrawn. It does not, however, have to be dismounted when pads are being renewed.

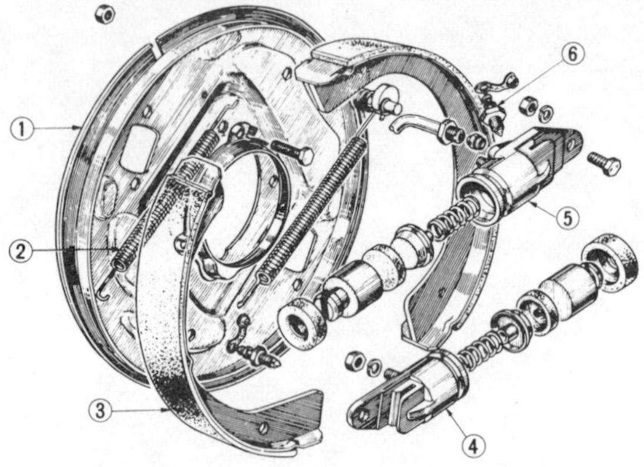

FIG 11:1 Components of front drum brake

Key to Fig 11:1 1 Backplate 2 Pull-off spring 3 Brake shoe 4 Upper wheel cylinder 5 Lower wheel cylinder 6 Bleed screw

Rear drum brakes:

The components of a rear drum type brake are shown in **FIG 11:3**. All models are provided with the same design of rear brakes. The single wheel cylinder assembly actuates both brake shoes, one directly and the other by reaction of the sliding cylinder. Routine adjustment to compensate for wear of the shoe friction linings is required. A single adjuster provides adjustment of both shoes.

Handbrake:

The handbrake operates mechanically through a flexible cable and lever system on the rear wheel brakes only. The design of the cable and lever system differs slightly between saloon and estate car models. Routine adjustment is required to compensate for the wear of the rear brake shoe friction linings.

11:2 Maintenance

Hydraulic fluid:

At least every 3000 miles (5000 km), check the fluid level in the master cylinder reservoirs and top up if

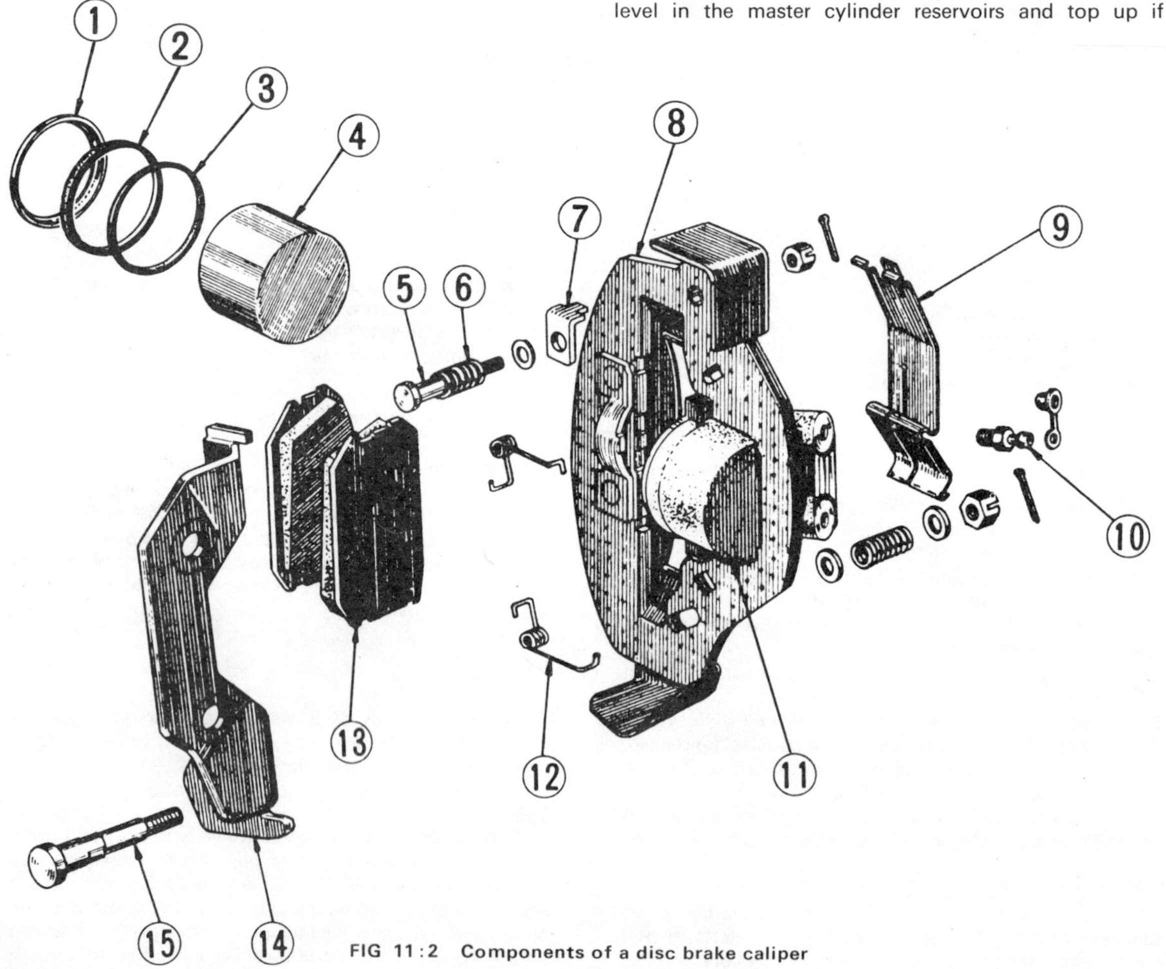

FIG 11:2 Components of a disc brake caliper

Key to Fig 11:2 1 Retainer 2 Seal 3 Piston seal 4 Piston 5 Holding down pin 6 Spring 7 Bracket 8 Caliper plate 9 Clip 10 Bleed screw 11 Cylinder 12 Spring 13 Pad 14 Bracket 15 Pivot pin

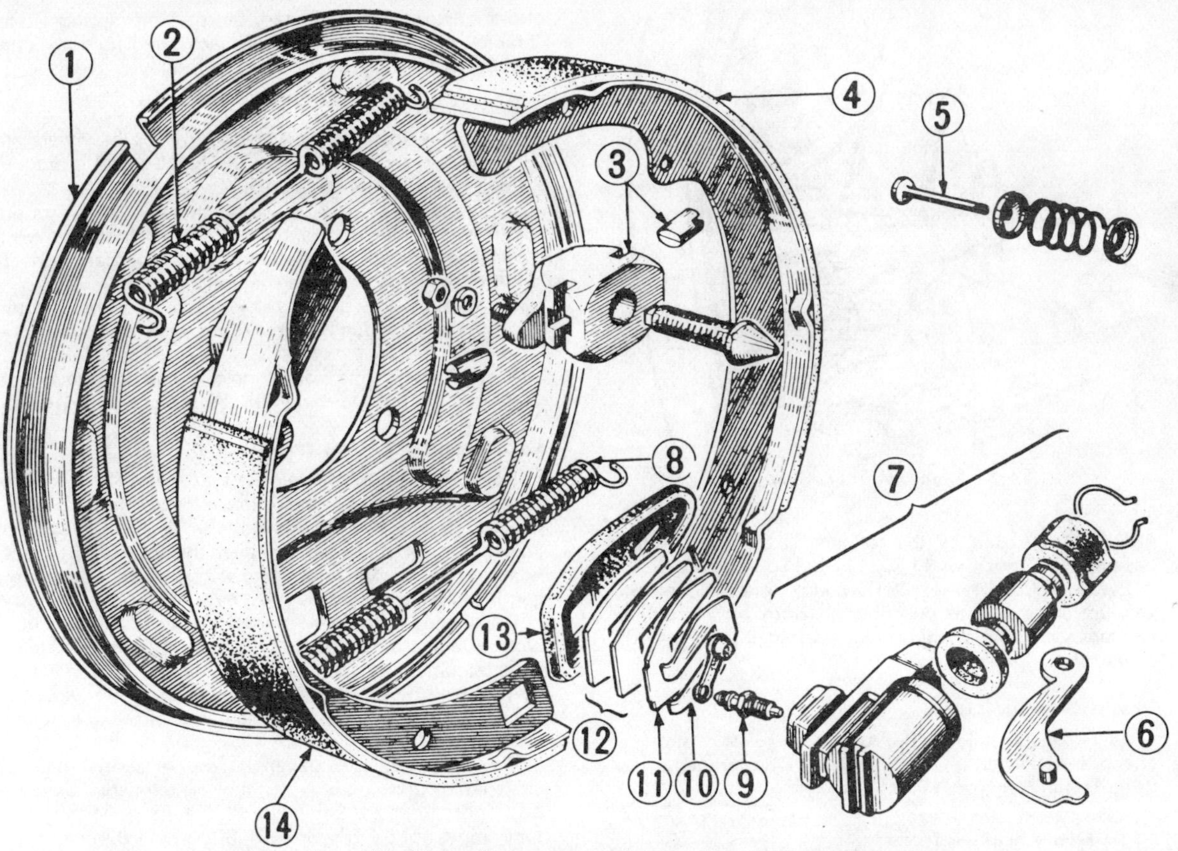

FIG 11 : 3 Components of a rear drum brake

Key to Fig 11 : 3 1 Backplate 2 Pull-off spring 3 Adjuster assembly 4 Brake shoe 5 Steady spring assembly 6 Lever 7 Wheel cylinder assembly 8 Pull-off spring 9 Bleed screw 10 Lock plate 11 Lock plate 12 Lock plates 13 Dust cover 14 Brake shoe

necessary. Use the same approved fluid as that already in the system. This should be heavy duty brake fluid of reputable brand to specification SAE J1703a.

Every 12,000 miles (20,000 km) in the case of models fitted with disc front brakes and every 24,000 miles (40,000 km) in the case of models fitted with drum front brakes, drain off and refill the system with fresh hydraulic fluid. The procedure is described in **Section 11 : 7**.

Brake pedal free play:

Every 6000 miles (10,000 km), check the brake pedal free play and adjust if necessary as described in **Section 11 : 6**.

Adjustment:

Every 6000 miles (10,000 km), to compensate for wear of the brake shoe linings, adjust the drum brake shoes as described in **Sections 11 : 3** and **11 : 4**. Follow this by checking the operation of the handbrake and, as described in **Section 11 : 10**, making any adjustment that is required.

No corresponding action is required on disc brakes as adjustment for pad wear is automatic.

Friction linings:

Every 3000 miles (5000 km), check the thickness of the disc brake pad linings and fit new pads when the thickness of a lining has worn down to .04 inch (1 mm). The procedure is described in **Section 11 : 5**. Always renew pads in pairs and never singly and on both front wheels even if only one brake has worn down to the limit.

Every 12,000 miles (20,000 km), check the thickness of drum brake shoe linings and renew when the thickness has worn down to .06 inch (1.5 mm). Renew linings in sets and never singly and on both sides of the axle. The procedure is described in **Section 11 : 3** for front drum brakes and in **Section 11 : 4** for rear brakes.

Lubrication:

Every 12,000 miles (20,000 km), refer to **Section 11 : 6** and lubricate the foot brake pedal pivots. Every 24,000 miles (40,000 km), refer to **Section 11 : 10** and lubricate the handbrake linkage.

Hydraulic system:

Every 30,000 miles (50,000 km), overhaul the master cylinder, the wheel cylinders and, in the case of models

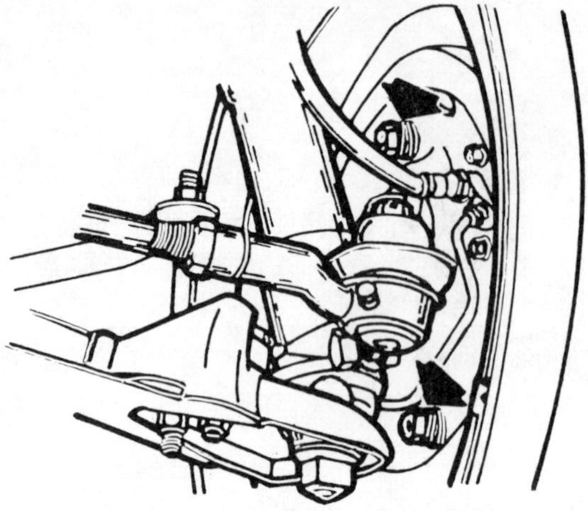

FIG 11:4 Front drum brake adjusters

fitted with disc brakes, the calipers. The procedures are described in **Sections 11:3, 11:4, 11:5** and **11:6**.

Every 12,000 miles (20,000 km), check over the vacuum servo unit as described in **Section 11:9**. The vacuum servo unit should be fully serviced every 24,000 miles (40,000 km).

Proportioning valve:

Every 24,000 miles (40,000 km) on relevant models, check the efficiency of this valve. The procedure is described in **Section 11:6**.

11:3 Drum brakes, front:

Each shoe is expanded against the internal diameter of a brake drum by a hydraulically operated piston in each wheel cylinder assembly and both operate as leading

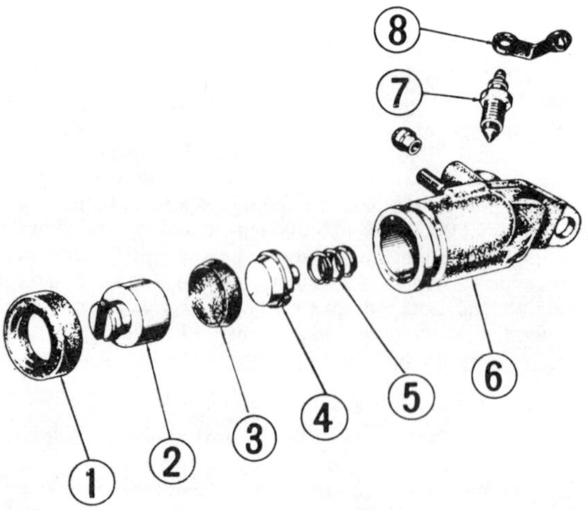

FIG 11:5 Components of a front wheel cylinder assembly

Key to Fig 11:5 1 Dust cover 2 Piston 3 Cup 4 Spring retainer 5 Spring 6 Cylinder 7 Bleed screw 8 Cap

shoes. Shoes are retracted by pull-off springs. The 'brakes off' clearance between each shoe friction lining and the drum must be adjusted as the lining wears.

Adjustment:

1 Raise the front of the vehicle until both wheels are clear of the ground. Pump the brake pedal a number of times to settle the shoes.
2 Refer to **FIG 11:4** in which the two adjusters are arrowed. Turn one of the adjusters (clockwise for a lefthand wheel, anticlockwise for a righthand wheel) until the shoe drags on the brake drum.
3 Now turn the adjuster by small amounts in the opposite direction until the drum is just free from shoe drag.
4 Repeat operations 2 and 3 on the second adjuster and then carry out the procedure on the opposite wheel.

Drum removal and fitment:

Raise the front of the vehicle and remove the relevant road wheel. Pull off the drum. If the drum is tight, use two 8 mm x 1.25 mm bolts in the holes provided adjacent to two of the studs to push the drum off the wheel retaining studs. The drum and the shoe friction linings can now be inspected.

Brake shoes should be renewed when the linings have worn down to a thickness of .06 inch (1.5 mm). If linings have become contaminated with grease or hydraulic fluid they should be renewed irrespective of the thickness of the linings. Trace and rectify the cause of the contamination.

Drums which are unevenly worn or scored may be salvaged by grinding provided that the refinished diameter does not exceed 8.945 inch (227.2 mm). Ovality and taper must not be greater than .008 inch (.02 mm).

Fitment of a drum is the reverse of the removal sequence and must be followed by adjustment of the brakes as described earlier.

Removing and fitting brake shoes:

Remove the relevant brake drum as described earlier. Refer to **FIG 11:1**. Unhook the two pull-off springs and dismount the brake shoes.

Fitment of shoes is the reverse of this sequence. Lubricate the shoe abutments and side contact pads sparingly with grease. Ensure that no grease will come in contact with the friction linings **or with the adjusters.**

Wheel cylinder removal and fitment:

Remove the brake shoes as described earlier. Refer to **Section 11:8** and disconnect the hydraulic flexible pipe. Remove the rigid pipe which links the two wheel cylinders. Identify the cylinders to their respective positions. Remove the nuts which secure the cylinders to the backplate and collect the washers. Dismount the cylinders.

Wheel cylinder fitment is the reverse of this sequence. Torque tighten the larger nuts to 11 to 13 lb ft (1.5 to 1.8 kgm) and the smaller nuts to 4 to 5 lb ft (.5 to .7 kgm). Torque tighten the rigid pipe connections to 11 to 13 lb ft (1.5 to 1.8 kgm) and the flexible pipe connections to 12 to 14 lb ft (1.7 to 2 kgm). On completion of the work, bleed the hydraulic system as described in **Section 11:7** and adjust the shoes as described earlier.

Wheel cylinder overhaul:

Remove the wheel cylinders as described earlier. Refer to **FIG 11 :5**. Remove dust cover 1. Apply low pressure air to the fluid orifice and carefully blow out the piston assembly. Discard the cup 3 even though it may appear serviceable.

Clean the parts in fresh brake fluid. Reject the piston if its diameter is corroded. Reject the cylinder if its bore is corroded. Reject the dust cover if it is cracked, torn or shows signs of perishing.

Assembly is the reverse of the dismantling sequence. Torque tighten the bleed nipple (if it was removed) to 5 to 6.5 lb ft (.7 to .9 kgm). Assemble the internal parts wetted with fresh brake fluid.

11 :4 Drum brakes, rear

On each rear wheel, both shoes are expanded against the internal diameter of a brake drum by a single hydraulically actuated piston operating in a sliding cylinder. One shoe is directly actuated by the piston and the other indirectly by the reaction of the sliding cylinder. This gives a leading and trailing shoe arrangement. The shoes are retracted by pull-off springs. A single adjustor (arrowed in **FIG 11 :6**) provides means for adjustment of the 'brakes off' clearance between both shoe linings and the drum simultaneously.

Adjustment:

1 Chock the front wheels securely and raise the rear of the vehicle until both wheels are clear of the ground. Release the handbrake and pump the brake pedal a number of times to settle the shoes.

2 Refer to **FIG 11 :6**. Turn the adjuster (clockwise for a lefthand wheel, anticlockwise for a righthand wheel) until the shoes drag on the brake drum.

3 Now turn the adjuster by small amounts in the opposite direction until the drum is just free from shoe drag.

4 Repeat operations 2 and 3 on the opposite wheel.

5 Adjust the handbrake as described in **Section 11 :10**.

Drum removal and fitment:

Chock the front wheels securely and raise the rear of the vehicle. Remove the relevant road wheel and release the handbrake. Pull off the drum. If the drum is tight, use two 8 mm x 1.25 mm bolts in the holes provided adjacent to two of the studs to push the drum off the wheel retaining studs. The drum and the shoe friction linings can now be inspected exactly as described in **Section 11 :3** for front drums and shoes.

Fitment of a drum is the reverse of the removal sequence and must be followed by adjustment of the brake shoes as described earlier and adjustment of the handbrake as described in **Section 11 :10**.

Removing and fitting brake shoes:

Remove the brake drums as described earlier. Refer to **FIG 11 :3**. Turn the steady spring pins 5 through $\frac{1}{4}$ turn and remove the spring assemblies. Unhook the pull-off springs and dismount the brake shoes.

Fitment of shoes is the reverse of this sequence. Lubricate the shoe abutments and side contact pads sparingly with grease. Ensure that no grease comes in contact with the friction linings or with the adjusters.

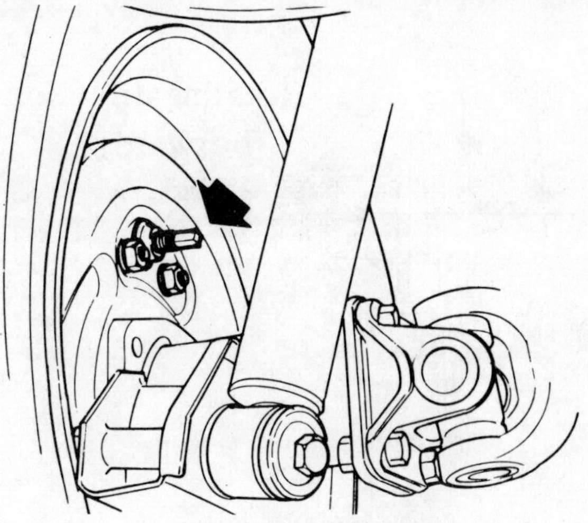

FIG 11 :6 Rear drum brake adjuster

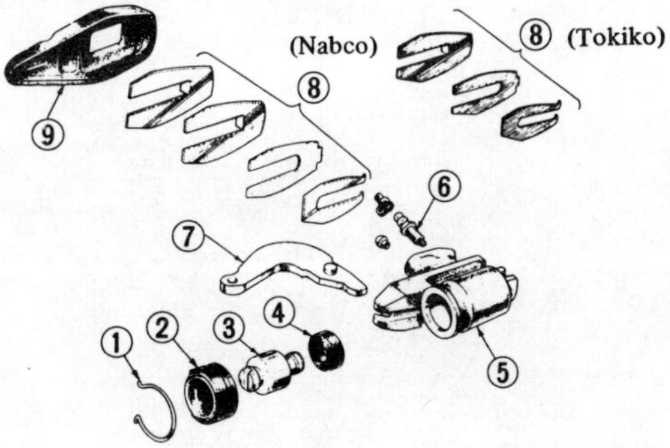

FIG 11 :7 Components of a rear wheel cylinder assembly

Key to Fig 11 :7 1 Circlip 2 Dust cover 3 Piston 4 Cup 5 Cylinder 6 Bleed screw 7 Lever (handbrake) 8 Lock plates 9 Dust cover

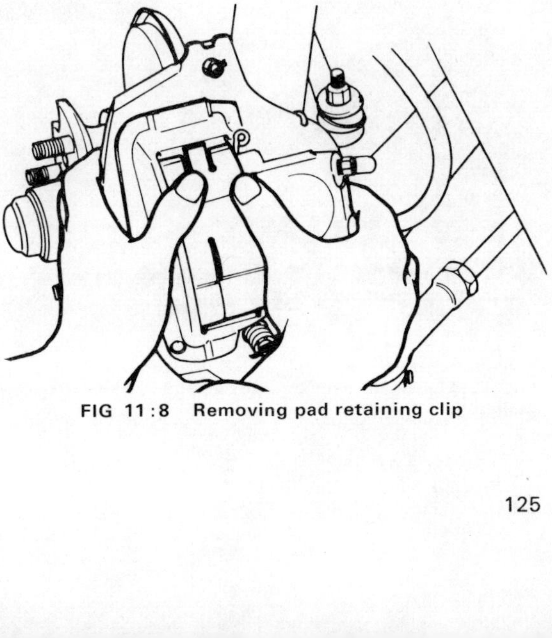

FIG 11 :8 Removing pad retaining clip

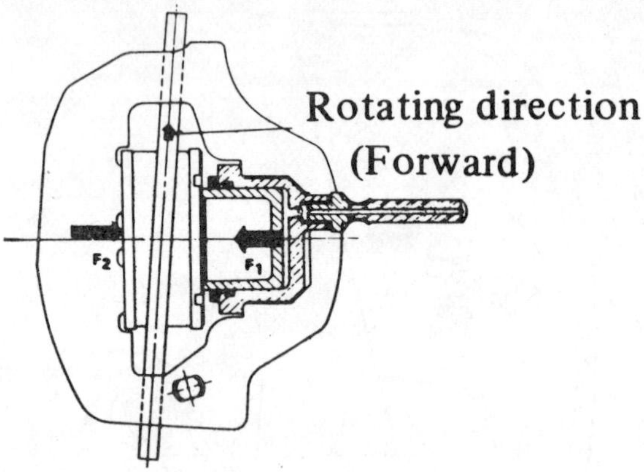

FIG 11:9 New pads in position

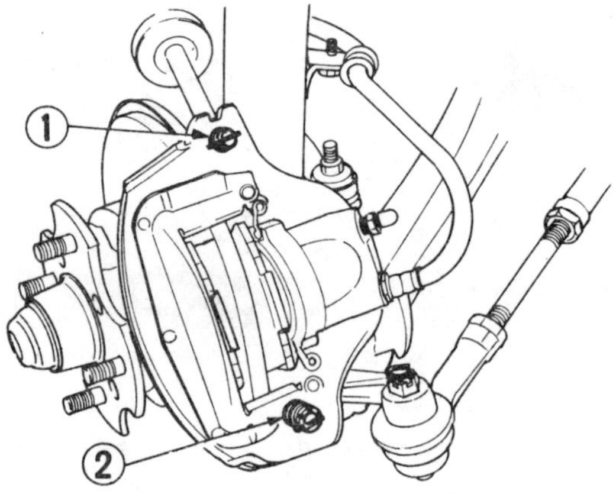

FIG 11:10 Removing a caliper

Key to Fig 11:10 1 Holding down pin 2 Pivot pin

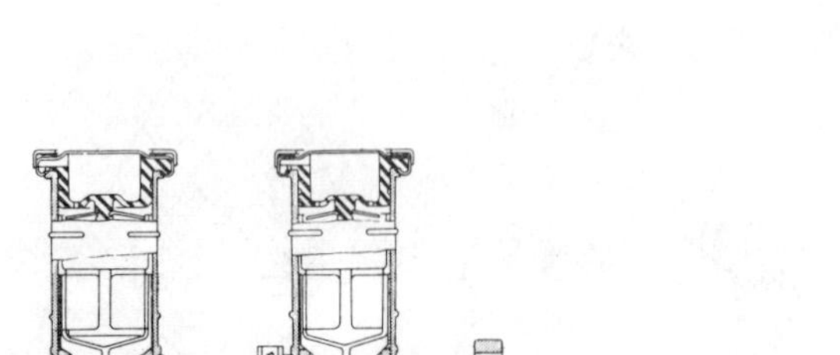

FIG 11:11 Cross-section through a Tokiko master cylinder

Wheel cylinder removal:

Remove the brake shoes as described earlier. Refer to **FIG 11:3**. Remove the two nuts and washers and withdraw the adjuster assembly 3. Disconnect the hydraulic pipe. Remove the clevis pin and uncouple the handbrake cable from the lever 6. Remove the dust cover 13 and the adjusting shims and lock plates 10, 11 and 12. Keep them in sequence and note that, as shown in **FIG 11:7**, these items differ between assemblies of Nabco and Tokiko manufacture. Withdraw the wheel cylinder.

If the backplate 1 is to be removed note that the procedure differs between saloon and estate car models. Refer to **Chapter 8, Section 8:7** and, in conjunction with removal of the axle shaft, remove four bolts to dismount the backplate.

Wheel cylinder fitment:

Insert lever 6 into the backplate and fit the wheel cylinder into position. Using a hammer, drive in the shims and lockplates in the same order as that in which they were originally fitted (see also **FIG 11:7**). Fit the adjuster assembly and torque tighten the retaining nuts to 10 to 13 lb ft (1.4 to 1.8 kgm). After fitting the shoes, use a spring balance to measure the load required to slide the wheel cylinder in the backplate. This load should be within the range of 4.4 to 15.4 lb (2 to 7 kg). On completion of the work, bleed the hydraulic system as described in **Section 11:7** and adjust the shoes as described earlier.

Wheel cylinder overhaul:

Refer to **FIG 11:7** and proceed as described under this heading in **Section 11:3**.

11:5 Disc brakes

Adjustment to compensate for pad friction lining wear is automatic.

Pad renewal:

Pads which are excessively worn or which have linings that are contaminated with oil, grease or brake fluid must be renewed. Renew pads when the linings have worn down to .04 inch (1 mm). Pads must always be renewed in sets (both pads in both calipers). Renewal in one caliper only will lead to uneven braking.

Pad removal:

Raise the front of the vehicle and remove both road wheels. Refer to **FIG 11:8** and release the clip (9 in **FIG 11:2**) by pushing on its upper portion. Remove the pads with the aid of a screwdriver.

Pad fitment:

Dry clean those parts of the caliper and piston against which the pads locate. Press the piston into the cylinder just far enough to give clearance for the new (thicker) pads and, while doing so, watch that the fluid in the relevant reservoir does not overflow. If necessary, remove an appropriate amount of fluid. Fit the new pads. Ensure that they are the correct way round as shown in **FIG 11:9**. Fit the retaining clip. Depress the brake pedal several times to settle the pads, check and adjust the brake fluid level.

Caliper removal and fitment:

Remove the pads as described earlier. Refer to **Section 11:8** and disconnect the hydraulic flexible pipe. Refer to **FIG 11:10**. Remove the splitpins from the nuts 1 and 2. Remove the nuts and withdraw the holding down and pivot pins (these are 5 and 15 in **FIG 11:2**). Dismount the caliper plate assembly from its mounting bracket.

Fitment is the reverse of this sequence and must be followed by bleeding the system as described in **Section 11:7**. Use new splitpins to lock the castellated nuts. Before fitting the pads, check that the caliper pivots smoothly.

Caliper overhaul:

1 Dismount the caliper as described earlier and, before proceeding with the dismantling, clean off all mud and and dust from the unit.
2 Refer to **FIG 11:2**. Remove springs 12 and withdraw the cylinder 11 from the caliper plate 8.
3 Using low pressure air applied to the hydraulic pipe connection and taking great care to control the piston as it emerges, carefully blow the piston from its cylinder.
4 Remove and discard the wiper seal 2 and also the piston seal 3. Clean the piston and the cylinder bore with fresh brake fluid.

Inspection:

Discard the seals 2 and 3 even if they appear serviceable. Slight corrosion or rusting of the cylinder bore may be rectified by careful polishing with very fine emery. The piston diameter is plated. Make no attempt to remove rust or corrosion but obtain a new component if the surface is so affected. Piston to bore diametrical clearance must not exceed .006 inch (.15 mm).

Reassembly:

This is the reverse of the dismantling sequence. Assemble the internal parts wetted with fresh brake fluid. Ensure that the seals are correctly fitted in their grooves.

Brake disc:

A scored disc may be reground. The salvaged thickness must not be less than .331 inch (8.4 mm). The retaining bolts should be torque tightened to 28 to 38 lb ft (3.9 to 5.3 kgm).

11:6 The hydraulic system

The master cylinder may be either a unit of Tokiko or of Nabco manufacture. Both are tandem piston (dual line) units. Cross-sections through these assemblies are shown in **FIGS 11:11** and **11:12**. A cross-section through a fluid level gauge is given in **FIG 11:13** and the components of a master cylinder (this illustration is relevant to both types) are shown in **FIG 11:14**.

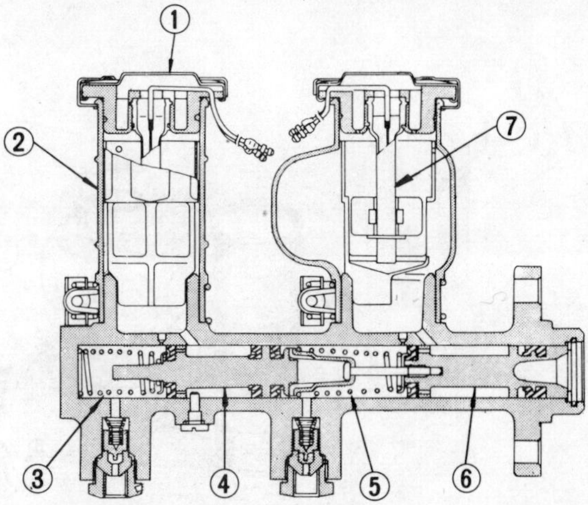

FIG 11:12 Cross-section through a Nabco master cylinder

Key to Fig 11:12 1 Reservoir cap 2 Reservoir 3 Secondary piston return spring 4 Secondary piston 5 Primary piston return spring 6 Primary piston 7 Fluid level gauge

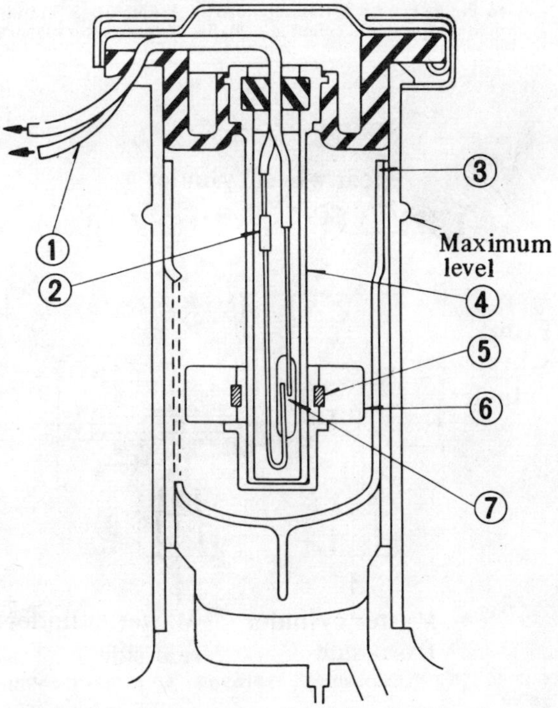

FIG 11:13 Cross-section through a fluid level gauge

Key to Fig 11:13 1 Wiring 2 Resistor 3 Filter 4 Case 5 Magnet 6 Float 7 Switch contacts

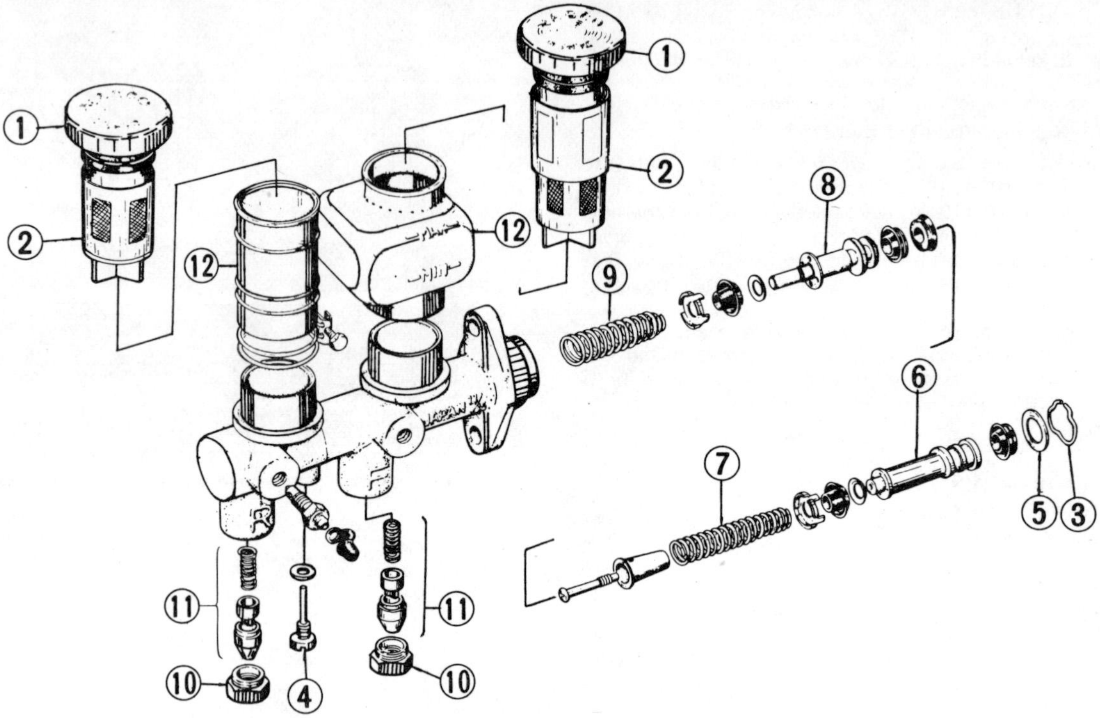

FIG 11:14 Components of a Nabco master cylinder

Key to Fig 11:14 1 Reservoir cap 2 Filter 3 Stop ring 4 Stop screw 5 Stop washer 6 Primary piston assembly 7 Primary piston return spring 8 Secondary piston assembly 9 Secondary piston return spring 10 Plug 11 Valve 12 Reservoir

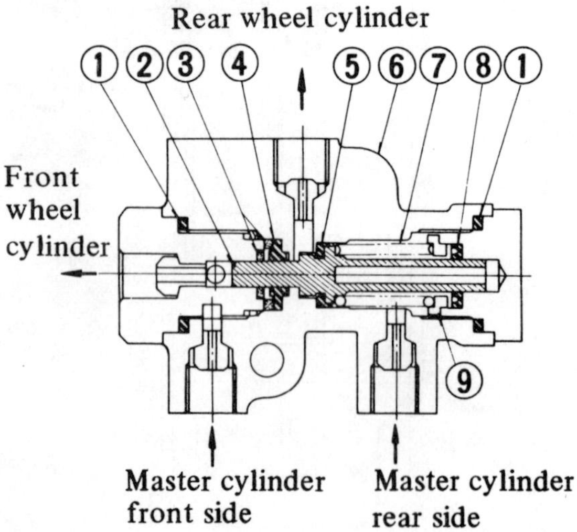

FIG 11:15 Cross-section through a proportioning valve

Key to Fig 11:15 1 'O' ring 2 Plunger 3 Ring 4 Seal 5 Seal 6 Valve body 7 Spring 8 Cup seal 9 Spring retainer

Vehicles fitted with disc brakes are provided with a proportioning valve which biases braking effort in favour of the front wheels. These models are also provided with vacuum servo assistance.

Observe scrupulous cleanliness when working on any part of the hydraulic system and use only fluid of reputable brand and to the approved specification.

Master cylinder removal and fitment:

The procedure differs between models having drum front brakes and those having disc front brakes.

Models with drum front brakes:

Remove the clevis pin which connects the master cylinder pushrod to the brake pedal. Uncouple both hydraulic pipes from the master cylinder and blank off all opened orifices to preclude entry of dirt. Remove the nuts and washers which attach the flange to the dash panel and dismount the master cylinder. The pushrod and the rubber boot may now be withdrawn.

Fitment is the reverse of this sequence. Check that the pushrod rubber boot is in good condition. Torque tighten the attachment nuts to 5.8 to 8 lb ft (.8 to 1 kgm) and the pipe connections to 11 to 13 lb ft (1.5 to 1.8 kgm). Adjust the pushrod free play as described later. Bleed the system as described in **Section 11:7**.

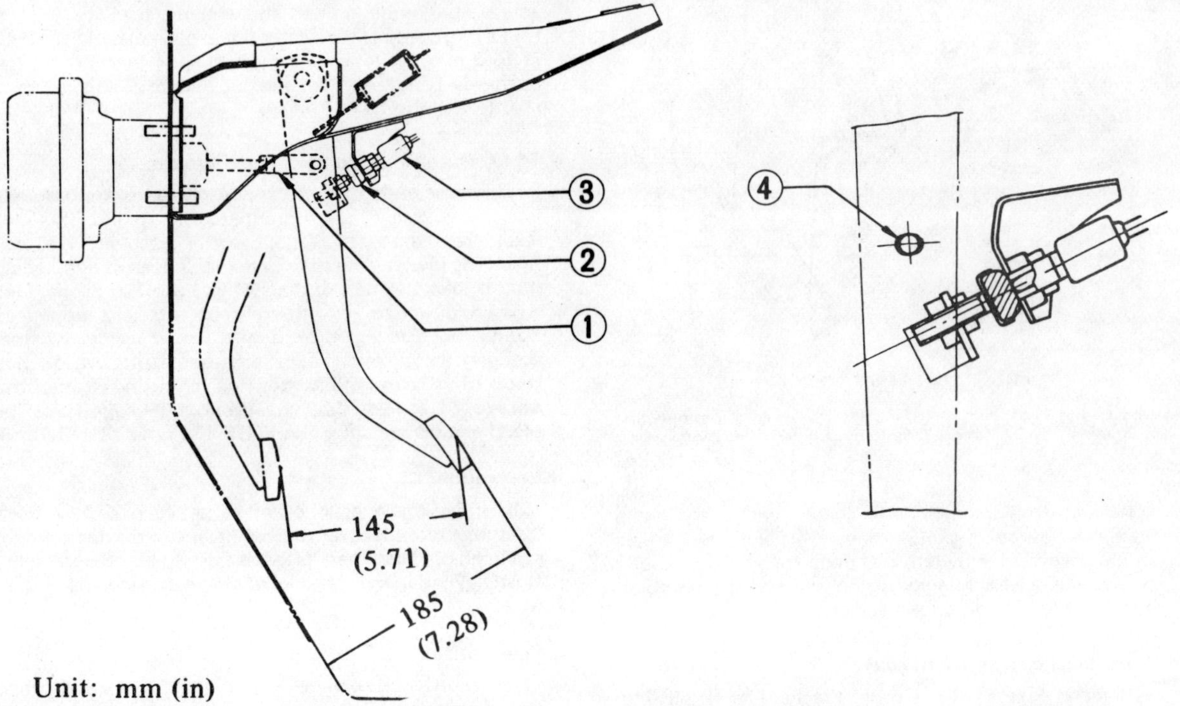

FIG 11:16 Brake pedal height setting

Key to Fig 11:16 1 Pushrod adjustment locknut 2 Stop 3 Switch 4 Clevis pin

Models with disc front brakes:

Disconnect the leads from the fluid level gauges. Uncouple both hydraulic pipes and blank off all opened orifices to preclude entry of dirt. Remove the nuts and washers which attach the flange to the vacuum servo unit and dismount the master cylinder.

Fitment is the reverse of this sequence but, before fitting the master cylinder to the servo unit, refer to **Section 11:9** and check that the pushrod protrusion is within limits. Torque tighten the attachment nuts and the pipe connections as for drum type brakes given earlier.

Servicing the master cylinder:

Remove the unit as described earlier and empty the fluid from the reservoirs. Refer to **FIG 11:14**. Pry out the stop ring and washer 3 and 5. Remove the stop screw 4. Withdraw the primary piston and return spring assembly and the secondary piston and return spring assembly. Remove the plugs 10 and withdraw the check valves 11. **Do not remove the reservoirs. Do not dismantle the fluid level gauges.** If a reservoir is damaged or if a fluid level gauge is defective obtain a replacement assembly. Use fresh brake fluid to clean the internal parts.

Discard valves and sealing cups even if they appear to be serviceable. Check piston diameters and the cylinder bore for wear, rust or corrosion. Piston to cylinder bore diametrical clearance should not exceed .006 inch (1.5 mm). Check return springs against the data given in the following tabulation in which dimensions are given in inches and lb with mm and kg equivalents in brackets.

	Primary		*Secondary*	
Return spring	*Tokiko*	*Nabco*	*Tokiko*	*Nabco*
Free length ..	2.165 (55.0)	**Do**	2.146 (54.5)	1.988 (50.5)
Fitted load ..	4.0 to 4.9 (1.8 to 2.2)	**not**	7.9 to 9.7 (3.6 to 4.4)	5.5 to 6.8 (2.5 to 3.1)
Fitted length ..	1.406 (35.7)	**dismantle**	1.358 (34.5)	1.303 (33.1)

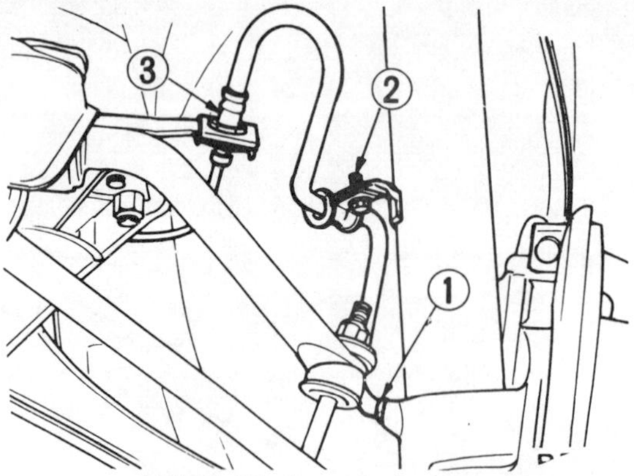

FIG 11:17 Front brake hose

Key to Fig 11:17 1 Flexible pipe to caliper connection 2 Bracket 3 Flexible pipe to rigid pipe connection

Assemble all internal parts wetted with fresh brake fluid. Use new sealing cups, new valves and new gaskets and, if necessary, new return springs (or, in the case of a Nabco unit, a new primary piston and spring assembly). Install the unit as described earlier.

Fluid level gauge (if fitted):

Refer to **FIG 11:13**. Should the fluid level fall until the float 6 reaches the stop (this condition is shown in the illustration), the magnet 5 closes the contacts of the switch 7 and the warning light will illuminate when the ignition is switched on.

A defective gauge cannot be repaired by an owner and should be replaced by a new unit.

Proportioning valve:

A cross-section through the valve is shown in **FIG 11:15**. At the mileage intervals recommended in **Section 11:2**, check the functional efficiency of the valve as follows.

Without passengers, drive on a dry concrete road at 30 mile/hr (50 km/hr). Apply the brakes hard. The front and rear wheels should lock simulataneously or the front wheels should lock before the rear wheels. If the rear wheels lock first, the valve is defective and should be replaced by a new unit.

Differential pressure warning light switch:

This unit, which operates if a pressure **difference** of 185 to 242 lb/sq inch (13 to 17 kg/sq cm) exists between the front and rear hydraulic systems, is fitted only to models exported to the USA or to Canada. A defective switch cannot be repaired by an owner and must be replaced by a new unit.

Brake pedal adjustments:

Refer to **FIG 11:16**. Adjust the brake light switch bolt until its end face is flush with the front face of the locknut. Torque tighten the locknut to 11 to 16 lb ft (1.6 to 2.2 kgm). Adjust the position of the pedal stop 2 until the specified pedal height of 7.28 inch (185 mm) is achieved. Torque tighten the locknut to 6 to 8 lb ft (.8 to 1 kg). Adjust the pushrod free play to .04 to .20 inch (1 to 5 mm) by loosening the locknut 1 and turning the pushrod. Torque tighten the locknut to 11 to 16 lb ft (1.6 to 2.2 kgm).

11:7 Bleeding the hydraulic system

This procedure, for which two operators are required, is only necessary if air has entered the system. This may result from the level of fluid in the reservoir(s) having fallen too low; because the system has been drained of old fluid or because part of the system has been dismantled. It is important to keep the relevant reservoir topped up during the bleeding procedure to avoid further air from entering the system. **Do not re-use fluid which has been bled from the system as it will have become aerated.** Use fresh fluid straight from the supply tin. The bleed screws are shown in **FIGS 11:1, 11:2** and **11:3**.

Sequence:

If only one-wheel cylinder or caliper has been disconnected, bleed at that point. If the master cylinder has been disconnected, bleed at the wheels nearest to the master cylinder. If the system has been drained, bleed at all wheels.

Procedure:

1 Position a ring spanner over the bleed screw and attach a length of rubber or plastic tube snugly over the bleed screw. Submerge the free end of the drain tube in a container which is partially filled with fluid. Loosen the bleed screw by approximately one turn.
2 Depress the brake pedal slowly through its full travel, close the bleed screw and slowly release the brake pedal. Repeat this procedure until air bubbles cease to issue from the drain tube through the fluid in the container.
3 Close the bleed screw, remove the drain tube and the spanner and repeat the procedure on any other wheel specified earlier under 'sequence'.

Draining the system:

Connect a drain tube to a bleed screw and lead it to a container. Open the bleed screw and pump' the brake pedal until no further fluid emerges from that bleed screw. Repeat this procedure at the remaining wheels.

11:8 Removing and fitting a flexible pipe

To avoid twisting, never attempt to remove a flexible pipe except by first disconnecting it from its rigid pipe and, where applicable, from its support bracket. As an example, refer to **FIG 11:17** and, to remove the flexible pipe, uncouple first at 3, then at 2 and finally remove the pipe from the caliper at 1.

Fitment is the reverse of this sequence. With the wheels in the straight-ahead position, fit the pipe to the caliper at 1 and torque tighten it to 11 to 13 lb ft (1.5 to 1.8 kgm). The installed angle at 2 should be 45 deg. Hold the fitting at 3 with a separate spanner while torque tightening the flexible pipe connection to 11 to 13 lb ft (1.5 to 1.8 kgm).

11:9 Vacuum servo unit

A cross-section through a vacuum servo unit is shown in **FIG 11:18**. Its connection with the engine intake manifold (via a check valve), its connection with the brake pedal and the mounting of the master cylinder on its forward face are shown in **FIG 11:19** together with a vacuum gauge test set up. The servo effort arises from the difference between atmospheric pressure acting upon the rear of the diaphragm and diaphragm plate 3 and 5 and the partial vacuum which is maintained in the front shell 18 by the depression in the engine intake manifold. When the brake pedal is depressed, a valve is opened and admits air at atmospheric pressure to the rear of the diaphragm via air silencer/filter 10. Differential pressure across the diaphragm forces it forward and added effort is applied to the master cylinder pistons through pushrod 2. When the brakes are released, the diaphragm is returned rearwards by spring 17.

Should the vacuum servo unit or the check valve be defective, should the pipe to the manifold leak or be disconnected, the master cylinder is operated directly by pushrods 11 and 12 and unassisted braking is available.

Checking for leaks:

Refer to **FIG 11:19**. Between the check valve 1 and the unit, fit a T-piece and a vacuum gauge 2. Run the engine until the gauge records a depression of 19.7 inch (500 mm) of Hg. If, fifteen seconds after stopping the engine, a depression drop of more than 1 inch (25 mm) of Hg has occurred, excessive air leakage is indicated. Leakage may result from a defective check valve, a leaking pushrod seal, valve body seal, valve plunger seat, a defective pipe or pipe connection.

Removing and fitting the servo unit:

Dismount the master cylinder as described in **Section 11:6**. Remove the clevis pin which connects the rear pushrod to the brake pedal. From inside the car, remove the the four nuts and washers which attach the unit to the dash panel and dismount the unit.

Fitment is the reverse of this sequence and must be followed by bleeding the hydraulic system and setting the rear pushrod free play as described in **Section 11:7**. On completion of the installation, check the unit for air leaks as described earlier.

Dismantling the unit:

1 Refer to **FIG 11:18**. Remove the clevis and locknut from pushrod 11 and withdraw guard 9
2 Mark shells 4 and 18 so that they may be reassembled in their original relative position and, using wrench ST08080000, remove the rear shell assembly. Withdraw the diaphragm plate assembly, front shell assembly, diaphragm spring and front pushrod assembly.
3 Pry the retainer from the rear shell and withdraw the bearing and seal. Unless absolutely necessary, do not dismantle the seal assembly.
4 Detach the diaphragm from the groove in the plate. Using a screwdriver, carefully pry off the air silencer/filter retainer.
5 With the key hole facing downwards, remove the valve plunger stop key by gently pushing the rod 11 while

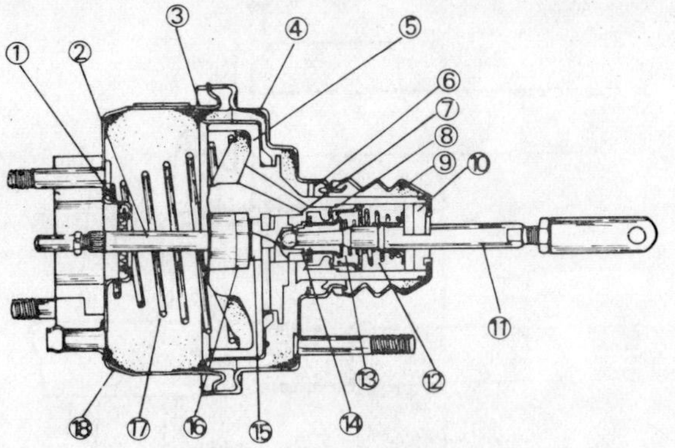

FIG 11:18 Vacuum servo unit

Key to Fig 11:18 1 Plate and seal 2 Forward pushrod 3 Diaphragm 4 Rear shell 5 Diaphragm plate 6 Seal 7 Valve 8 Poppet assembly 9 Valve body guard 10 Air silencer/filter 11 Rear pushrod (valve operating rod) 12 Valve return spring 13 Poppet return spring 14 Exhaust valve 15 Valve plunger 16 Reaction disc 17 Diaphragm return spring 18 Front shell

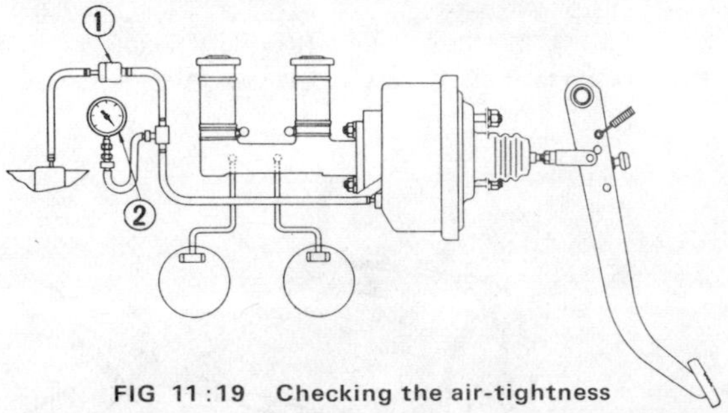

FIG 11:19 Checking the air-tightness

Key to Fig 11:19 1 Check valve 2 Vacuum gauge

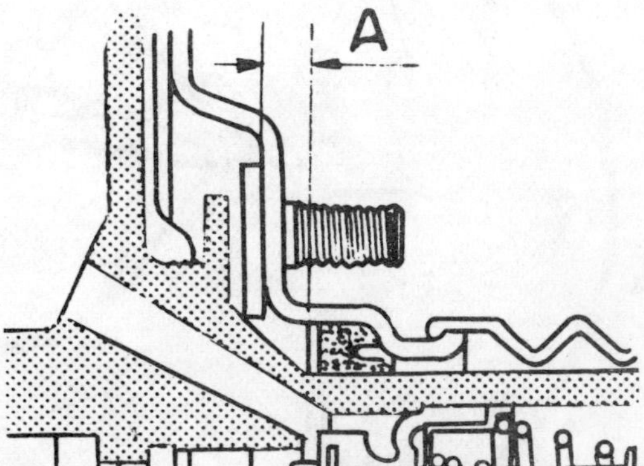

FIG 11:20 Seal installation

Key to Fig 11:20 **A** .264 to .276 inch (6.7 to 7.0 mm)

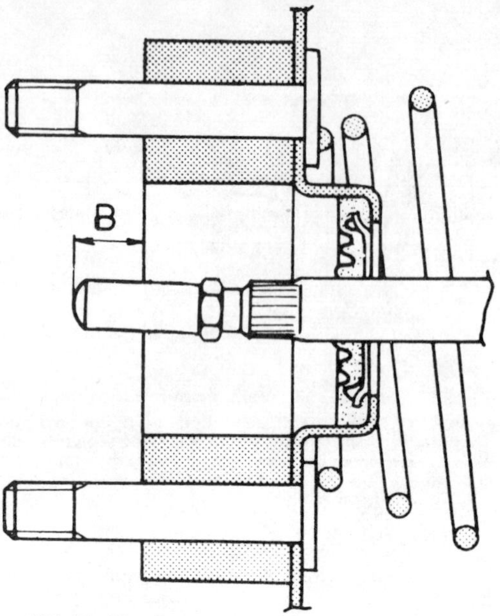

FIG 11:21 **Protrusion of forward pushrod**

Key to Fig 11:21 B .384 to .394 inch (9.75 to 10.0 mm)

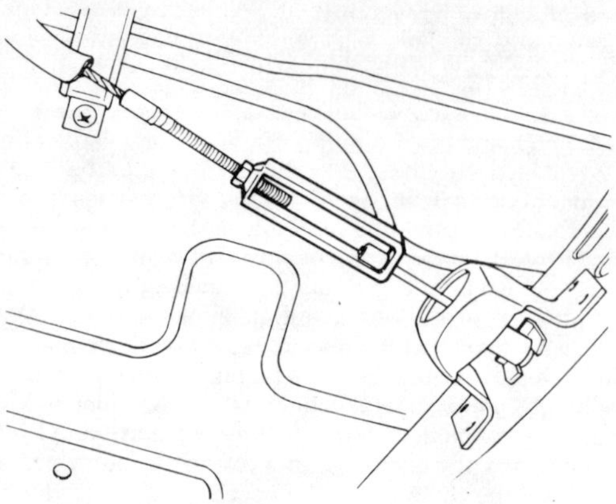

FIG 11:23 **Handbrake rear cable adjuster**

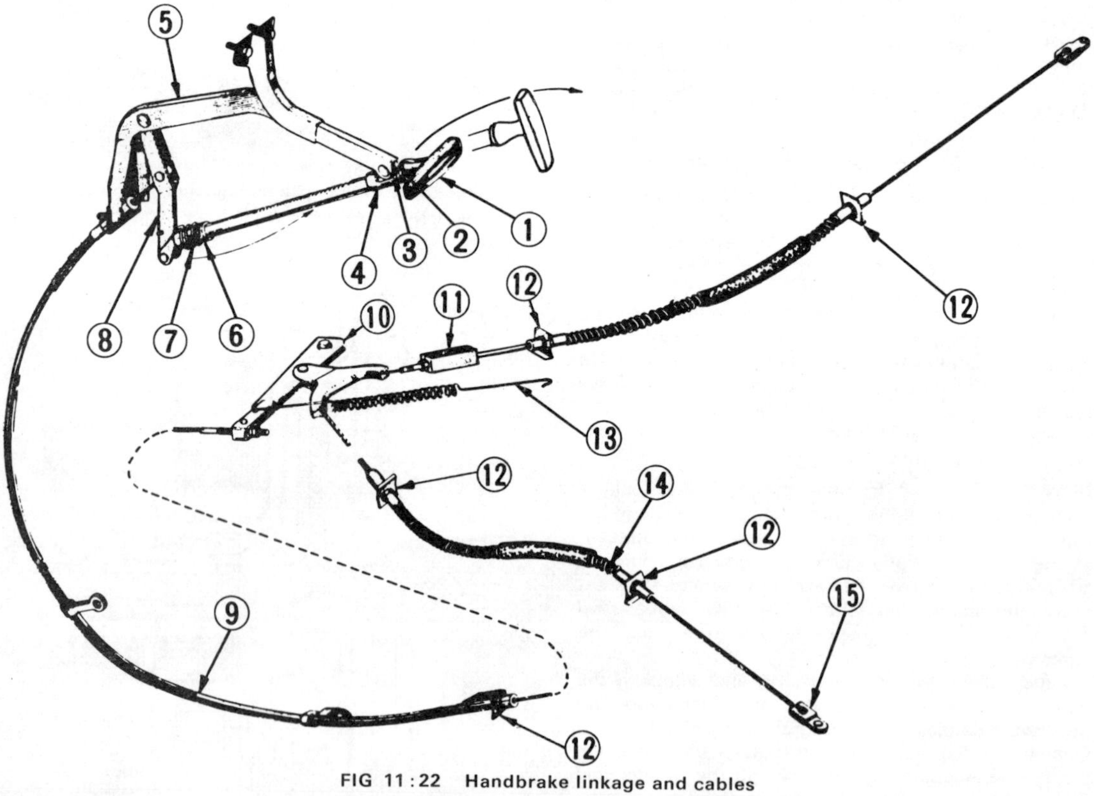

FIG 11:22 **Handbrake linkage and cables**

Key to Fig 11:22 1 Handbrake control 2 Ratchet spring 3 Ratchet 4 Guide 5 Bracket 6 Yoke 7 Spring 8 Lever 9 Front cable 10 Centre lever 11 Rear cable adjuster 12 Cable lock plate 13 Return spring 14 Rear cable 15 Clevis simultaneously vibrating it. Withdraw the silencer/filter and plunger assembly. Withdraw the reaction disc 16. Detach the flange from the front shell and withdraw the front seal assembly 1.

Inspection:

Discard the seals even if they appear serviceable. Check the diaphragm carefully and, if there is any indication of cracking, hardening or perishing, obtain a replacement. Check the bakelite diaphragm plate for damage or cracks. Check other parts for wear or damage and, in particular, check the poppet assembly and valve operating rod assembly (rear pushrod). Renew parts or assemblies as necessary.

Assembling the unit:

Assembly is the reverse of the dismantling sequence. Apply Master-Vac grease to the sealing surfaces and lips of the seals. Use drift ST08060000 to fit the seal 6 to the rear shell and ensure that the pawl of the tool aligns with the seal hole. Refer to **FIG 11:20**. Dimension **A** must be within .264 to .276 inch (6.7 to 7.0 mm). Apply a thin coating of mica powder to the diaphragm before fitting it to the plate but keep the powder off the outer diameter and seating portion with which the shell comes in contact. Apply grease sparingly to the sliding contact diameters of the plunger assembly, the reaction disc, pushrod and sliding portion of the diaphragm plate. Observe the shell alignment marks made earlier and, finally, refer to **FIG 11:21** and set dimension **B** to .384 to .394 inch (9.75 to 10.0 mm).

11:10 Handbrake

The handbrake linkage and cables are shown in **FIG 11:22**. The handbrake operates only on the rear drums. A single front cable 9, which is actuated by the handbrake control 1, pulls on one end of the central lever 10 and operates the balanced rear cable through an equalizer yoke. The contacts of a brake applied warning light are closed when the handbrake control is operated. This illuminates the same light in the instrument panel as the brake fluid level or the brake differential pressure warning. The rear cable is adjusted at 11; the front cable is adjusted at the centre lever 10.

Adjustment:

1 Adjust the rear brake shoes as described in **Section 11:4**.
2 Refer to **FIG 11:23**. With the wheels chocked and the handbrake released, loosen the rear cable adjuster locknut and, by turning the turnbuckle, take up all the slack in the rear cable. Ensure, however, that neither backplate lever (6 in **FIG 11:3**) has been pulled away from the brakes fully released position. Tighten the locknut.
3 Refer to **FIG 11:24**. Loosen the locknut and adjust the front cable by means of nut 1 so that, when the handbrake control is pulled by a force of 44 lb (20 kg), the stoke of the control is 3.5 to 4 inch (90 to 100 mm). Tighten the locknut.
4 Confirm that when the handbrake is released both backplate levers return to the brakes fully released position and that there is no brake shoe drag.

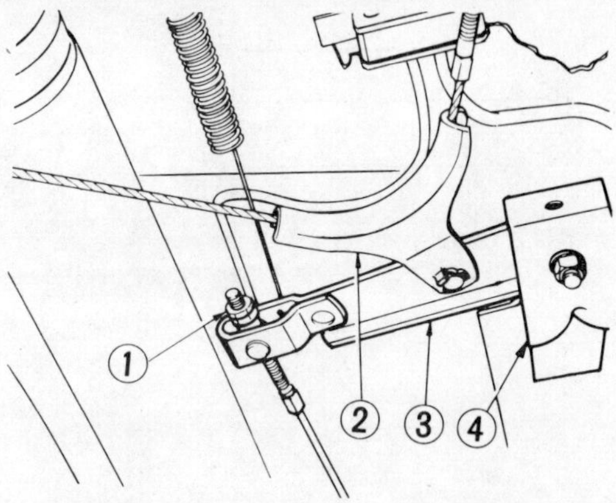

FIG 11:24 Handbrake front cable adjuster

Key to Fig 11:24 1 Cable adjuster 2 Equalizer yoke 3 Centre lever 4 Bracket

11:11 Fault diagnosis

(a) 'Spongy' pedal

1 Leak in hydraulic system
2 Worn master cylinder
3 Defective master cylinder sealing cups
4 Defective wheel cylinder or caliper seals
5 Air in hydraulic system

(b) Excessive pedal movement

1 Check 1 and 5 in (a)
2 Brake shoes require adjustment
3 Excessive shoe or pad friction lining wear
4 Very low fluid level in reservoir(s)

(c) Brakes grab or pull to one side

1 Distorted drum or disc
2 Contaminated shoe or pad friction lining
3 Loose caliper unit
4 Loose disc
5 Uneven tyre pressures
6 Seized piston in wheel or caliper cylinder
7 Blocked flexible or rigid pipe
8 Seized handbrake cable or linkage pivot
9 Broken pull-off spring

(d) Absence of servo assistance

1 Air silencer/filter blocked
2 Vacuum pipe blocked or fractured
3 Check valve defective
4 Servo unit defective

(e) Only front or rear brakes operate

1 One reservoir empty
2 One section of master defective
3 Pipeline(s) to front or rear brakes blocked or fractured

(f) Rear brakes lock before front brakes

1 Check front section of (e)
2 Defective proportioning valve

NOTES

CHAPTER 12

THE ELECTRICAL EQUIPMENT

12:1 Description
12:2 Battery
12:3 The starter motor
12:4 The alternator
12:5 The alternator regulator
12:6 Windscreen wiper and washer
12:7 Headlamps
12:8 Lighting circuits and flasher units
12:9 Fuses and fusible links
12:10 Instruments
12:11 Horns
12:12 Fault diagnosis

12:1 Description

All models covered by this manual have 12-volt electrical systems in which the negative battery terminal is earthed. A wiring diagram is included in the Technical Data section of the Appendix.

The battery is housed in the engine compartment. The fuse block is located beneath the instrument panel and fusible links, which protect the starting, ignition, charging and headlamp circuits are incorporated in the wiring.

The starter motor incorporates positive engagement of the drive pinion. The starter switch, which is part of the ignition switch, operates a relay which is integral with the starter motor assembly.

The generator is belt driven from the crankshaft by the same belt that drives the cooling fan and the water pump. It is a 3-phase AC machine with an air-cooled transistorized rectifier. An electro-mechanical voltage regulator controls the charging circuit and a 'no charge' warning light is provided.

Although instructions for servicing of electrical equipment are given in this Chapter, it must be accepted that it is not sensible to attempt repairs to units which are seriously defective, electrically or mechanically. Such defective equipment should be replaced by new units obtained on an exchange basis. The testing and adjustment of certain equipment requires specialist services and facilities.

12:2 The battery

The negative terminal is earthed. **Do not, under any circumstance, reverse the terminal connections.** The cables must be tight in their terminals and the terminals must be tight on the battery posts. A light coating of non-metalic grease should be applied to the terminals and posts to retard corrosion and oxidation. If the terminals and posts are corroded, remove the terminals and wash them in a solution of bicarbonate of soda. Dry them thoroughly, apply non-metalic grease and fit the terminals tightly.

Keep the fluid in each cell up to the level of the ring in the bottom of the filler well by adding distilled water.

Never add undiluted acid. If it is necessary to prepare a new solution of electrolyte due to spillage or loss, add the sulphuric acid to the distilled water. It is highly dangerous to add water to acid.

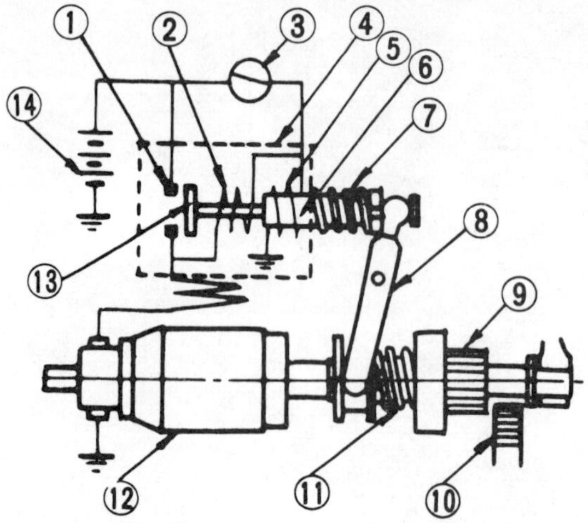

FIG 12:1 Starter motor circuit

Key to Fig 12:1 1 Stationary contacts 2 Series coil 3 Ignition switch 4 Solenoid 5 Shunt coil 6 Plunger 7 Spring 8 Lever 9 Starter pinion 10 Flywheel ring gear 11 Spring 12 Armature 13 Moving contact 14 Battery

If the charge state of the battery is suspect, test the electrolyte with a hydrometer. The indications from the specific gravity readings given by the hydrometer are, at 68°F (20°C), approximately as follows:

Cells fully charged	Specific gravity 1.240 to 1.260
Cells half charged	Specific gravity 1.170 to 1.190
Cells discharged	Specific gravity 1.100 to 1.120

For the same cell condition, specific gravity will increase when the electrolyte temperature is less than 68°F and vice versa. Add .002 for every 5°F (3°C) below 68°F and subtract .002 for every 5°F (3°C) above 68°F.

If the state of the battery is low, take the car for a long daylight run or put the battery on charge at 5 amp. If this does not correct the battery charge state, have the individual cells voltage tested to ascertain whether the battery should be replaced by a new one.

If the battery is to stand for a long period, give it a freshening-up charge every month. If it is left discharged, it will deteriorate and be ruined.

12:3 The starter motor

The starter motor circuit is shown in **FIG 12:1**. The solenoid has a series and a shunt coil. When the starter switch is operated, both coils are energized and move the solenoid plunger which, through lever 8, engages the pinion 9 with the flywheel ring gear 10. At the end of the plunger travel, moving contact 13 closes the stationary contacts 1 and (a) operates the motor and (b) short circuits the series coil 2. The shunt coil 5 holds the engaged position of the plunger. It will be noted that the motor cannot begin to turn the engine until the pinion gear is fully engaged. When the engine starts, the flywheel is precluded from driving the motor by the over-run clutch. When the starter switch is opened, the solenoid is no longer energized, the spring 7 returns the plunger to the initial position and the pinion is disengaged from the flywheel ring gear.

Tests for a starter which does not operate:

Check the condition of the battery and its connections. If these are in order, switch on the lights and operate the starter switch. Current is reaching the starter if the lights go dim. If the lights do not dim, check with a voltmeter or test light if there is voltage at the solenoid when the switch is operated. If there is, suspect a defective solenoid. If there is not, suspect the ignition switch or the wiring continuity. If these and the solenoid are in order, check the brush gear as described later.

Starter removal and installation:

Disconnect both battery cables. Identify and disconnect the wiring from the solenoid. Remove the two bolts which retain the motor to the clutch/flywheel housing, pull the motor forwards and dismount it.

Installation is the reverse of this sequence.

Dismantling the starter:

1 Remove the starter as described earlier. Refer to **FIG 12:2**. Loosen the nut which secures the solenoid 6 to the **M** terminal. Remove three screws and dismount the solenoid.
2 Remove the two through-bolts 24 and take off the bush cover. Disengage the brush springs and withdraw the brushes from the brush holders.
3 Using a soft hammer, remove yoke 17 and withdraw the armature and the engagement lever.
4 Push the pinion stop 13 towards the over-run clutch 15 and remove clip ring 12. Remove the pinion stop. Withdraw the over-run clutch assembly from the armature shaft.
5 If necessary, unsolder the brush leads and remove the brushes.

Cleaning and inspecting:

Use a brush to clean dust from the field coils, armature, casings and brush holder assembly. Do not use solvent to clean the over-run clutch assembly as it is prepacked with grease. Check the insulation of the brush holders. Check the brushes and their springs against the information given later. Check the armature and field coils for open circuit and for insulation. Armature shaft bend must not exceed .003 inch (.08 mm). Polish the commutator with very fine (00 or 000 grade) sandpaper. Check the ovality of the commutator. This must not exceed .008 inch (.2 mm). Skim a badly worn commutator in a lathe. Use a high speed and take light cuts with a sharp tool. Remove the minimum amount to clean up (a refinished diameter of 1.299 inch (33 mm) is a minimum) and undercut the mica insulation by .02 to .03 inch (.5 to .8 mm).

The clearance between the bushes 9 and 22 and the armature shaft should not exceed .008 inch (.2 mm). If necessary, fit new bushes and ream to give a diametrical clearance of .0012 to .004 inch (.03 to .1 mm). Check the over-run clutch. There must be neither slip in the drive direction nor drag in the opposite direction. Renew the assembly if it is defective. Check that the pinion teeth are in good order and that the sleeve can slide freely along the armature shaft splines. Renew if excessively worn or damaged.

If the solenoid was suspect, check the coils by connecting a 12-volt battery across the **S** and **M** terminals.

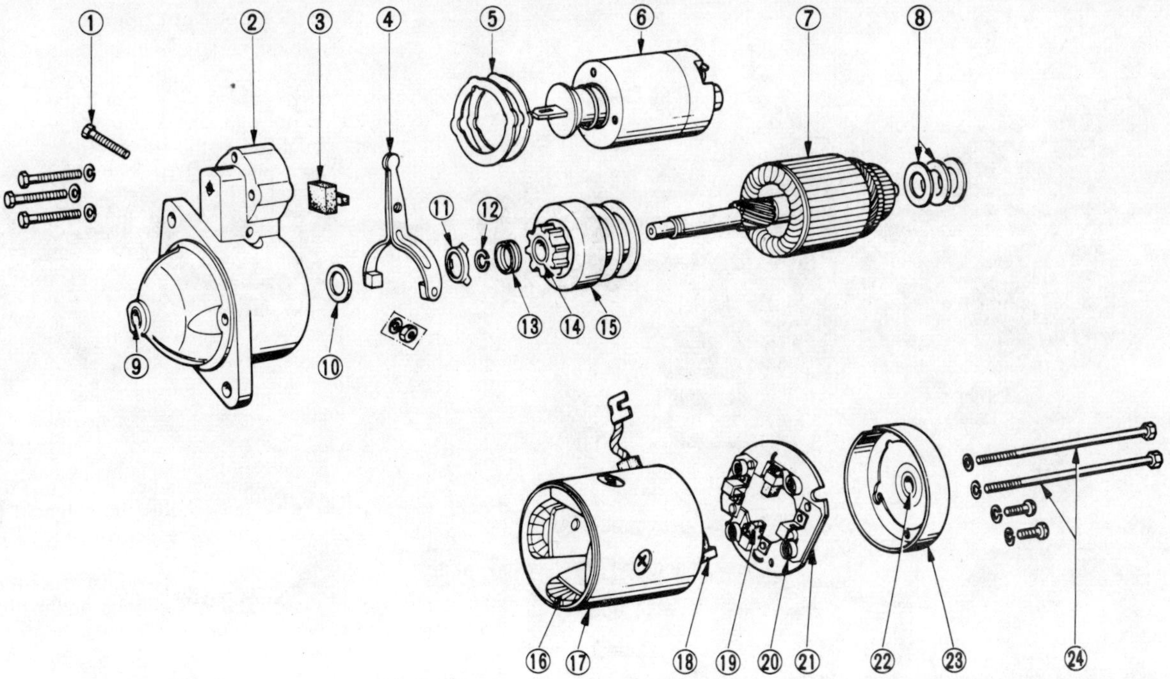

FIG 12:2 Components of the starter motor

Key to Fig 12:2 1 Lever pin 2 End housing 3 Dust cover 4 Lever 5 Gasket 6 Solenoid assembly 7 Armature 8 Thrust washer 9 Bush 10 Thrust washer 11 Stop washer 12 Clip ring 13 Pinion stop 14 Pinion 15 Over-run clutch 16 Field coil 17 Yoke 18 Brush (+) 19 Brush (—) 20 Brush spring 21 Brush holder assembly 22 Bush 23 Cover 24 Through-bolt

The series coil is normal if the solenoid plunger operates. Repeat this test with the **M** terminal earthed to the solenoid body. With the plunger operating, disconnect from the **M** terminal. The shunt coil is normal if the plunger continues to operate. Reference to **FIG 12:1** will clarify these test connections.

Starter assembly:

This is the reverse of the dismantling sequence. Apply grease sparingly to the armature shaft splines and to the lever pivot. Apply a little oil to the bearings and pinion.

On completion of the assembly, check the pinion to pinion stop operational clearance by connecting a 12-volt battery and switch across terminals **M** and **S** with the battery positive (+) connected to the **S** terminal. Close the switch and, as shown in **FIG 12:3**, measure the gap between the front of the pinion and the pinion stop. This gap should be within the range of .0118 to .0591 inch (.3 to 1.5 mm).

Brush gear:

Failure of the starter to operate can be due to worn or sticking brushes. Access to the brushes requires removal of the rear cover 23 in **FIG 12:2**. Relieve any sluggishness by polishing the sides of the brushes with a smooth file. Renew brushes when worn down to .236 inch (6 mm) and confirm that the new brushes move freely in the brush holders. Check each brush spring load. This should be approximately 3.5 lb (1.6 kg).

12:4 The alternator

The components of the alternator are shown in **FIG 12:4**. It is an AC machine and is belt driven together with the cooling fan and water pump from a pulley on the crankshaft. The stationary 3-phase output coils 6 are connected to the intergral six diode rectifier 9. The field coils are wound on the rotor 4 and are connected to two slip rings on which brushes 8 run. A cooling fan is incorporated with the drive pulley.

Brushes must be renewed when they have worn down to the limiting lines shown in **FIG 12:5**. The procedure is described later.

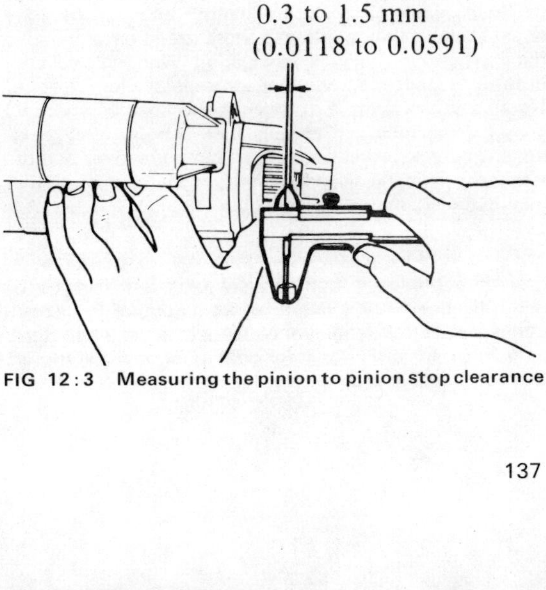

FIG 12:3 Measuring the pinion to pinion stop clearance

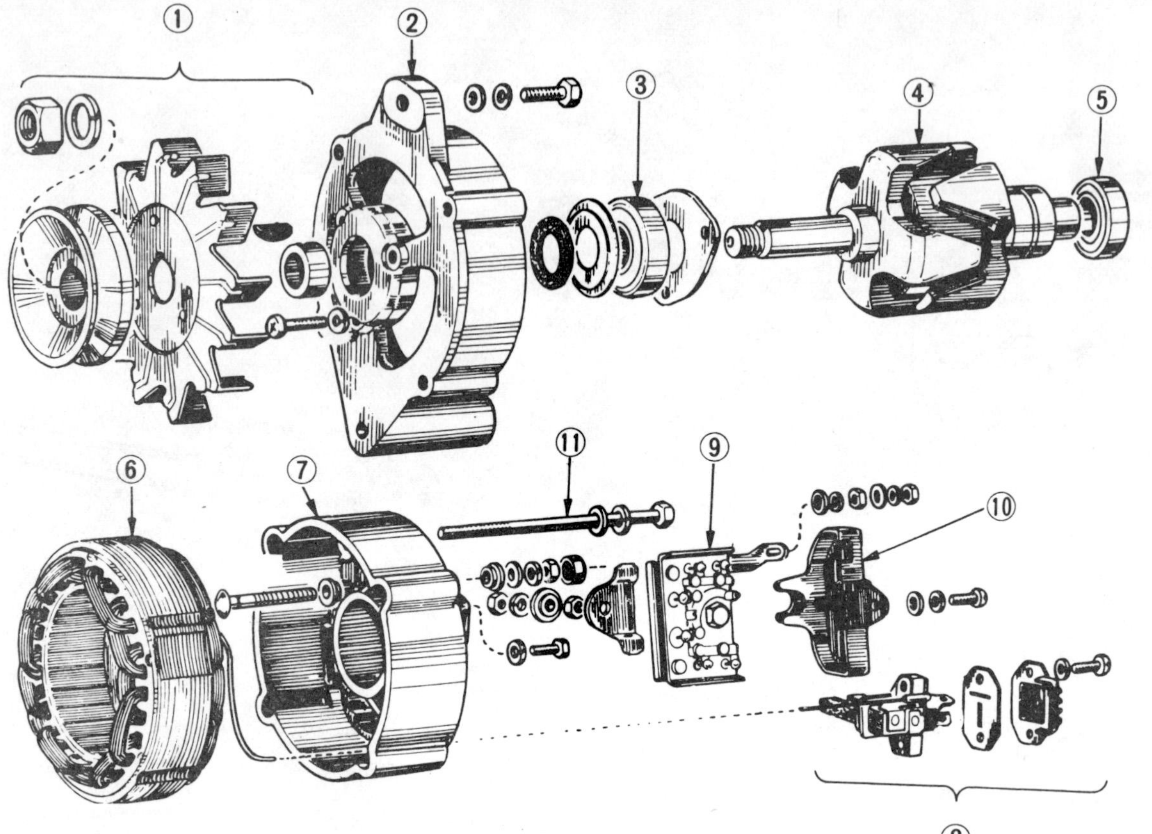

FIG 12:4 Components of the alternator

Key to Fig 12:4 1 Drive pulley assembly 2 Front cover 3 Front bearing 4 Rotor 5 Rear bearing 6 Stator 7 Rear cover 8 Brush assembly 9 Rectifier assembly 10 Cover 11 Through-bolt

Tests on an alternator which is not charging:

During normal driving, if the ignition (no charge) warning light does not go out, investigate the reason why the alternator is not charging. Check that the connections to the battery, alternator and regulator are intact and firm. Check that the belt drive is intact and, as described later, that it is correctly tensioned. Check that the brushes are of serviceable length and that they are not sticking in their holders. If these are in order, remove the alternator for further investigation. With the alternator dismounted, apply an ohmeter across lead wire **F** (white/black) and lead wire **E** (black). If the brushes and field coils are satisfactory, the resistance should be approximately 5 ohms. If there is an open circuit reading or if the resistance is markedly different from that specified, dismantle the alternator for inspection.

Output check:

If the regulator is correctly set (see **Section 12:5**) and if the alternator is charging but its output is suspect, connect a 30-volt range voltmeter across the alternator **E** and **A** terminals. Full battery voltage should be shown. Do not proceed with this test if the battery is not fully charged. With the battery fully charged, switch on the headlights (main beam) and start the engine. Run the engine at approximately 1100 rev/min (do not exceed this speed) and note the voltmeter reading. If the reading is less than 12.5 volts, remove the alternator for inspection.

Alternator removal and fitment:

Disconnect the battery earth lead. Identify and disconnect the wiring from the alternator. Remove the drive belt as described later. Remove the attachment bolts and dismount the alternator.

Fitment is the reverse of this sequence. Fitting and tensioning the drive belt is described later.

Drive belt removal, fitment and tensioning:

Loosen the adjuster bolt which secures the top of the alternator to the adjuster strap quadrant. Loosen the bolts which attach the alternator to the engine. Swing the alternator body towards the engine, disengage the drive belt from the alternator pulley, the fan pulley and the crankshaft pulley.

Fitment of a new belt is the reverse of this sequence.

Tension the belt by swinging the alternator away from the engine and while holding it so, tighten the adjuster bolt and the two attaching bolts. The belt is correctly tensioned when it can be depressed by .3 to .5 inch (8 to 12 mm) midway between the fan and alternator pulleys by a force of 22 lb (10 kg).

Brush gear:

The brushes and brush holder are shown in **FIG 12:5** (see also 8 in **FIG 12:4**). Remove the retaining screws and dismount the cover. Remove the brush holder complete with the brushes. Brushes should be discarded when they have worn down to the limiting lines (see **FIG 12:5**). Brushes of serviceable length which do not move freely in their holders should be eased by polishing their sides on a smooth file. Check that new brushes move freely in the holders and, if necessary, ease them.

With a brush projecting .08 inch (2 mm) from the holder, the spring load should be 9 to 12 oz (.25 to .35 kg) for a new spring. As the brush wears, spring load decreases by approximately $\frac{3}{4}$ oz per .04 inch (20 gr per mm) of brush wear.

Dismantling the alternator:

1 Remove the alternator as described earlier. Refer to **FIG 12:4**. Remove the retaining nut, pulley, fan and spacer. Remove the brush gear as described earlier.
2 Remove the through-bolts 11 and separate the rear cover 7 from the front cover 2 by tapping the front cover bracket with a soft hammer.
3 Remove the screws which secure the retainer of bearing 3 to the front cover and withdraw rotor 4.
4 Remove the diode cover (6 in **FIG 12:6**) retaining screw and dismount the cover. Disconnect the three stator coil connecting wires from the diode terminals. A soldering iron is required for this operation.
5 Remove the **A** terminal nut (see 5 in **FIG 12:6**) and diode assembly nut and, using the minimum of force, dismount the diode assembly.

Inspection:

Renew the bearings if necessary. At normal ambient temperature the resistance measured slip ring to slip ring should be approximately 4.4 ohms. Check the rotor insulation from the core to each slip ring. Check the insulation of the stator from the core to each of the four leads. Diodes may be individually tested by checking that current will only flow in the relevant direction (see **FIG 12:7**). An individual diode cannot be renewed however and, should there be a diode failure, the diode assembly must be renewed.

Assembling the alternator:

This is the reverse of the dismantling sequence. When soldering the leads to the diode assembly, work quickly and, to protect the diodes from the conducted heat, use an appropriate 'heat sink'. Ensure that the insulation bushing and tube (see **FIG 12:6**) are fitted when installing the diode terminal **A**. Torque tighten the pulley retaining nut to 25 to 28.5 lb ft (3.0 to 3.44 kgm).

Testing an alternator requires a variable speed drive test bench, specialist facilities and special equipment.

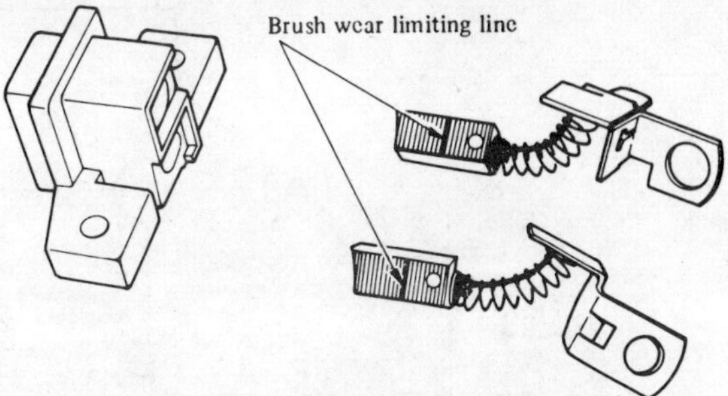

FIG 12:5 Alternator brush wear

12:5 The alternator regulator

The circuit of the regulator is included in **FIG 12:7** and shows the moving contact P5 in the 'no charge' position and closed with the P4 contact. The ignition warning light is illuminated. As the alternator speed increases, current excites the VC1 coil and the P5 contact moves over and closes with the P6 contact. The warning light will then no longer be illuminated. When the voltage rises excessively, moveable contact P2 closes with contact P3 and resistance R1 comes into circuit and reduces the field excitation current. P2 makes and breaks with P1 and P3 and by shorting and unshorting R1, maintains a substantially constant output voltage. An ambient temperature compensator is incorporated. This prevents under-charge in winter and overcharge in summer.

Regulating voltage measurement:

Refer to **FIG 12:8** and install a resistance, an ammeter and a voltmeter as shown. The regulator must be mounted in its normal position; the resistance must have a value of .25 ohms; the ammeter must have a capacity of 10 amp; the voltmeter must have a range of 30 volt. **All electrical load** (lights, heater blower motor, radio etc.)

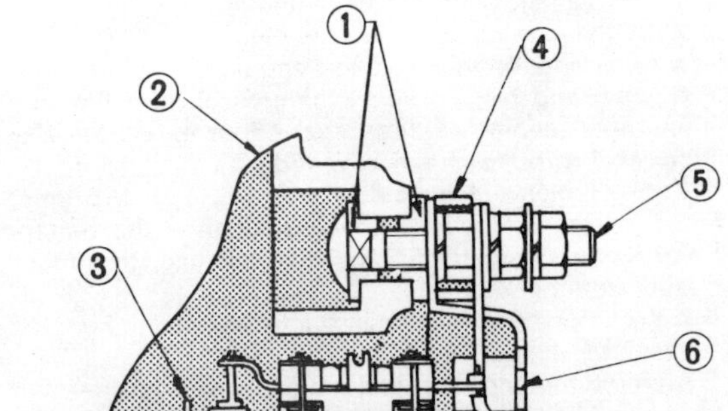

FIG 12:6 Alternator rectifier

Key to Fig 12:6 1 Insulating bushes 2 Rear cover 3 Rectifier (diode) assembly 4 Insulating tube 5 **A** Terminal bolt 6 Cover

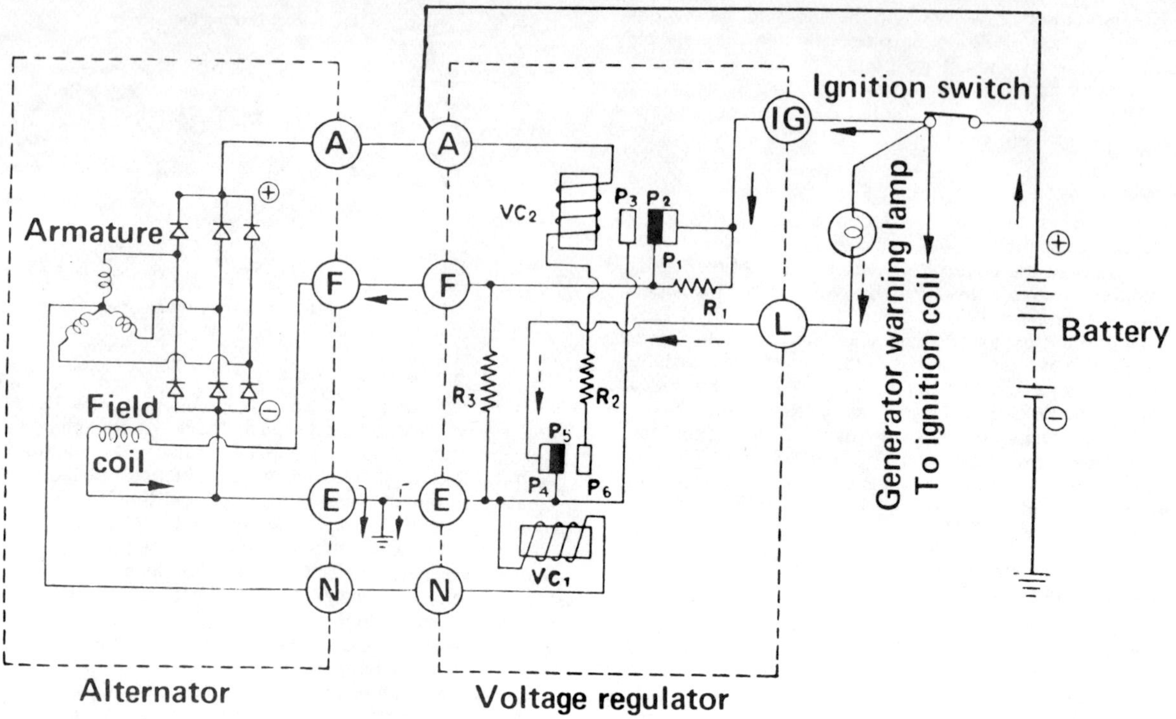

FIG 12:7 Alternator and regulator circuit

except the ignition must be switched off. Fit a tachometer to the engine if one is not already installed. A thermometer must be available to measure the ambient temperature near the regulator. Carry out the measurement when the regulator is cold and not immediately after a run. Proceed then as follows:

1 Short circuit the ammeter and resistance (dotted line in **FIG 12:8**). Start up the engine.

2 With the engine running, remove the short circuit wire. Gradually increase the engine speed to 2500 rev/min and run for some minutes. Ensure that the ammeter reading **is less than 5 amp when the several minutes have elapsed.**

3 If the ammeter reading does not drop below 5 amp, the battery is not fully charged. Change the battery for a fully charged one and recommence the procedure from operation 1.

4 If the amperage is less than 5 amp, reduce the engine speed to idling.

5 Increase the engine speed gradually to 2500 rev/min and read the voltage and the ambient temperature near the regulator. Compare the readings with the following tabulation and, if necessary, adjust the voltage as described later.

Ambient temperature		*Regulator voltage*
—10°C	(14°F)	14.75 to 15.25
0°C	(32°F)	14.60 to 15.10
10°C	(50°F)	14.45 to 14.95
20°C	(68°F)	14.30 to 14.80
30°C	(86°F)	14.15 to 14.65
40°C	(104°F)	14.00 to 14.50

A regulator which does not respond to adjustment should be passed to a specialist for repair or a replacement unit fitted.

Core gaps and points gaps adjustment:

Check that the core gap surfaces are clean and smooth. Check that the points are in good condition.

Measure the core gaps and adjust if necessary. **FIG 12:9** shows the voltage regulator core gap being adjusted. This gap should be .024 to .040 inch (.6 to 1 mm) and that of the charge relay should be .032 to .040 inch (.8 to 1 mm). Measure the points gaps and adjust if necessary. **FIG 12:10** shows the voltage regulator points gap being adjusted. This gap should be .012 to .016 inch (.3 to .4 mm) and that of the charge relay should be .016 to .024 inch (.4 to .6 mm).

Voltage adjustment:

The regulator voltage is adjusted as shown in **FIG 12:11**. Loosen locknut 4. To increase the voltage, turn the screw 3 clockwise. To reduce the voltage, turn the adjusting screw 3 counterclockwise. Tighten the locknut and check that the voltage is within the specified range as tabulated earlier.

12:6 Windscreen wiper and washer

The layout of the windscreen wipers, the 2-speed wiper motor and the actuating linkage are shown in **FIG 12:12**. The wiper motor incorporates self-parking and the wiper motor circuit and washer motor circuit are shown in **FIG 12:13**.

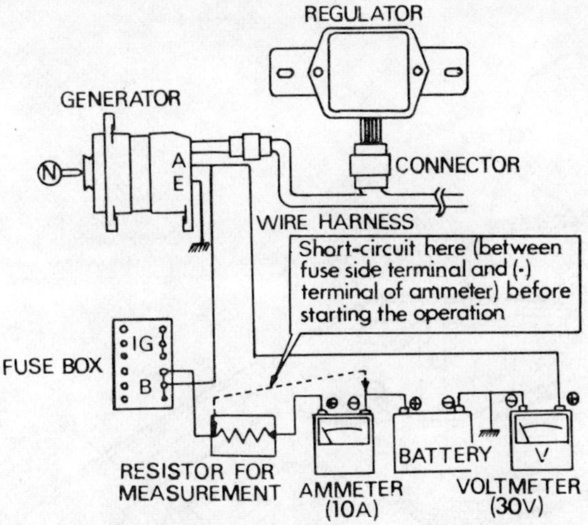

FIG 12:8 Regulator voltage measurement

Ensure that the fluid used to keep the washer tank (6 in **FIG 12:12**) filled **is absolutely free of grit and foreign matter**. Blockage of washer nozzles by dirt is the main reason for defective operation. If either the wiper motor or the washer motor fails to operate, check, by using jump wires, that the relevant switch is not at fault. If the switch is serviceable but there is no voltage at a motor, check the fuse and wiring continuity. If there is voltage at a motor but it fails to operate, fit an exchange replacement. No servicing or overhaul procedures are prescribed for wiper or washer motors.

Wiper motor removal and fitment:

1 Disconnect the wiring from the motor after identifying them. Remove the three bolts which attach the motor and collect the washers.
2 Remove the nut which connects the shaft of the motor to the wiper link and dismount the motor.

Installation of a wiper motor is the reverse of this sequence.

Washer unit removal and fitment:

Identify and disconnect the wiring from the unit. Uncouple the fluid piping, remove the attachment and dismount the unit.

Fitment is the reverse of this sequence.

12:7 Headlamps

Sealed beam unit renewal:

1 Refer to **FIG 12:14**. Remove the retaining screws and dismount the bezel. Remove the three retaining ring screws but **do not disturb the alignment screws**.
2 Remove the retaining ring 2 by turning it clockwise. Withdraw the sealed beam unit from the mounting ring 1 and withdraw the wiring connector.
3 Position the new sealed beam unit and ensure that the three location tabs register with the hollows in the mounting ring. Check that TOP is uppermost.
4 The remaining operations are the reverse of the removal operations.

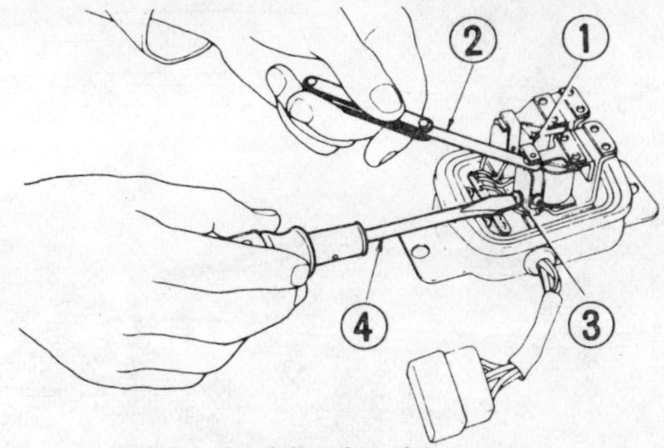

FIG 12:9 Adjusting the core gap

Key to Fig 12:9 1 Points 2 Feeler guage 3 4 mm diameter screw 4 Screwdriver

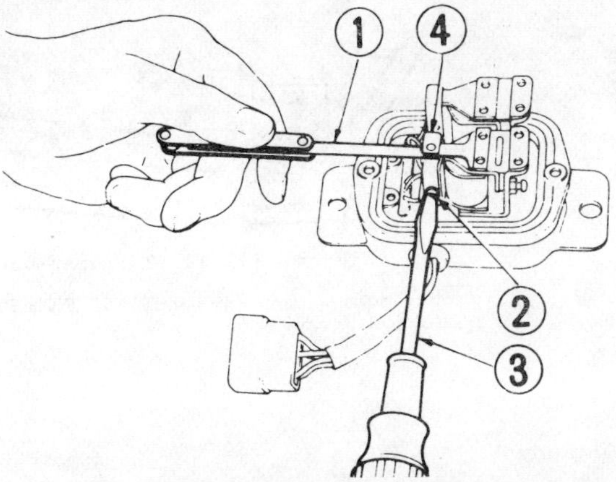

FIG 12:10 Adjusting the points gap

Key to Fig 12:10 1 Feeler gauge 2 3 mm diameter screw 3 Screwdriver 4 Points

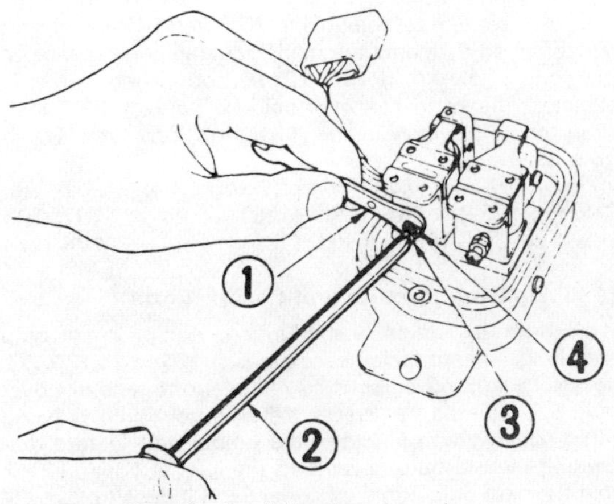

FIG 12:11 Adjusting the voltage

Key to Fig 12:11 1 Spanner 2 Screwdriver 3 Adjusting screw 4 Locknut

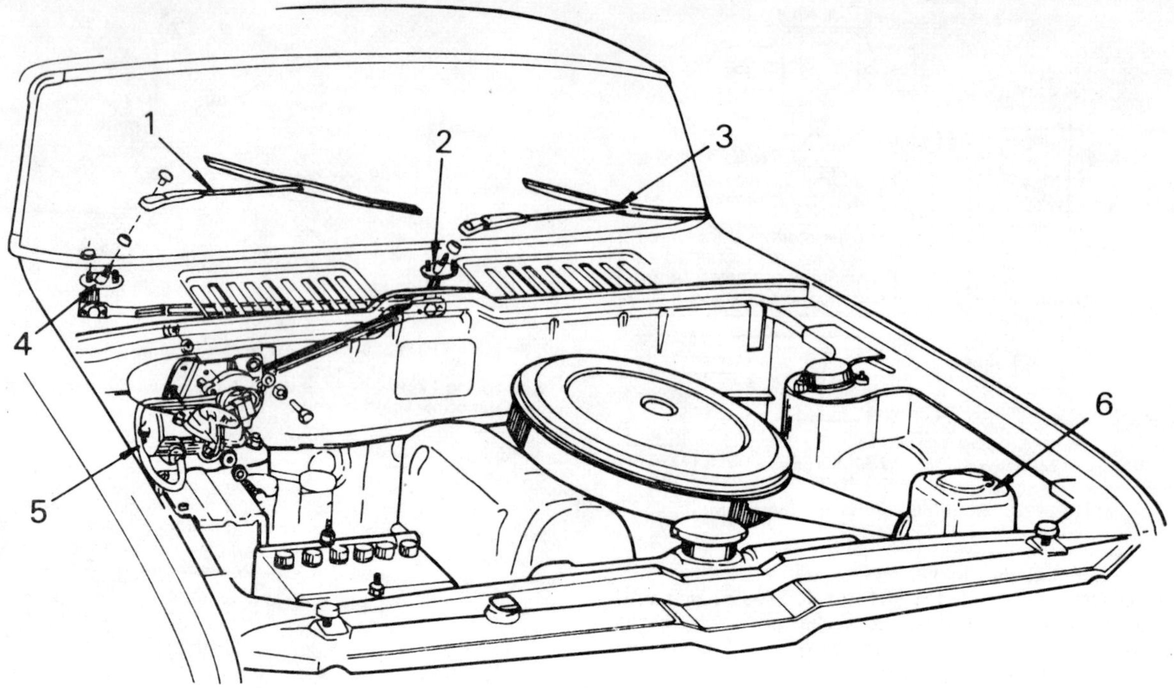

FIG 12:12 Wiper motor and linkage and washer unit

Key to Fig 12:12 1 Wiper arm (righthand) 2 Pivot (lefthand) 3 Wiper arm (lefthand) 4 Pivot (lefthand) 5 Wiper motor 6 Washer tank and motor unit

Alignment:

Professional facilities are required for complete and accurate alignment of the main and dipped beams but acceptable adjustments may be made by checking the main beam (undipped) alignment as follows.

With the tyres correctly inflated, the unladen vehicle should be positioned on level ground 33 ft (10 m) from a wall or a screen as shown in **FIG 12:15**. Vertical and horizontal adjustments are made separately by means of the screws shown in **FIG 12:16** and, when correctly adjusted, the main beams should be parallel, 32.7 inch (830 mm) (this is **W** in the illustration) apart and **H—h** from the ground.

	H inch (mm)	*h inch (mm)*	*A min*	*L ft (m)*
Saloon	25.8 (655)	5.0 (128)	44	167 (51)
Estate car	26.8 (680)	5.0 (128)	44	174 (53)

12:8 Lighting circuits and flasher units

With the exception of the luggage compartment bulb and the headlamp sealed beam units (see **Section 12:7**), access to lighting bulbs is by removal of a lens or cover which is retained by screws. When a new bulb is being fitted, clean the contacts in the holder and, before discarding the old bulb or refitting the lens or cover, check that the new bulb lights up correctly. If it does not, check the relevant fuse (see **Section 12:9** and **FIG 14:1** in the Appendix). If the fuse is in order, check the relevant switch and the wiring continuity.

Bulbs burn out frequently:

Suspect that the voltage regulator is out of adjustment or is defective. Check the regulator as described in **Section 12:5**.

Brilliance of lights varies with engine speed:

Check the condition of the battery connections, clean the battery terminal posts, renew defective cables, ensure that they fit tightly on the terminal posts and make sure that the battery earth connection is making good contact.

Confirm that the alternator drive belt is in good condition and that it is correctly tensioned as described in **Section 12:4**.

Flasher units:

The wiring circuits of the direction indicator flasher unit and the hazard warning flasher unit are included in **FIG 14:1** in the Appendix. Note that each flasher unit is protected by a different fuse. Before suspecting that a flasher unit has become defective, check that the bulbs are serviceable, that the relevant fuse is intact, that the switch is operative and that there is no disconnection in the wiring continuity. Flasher units cannot be repaired by an owner and a defective unit must be renewed.

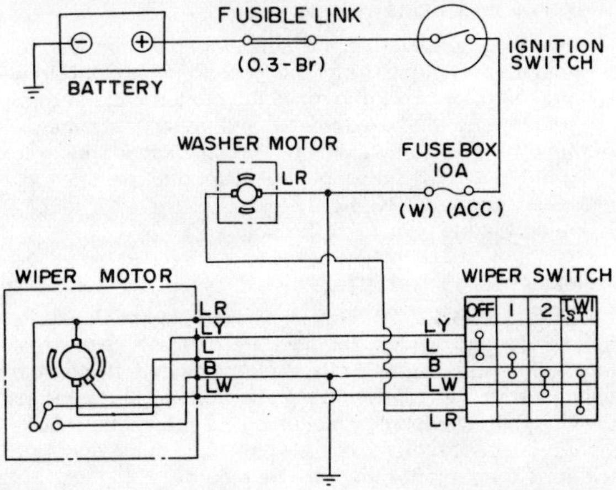

FIG 12:13 Windscreen wiper motor and washer motor circuits

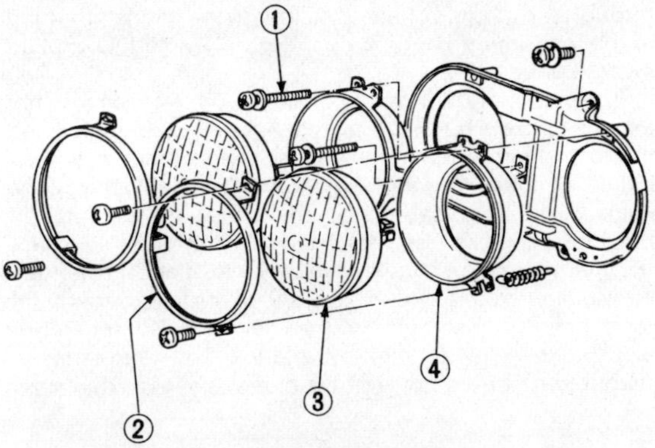

FIG 12:14 Headlamp components

Key to Fig 12:14 1 Alignment screw 2 Retaining ring 3 Sealed beam unit 4 Mounting ring

12:9 Fuses and fusible links

Fuses:

The fuse box is located beneath the instrument panel and is shown in **FIG 12:17**. There are ten fuses. Four are of 20 amp, 5 are of 10 amp and one is of 5 amp capacity and the specifications are listed on the fuse box cover. A separate fuse is provided for the defrosting circuit for the heated (optional) rear window. All fuses are included in wiring diagram **FIG 14:1** in the Appendix.

Never fit a replacement fuse of greater capacity than that specified for the position in the fuse box since, by doing so the protection of the relevant circuit may be jeopardized. If a fuse blows repeatedly, trace the cause of it doing so without delay.

Fusible links:

Two fusible links of different capacities are provided and are included in wiring diagram **FIG 14:1** in the Appendix. Their location is shown in **FIG 12:18**. The brown link has a continuous rating of 11 amp and a 5

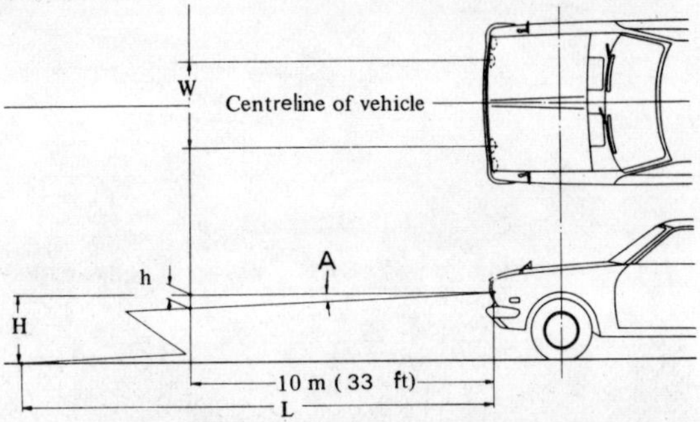

FIG 12:15 Headlamp beam adjustment

Key to Fig 12:15 H, h, W, L and A are given in the text

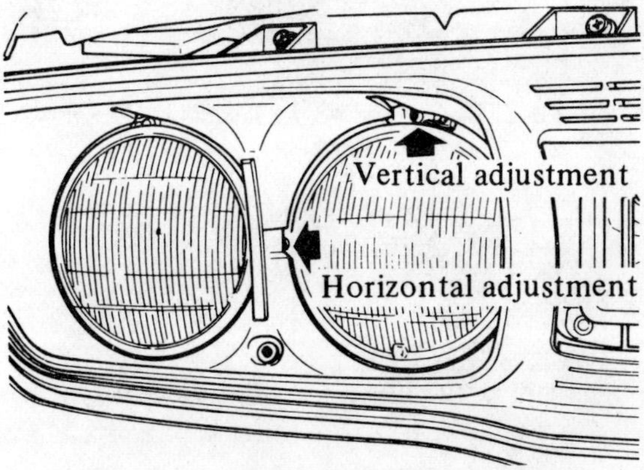

FIG 12:16 Headlamp adjustment screws

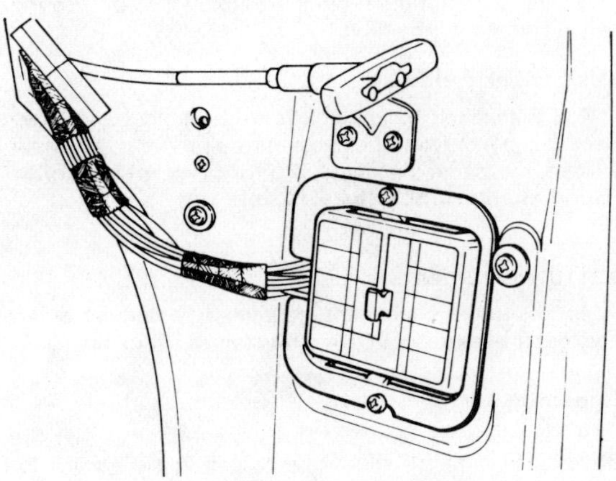

FIG 12:17 The fuse box

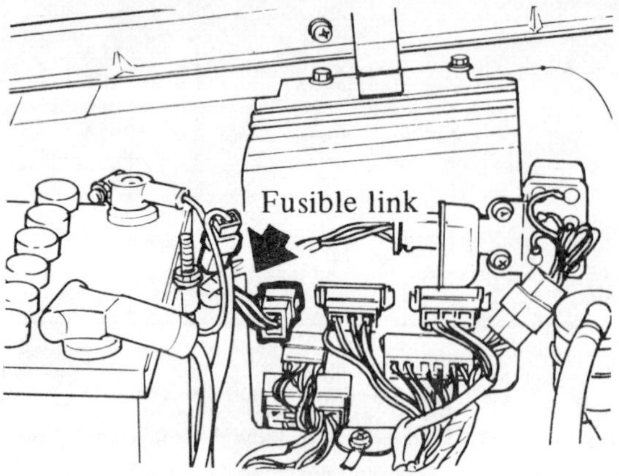

FIG 12:18 The fusible links

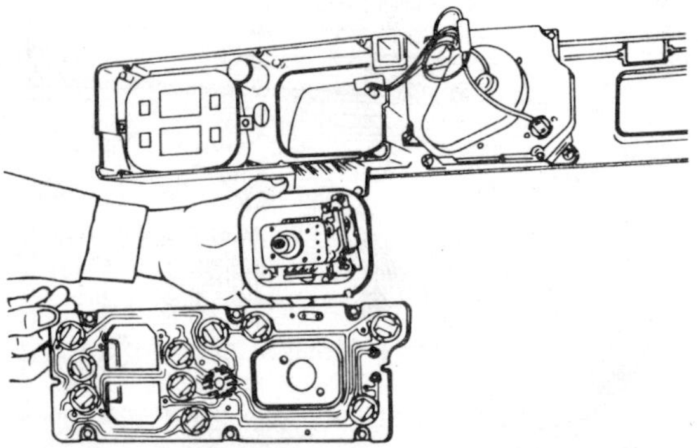

FIG 12:19 Removing the speedometer

second melt current of approximately 60 amp. This link protects the ignition circuit, circuits controlled by the ignition switch and, through a supplementary fuse, the defrosting circuit for the heated (optional) rear window. The red link has a continuous rating of 26 amp and a 5 second melt current of approximately 250 amp. This link protects all circuits not protected by the brown link.

It is most important, if a fusible link melts, to trace the cause and rectify the fault.

Fusible link renewal:

Pull the melted fusible link from the holder and, after tracing and rectifying the cause of the burn out, fit a new link of the same capacity. **Do not wrap anything round the periphery of a fusible link.**

12:10 Instruments

Access to the instruments requires the removal of the cluster panel as described in **Chapter 13, Section 13:9**.

Speedometer:

A speedometer which is inoperative (check that the drive cable is intact) should be passed to a specialist for repair or an exchange replacement unit fitted.

Removal and fitment:

Following removal of the cluster panel, remove the odometer reset knob from the speedometer, withdraw six attaching screws and remove the printed circuit housing together with speedometer and other instruments. Remove the two screws which retain the speedometer to the printed circuit housing and dismount the speedometer as shown in **FIG 12:19**.

Fitment is the reverse of this sequence.

Gauge voltage stabilizer:

Refer to **FIG 12:20**. This shows the electrical circuits for the cooling system temperature gauge and the fuel tank contents gauge. Both circuits are fed through a voltage stabilizer (shown as 'meter voltage regulator' in the illustration) which, by maintaining a substantially constant voltage to these circuits, ensures more accurate readings than might otherwise be recorded.

Temperature gauge:

The coolant temperature transmitter is connected through the gauge voltage stabilizer to the gauge mounted in the instrument panel. It operates only with the ignition switched on.

If the temperature gauge does not operate, check that the fuse (see **FIG 14:1** in the Appendix) is intact and that the wiring connections to the transmitter are secure. If the fuel contents gauge is operating normally, the gauge voltage stabilizer cannot be the cause of the fault. If the fuel gauge is also inoperative but the fuse is intact, the gauge voltage stabilizer must be suspect. If the fuse, wiring and voltage stabilizer are in order, suspect the temperature transmitter and fit a new one. If temperature is not then indicated, fit a new gauge. The gauge may be withdrawn after removal of the cluster panel as described earlier.

Fuel tank contents gauge:

The contents of the fuel tank is indicated by the transmitter unit in the fuel tank. The transmitter is a resistance coil and slider and the resistance is progressively altered by changes in the position of the arm which is controlled by the float. The transmitter, float and arm are shown diagramatically in **FIG 12:20**. The transmitter unit is connected through the gauge voltage stabilizer to the contents gauge mounted in the instrument panel. The circuit is shown in **FIG 12:20**. The gauge can only operate with the ignition switched on.

If the fuel tank contents gauge does not register, check the fuse (see **FIG 14:1** in the Appendix) and the wiring connections. If the coolant temperature gauge is operating normally, the gauge voltage stabilizer is functioning. If the temperature gauge is also inoperative but the fuse is intact, the gauge voltage stabilizer must be suspect. If the fuse, wiring and voltage stabilizer are in order, suspect the fuel gauge or the transmitter unit. Check by shorting the transmitter lead to earth and briefly switching on the ignition. A serviceable gauge will give a reading. If it does not, it must be suspect. The gauge may be removed after dismounting the cluster panel as described earlier. The transmitter unit is retained in the fuel tank by a locking plate which may be removed by turning it anticlockwise with a screwdriver.

Oil pressure gauge:

The oil pressure gauge (if fitted) is operated by the engine oil pressure transmitter. The circuit is included in **FIG 14:1** in the Appendix and, it will be noted, is not connected through the gauge voltage stabilizer since the accuracy of the pressure reading is not critical.

Oil pressure warning light:

Models not equipped with an oil pressure gauge are provided with an oil pressure warning light.

With the engine stationary but with the ignition switched on, the warning light should light up. If it does not do so, suspect that the bulb has failed or that the fuse has blown. The fuse may be identified in **FIG 14:1** in the Appendix. If the bulb, fuse and wiring continuity are in order, the oil pressure transmitter switch must be suspect. The contacts of this pressure switch open at 6 to 8.5 lb/sq in (.4 to .6 kg/sq cm) to extinguish the warning light.

Tachometer:

The impulse type tachometer is wired into the ignition coil LT circuit but is not standard equipment on all models. Models which are not initially equipped may, optionally, be fitted with either a tachometer or a clock. The tachometer is wired in by disconnecting the black/white-black/green wire (laid along the lower portion of the cluster panel) at the connector, connecting in the tachometer to these points and connecting the illumination wiring to the cluster illumination circuit.

Clock:

A clock is not standard equipment on all models. Its wiring is independent of the ignition switch and it is continuously in operation. Models which are not initially equipped with a clock may be optionally fitted with either a clock or a tachometer. The clock is wired to the blue/white wire which is laid along the lower portion of the cluster panel and its illumination wiring is connected to the cluster illumination circuit.

12:11 Horns

The horn circuit incorporates a relay and the steering wheel horn switch button consequently only carries relay current. The circuit is included in wiring diagram **FIG 14:1** in the Appendix.

Tests:

If only one horn will operate, the inoperative horn should be removed for inspection and possible renewal.

If both horns are inoperative, refer to **FIG 14:1** in the Appendix and check the relevant fuse. By means of a test lamp or voltmeter, check that there is voltage at the **B** terminal of the relay. If the fuse is intact but there is no voltage, check the wiring continuity. If the horns operate when the relay **S** terminal is shorted to earth, the horn switch button or its wiring is defective. If the serviceability of the relay is suspect, disconnect the lead from the relay **H** terminal and, using a jump wire, connect direct to the battery positive. If the horns sound, the relay must be defective.

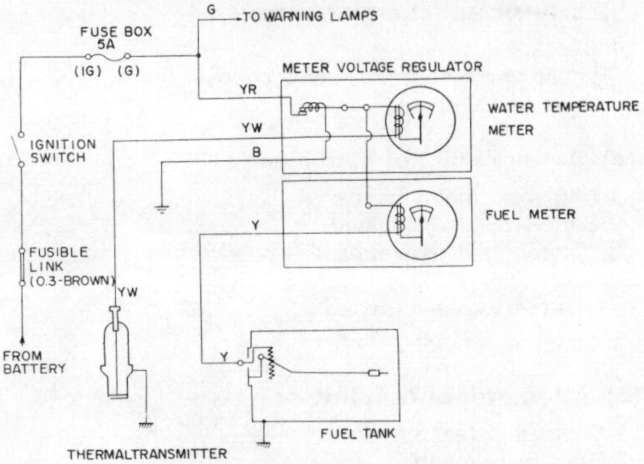

FIG 12:20 Fuel and temperature gauge circuits

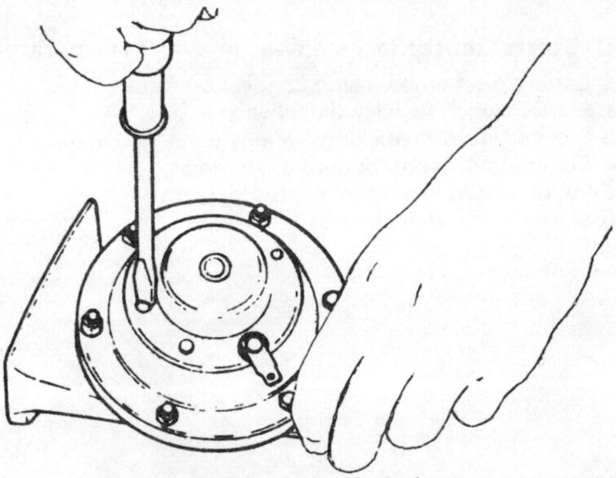

FIG 12:21 Adjusting a horn

Sound adjustment:

Identify the wiring and disconnect and dismount the horns. Adjustment, which is made as shown in **FIG 12:21**, is carried out on each horn separately.

Connect up a horn, a switch and an ammeter in series with a 12-volt battery. Connect a voltmeter across the horn. Close the switch, confirm that the voltage is normal and note the ammeter reading. Open the switch. The current consumption should be 1.5 to 3.5 amp for a 'flat' type horn or 3 to 5 amp for a 'spiral' type horn. When correctly adjusted, a horn should have a clear mellow sound at or below the rated current. If necessary, loosen the locknut and turn the adjustment screw clockwise to increase the current and vice versa. After adjustment, retighten the locknut securely.

12:12 Fault diagnosis

(a) Battery discharged

1 Lights left on
2 Short circuit in electrical system
3 Alternator not charging
4 Regulator defective or out of adjustment
5 Battery internally defective

(b) Insufficient charging rate

1 Check 4 in (a)
2 Loose or dirty terminal connections
3 Drive belt slipping

(c) Battery will not hold charge

1 Neglected maintenance
2 Battery plates sulphated
3 Battery plate separators defective

(d) Battery overcharged

1 Check 4 in (a)

(e) Alternator output low or nil

1 Check 4 in (a); 3 in (b)
2 Drive belt broken
3 Stator and/or rotor windings defective
4 Slip rings worn, burned or shorted
5 Brushes worn or sticking, springs weak or broken

(f) Starter motor lacks power or will not operate

1 Battery discharged, cable connection loose
2 Starter switch or relay defective
3 Brushes worn or sticking, springs weak or broken
4 Commutator worn, burned or shorted
5 Pinion engagement mechanism defective
6 Starter motor defective

(g) Starter motor rough or noisy

1 Retaining bolts loose
2 Damaged teeth on pinion or flywheel ring gear

(h) Lights inoperative or erratic

1 Battery discharged, bulb(s) burned out
2 Faulty earth connection of battery or light(s)
3 Defective switch, loose or broken connection(s)

(j) Wiper motor sluggish

1 Defective motor
2 Seized linkage pivot

(k) Temperature or fuel gauge inoperative

1 Gauge voltage stabilizer defective
2 Transmitter disconnected or defective
3 Gauge defective
4 Blown fuse, loose or broken wiring

(l) Oil pressure gauge inoperative

1 Check 2, 3 and 4 in (k)

(m) Warning light(s) inoperative

1 Blown bulb or fuse
2 Pressure switch defective (oil pressure)
3 Wiring discontinuity

CHAPTER 13

THE BODYWORK

13:1 Bodywork finish
13:2 Bonnet removal and fitment
13:3 Front wings and grilles
13:4 Bumpers
13:5 Doors, locks and hinges
13:6 Luggage compartment lid and tail door
13:7 Door and window glass
13:8 Windscreen and backlight glass
13:9 Dashboard
13:10 Console
13:11 Heater
13:12 Exhaust system

13:1 Bodywork finish

Large-scale repairs to body panels are best left to expert panel beaters. Even small dents can be tricky, as too much hammering will stretch the metal and make things worse instead of better. Filling minor dents and scratches is probably the best method of restoring the surface. The touching-up of paintwork is well within the powers of most owners, particularly as self-spraying cans of paint of the correct colours are now readily available. Paint may change colour with age and it is better to spray a whole wing or door rather than to touch-up a small area.

Before spraying, remove all traces of wax polish with white spirit. More drastic treatment is required if silicone polishes have been applied. Use a primer surfacer or paste stopper according to the amount of filling required, and when it is dry, rub it down with 400 grade 'Wet or Dry' paper until the surface is smooth and flush with the surrounding area. Spend time on getting the best finish as this will control the final effect. Apply a retouching paint keeping it wet in the centre and light and dry round the edges. After a few hours of drying, use a cutting compound to remove the dry spray and finish off with a liquid polish.

13:2 Bonnet removal and fitment

Two operators are required to dismount the bonnet.

Open the bonnet and mark round the hinges. This will minimize the need for adjustment on refitment. While holding the bonnet at both sides, remove the bolts which secure the hinges to the bonnet panel. Disengage the the rod from the stay rail and lift off the bonnet.

Fitment of the bonnet is the reverse of this sequence. Before finally tightening the hinge securing bolts, position the bonnet panel to the marks which were made round the hinges. When fitted, the gap between the bonnet and the wing rails should be equal and even. The bonnet buffer stops should be adjusted so that, when the bonnet is depressed by hand, the difference between the top surface of the bonnet and the wings is .04 to .12 inch (1 to 3 mm).

Bonnet catch:

Adjustment is made at the male catch. This catch may be aligned with the female catch by loosening the attachment bolts and moving the catch assembly fore or aft or from side to side. The male catch vertical adjustment is made by loosening the locknut and turning the catch post clockwise or anticlockwise. Check that the catches

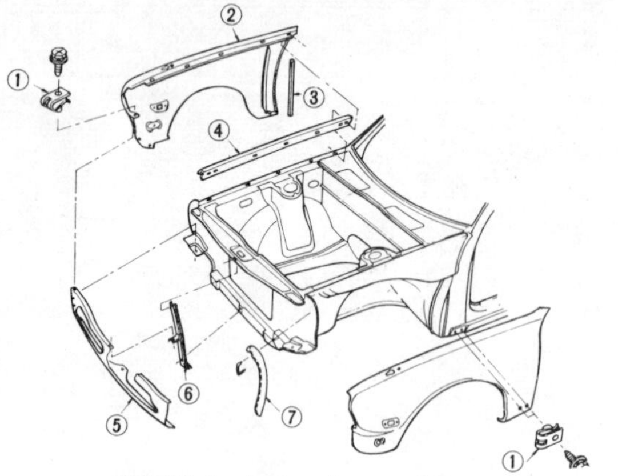

FIG 13:1 Front wings and apron

Key to Fig 13:1 1 Spring nut 2 Front wing (righthand) 3 Filler 4 Rubber 5 Apron 6 Stay 7 Rubber

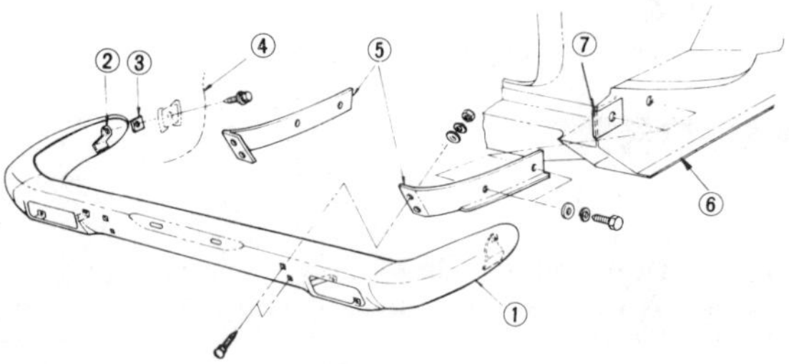

FIG 13:2 Front bumper

Key to Fig 13:2 1 Bumper 2 Bumper side bracket 3 Shim 4 Outline of wing 5 Bumper stay 6 Body side member 7 Spring nut

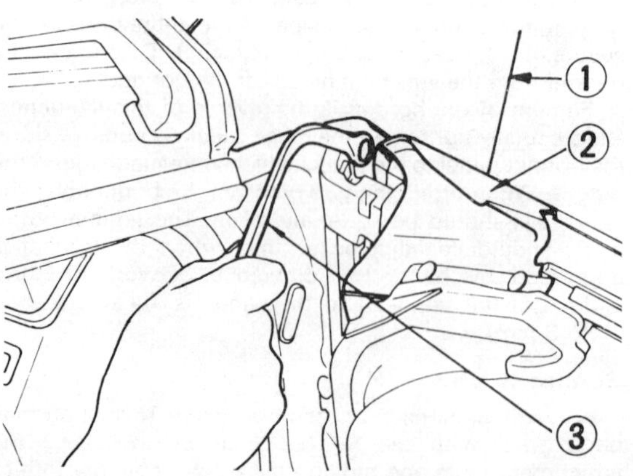

FIG 13:3 Front door hinge special spanner

Key to Fig 13:3 1 Wing 2 Front door 3 Spanner ST08720000

engage securely when the bonnet is closed and that, when the bonnet lock is released, the safety catch retains the bonnet until the manual latch is operated.

13:3 Front wings and grilles

Front grille:

The front grille is retained by eleven bolts. Six of these are along the top, three along the bottom and one between each pair of headlamps. Each bolt has a plain and a spring washer.

Top grille:

To remove the top grille proceed as follows.

Dismount the bonnet as described in **Section 13:2**. Remove the windscreen wiper blades. Using a screwdriver, disengage the inner and outer fasteners which retain the forward edge of the top grille. Draw the top grille forwards to dismount it.

Wings:

The front wing panels and front apron are shown in **FIG 13:1**. The front bumper (see **Section 13:4**), the apron and the top grille must be removed before either wing panel can be dismounted. Proceed as follows:

1 Open the bonnet and remove the front grille as described earlier. Remove the front bumper as described in **Section 13:4**.

2 Remove the four screws which attach the apron 5 to each wing panel 2. Remove the two screws which attach the apron to the stay 6 and dismount the apron. Remove the top grille as described earlier.

3 Remove the sill mouldings. Remove the four bolts from the top edge of the wing panel. Remove the bolt attaching the top cowl to the wing panel. Remove two bolts attaching the sill to the wing panel lower end.

4 Dismount the wing panel and, if necessary, repeat operations 1 to 3 on the opposite side.

Fitment of the front grille, top grille and wing panel(s) is, in each case, the removal sequence in reverse.

13:4 Bumpers

Front bumper removal and fitment:

1 Disconnect the wiring from the direction indicator lamps.

2 Refer to **FIG 13:2** and, from each side, remove the bolt which retains the bumper side bracket to the bottom of the wing panel.

3 Remove the bolts which retain the bumper stays to the body side members and dismount the front bumper.

Fitment is the reverse of this sequence. Before finally tightening the attachment bolts, ensure that the bumper is evenly positioned.

Rear bumper removal and fitment:

1 In the case of saloon models, disconnect the wiring from the rear number plate lighting. On estate car models this does not have to be done.

2 From each side, remove the two bolts which retain the bumper stay to the body side member and withdraw the bumper.

3 Note that, in the case of estate car models it is not necessary to remove the rear number plate as this is fitted directly to the body.

Fitment is the reverse of the removal sequence.

13:5 Doors, locks and hinges

Door alignment:

By loosening the three bolts which attach each hinge to the body, a door may be moved upwards and downwards or inwards and outwards within the limit of the enlarged attachment holes. Similarly, by loosening the two bolts which attach the lock striker, the striker may be moved upwards or downwards and inwards and outwards.

When correctly adjusted, there should be an even and parallel gap all round between the door and the body panels.

Access to front door hinge attachment bolts is simplified (without removing the relevant wing) by using hinge spanner ST08720000 or an equivalent cranked ring spanner as shown in **FIG 13:3**.

Front door removal:

Remove the relevant front wing and the top grille as as described in **Section 13:3**. Open the door and support it from beneath with a padded jack. Remove the three bolts which attach each hinge to the body and dismount the door.

Rear door removal:

Open both the relevant rear door and also the front door. Support the rear door from beneath with a padded jack. Remove the three bolts which attach each hinge to the body and dismount the door.

Door fitment:

Door fitment is the removal sequence in reverse. Adjust the alignment as described earlier.

Door trim removal and fitment:

With the door open, raise the lock knob, turn it anticlockwise and remove it and its grommet. Remove the attachment bolts and dismount the arm rest. Remove the screw which retains the handle escutcheon and remove the lock dial and escutcheon. With the window glass fully raised, note the disposition of the window regulator handle so that it may be refitted in the same attitude. Remove the spring retainer and dismount the regulator handle and its washer. Using a thin bladed screwdriver, prise off the door trim which is retained by spring clips engaging holes in the door inner panel. Remove the watertight seal from the door panel.

Fitment is the reverse of this sequence.

Door lock and striker removal and fitment:

Remove the door trim as described earlier. Remove the two screws which are arrowed in **FIG 13:4** and dismount the door inside handle. Remove the screws which attach the remote control and lock knob rods and detach the rods. Remove the two attachment nuts and dismount the door outside handle. Remove the remote control rod from the door lock cylinder. Remove the three screws which retain the door lock and withdraw the lock. As described earlier, the lock striker is retained by two bolts.

Fitment is the reverse of the removal sequence. If necessary, adjust the outside and inside handles as described later.

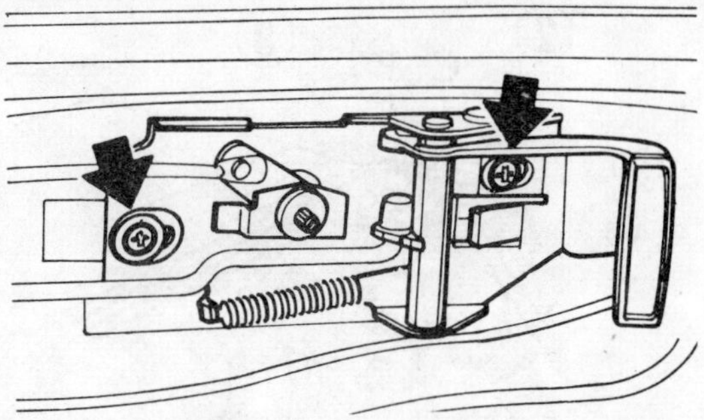

FIG 13:4 Removing inside handle

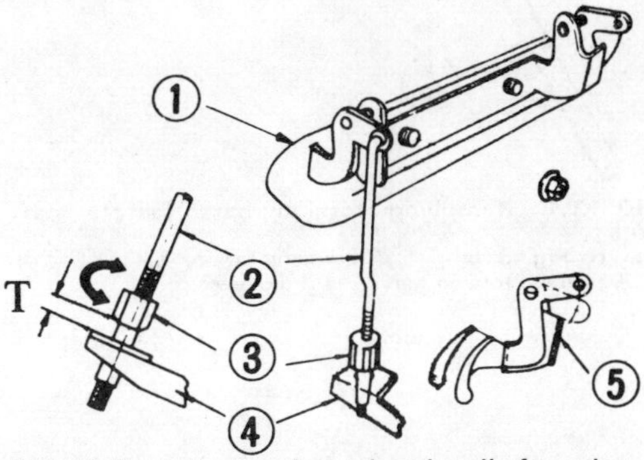

FIG 13:5 Adjusting front door handle free play

Key to Fig 13:5 1 Outside door handle 2 Remote control rod 3 Adjusting nut 4 Door lock lever 5 Stop

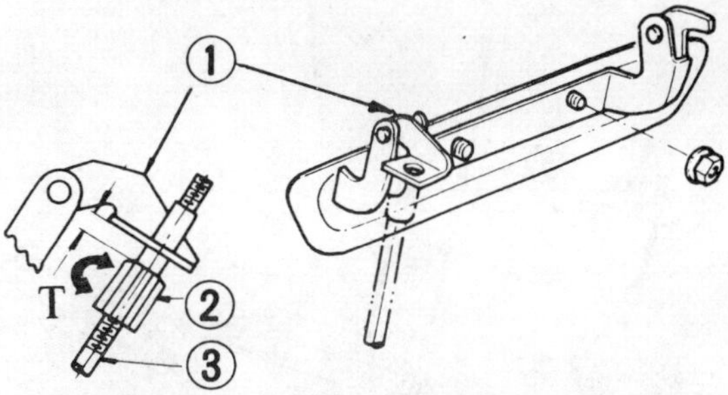

FIG 13:6 Adjusting rear door handle free play

Key to Fig 13:6 1 Outside door handle 2 Adjusting nut 3 Remote control rod

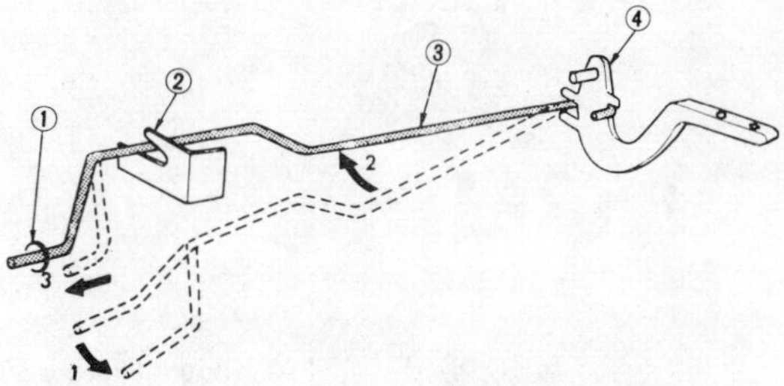

FIG 13:7 Luggage compartment lid torsion bar

Key to Fig 13:7 1 Hole in panel 2 Bracket 3 Lefthand torsion bar 4 Hinge

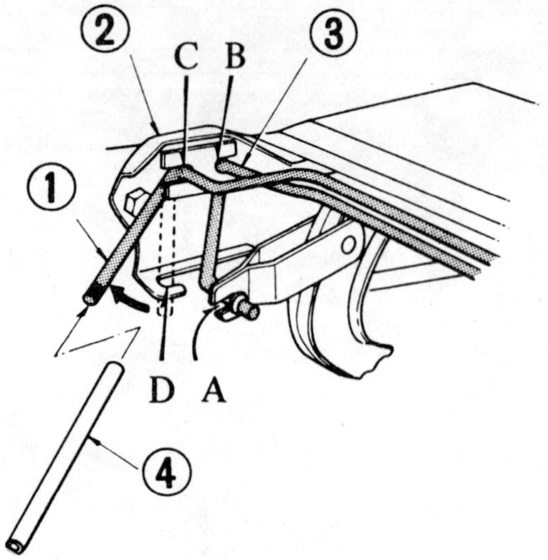

FIG 13:8 Removing torsion bars (estate car tail door)

Key to Fig 13:8 1 Lefthand torsion bar 2 Hinge 3 Righthand torsion bar 4 Pipe lever

Door outside handle adjustment:

This handle is adjusted by turning the remote control rod nut in the appropriate direction to bring clearance **T** in **FIG 13:5** (front door) or in **FIG 13:6** (rear door) to below .04 inch (1 mm). The adjusting nut is 3 in **FIG 13:5** and 2 in **FIG 13:6**.

Door inside handle adjustment:

To adjust the inside handle free play, loosen the two screws which are arrowed in **FIG 13:4** and move the handle fore or aft to bring the free play to below .04 inch (1 mm). Do not attempt to adjust the free play by bending the door lock lever.

Door lock cylinder removal and fitment:

Remove the door trim as described earlier. Disconnect the control rod from the door lock cylinder. Remove the locking spring which secures the lock cylinder to the door outside panel. Withdraw the lock cylinder.

Fitment is the reverse of this sequence. If necessary, adjust the handles as described earlier.

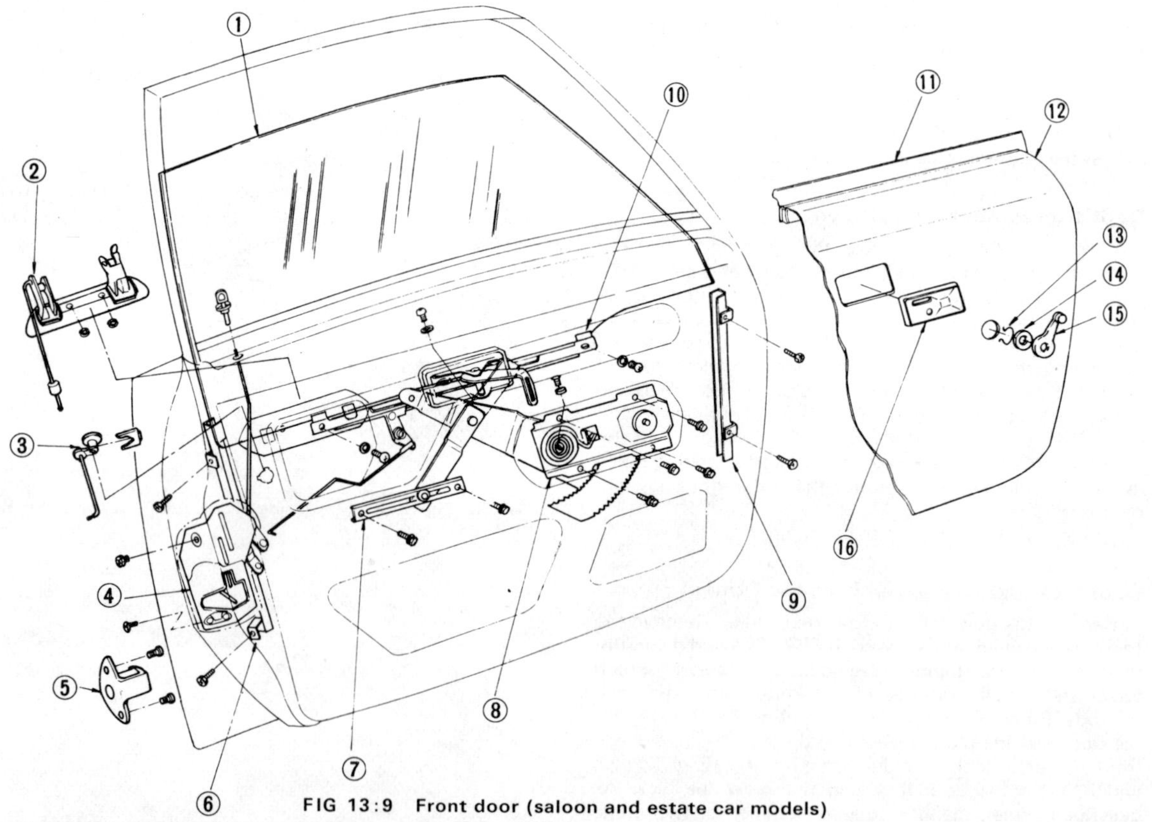

FIG 13:9 Front door (saloon and estate car models)

Key to Fig 13:9 1 Door window glass 2 Door outside handle 3 Lock cylinder 4 Door lock assembly 5 Striker 6 Rear lower sash 7 Guide channel **A** 8 Regulator 9 Front lower sash 10 Guide channel **B** 11 Watertight seal cover 12 Door finisher 13 Spring 14 Washer 15 Handle 16 Door inside handle escutcheon

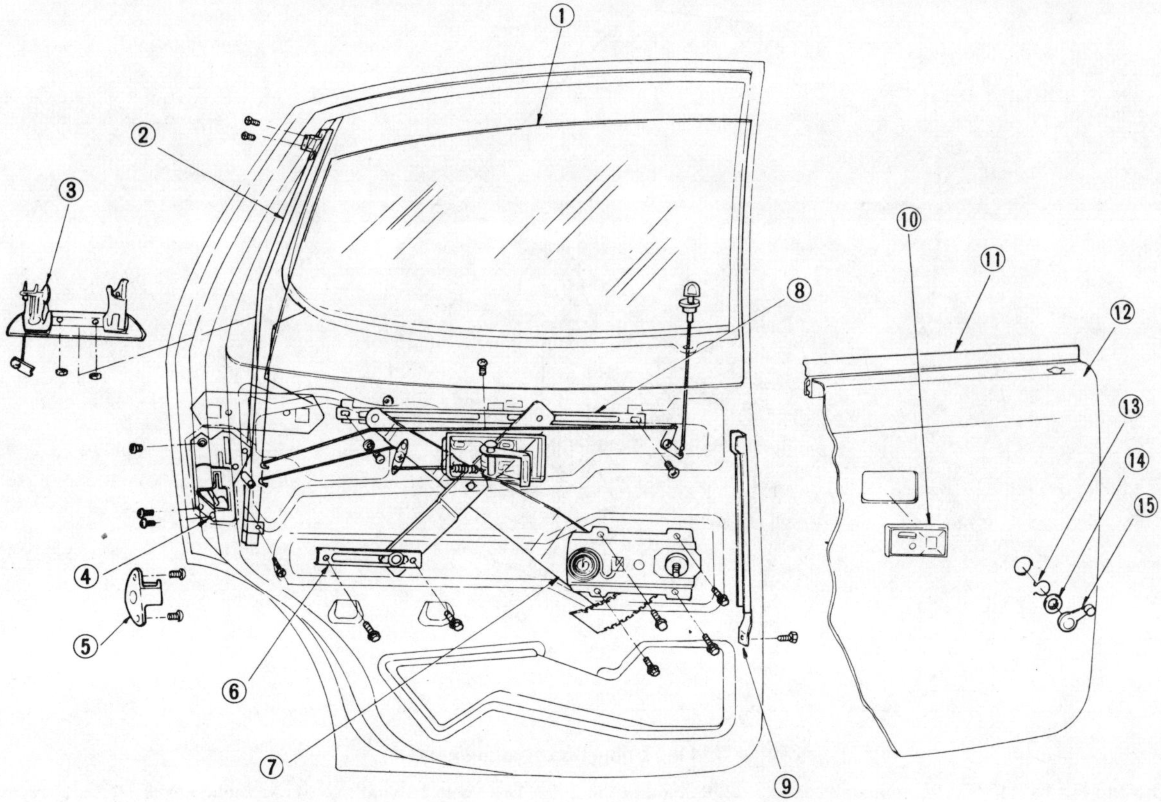

FIG 13:10 Rear door (saloon and estate car models)

Key to Fig 13:10 1 Door window glass 2 Rear sash 3 Door outside handle 4 Door lock assembly 5 Striker 6 Guide channel **A** 7 Regulator 8 Guide channel **B** 9 Front lower sash 10 Inside handle escutcheon 11 Watertight glass seal 12 Door finisher 13 Spring 14 Washer 15 Handle

13:6 Luggage compartment lid and tail door

Saloon and coupe models:

The first part of this Section covers the luggage compartment lid and applies only to saloon and coupe models.

Luggage compartment lid removal and fitment:

Two operators are required to dismount the luggage compartment lid. Take great care not to damage the rear wing paintwork.

Open the lid and mark round the hinges. This will minimize the need for adjustment when the lid is being refitted. While holding the lid at both sides, remove the two bolts which attach each hinge to the lid and lift off the lid.

Following fitment of the lid which is the removal sequence in reverse, check the alignment of the lid and, if necessary, adjust as described later.

Luggage compartment lid adjustment:

Loosen the two bolts which attach each hinge to the lid. The lid may now be moved fore and aft or side to side to align it with the lock striker and to even the gap round the lid.

To obtain a snug fit between the lid and the weatherstrip, the striker, which is retained by three bolts may have to be moved up or down or from side to side in conjunction with the adjustment of the lid itself.

Luggage compartment lid torsion bars:

The weight of the lid is counterbalanced by torsion bar 'spring' load. The connections of one of the torsion bars with its hinge is illustrated in **FIG 13:7**.

To remove the torsion bars, open the lid, remove the retaining screws and withdraw the trim which covers the bars. Support the lid in the open position and, by hand, draw the end of the lefthand torsion bar from the hole 1 at the side of the panel. Disengage the bar from the bracket 2 and then unhook it from the hinge 4. Similarly disengage the righthand torsion bar and unhook it from the hinge.

Fitment of the torsion bars is the reverse of this removal sequence.

Luggage compartment hinge removal and fitment:

Remove the lid as described earlier. Remove the torsion bars as described earlier. Pull the clips out of the hinges, remove the washers and dismount the hinges.

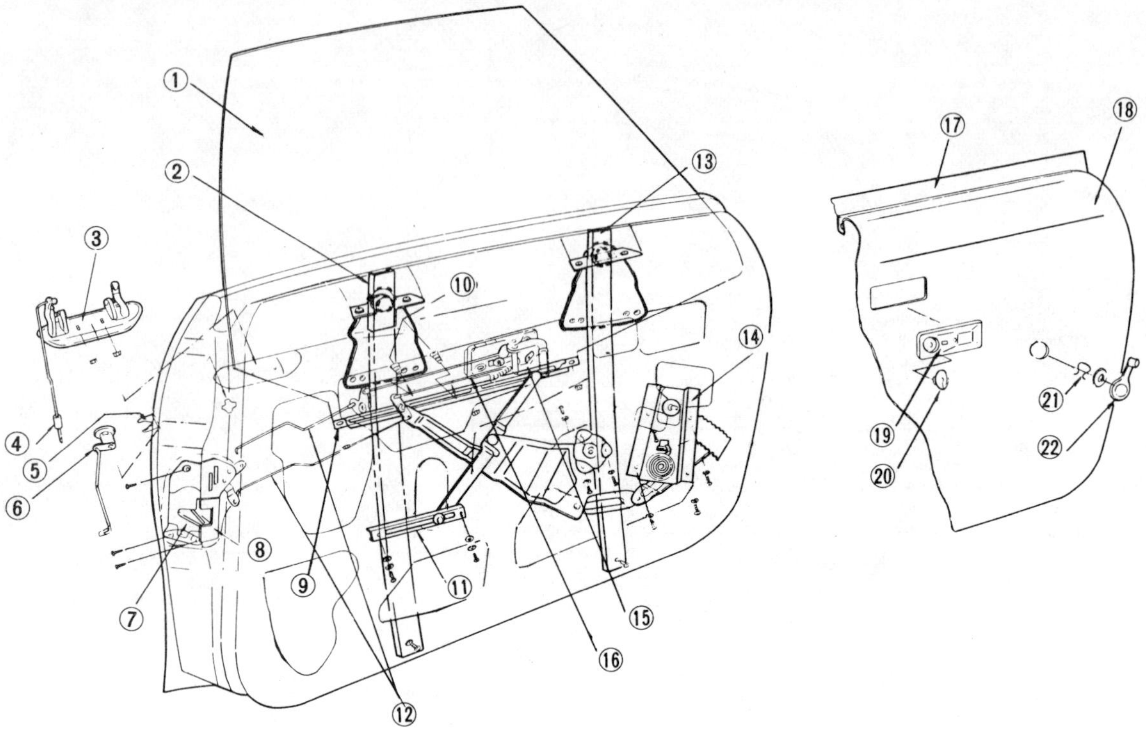

FIG 13:11 Single door (coupe models)

Key to Fig 13:11 1 Door window glass 2 Rear guide rail 3 Door outside handle 4 Adjusting nut 5 Lock spring 6 Lock cylinder 7 Door lock assembly 8 Spacer 9 Guide channel **B** 10 Rod holder 11 Guide channel **A** 12 Door lock rod 13 Front guide rail 14 Regulator 15 Door inside handle 16 Dust cover 17 Watertight seal cover 18 Door finisher. 19 Inside handle escutcheon 20 Lock dial 21 Spring 22 Handle

Estate car models:

The remainder of this Section is relevant only to estate car models.

Tail door removal and fitment:

Two operators are required to dismount the tail door and care must be taken not to damage the adjacent paintwork.

Open the tail door and support it in the open position. Mark round the hinges. This will minimize the need for adjustment on refitment. Remove the three bolts which attach each hinge to the door and lift off the door.

Fitment is the reverse of this sequence. On completion, check and, if necessary, adjust the alignment of the door as described later.

Tail door adjustment:

Up and down and side to side adjustments may be made after loosening the three bolts which attach each hinge to the door. Fore and aft adjustment may be made after removing the hinge covers and loosening the two bolts which attach each hinge to the body.

Adjust the door alignment so that it is level with the body panels and has an even and parallel gap all round.

Tail door torsion bars:

The weight of the door is counterbalanced by torsion bar 'spring' load. To remove the torsion bars, proceed as follows.

Open the tail door. Remove the hinge covers. Remove the screws which retain the rear of the head lining and withdraw the lining from the rear panel to give access to the torsion bars. Support the door in the open position. Refer to **FIG 13:8**. Disengage the lefthand torsion bar (is is painted yellow) from, first, the **D** bracket and then from the **C** bracket using a suitable pipe lever 4 over the end of the bar. Withdraw the bar. Similarly disengage and withdraw the righthand torsion bar.

Fitment is the reverse of this procedure.

Tail door hinge removal and fitment:

Remove the tail door as described earlier. Remove the torsion bars as described earlier. Remove the two bolts which attach each hinge to the body and dismount the hinges.

Fitment is the reverse of this sequence and should be followed by adjustment of the door alignment as described earlier.

Taildoor catch adjustment:

The tail door catch, striker and down stops are each retained by two bolts. After loosening the retaining bolts, the catch may be moved from side to side, the striker may be moved fore and aft and each stop may be moved up or down.

13:7 Door and window glass

Door illustrations:

The front door illustrated in **FIG 13:9** is relevant to both saloon and estate car models. The rear door shown in **FIG 13:10** relates also to these models and the door shown in **FIG 13:11** relates only to coupe (single door) models.

Door glass and regulator removal and fitment:

1 Lower the door glass and, as described in **Section 13:5**, remove the door trim. Remove the door outside weatherstrip and, in the case of a rear door, the rear sash. In the case of coupe models, drive out the inner pin of the outside finisher retaining clip, remove the clip, the finisher and the weatherstrip.
2 In the case of a front or rear door, remove the front lower sash 9 in **FIGS 13:9** and **13:10** although for glass removal only this is not essential. In the case of a coupe door, raise the glass until the upper stops appear in the panel upper openings, remove the stops and lower the glass.
3 Support the glass and remove the screws which retain channel **B** to the glass backplate. Withdraw the glass.
4 Remove the screws which attach guide channel **A** and the regulator base. In the case of coupe models, remove the guide rails 2 and 13 in **FIG 13:11**. In the case of a front door, remove the rear sash and, if not done at operation 2, the front lower sash. Withdraw the regulator through the panel lower opening.

Fitment is the reverse of the removal sequence in each case. Adjustment will be required to centre and align the glass.

Door glass adjustment:

In the case of saloon and estate car front doors, glass alignment is achieved by adjusting the front and rear lower sashes and guide channel **A** (9, 6 and 7 in **FIG 13:9**).

In the case of saloon rear doors, alignment is achieved by adjusting the front lower sash, the rear sash and guide channel **A** (9, 2 and 6 in **FIG 13:10**).

In the case of a coupe door, with the glass raised, temporarily tighten the upper guide rail adjustment bolt in the centre of the elongated hole and fully tighten the lower adjusting bolt before backing it off by nine turns and tightening the locknut. Alignment is achieved by adjusting the guide rails and the guide channel **A** (2, 13 and 11 in **FIG 13:11**). With the glass raised, adjust the upper stops to give a clearance of zero to .04 inch (0 to 1 mm) between the top of the glass and the body side weatherstrip. The clearance between the top of the glass and the end of the guide must be between zero and .02 inch (0 to .5 mm) just before the glass and the side weatherstrip meet.

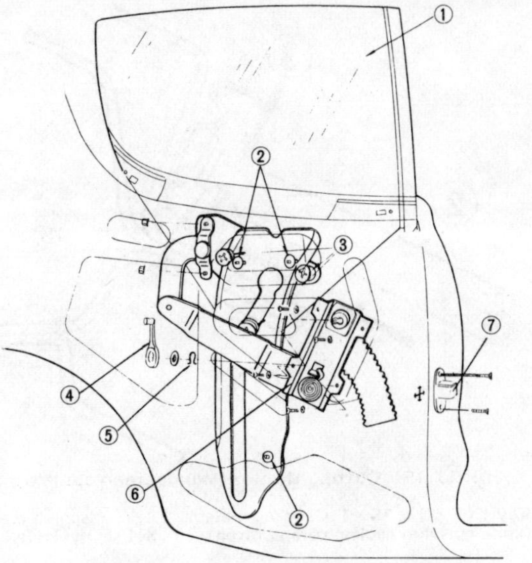

FIG 13:12 Side window (coupe models)

Key to Fig 13:12 1 Window glass 2 Guide plate adjusting bolts 3 Guide roller 4 Handle 5 Spring 6 Regulator 7 Striker

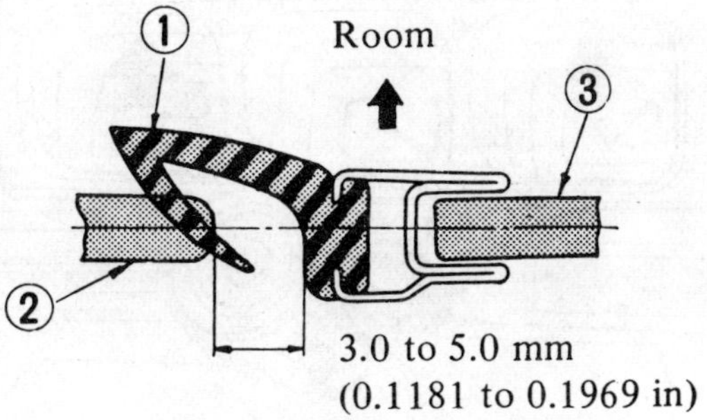

FIG 13:13 Window glass to weatherstrip clearance (coupe models)

Key to Fig 13:13 1 Weatherstrip 2 Door window glass 3 Side window glass

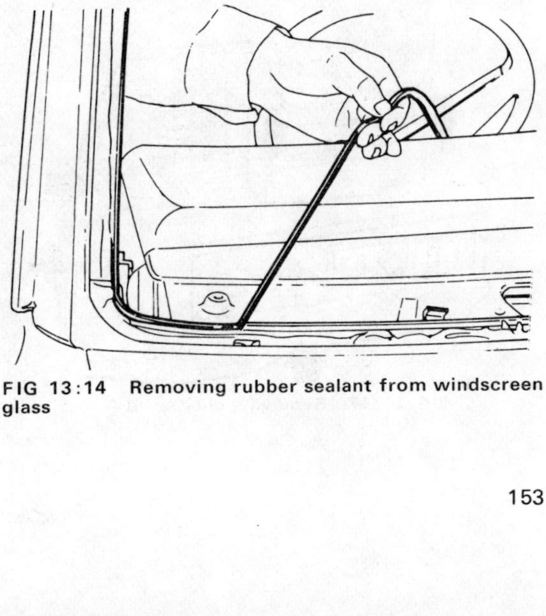

FIG 13:14 Removing rubber sealant from windscreen glass

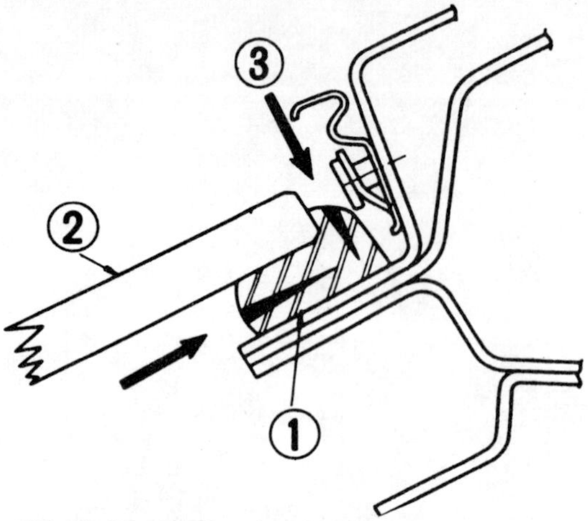

FIG 13:15 Cutting through windscreen caulking

Key to Fig 13:15 1 Caulking material 2 Windscreen glass (knife cuts into caulking are arrowed) 3 External knife cut

FIG 13:16 Removing cluster panel

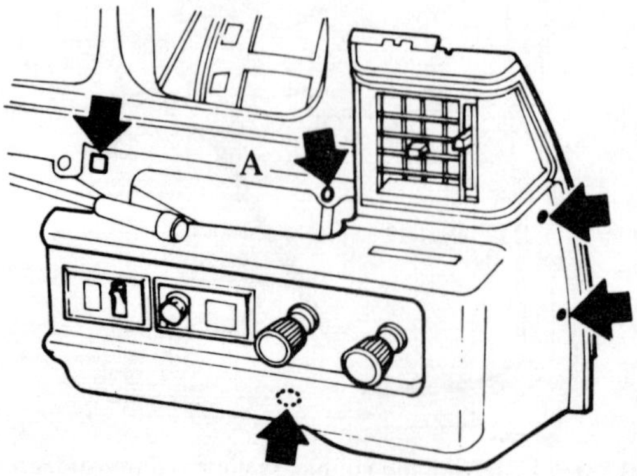

FIG 13:17 Removing cluster lid A

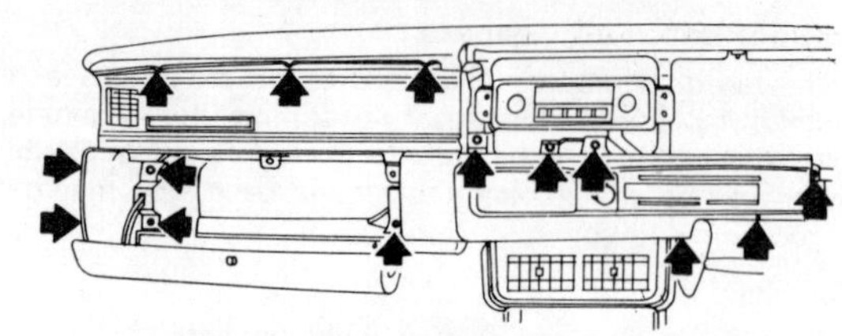

FIG 13:18 Removing cluster lid B

Rear side window, coupe models:

The window regulator is shown in **FIG 13:12**. To remove the regulator and window glass, proceed as follows:

1 Remove the rear seat and swab. If fitted, remove the the rear seat safety belt anchorages. Remove the kicking plate. Lower the window glass.

2 Remove the arm rest, regulator handle, rear side finisher and watertight seal. Remove the draught finisher and the rear corner finisher. Remove the inner seal and bracket.

3 Raise the glass until the regulator arm bracket appears in the panel upper opening. Support the glass and remove the nuts which attach the arm bracket to the glass backplate.

4 Loosen the guide plate upper and lower adjusting bolt locknuts and remove the bolts from the guide plate. Raise the glass and guide panel and remove them inwards.

5 Remove the regulator base attaching screws and withdraw the regulator assembly through the panel lower opening.

The procedure for fitting the regulator and window glass is the reverse of the removal sequence. Adjustment will be required to centre and align the glass.

Rear side window adjustment, coupe models:

With the glass lowered, temporarily tighten the guide plate adjusting bolts in the centre of the elongated holes. Tighten them fully and then back off by eight turns. The clearance between the wing panel and the outer face of the glass should be .33 to .41 inch (8.5 to 10.5 mm) and is adjusted by the guide plate upper adjusting bolts. With the glass fully raised the clearance between the glass and the weatherstrip should be .12 to .2 inch (3 to 5 mm) as shown in **FIG 13:13** and this also is adjusted at the guide plate.

13:8 Windscreen and backlight glass

A replacement windscreen or backlight is retained by a special adhesive and is caulked using a cartridge of caulking material in a caulking gun. The procedure also requires the use of primers, masking and suction glass holders and, on completion, a water leakage correction procedure. It is advised that since the complete procedure is not suitable for action by an owner, a main agent who is suitably equipped should replace a windscreen or backlight.

In an emergency, a broken windscreen may be removed as follows:

1 Protect the bonnet, front wings, instrument panel and front seats with suitable covers. Remove the windscreen wipers, front pillar garnish and welt.

2 Remove the windscreen mouldings. Strip the rubber sealant from around the glass as shown in **FIG 13:14** (when the special sealant is used, the rubber sealant need not be refitted).

3 Using a sharp knife, cut into the caulking material along the edge of the entire windscreen opening as shown in **FIG 13:15**.

4 Working from inside the vehicle, push the windscreen glass outwards and remove fragments as necessary.

13:9 Dashboard

Although removal of the steering wheel as described in **Chapter 8, Section 8:8** will provide easier access when removing the dashboard panel and lids, it is not essential to do so.

Identify all wiring and connectors before dismantling or uncoupling.

Instrument cluster panel removal and fitment:

1 Disconnect both cables from the battery. Remove four screws and dismount the steering column shell covers.

2 Refer to **FIG 13:16**. Remove the four arrowed retaining screws. Pull the cluster panel rearwards and, from behind the panel, disconnect the multi-way plug from the printed circuit housing.

3 Uncouple the speedometer drive cable from the speedometer head. Disconnect other linking connections from the printed circuit as may apply to the specific model and dismount the cluster panel.
Fitment is the reverse of this sequence.

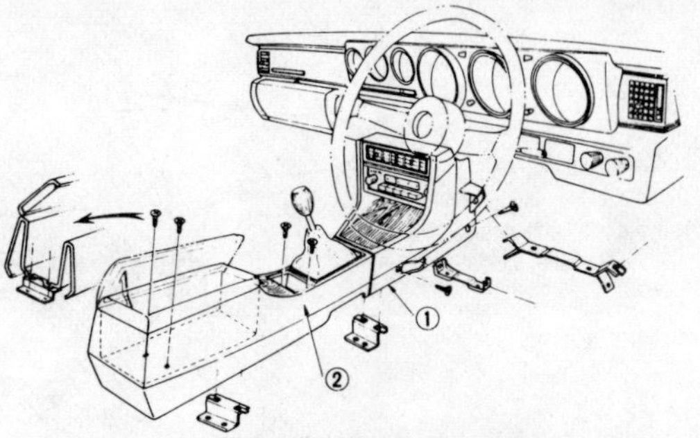

FIG 13:19 Centre console

Key to Fig 13:19 1 Console front section 2 Console rear section

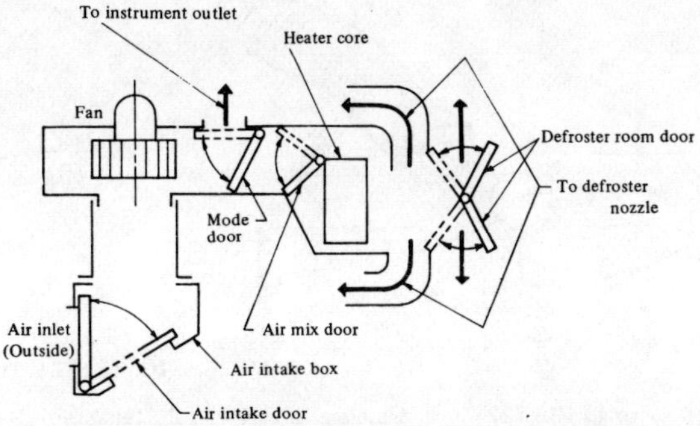

FIG 13:20 Diagrammatic cross-section through heater ducting

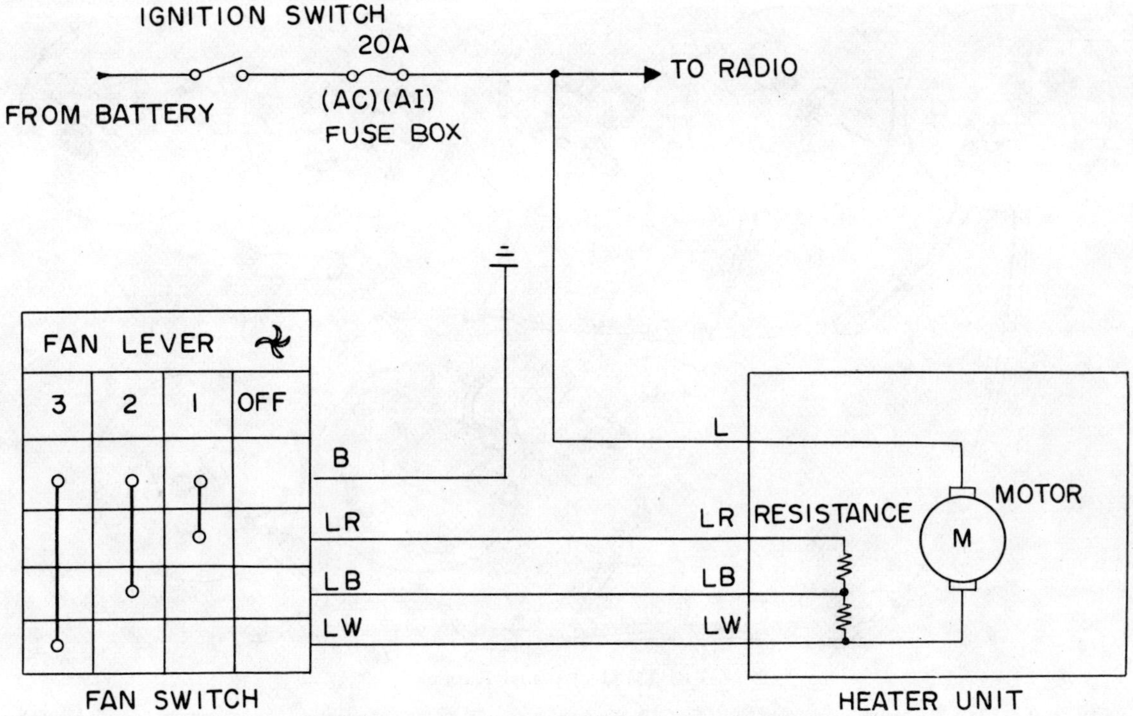

FIG 13:21 3-speed switch circuit, heater motor

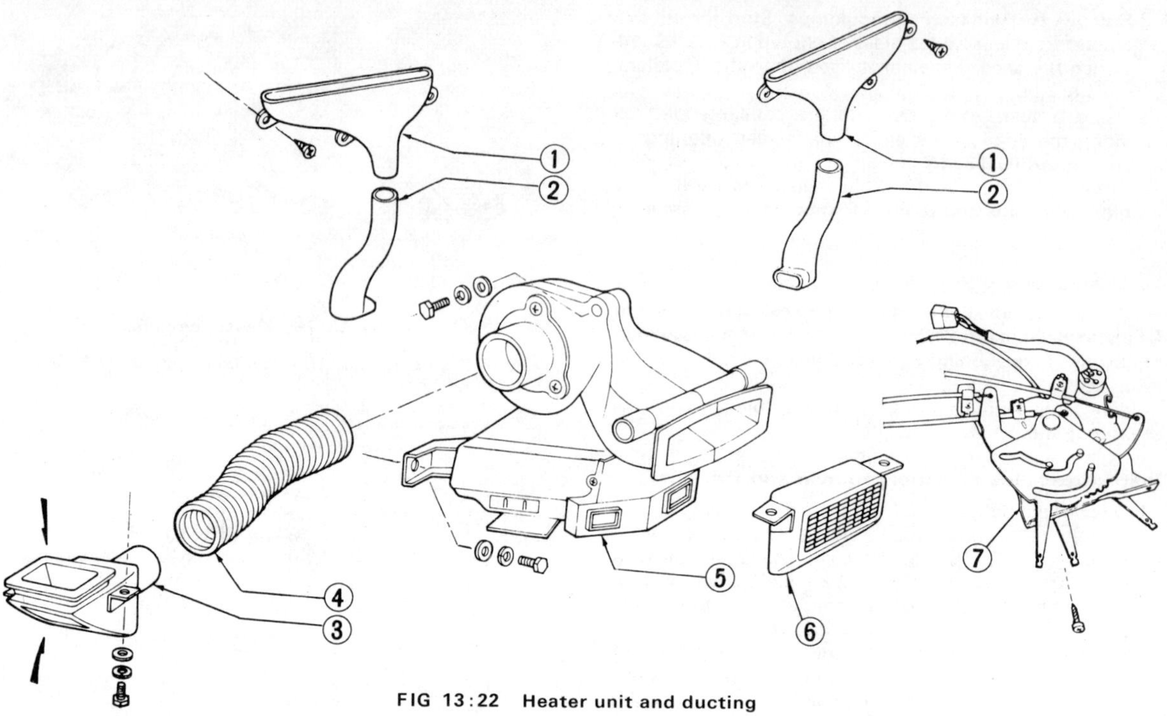

FIG 13:22 Heater unit and ducting

Key to Fig 13:22 1 Demister nozzle 2 Demister hose 3 Air intake 4 Duct 5 Heater unit 6 Centre ventilator 7 Control assembly

FIG 13:23 Exhaust system

Key to Fig 13:23 1 Front pipe assembly 2 Presilencer 3 Rear pipe assembly 4 Silencer 5 Heat shield 6 Presilencer assembly 7 Silencer and rear pipe assembly

Cluster lid A. Removal and fitment:

Remove the cluster panel as described earlier. Refer to **FIG 13:17**. The cluster lid **A** is retained by the five screws which are arrowed in the illustration. Remove these screws and dismount the lid.

Fitment is the reverse of this sequence.

Cluster lid B. Removal and fitment:

Remove the cluster panel as described earlier. Remove the cluster lid **A** also as described earlier. Remove the heater control knobs (if fitted). Refer to **FIG 13:18**. The cluster lid **B** is retained by the fourteen screws which are arrowed in the illustration. Remove these screws and dismount the cluster lid **B**.

Fitment is the reverse of this sequence.

13:10 Console

Removal:

1 Remove the knob from the gearchange lever. In the case of automatic transmission models, refer to **Chapter 7, FIG 7:11**, remove two small screws and pull the control handle off the lever.
2 Refer to **FIG 13:19**. Remove the screws which retain the rear section of the console. Withdraw this section of the console.
3 If a radio is fitted to the forward section of the console, disconnect the aerial and other wiring from it.
4 Remove the screws which attach the forward section of the console to the parcel tray. Remove the side attaching screws and withdraw the forward section of the console.

Fitment:

Fitment of the console is the reverse of the removal sequence in each case. On automatic transmission models, refer to **Chapter 7, Section 7:4** and, as described in 'Floor level control adjustment', check that the relevant adjustments are within the prescribed limits.

13:11 Heater

The layout of the heater ducting is shown diagramatically in **FIG 13:20** and the electrical circuit for the three-speed blower fan motor is shown in **FIG 13:21**. The components of the assembly are illustrated in **FIG 13:22**.

Removal:

1 Disconnect the cables from the battery. Drain the engine cooling system as described in **Chapter 4, Section 4:2** and disconnect the hoses from the heater unit.
2 Remove the centre ventilator and the console (see **Section 13:10**). Refer to **FIG 13:22**. Remove the duct hose 4 and the demister hoses 2. Remove the control cable retaining clamps and disconnect the cables from the control levers.
3 Disconnect the wiring at two connectors. Remove three securing bolts (one from each side of the heater unit and one from the top) and dismount the unit. If necessary, the fan motor may be withdrawn after removing three retaining screws.

Fitment:

Fitment of a heater unit is the reverse of the removal sequence. Connect the control cables as follows:

1 Move the AIR lever to the OFF position.
2 While pulling on the cable outer casing with a force of approximately 2 to 4 lb (1 to 2 kg), fit the inner cable to the lever and retain it with a cable clamp.
3 Move the AIR lever to the DEF position. Connect the control cable as described in operation 2.
4 Fit the cable to the 'mode' lever. Connect the control cable as described in operation 2.
5 Move the TEMP lever fully to the left. Check that it is against the stop. Connect the control cable as described in operation 2.

13:12 Exhaust system

The exhaust system carries a presilencer and a main silencer and is suspended from the body on mounting hangers and brackets. In **FIG 13:23**, the upper part of the illustration relates to saloon and coupe models and the lower part to estate car models.

Removal:

Remove the nuts which secure the front exhaust pipe assembly to the engine exhaust manifold. Remove the bolts from the clamps and dismount the complete system. Discard the gasket from between the front pipe assembly and the engine manifold. If necessary, separate the presilencer assembly from the rear exhaust pipe. In case of difficulty, refer to to 2 in Hints on Maintenance and Overhaul in the Appendix.

Inspection:

Check that neither the presilencer nor the main silencer is cracked, corroded or punctured by road stones. Confirm that the pipes are sound and that the mountings are serviceable. Renew as necessary.

Fitment:

This the reverse of the removal procedure. Use a new gasket between the engine manifold and the front pipe assembly. Ensure that there is a clearance of at least .71 inch (18 mm) between the exhaust system and adjacent body panels or members.

Torque tightening recommendations are: manifold to front pipe assembly nuts, 12 to 15 lb ft (1.6 to 2.1 kgm); other nuts and bolts, 7 to 11 lb ft (1 to 1.5 kgm).

After running the vehicle for, say, 100 miles (160 km), retighten the manifold and pipe clamp connections.

NOTES

APPENDIX

TECHNICAL DATA

Engine Fuel system Cooling system Ignition system
Clutch Transmission Suspension Steering Brakes
Electrical equipment Capacities Dimensions

WIRING DIAGRAM

FIG 14:1 Wiring diagram

METRIC CONVERSION TABLE

HINTS ON MAINTENANCE AND OVERHAUL

GLOSSARY OF TERMS

INDEX

NOTES

TECHNICAL DATA

Dimensions are in inches unless otherwise stated

ENGINE

Engine capacity	1595 cc (L16)	1770 cc (L18)
Bore and stroke	83 mm x 73.7 mm	85 mm x 78 mm
Compression ratio	8.5 or 9.5	
Crankshaft:		
Main bearings	5	
Bearing shell thickness:		
Standard	.0717 to .0722	
Undersize (thicker than standard)	4 sizes (see Chapter 1, Section 1:13)	
Journal diameter (new)	2.1631 to 2.1636	
Clearance with new main bearing	.0008 to .0024	
Maximum acceptable clearance	.0047	
Crankpin diameter (new)	1.9670 to 1.9675	
Maximum ovality and taper	.0004 (main and crankpin journals)	
Axial clearance (new)	.0020 to .0071	
Maximum acceptable	.0120	
Connecting rods:		
Maximum bend or twist	.002 per 3.94 of length	
Weight variation per rod per set	.25 oz maximum	
Big-end bearing shell thickness:		
Standard	.0588 to .0593	
Undersize (thicker than standard)	6 sizes (see Chapter 1, Section 1:13)	
Clearance with crankpin (new)	.0010 to .0022	
Maximum acceptable clearance	.016	
Gudgeon pin:		
Diameter	.8266 to .8268	
Length	2.8445 to 2.8740	
Clearance with piston	.0003 to .0004 at 20°C (68°F)	
Interference with small-end	.0006 to .0013	
Pistons:		
Diameters:	*L16*	*L18*
Standard	3.2671 to 3.2691	3.3459 to 3.3478
Oversize (.25 mm)	3.2762 to 3.2781	—
Oversize (.50 mm)	3.2860 to 3.2880	3.3648 to 3.3667
Oversize (.75 mm)	3.2959 to 3.2978	—
Oversize (1.00 mm)	3.3057 to 3.3077	3.3844 to 3.3864
Oversize (1.25 mm)	3.3254 to 3.3274	—
Ovality (maximum)	.013 to .014	
Clearance with cylinder bore (new)	.0010 to .0018	
Overhaul at	.0078	
Piston rings:		
Side clearance in groove:	*L16*	*L18*
Top compression	.0016 to .0031	.0018 to .0031
Second compression	.0012 to .0028	
Wear limit	.039	
Gaps	See Chapter 1, Section 1:10	
Cylinder block:		
Head face flatness	.004 maximum	
Bore clearance with piston (new)	.0010 to .0018	
Overhaul at	.0078	
Ovality (new)	.0006 maximum	
Liners:		
OD of 4.0 mm undersize	3.4252 to 3.4272	
OD of 4.5 mm undersize	3.4449 to 3.4468	
OD of 5.0 mm undersize	3.4646 to 3.4665	

Camshaft:			
Journal diameter (standard)	1.8877 to 1.8883		
Clearance with journal bearings	.0015 to .0026		
Bearing ID (standard)	1.8894 to 1.8904		
Bend (maximum)	.0007		
Cam lift:	*Single carburetter*	*Twin carburetter*	
Inlet	.2618	.2753	
Exhaust	.2753	.2753	
End play	.003 to .015		
Valves:			
Dimensions	See Chapter 1, FIG 1:15		
Stem to guide clearance:			
Inlet	.0008 to .0021		
Exhaust	.0016 to .0029		
Wear limit	.004		
Valve seat inserts	See Chapter 1, FIG 1:16		
Valve guides	See Chapter 1, FIG 1:17		
Valve springs:			
Free length, inlet and exhaust:			
Outer	1.968		
Inner	1.766		
Assembled height:			
Outer	1.573		
Inner	1.378		
Effective number of turns:			
Outer	5		
Inner	$5\frac{1}{2}$		
Valve clearance:	*Cold*	*Warm*	
Inlet	.008	.010	
Exhaust	.010	.012	
Valve timing:			
Single carburetter models:			
Inlet opens	12 deg. BTDC		
Inlet closes	48 deg. ABDC		
Exhaust opens	54 deg. BBDC		
Exhaust closes	18 deg. ATDC		
Twin carburetter models:			
Inlet opens	16 deg. BTDC		
Inlet closes	52 deg. ABDC		
Exhaust opens	54 deg. BBDC		
Exhaust closes	18 deg. ATDC		
Oil pump and filter:			
Pump	Dual rotor		
Relief valve opens at	50 to 70 lb/sq inch		
Pressure at idling	11 to 40 lb/sq inch		
Filter	Full flow, disposable element		

FUEL SYSTEM

Filters:	
Air cleaner	Viscous paper, disposable element
Fuel	In-line, disposable element
Fuel pump	Mechanical, diaphragm
Pressure at 1000 rev/min	2.6 to 3.4 lb/sq inch
Capacity at 1000 rev/min	$1\frac{3}{4}$ pints in 60 seconds or less
Fuel octane ratings:	
Single carburetter models	90 (2- or 3-star)
Twin carburetter models	95 (3- or 4-star)

Carburetter(s):			
Single carburetter models	.. .. ..	Twin venturi, downdraught	
Manual transmission, L16	.. .. ..	Type 213282-331	
Automatic transmission, L16	.. .. ..	Type 213282-341	
Manual transmission, L18	.. .. ..	Type 213304-361	
Automatic transmission, L18	.. .. ..	Type 213304-421	
Type 213282-331 and 341:		*Primary*	*Secondary*
Venturi diameter	.. ..	22 mm	29 mm
Main jet	.. ..	102	165
Main air bleed	.. ..	60	60
First slow air bleed	.. ..	1 mm	—
Second slow air bleed	.. ..	180	100
Slow economizer	.. ..	1.6 mm	—
Power jet	.. ..	—	45
Main nozzle	.. ..	2.3 mm	2.5 mm
Type 213304-361 and 421:		*Primary*	*Secondary*
Venturi diameter	.. ..	23 mm	30 mm
Main jet	.. ..	102	170
Main air bleed	.. ..	60	60
First slow air bleed	.. ..	1 mm	—
Second slow air bleed	.. ..	210	100
Slow economizer	.. ..	1.6 mm	—
Power jet	.. ..	—	55
Main nozzle	.. ..	2.3 mm	2.8 mm
Twin carburetter models	.. ..	Two sidedraught	
Type	.. ..	HJL 38W6 (SU type), variable ventiri	
Bore	.. ..	38 mm	
Piston lift	.. ..	29 mm	
Jet needle number	.. ..	M-76	
Jet nozzle diameter	.. ..	2.34 mm	
Slow running rev/min:			
Transmission type:		*Manual*	*Automatic*
Single carburetter models	.. .. ..	600	650
Twin carburetter models	.. .. ..	650	700
Emission control models	.. .. ..	700	720

IGNITION SYSTEM

Firing order	.. ..	1, 3, 4, 2
Sparking plugs:		
Diameter and reach	.. ..	14 mm x 19 mm
Type:		
Single carburetter models	.. .. ..	NGK, BP-5ES or equivalent
Twin carburetter models	.. .. ..	NGK, BP-6ES or equivalent
Gap	.. ..	.031 to .035
Distributor	.. ..	Hitachi D411-58K or D409-54K
Type	.. ..	Centrifugal and vacuum advance/ retard
Series number:		
Single carburetter models	.. .. ..	D411-58K
Twin carburetter models	.. .. ..	D409-54K
Points gap	.. ..	.018 to .022
Coil	.. ..	Hitachi 6R-200
Ignition timing at idling rev/min:		
Single carburetter models	.. .. ..	10 deg. BTDC
Twin carburetter models	.. .. ..	14 deg. BTDC

Refer to Chapter 3, Section 3:6 for timing procedures

COOLING SYSTEM

Filler cap pressure rating	13 lb/sq inch	
Thermostat opens at:		
Standard	82°C (180°F)	
Cold climate	88°C (190°F)	
Tropical climate	76.5°C (170°F)	

CLUTCH

Lining:		
Outer diameter	7.87	
Inner diameter	5.12	
Thickness	.138	
Wear limit	.012 above rivet head	
Driven plate assembly:		
Face runout	.020 maximum	
Thickness:		
New linings and 'free'	.338 to .354	
New linings but 'compressed'	.301 to .313	

TRANSMISSION

Manual type	R3W65	F4W63 or F4C63
Number of forward speeds	3	4
Gear ratios:		
1st	3.263	3.382
2nd	1.645	2.013
3rd	1.000	1.312
4th	—	1.000
Reverse	3.355	3.365
Automatic type	3N71B	
Gear ratios:		
1st	2.458	
2nd	1.458	
3rd	1.000	
Reverse	2.182	
Torque converter	3-element, 1-stage, 2-phase	
Maximum ratio	2.0:1	
Final drive ratio:		
Engine type:	*L16*	*L18*
Saloon	3.900	3.700
Estate car	3.889	3.889
Coupe	—	3.700
USA and Canada:		
Saloon and coupe	3.700 or 3.900	
Estate car	3.889	

SUSPENSION

Front	MacPherson strut, coil type independent	
Dampers	Integral with strut, telescopic hydraulic	
Rear:		
Saloon and coupe models	Coil, independent	
Estate car models	Leaf, semi-elliptical	
Dampers	Telescopic, hydraulic	
Axle:		
Saloon and coupe models	Suspension arms and drive shafts	
Estate car models	'Banjo' axle assembly	
Tyre pressure	23 to 27 lb/sq inch (1.6 to 1.9 kg/sq cm)	

STEERING

Type	Recirculating ball
Ratio	15:1
Steering wheel turns, lock to lock	3.3
Turning angle:	
Inner	37 to 38 deg.
Outer	$30\frac{3}{4}$ to $32\frac{3}{4}$ deg.
Wheel alignment:	
Inclination	Preset, not adjustable
Castor angle	Preset, not adjustable
Camber angle	Preset, not adjustable
Toe-in	See Chapter 10, Section 10:6

BRAKES

Operation:	
Foot	Hydraulic
Hand	Mechanical (rear drums only)
Drums:	
Maximum regrind ID	9.055 (front and rear)
Minimum lining thickness	.06
Discs:	
Minimum thickness	.331
Minimum pad lining thickness	.04
Friction linings:	
Shoes (front and rear)	1.575 x 8.642 x .177
Caliper pads	1.563 x 3.386 x .354

ELECTRICAL EQUIPMENT

Battery:	
Voltage	12-volt
Earth system	Negative earth
Starter motor:	Hitachi S114-103P
Pinion engagement	Positive
Brush minimum length	.236
Commutator diameter	1.299 minimum
Alternator	Hitachi LT150-05
Rectifier	Integral diodes
Brush minimum length	.295
Alternator regulator	Hitachi TL 1Z-58
Fuses (see FIG 14:1)	One 5 amp; five 10 amp; four 20 amp
Fusible links (see FIG 14:1)	One brown; one red
Continuous rating:	
Brown	11 amp
Red	26 amp

CAPACITIES

	Imperial	*USA*	*Litre*
Engine:			
Sump only	7 pts	$8\frac{1}{2}$ pts	3.8
Sump and oil filter	$7\frac{1}{2}$ pts	9 pts	4.3
Cooling system:			
Engine system only	11 pts	13 pts	6
Engine and heater systems	$11\frac{1}{2}$ pts	$13\frac{1}{2}$ pts	6.5
Fuel tank:			
Saloon and coupe	12 galls	14 galls	55
Estate car	$11\frac{1}{2}$ galls	$13\frac{1}{2}$ galls	52

Transmission:			
Manual gearbox:			
3-speed	$2\frac{7}{8}$ pts	$3\frac{1}{2}$ pts	1.7
4-speed	$3\frac{3}{8}$ pts	$4\frac{1}{8}$ pts	2
Automatic (including converter)	$9\frac{1}{2}$ pts	$11\frac{1}{4}$ pts	5.5
Rear axle:			
Saloon and coupe	$1\frac{3}{8}$ pts	$1\frac{5}{8}$ pts	.8
Estate car	$2\frac{3}{8}$ pts	$2\frac{7}{8}$ pts	1.3
Steering gearbox	$\frac{1}{2}$ pts	$\frac{5}{8}$ pts	.27
Brakes:			
Master cylinder reservoirs:			
Drum front brakes			.045
Disc front brakes			.110
Front suspension:			
Ampco dampers			.325
Kayaba dampers			.332

DIMENSIONS

Overall length:	
Saloon and coupe	13 ft 10 inch (4.215 m)
Estate car	14 ft $\frac{1}{2}$ inch (4.280 m)
Overall width (all models)	5 ft 3 inch (1.600 m)
Overall height:	
Saloon	4 ft $7\frac{1}{4}$ inch (1.405 m)
Coupe	4 ft $6\frac{1}{2}$ inch (1.385 m)
Estate car	4 ft $8\frac{1}{2}$ inch (1.435 m)
Track	
Front (all models)	4 ft $3\frac{5}{8}$ inch (1.310 m)
Rear:	
Saloon and coupe	4 ft 4 inch (1.320 m)
Estate car	4 ft $4\frac{3}{8}$ inch (1.330 m)
Wheelbase (all models)	8 ft $2\frac{3}{8}$ inch (2.500 m)
Ground clearance:	
Saloon and coupe	$7\frac{1}{4}$ inch (.185 m)
Estate car	$6\frac{3}{4}$ inch (.170 m)

TORQUE WRENCH SETTINGS

Torques are in lb ft unless otherwise stated

Engine:	
Connecting rod cap nuts	33 to 40
Crankshaft pulley bolt	87 to 116
Cylinder head bolts	47 to 61, but see Chapter 1, Section 1:5
Flywheel bolts	101 to 116
Main bearing cap bolts	33 to 40
Oil sump bolts	4.3 to 6.3
Ignition system:	
Sparking plugs	11 to 15
Clutch:	
Clutch to flywheel bolts	12 to 16
Transmission:	
Manual:	
Bellhousing to engine bolts	18 to 29
Mainshaft nut	65 to 80
Bottom cover	8 to 12
Check ball plug	12 to 15
Automatic:	
Bellhousing to engine bolts	30 to 36
Piston stem (brake band)	8.7 to 10.8
Sump bolts	2.5 to 3.2
Drive shaft coupling bolts	36 to 43
Front suspension	
Strut:	
Upper mounting bolts	18 to 25
Strut to steering arm	53 to 72
Spring (self-locking nut)	43 to 54
Tension rod:	
Bracket bolts	37 to 50
Rod to bracket nut	33 to 40
Anti-roll bar:	
Bracket bolt	10 to 13
Suspension arm attachment	8.7 to 12
Suspension arm pivot bolts	65 to 72
Ball joint:	
Castellated nut	40 to 55
Joint to arm nuts	14 to 18
Rear suspension:	
Spring U-bolts (estate car)	43 to 47
Damper:	
Saloon and coupe	12 to 16 (both ends)
Estate car, upper	6.5 to 8.7
Estate car, lower	25 to 33
Suspension arm pivot bolts	58 to 72
Steering:	
Coupling clamp bolt	29 to 36
Ball joint nuts	40 to 55
Side rod locknuts	32 to 44
Steering wheel nut	29 to 36
Brakes:	
Pipe connections	11 to 13
Front wheel cylinder:	
Larger nuts	11 to 13
Smaller nuts	4 to 5
Disc retaining bolts	28 to 38

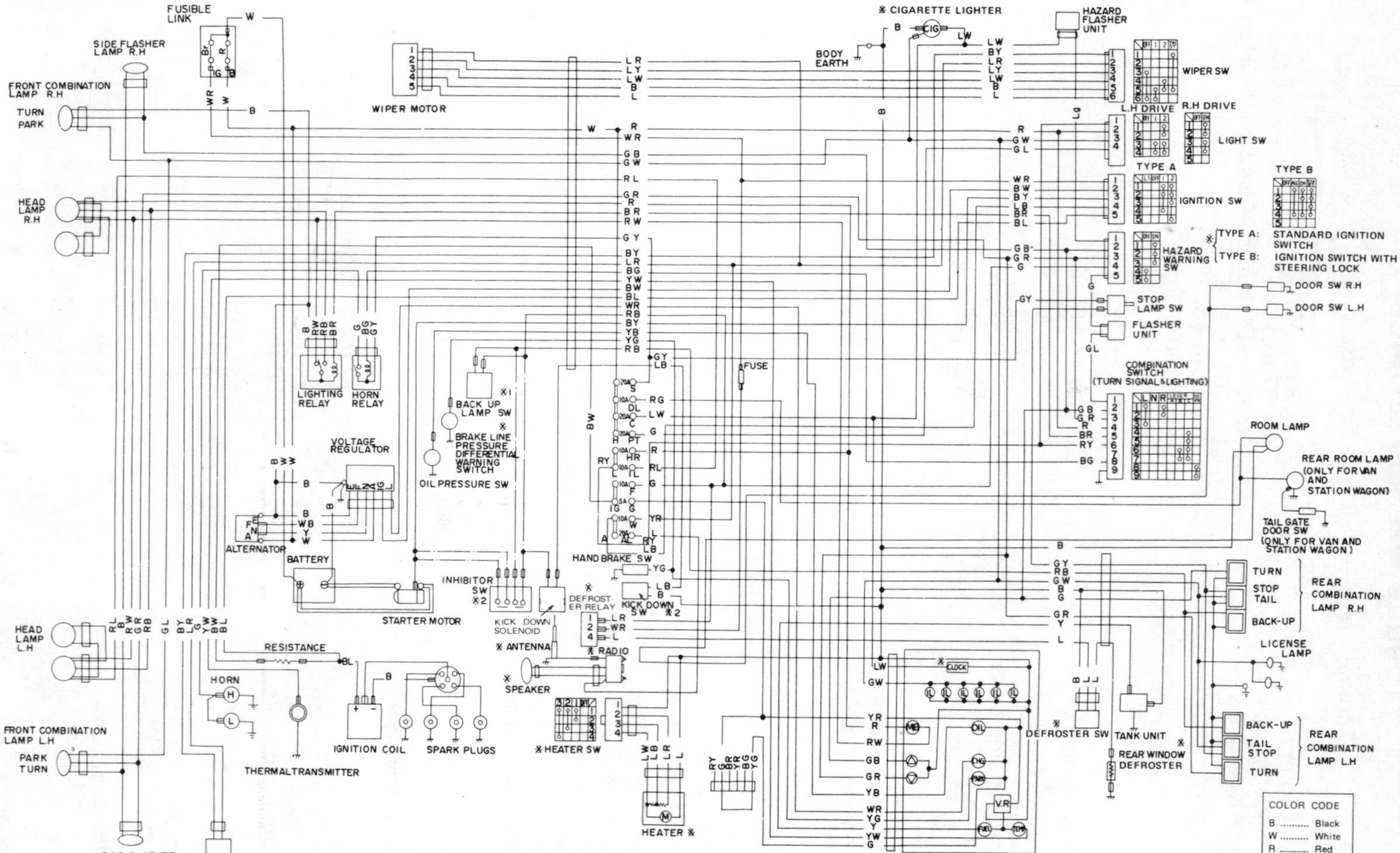

※1 ONLY FOR VEHICLE EQUIPPED WITH MANUAL TRANSMISSION
※2 ONLY FOR VEHICLE EQUIPPED WITH AUTOMATIC TRANSMISSION
※ OPTIONAL EQUIPMENT

FIG 14:1 Wiring diagram

Key to Fig 14:1 Colour code **B** Black **W** White **R** Red **Y** Yellow **G** Green **L** Blue

Inches	Decimals	Millimetres	Inches to Millimetres		Millimetres to Inches	
			Inches	mm	mm	Inches
1/64	.015625	.3969	.001	.0254	.01	.00039
1/32	.03125	.7937	.002	.0508	.02	.00079
3/64	.046875	1.1906	.003	.0762	.03	.00118
1/16	.0625	1.5875	.004	.1016	.04	.00157
5/64	.078125	1.9844	.005	.1270	.05	.00197
3/32	.09375	2.3812	.006	.1524	.06	.00236
7/64	.109375	2.7781	.007	.1778	.07	.00276
1/8	.125	3.1750	.008	.2032	.08	.00315
9/64	.140625	3.5719	.009	.2286	.09	.00354
5/32	.15625	3.9687	.01	.254	.1	.00394
11/64	.171875	4.3656	.02	.508	.2	.00787
3/16	.1875	4.7625	.03	.762	.3	.01181
13/64	.203125	5·1594	.04	1.016	.4	.01575
7/32	.21875	5.5562	.05	1.270	.5	.01969
15/64	.234375	5.9531	.06	1.524	.6	.02362
1/4	.25	6.3500	.07	1.778	.7	.02756
17/64	.265625	6.7469	.08	2.032	.8	.03150
9/32	.28125	7.1437	.09	2.286	.9	.03543
19/64	.296875	7.5406	.1	2.54	1	.03937
5/16	.3125	7.9375	.2	5.08	2	.07874
21/64	.328125	8.3344	.3	7.62	3	.11811
11/32	.34375	8.7312	.4	10.16	4	.15748
23/64	.359375	9.1281	.5	12.70	5	.19685
3/8	.375	9.5250	.6	15.24	6	.23622
25/64	.390625	9.9219	.7	17.78	7	.27559
13/32	.40625	10.3187	.8	20.32	8	.31496
27/64	.421875	10.7156	.9	22.86	9	.35433
7/16	.4375	11.1125	1	25.4	10	.39370
29/64	.453125	11.5094	2	50.8	11	.43307
15/32	.46875	11.9062	3	76.2	12	.47244
31/64	.484375	12.3031	4	101.6	13	.51181
1/2	.5	12.7000	5	127.0	14	.55118
33/64	.515625	13.0969	6	152.4	15	.59055
17/32	.53125	13.4937	7	177.8	16	.62992
35/64	.546875	13.8906	8	203.2	17	.66929
9/16	.5625	14.2875	9	228.6	18	.70866
37/64	.578125	14.6844	10	254.0	19	.74803
19/32	.59375	15.0812	11	279.4	20	.78740
39/64	.609375	15.4781	12	304.8	21	.82677
5/8	.625	15.8750	13	330.2	22	.86614
41/64	.640625	16.2719	14	355.6	23	.90551
21/32	.65625	16.6687	15	381.0	24	.94488
43/64	.671875	17.0656	16	406.4	25	.98425
11/16	.6875	17.4625	17	431.8	26	1.02362
45/64	.703125	17.8594	18	457.2	27	1.06299
23/32	.71875	18.2562	19	482.6	28	1.10236
47/64	.734375	18.6531	20	508.0	29	1.14173
3/4	.75	19.0500	21	533.4	30	1.18110
49/64	.765625	19.4469	22	558.8	31	1.22047
25/32	.78125	19.8437	23	584.2	32	1.25984
51/64	.796875	20.2406	24	609.6	33	1.29921
13/16	.8125	20.6375	25	635.0	34	1.33858
53/64	.828125	21.0344	26	660.4	35	1.37795
27/32	.84375	21.4312	27	685.8	36	1.41732
55/64	.859375	21.8281	28	711.2	37	1.4567
7/8	.875	22.2250	29	736.6	38	1.4961
57/64	.890625	22.6219	30	762.0	39	1.5354
29/32	.90625	23.0187	31	787.4	40	1.5748
59/64	.921875	23.4156	32	812.8	41	1.6142
15/16	.9375	23.8125	33	838.2	42	1.6535
61/64	.953125	24.2094	34	863.6	43	1.6929
31/32	.96875	24.6062	35	889.0	44	1.7323
63/64	.984375	25.0031	36	914.4	45	1.7717

UNITS	Pints to Litres	Gallons to Litres	Litres to Pints	Litres to Gallons	Miles to Kilometres	Kilometres to Miles	Lbs. per sq. In. to Kg. per sq. Cm.	Kg. per sq. Cm. to Lbs. per sq. In.
1	.57	4.55	1.76	.22	1.61	.62	.07	14.22
2	1.14	9.09	3.52	.44	3.22	1.24	.14	28.50
3	1.70	13.64	5.28	.66	4.83	1.86	.21	42.67
4	2.27	18.18	7.04	.88	6.44	2.49	.28	56.89
5	2.84	22.73	8.80	1.10	8.05	3.11	.35	71.12
6	3.41	27.28	10.56	1.32	9.66	3.73	.42	85.34
7	3.98	31.82	12.32	1.54	11.27	4.35	.49	99.56
8	4.55	36.37	14.08	1.76	12.88	4.97	.56	113.79
9		40.91	15.84	1.98	14.48	5.59	.63	128.00
10		45.46	17.60	2.20	16.09	6.21	.70	142.23
20				4.40	32.19	12.43	1.41	284.47
30				6.60	48.28	18.64	2.11	426.70
40				8.80	64.37	24.85		
50					80.47	31.07		
60					96.56	37.28		
70					112.65	43.50		
80					128.75	49.71		
90					144.84	55.92		
100					160.93	62.14		

UNITS	Lb ft to kgm	Kgm to lb ft	UNITS	Lb ft to kgm	Kgm to lb ft
1	.138	7.233	7	.967	50.631
2	.276	14.466	8	1.106	57.864
3	.414	21.699	9	1.244	65.097
4	.553	28.932	10	1.382	72.330
5	.691	36.165	20	2.765	144.660
6	.829	43.398	30	4.147	216.990

NOTES

HINTS ON MAINTENANCE AND OVERHAUL

There are few things more rewarding than the restoration of a vehicle's original peak of efficiency and smooth performance.

The following notes are intended to help the owner to reach that state of perfection. Providing that he possesses the basic manual skills he should have no difficulty in performing most of the operations detailed in this manual. It must be stressed, however, that where recommended in the manual, highly-skilled operations ought to be entrusted to experts, who have the necessary equipment, to carry out the work satisfactorily.

Quality of workmanship:

The hazardous driving conditions on the roads to-day demand that vehicles should be as nearly perfect, mechanically, as possible. It is therefore most important that amateur work be carried out with care, bearing in mind the often inadequate working conditions, and also the inferior tools which may have to be used. It is easy to counsel perfection in all things, and we recognize that it may be setting an impossibly high standard. We do, however, suggest that every care should be taken to ensure that a vehicle is as safe to take on the road as it is humanly possible to make it.

Safe working conditions:

Even though a vehicle may be stationary, it is still potentially dangerous if certain sensible precautions are not taken when working on it while it is supported on jacks or blocks. It is indeed preferable not to use jacks alone, but to supplement them with carefully placed blocks, so that there will be plenty of support if the car rolls off the jacks during a strenuous manoeuvre. Axle stands are an excellent way of providing a rigid base which is not readily disturbed. Piles of bricks are a dangerous substitute. Be careful not to get under heavy loads on lifting tackle, the load could fall. It is preferable not to work alone when lifting an engine, or when working underneath a vehicle which is supported well off the ground. To be trapped, particularly under the vehicle, may have unpleasant results if help is not quickly forthcoming. Make some provision, however humble, to deal with fires. Always disconnect a battery if there is a likelihood of electrical shorts. These may start a fire if there is leaking fuel about. This applies particularly to leads which can carry a heavy current, like those in the starter circuit. While on the subject of electricity, we must also stress the danger of using equipment which is run off the mains and which has no earth or has faulty wiring or connections. So many workshops have damp floors, and electrical shocks are of such a nature that it is sometimes impossible to let go of a live lead or piece of equipment due to the muscular spasms which take place.

Work demanding special care:

This involves the servicing of braking, steering and suspension systems. On the road, failure of the braking system may be disastrous. Make quite sure that there can be no possibility of failure through the bursting of rusty brake pipes or rotten hoses, nor to a sudden loss of pressure due to defective seals or valves.

Problems:

The chief problems which may face an operator are:

1 External dirt.
2 Difficulty in undoing tight fixings
3 Dismantling unfamiliar mechanisms.
4 Deciding in what respect parts are defective.
5 Confusion about the correct order for reassembly.
6 Adjusting running clearances.
7 Road testing.
8 Final tuning.

Practical suggestion to solve the problems:

1 Preliminary cleaning of large parts—engines, transmissions, steering, suspensions, etc.,—should be carried out before removal from the car. Where road dirt and mud alone are present, wash clean with a high-pressure water jet, brushing to remove stubborn adhesions, and allow to drain and dry. Where oil or grease is also present, wash down with a proprietary compound (Gunk, Teepol etc.,) applying with a stiff brush—an old paint brush is suitable—into all crevices. Cover the distributor and ignition coils with a polythene bag and then apply a strong water jet to clear the loosened deposits. Allow to drain and dry. The assemblies will then be sufficiently clean to remove and transfer to the bench for the next stage.

On the bench, further cleaning can be carried out, first wiping the parts as free as possible from grease with old newspaper. Avoid using rag or cotton waste which can leave clogging fibres behind. Any remaining grease can be removed with a brush dipped in paraffin. If necessary, traces of paraffin can be removed by carbon tetrachloride. Avoid using paraffin or petrol in large quantities for cleaning in enclosed areas, such as garages, on account of the high fire risk.

When all exteriors have been cleaned, and not before, dismantling can be commenced. This ensures that dirt will not enter into interiors and orifices revealed by dismantling. In the next phases, where components have to be cleaned, use carbon tetrachloride in preference to petrol and keep the containers covered except when in use. After the components have been cleaned, plug small holes with tapered hard wood plugs cut to size and blank off larger orifices with grease-proof paper and masking tape. Do not use soft wood plugs or matchsticks as they may break.

2 It is not advisable to hammer on the end of a screw thread, but if it must be done, first screw on a nut to protect the thread, and use a lead hammer. This applies particularly to the removal of tapered cotters. Nuts and bolts seem to 'grow' together, especially in exhaust systems. If penetrating oil does not work, try the judicious application of heat, but be careful of starting a fire. Asbestos sheet or cloth is useful to isolate heat.

Tight bushes or pieces of tail-pipe rusted into a silencer can be removed by splitting them with an open-ended hacksaw. Tight screws can sometimes be started by a tap from a hammer on the end of a suitable screwdriver. Many tight fittings will yield to the judicious use of a hammer, but it must be a soft-faced hammer if damage is to be avoided, use a heavy block on the opposite side to absorb shock. Any parts of the steering system which have been damaged should be renewed, as attempts to repair them may lead to cracking and subsequent failure, and steering ball joints should be disconnected using a recommended tool to prevent damage.

3 If often happens that an owner is baffled when trying to dismantle an unfamiliar piece of equipment. So many modern devices are pressed together or assembled by spinning-over flanges, that they must be sawn apart. The intention is that the whole assembly must be renewed. However, parts which appear to be in one piece to the naked eye, may reveal close-fitting joint lines when inspected with a magnifying glass, and, this may provide the necessary clue to dismantling. Left-handed screw threads are used where rotational forces would tend to unscrew a righthanded screw thread.

Be very careful when dismantling mechanisms which may come apart suddenly. Work in an enclosed space where the parts will be contained, and drape a piece of cloth over the device if springs are likely to fly in all directions. Mark everything which might be reassembled in the wrong position, scratched symbols may be used on unstressed parts, or a sequence of tiny dots from a centre punch can be useful. Stressed parts should never be scratched or centre-popped as this may lead to cracking under working conditions. Store parts which look alike in the correct order for reassembly. Never rely upon memory to assist in the assembly of complicated mechanisms, especially when they will be dismantled for a long time, but make notes, and drawings to supplement the diagrams in the manual, and put labels on detached wires. Rust stains may indicate unlubricated wear. This can sometimes be seen round the outside edge of a bearing cup in a universal joint. Look for bright rubbing marks on parts which normally should not make heavy contact. These might prove that something is bent or running out of truth. For example, there might be bright marks on one side of a piston, at the top near the ring grooves, and others at the bottom of the skirt on the other side. This could well be the clue to a bent connecting rod. Suspected cracks can be proved by heating the component in a light oil to approximately 100°C, removing, drying off, and dusting with french chalk, if a crack is present the oil retained in the crack will stain the french chalk.

4 In determining wear, and the degree, against the permissible limits set in the manual, accurate measurement can only be achieved by the use of a micrometer. In many cases, the wear is given to the fourth place of decimals; that is in ten-thousandths of an inch. This can be read by the vernier scale on the barrel of a good micrometer. Bore diameters are more difficult to determine. If, however, the matching shaft is accurately measured, the degree of play in the bore can be felt as a guide to its suitability. In other cases, the shank of a twist drill of known diameter is a handy check.

Many methods have been devised for determining the clearance between bearing surfaces. To-day the best and simplest is by the use of Plastigage, obtainable from most garages. A thin plastic thread is laid between the two surfaces and the bearing is tightened, flattening the thread. On removal, the width of the thread is compared with a scale supplied with the thread and the clearance is read off directly. Sometimes joint faces leak persistently, even after gasket renewal. The fault will then be traceable to distortion, dirt or burrs. Studs which are screwed into soft metal frequently raise burrs at the point of entry. A quick cure for this is to chamfer the edge of the hole in the part which fits over the stud.

5 **Always check a replacement part with the original one before it is fitted.**

If parts are not marked, and the order for reassembly is not known, a little detective work will help. Look for marks which are due to wear to see if they can be mated. Joint faces may not be identical due to manufacturing errors, and parts which overlap may be stained, giving a clue to the correct position. Most fixings leave identifying marks especially if they were painted over on assembly. It is then easier to decide whether a nut, for instance, has a plain, a spring, or a shakeproof washer under it. All running surfaces become 'bedded' together after long spells of work and tiny imperfections on one part will be found to have left corresponding marks on the other. This is particularly true of shafts and bearings and even a score on a cylinder wall will show on the piston.

6 Checking end float or rocker clearances by feeler gauge may not always give accurate results because of wear. For instance, the rocker tip which bears on a valve stem may be deeply pitted, in which case the feeler will simply be bridging a depression. Thrust washers may also wear depressions in opposing faces to make accurate measurement difficult. End float is then easier to check by using a dial gauge. It is common practice to adjust end play in bearing assemblies, like front hubs with taper rollers, by doing up the axle nut until the hub becomes stiff to turn and then backing it off a little. Do not use this method with ballbearing hubs as the assembly is often preloaded by tightening the axle nut to its fullest extent. If the splitpin hole will not line up, file the base of the nut a little.

Steering assemblies often wear in the straight-ahead position. If any part is adjusted, make sure that it remains free when moved from lock to lock. Do not be surprised if an assembly like a steering gearbox, which is known to be carefully adjusted outside the car, becomes stiff when it is bolted in place. This will be due to distortion of the case by the pull of the mounting bolts, particularly if the mounting points are not all touching together. This problem may be met in other equipment and is cured by careful attention to the alignment of mounting points.

When a spanner is stamped with a size and A/F it means that the dimension is the width between the jaws and has no connection with ANF, which is the designation for the American National Fine thread. Coarse threads like Whitworth are rarely used on cars to-day except for studs which screw into soft aluminium or cast iron. For this reason it might be found that the top end of a cylinder head stud has a fine thread and the lower end a coarse thread to screw into the cylinder block. If the car has mainly UNF threads then it is likely that any coarse threads will be UNC, which are not the same as Whitworth. Small sizes have the same number of threads in Whitworth and UNC, but in the $\frac{1}{2}$ inch size for example, there are twelve threads to the inch in the former and thirteen in the latter.

7 After a major overhaul, particularly if a great deal of work has been done on the braking, steering and suspension systems, it is advisable to approach the problem of testing with care. If the braking system has been overhauled, apply heavy pressure to the brake pedal and get a second operator to check every possible source of leakage. The brakes may work extremely well, but a leak could cause complete failure after a few miles.

Do not fit the hub caps until every wheel nut has been checked for tightness, and make sure the tyre pressures are correct. Check the levels of coolant, lubricants and hydraulic fluids. Being satisfied that all is well, take the car on the road and test the brakes at once. Check the steering and the action of the handbrake. Do all this at moderate speeds on quiet roads, and make sure there is no other vehicle behind you when you try a rapid stop.

Finally, remember that many parts settle down after a time, so check for tightness of all fixings after the car has been on the road for a hundred miles or so.

8 It is useless to tune an engine which has not reached its normal running temperature. In the same way, the tune of an engine which is stiff after a rebore will be different when the engine is again running free. Remember too, that rocker clearances on pushrod operated valve gear will change when the cylinder head nuts are tightened after an initial period of running with a new head gasket.

Trouble may not always be due to what seems the obvious cause. Ignition, carburation and mechanical condition are interdependent and spitting back through the carburetter, which might be attributed to a weak mixture, can be caused by a sticking inlet valve.

For one final hint on tuning, never adjust more than one thing at a time or it will be impossible to tell which adjustment produced the desired result.

NOTES

GLOSSARY OF TERMS

Allen key	Cranked wrench of hexagonal section for use with socket head screws.
Alternator	Electrical generator producing alternating current. Rectified to direct current for battery charging.
Ambient temperature	Surrounding atmospheric temperature.
Annulus	Used in engineering to indicate the outer ring gear of an epicyclic gear train.
Armature	The shaft carrying the windings, which rotates in the magnetic field of a generator or starter motor. That part of a solenoid or relay which is activated by the magnetic field.
Axial	In line with, or pertaining to, an axis.
Backlash	Play in meshing gears.
Balance lever	A bar where force applied at the centre is equally divided between connections at the ends.
Banjo axle	Axle casing with large diameter housing for the crownwheel and differential.
Bendix pinion	A self-engaging and self-disengaging drive on a starter motor shaft.
Bevel pinion	A conical shaped gearwheel, designed to mesh with a similar gear with an axis usually at 90 deg. to its own.
bhp	Brake horse power, measured on a dynamometer.
bmep	Brake mean effective pressure. Average pressure on a piston during the working stroke.
Brake cylinder	Cylinder with hydraulically operated piston(s) acting on brake shoes or pad(s).
Brake regulator	Control valve fitted in hydraulic braking system which limits brake pressure to rear brakes during heavy braking to prevent rear wheel locking.
Camber	Angle at which a wheel is tilted from the vertical.
Capacitor	Modern term for an electrical condenser. Part of distributor assembly, connected across contact breaker points, acts as an interference suppressor.
Castellated	Top face of a nut, slotted across the flats, to take a locking splitpin.
Castor	Angle at which the kingpin or swivel pin is tilted when viewed from the side.
cc	Cubic centimetres. Engine capacity is arrived at by multiplying the area of the bore in sq cm by the stroke in cm by the number of cylinders.
Clevis	U-shaped forked connector used with a clevis pin, usually at handbrake connections.
Collet	A type of collar, usually split and located in a groove in a shaft, and held in place by a retainer. The arrangement used to retain the spring(s) on a valve stem in most cases.
Commutator	Rotating segmented current distributor between armature windings and brushes in generator or motor.
Compression ratio	The ratio, or quantitative relation, of the total volume (piston at bottom of stroke) to the unswept volume (piston at top of stroke) in an engine cylinder.
Condenser	See capacitor.
Core plug	Plug for blanking off a manufacturing hole in a casting.
Crownwheel	Large bevel gear in rear axle, driven by a bevel pinion attached to the propeller shaft. Sometimes called a 'ring gear'.
'C'-spanner	Like a 'C' with a handle. For use on screwed collars without flats, but with slots or holes.
Damper	Modern term for shock-absorber, used in vehicle suspension systems to damp out spring oscillations.
Depression	The lowering of atmospheric pressure as in the inlet manifold and carburetter.
Dowel	Close tolerance pin, peg, tube, or bolt. which accurately locates mating parts.
Drag link	Rod connecting steering box drop arm (pitman arm) to nearest front wheel steering arm in certain types of steering systems.
Dry liner	Thinwall tube pressed into cylinder bore
Dry sump	Lubrication system where all oil is scavenged from the sump, and returned to a separate tank.
Dynamo	See Generator.
Electrode	Terminal, part of an electrical component, such as the points or 'Electrodes' of a sparking plug.
Electrolyte	In lead-acid car batteries a solution of sulphuric acid and distilled water.
End float	The axial movement between associated parts, end play.
EP	Extreme pressure. In lubricants, special grades for heavily loaded bearing surfaces, such as gear teeth in a gearbox, or crownwheel and pinion in a rear axle.

Fade	Of brakes. Reduced efficiency due to overheating.
Field coils	Windings on the polepieces of motors and generators.
Fillets	Narrow finishing strips usually applied to interior bodywork.
First motion shaft	Input shaft from clutch to gearbox.
Fullflow filter	Filters through which all the oil is pumped to the engine. If the element becomes clogged, a bypass valve operates to pass unfiltered oil to the engine.
FWD	Front wheel drive.
Gear pump	Two meshing gears in a close fitting casing. Oil is carried from the inlet round the outside of both gears in the spaces between the gear teeth and casing to the outlet, the meshing gear teeth prevent oil passing back to the inlet, and the oil is forced through the outlet port.
Generator	Modern term for 'Dynamo'. When rotated produces electrical current.
Grommet	A ring of protective or sealing material. Can be used to protect pipes or leads passing through bulkheads.
Grubscrew	Fully threaded headless screw with screwdriver slot. Used for locking, or alignment purposes.
Gudgeon pin	Shaft which connects a piston to its connecting rod. Sometimes called 'wrist pin', or 'piston pin'.
Halfshaft	One of a pair transmitting drive from the differential.
Helical	In spiral form. The teeth of helical gears are cut at a spiral angle to the side faces of the gearwheel.
Hot spot	Hot area that assists vapourisation of fuel on its way to cylinders. Often provided by close contact between inlet and exhaust manifolds.
HT	High Tension. Applied to electrical current produced by the ignition coil for the sparking plugs.
Hydrometer	A device for checking specific gravity of liquids. Used to check specific gravity of electrolyte.
Hypoid bevel gears	A form of bevel gear used in the rear axle drive gears. The bevel pinion meshes below the centre line of the crownwheel, giving a lower propeller shaft line.
Idler	A device for passing on movement. A free running gear between driving and driven gears. A lever transmitting track rod movement to a side rod in steering gear.
Impeller	A centrifugal pumping element. Used in water pumps to stimulate flow.
Journals	Those parts of a shaft that are in contact with the bearings.
Kingpin	The main vertical pin which carries the front wheel spindle, and permits steering movement. May be called 'steering pin' or 'swivel pin'.
Layshaft	The shaft which carries the laygear in the gearbox. The laygear is driven by the first motion shaft and drives the third motion shaft according to the gear selected. Sometimes called the 'countershaft' or 'second motion shaft.'
lb ft	A measure of twist or torque. A pull of 10 lb at a radius of 1 ft is a torque of 10 lb ft.
lb/sq in	Pounds per square inch.
Little-end	The small, or piston end of a connecting rod. Sometimes called the 'small-end'.
LT	Low Tension. The current output from the battery.
Mandrel	Accurately manufactured bar or rod used for test or centring purposes.
Manifold	A pipe, duct, or chamber, with several branches.
Needle rollers	Bearing rollers with a length many times their diameter.
Oil bath	Reservoir which lubricates parts by immersion. In air filters, a separate oil supply for wetting a wire mesh element to hold the dust.
Oil wetted	In air filters, a wire mesh element lightly oiled to trap and hold airborne dust.
Overlap	Period during which inlet and exhaust valves are open together.
Panhard rod	Bar connected between fixed point on chassis and another on axle to control sideways movement.
Pawl	Pivoted catch which engages in the teeth of a ratchet to permit movement in one direction only.
Peg spanner	Tool with pegs, or pins, to engage in holes or slots in the part to be turned.
Pendant pedals	Pedals with levers that are pivoted at the top end.
Phillips screwdriver	A cross-point screwdriver for use with the cross-slotted heads of Phillips screws.
Pinion	A small gear, usually in relation to another gear.
Piston-type damper	Shock absorber in which damping is controlled by a piston working in a closed oil-filled cylinder.
Preloading	Preset static pressure on ball or roller bearings not due to working loads.
Radial	Radiating from a centre, like the spokes of a wheel.

Radius rod	Pivoted arm confining movement of a part to an arc of fixed radius.
Ratchet	Toothed wheel or rack which can move in one direction only, movement in the other being prevented by a pawl.
Ring gear	A gear tooth ring attached to outer periphery of flywheel. Starter pinion engages with it during starting.
Runout	Amount by which rotating part is out of true.
Semi-floating axle	Outer end of rear axle halfshaft is carried on bearing inside axle casing. Wheel hub is secured to end of shaft.
Servo	A hydraulic or pneumatic system for assisting, or, augmenting a physical effort. See 'Vacuum Servo'.
Setscrew	One which is threaded for the full length of the shank.
Shackle	A coupling link, used in the form of two parallel pins connected by side plates to secure the end of the master suspension spring and absorb the effects of deflection.
Shell bearing	Thinwalled steel shell lined with anti-friction metal. Usually semi-circular and used in pairs for main and big-end bearings.
Shock absorber	See 'Damper'.
Silentbloc	Rubber bush bonded to inner and outer metal sleeves.
Socket-head screw	Screw with hexagonal socket for an Allen key.
Solenoid	A coil of wire creating a magnetic field when electric current passes through it. Used with a soft iron core to operate contacts or a mechanical device.
Spur gear	A gear with teeth cut axially across the periphery.
Stub axle	Short axle fixed at one end only.
Tachometer	An instrument for accurate measurement of rotating speed. Usually indicates in revolutions per minute.
TDC	Top Dead Centre. The highest point reached by a piston in a cylinder, with the crank and connecting rod in line.
Thermostat	Automatic device for regulating temperature. Used in vehicle coolant systems to open a valve which restricts circulation at low temperature.
Third motion shaft	Output shaft of gearbox.
Threequarter floating axle	Outer end of rear axle halfshaft flanged and bolted to wheel hub, which runs on bearing mounted on outside of axle casing. Vehicle weight is not carried by the axle shaft.
Thrust bearing or washer	Used to reduce friction in rotating parts subject to axial loads.
Torque	Turning or twisting effort. See 'lb ft'.
Track rod	The bar(s) across the vehicle which connect the steering arms and maintain the front wheels in their correct alignment.
UJ	Universal joint. A coupling between shafts which permits angular movement.
UNF	Unified National Fine screw thread.
Vacuum servo	Device used in brake system, using difference between atmospheric pressure and inlet manifold depression to operate a piston which acts to augment brake pressure as required. See 'Servo'.
Venturi	A restriction or 'choke' in a tube, as in a carburetter, used to increase velocity to obtain a reduction in pressure.
Vernier	A sliding scale for obtaining fractional readings of the graduations of an adjacent scale.
Welch plug	A domed thin metal disc which is partially flattened to lock in a recess. Used to plug core holes in castings.
Wet liner	Removable cylinder barrel, sealed against coolant leakage, where the coolant is in direct contact with the outer surface.
Wet sump	A reservoir attached to the crankcase to hold the lubricating oil.

NOTES

INDEX

A

Accelerator control .. 34
Air bleed sizes, twin venturi carburetter .. 163
Air cleaner .. 41
Air injection system .. 28
Air pump .. 29
Aligning headlamps .. 142
Alignment, wheel .. 118
Alternator .. 137
Alternator brushes .. 139
Alternator regulator .. 139
Alternator removal and fitment .. 138
Altitude tuning .. 41
Anti-backfire valve .. 29
Antifreeze .. 56
Armature, starter motor .. 136
Automatic advance/retard, ignition .. 45
Automatic transmission adjustments .. 85
Automatic transmission description .. 79
Automatic transmission fluid cooler .. 54, 79
Automatic transmission gearchange speeds 84
Automatic transmission operation .. 80
Automatic transmission removal and fitment 87
Automatic transmission testing .. 81
Axle, rear .. 102

B

Backlight glass .. 154
Ball joints .. 105, 110
Battery .. 135
Belt tension, alternator/fan drive .. 138
Big-end bearings .. 20
Bleeding brake system .. 130
Bleeding clutch system .. 65
Bleeding front dampers .. 109
Bodywork finish .. 147
Bonnet removal and fitment .. 147
Brake adjustment, front .. 124
Brake adjustment, handbrake .. 133
Brake adjustment, rear .. 125
Brake calipers .. 127
Brake discs .. 127
Brake drums, front .. 124
Brake drums, rear .. 125
Brake hydraulic system .. 127
Brake shoes .. 124, 125
Braking system, description .. 121
Brushes, alternator .. 139
Brushes, starter motor .. 137
Bumper removal and fitment .. 148

C

Caliper overhaul .. 127
Caliper pad renewal .. 126
Camber angle .. 110
Camshaft bearings .. 22, 162
Camshaft drive .. 22
Capacities .. 165
Capacitor, distributor .. 48
Carburetter adjustments .. 36, 40
Carburetter data .. 163
Carburetter dismantling and assembly, SU type 39
Carburetter dismantling and assembly,
twin venturi type .. 36
Carburetter float adjustment .. 37, 41
Carburetter removal and fitment, SU type .. 38
Carburetter removal and fitment, twin venturi type 35
Carburetter (SU type) damper .. 32, 38
Carburetter synchronization (SU type) .. 40
Carburetter throttle interlocks .. 37, 40
Castor angle .. 110
Centrifugal advance/retard, ignition .. 45
Choke control .. 35
Clock .. 145
Closed breather system .. 26
Clutch adjustments .. 59
Clutch description .. 59
Clutch free play .. 65
Clutch hydraulic system .. 64
Clutch removal and fitment .. 60
Coil, ignition .. 49
Commutator, starter motor .. 136
Compression ratio .. 9, 161
Condenser (capacitor), distributor .. 48
Connecting rod data .. 19, 161
Connecting rod removal and fitment .. 18
Console .. 157
Contact breaker points .. 45, 49, 51
Coolant pump .. 55
Coolant thermostat .. 56
Cooler, transmission fluid .. 54, 79
Cooling system description .. 53
Corrosion, radiator .. 54, 56
Crankshaft .. 9, 20
Cylinder block .. 9, 26
Cylinder bores .. 19, 26
Cylinder head bolt tightening sequence .. 14
Cylinder head removal and fitment .. 13
Cylinder head servicing .. 14
Cylinder sleeves (liners) .. 19, 26, 161

D

Dampers, front .. 108
Dampers, rear .. 95
Dashboard .. 155
Dashpot (throttle) adjustment .. 37, 85
Decarbonizing .. 14
Differential gearing .. 98, 102
Dimensions (vehicle) .. 166
Disc brakes .. 126
Distributor dismantling and reassembly .. 49
Distributor drive .. 11, 25
Distributor maintenance .. 45, 51
Distributor points renewal .. 49
Distributor removal and fitment .. 48
Door and window glass .. 153
Door fittings .. 149
Door trim .. 149
Draining engine oil .. 11
Draining hydraulic system (brakes) .. 130

Draining radiator 53
Draining transmission, automatic 88
Draining transmission, manual 69
Drive shaft removal and fitment 96
Drum brakes 124, 125

E
Electrical equipment 135, 165
Electrolyte, battery 136
Emission control, air injection 28
Emission control, closed breather 26
Emission control, fuel system 41
Emission control, ignition system 51
Engine assembly 26
Engine data 9, 161
Engine description 9
Engine dismantling 17
Engine installation 26
Engine mountings 26
Engine removal 17
Exhaust system 157

F
Fan, cooling 55
Fan drive belt tension 138
Filler cap pressure rating 53
Filter, air 41
Filter, fuel 32
Filter, oil 11
Firing order 45, 163
Float level, single carburetter 37
Float level, twin carburetters 41
Fluid, brake hydraulic system 122
Fluid, clutch hydraulic system 59
Flushing cooling system 54
Flywheel 20
Friction linings, brake shoes .. 124, 125
Friction linings, clutch 63
Friction pads, disc brakes 126
Front brakes, disc 126
Front brakes, drum 124
Front dampers 108
Front hubs 106
Front road springs 108
Front suspension arms 110
Front suspension, description 105
Front suspension struts 108
Frost precautions 56
Fuel filter 32
Fuel gauge and transmitter 144
Fuel mixture adjustment, single carburetters 36
Fuel mixture adjustment, twin carburetters .. 42
Fuel octane ratings 162
Fuel pump 33
Fuel system, description 31
Fuel system emission control 41
Fuses and fusible links 143

G
Gauges 144
Gearbox assembly, manual 74
Gearbox description, automatic 79
Gearbox description, manual 67
Gearbox dismantling, manual 70
Gearbox ratios 164
Gearbox removal, automatic 87
Gearbox removal, manual 69
Gearchange linkage 76
Glossary of terms 175
Grille, front and top 148
Grinding-in valves 15
Gudgeon pins 19, 161
Guides, valve 16

H
Handbrake 133
Headlamp alignment 142
Heater 157
Hinges, door 149
Hints on Maintenance and Overhaul .. 171
Horns 145
Hubs, front 106
Hubs, rear 97
Hydraulic system, brakes 127
Hydraulic system, clutch 64
Hydrometer tests (battery electrolyte) .. 136

I
Idle speed adjustment 32, 36, 40
Ignition faults 47
Ignition system, description 45
Ignition timing data 49, 52, 163
Ignition timing marks 48
Ignition timing procedure 49
Inhibitor starting switch 83, 86
Instruments 144

J
Jet needle, SU type carburetter 38, 163
Jet sizes 163
Jets, twin venturi carburetters 37
Jet, SU type carburetter 38, 163

K
Kick-down, automatic transmission 80

L
Lighting circuits 142
Lock, bonnet 147
Locks, door 149
Luggage compartment lid 151

M
Main bearings 21, 161
Master cylinder, brakes 127
Master cylinder, clutch 64
Metric conversion tables 169

N
Needle, jet (SU type carburetter) 38, 163

O
Oil filter, renewing element 11
Oil pressure gauge and transmitter 145
Oil pressure relief valve 11
Oil pressure warning light 145
Oil pump 11
Oil seals, crankshaft 22, 26
Oil seals, transmission 73
Oil sump 25

P

Piston removal and fitment . . 18
Piston ring gaps and side clearances . . 19
Pistons, oversize . . 19
Plastigage . . 22, 172
Pump, air (emission control) . . 29
Pump, coolant . . 56
Pump, fuel . . 33
Pump, oil . . 11
Pump, windscreen washer . . 140

R

Rack, steering . . 113
Radiator flushing . . 54
Radiator removal and fitment . . 54
Ratios, transmission . . 164
Rear axle . . 102
Rear brakes . . 125
Rear dampers . . 95
Rear hubs . . 97
Rear road springs . . 94
Rear suspension, description . . 93
Rectifier, alternator . . 137
Reversing light switch . . 69, 87
Ring gear, flywheel . . 20

S

Selector, automatic transmission . . 85
Shackles, spring . . 94
Side windows . . 154
Slow-running speeds . . 32
Sparking plug gap . . 49, 163
Sparking plug types, diameter and reach 49, 52, 163
Speed detector switch (emission control) . . 83
Speedometer . . 144
Springs, front suspension . . 108
Springs, rear suspension . . 94
Springs, valve . . 15, 162
Starter motor . . 136
Starting inhibitor switch . . 83, 86
Steering angles . . 118
Steering column . . 118
Steering data . . 165
Steering gear description . . 113
Steering gear removal and fitment . . 114
Steering wheel . . 118
Strut, front suspension . . 108
Suspension, front . . 105
Suspension, rear . . 93

T

Tachometer . . 145
Tail door . . 152
TDC mark . . 48
Technical data . . 161
Temperature gauge, coolant . . 144
Tensioner, camshaft drive chain . . 22
Tensioning alternator/fan drive belt . . 138
Thermostat, coolant . . 56
Throttle interlocks . . 37, 40
Timing data, ignition . . 163
Timing data, valve . . 162
Timing procedure, ignition . . 49
Timing procedure, valve . . 23
Toe-in, wheel alignment . . 118
Torque wrench settings . . 167
Torsion bars, luggage compartment lid . . 151
Torsion bars, tail door . . 152
Transmission assembly, manual . . 74
Transmission description, automatic . . 79
Transmission description, manual . . 67
Transmission dismantling, manual . . 70
Transmission ratios . . 164
Transmission removal and fitment, automatic 87
Transmission removal and fitment, manual . . 69
Trim, door . . 149
Tyre pressure . . 164

U

Universal joints, drive shafts . . 96
Universal joints, propeller shaft . . 91

V

Vacuum servo . . 131
Valve clearances . . 12, 162
Valve data . . 15, 162
Valve grinding-in . . 15
Valve guides . . 16
Valve removal and fitment . . 15
Valve seat inserts . . 16
Valve springs . . 15, 162
Valve timing data . . 162
Valve timing procedure . . 23
Ventilation control valve (emission control) 27
Voltage regulator, alternator . . 140
Voltage stabilizer, gauge circuits . . 144

W

Water (coolant) pump . . 55
Wheel alignment . . 118
Wheel hubs, front . . 106
Wheel hubs, rear . . 96
Wheel interchange scheme . . 105
Window glass, door . . 153
Window glass, side . . 154
Window regulators . . 153
Windscreen glass . . 154
Windscreen wipers and washer . . 140
Wing removal and fitment, front . . 148
Wiring diagram . . 168

NOTES

Alfa Romeo Giulia 1600, 1750, 2000 1962 on
Aston Martin 1921-58
Auto Union Audi 70, 80, Super 90, 1966-72
Audi 100 1969 on
Austin, Morris etc. 1100 Mk. 1 1962-67
Austin, Morris etc. 1100 Mk. 2, 3, 1300 Mk. 1, 2, 3 America 1968 on
Austin A30, A35, A40 Farina 1951-67
Austin A55 Mk. 2, A60 1958-69
Austin A99, A110 1959-68
Austin J4 1960 on
Austin Allegro 1973 on
Austin Maxi 1969 on
Austin, Morris 1800 1964 on
Austin, Morris 2200 1972 on
Austin Kimberley, Tasman 1970 on
Austin, Morris 1300, 1500 Nomad 1969 on
BMC 3 (Austin A50, A55 Mk. 1, Morris Oxford 2, 3 1954-59)
Austin Healey 100/6, 3000 1956-68
Austin Healey, MG Sprite, Midget 1958 on
Bedford CA Mk. 2 1964-69
Bedford CF Vans 1969 on
Bedford Beagle HA Vans 1964 on
BMW 1600 1966 on
BMW 1800 1964-71
BMW 2000, 2002 1966 on
Chevrolet Corvair 1960-69
Chevrolet Corvette V8 1957-65
Chevrolet Corvette V8 1965 on
Chevrolet Vega 2300 1970 on
Chrysler Valiant V8 1965 on
Chrysler Valiant Straight Six 1963 on
Citroen DS 19, ID 19 1955-66
Citroen ID 19, DS 19, 20, 21 1966 on
Citroen Dyane Ami 1964 on
Daf 31, 32, 33, 44, 55 1961 on
Datsun Bluebird 610 series 1972 on
Datsun Cherry 100A, 120A 1971 on
Datsun 1000, 1200 1968 on
Datsun 1300, 1400, 1600 1968 on
Datsun 240C 1971 on
Datsun 240Z Sport 1970 on
Fiat 124 1966 on
Fiat 124 Sport 1966 on
Fiat 125 1967-72
Fiat 127 1971 on
Fiat 128 1969 on
Fiat 500 1957 on
Fiat 600, 600D 1955-69
Fiat 850 1964 on
Fiat 1100 1957-69
Fiat 1300, 1500 1961-67
Ford Anglia Prefect 100E 1953-62
Ford Anglia 105E, Prefect 107E 1959-67
Ford Capri 1300, 1600 OHV 1968 on
Ford Capri 1300, 1600, 2000 OHC 1972 on
Ford Capri 2000 V4, 3000 V6 1969 on
Ford Classic, Capri 1961-64
Ford Consul, Zephyr, Zodiac, 1, 2 1950-62
Ford Corsair Straight Four 1963-65
Ford Corsair V4 1965-68
Ford Corsair V4 2000 1969-70
Ford Cortina 1962-66
Ford Cortina 1967-68
Ford Cortina 1969-70
Ford Cortina Mk. 3 1970 on
Ford Escort 1967 on
Ford Falcon 6 1964-70
Ford Falcon XK, XL 1960-63
Ford Falcon 6 XR/XA 1966 on
Ford Falcon V8 (U.S.A.) 1965-71
Ford Falcon V8 (Aust.) 1966 on
Ford Pinto 1970 on
Ford Maverick 6 1969 on
Ford Maverick V8 1970 on
Ford Mustang 6 1965 on
Ford Mustang V8 1965 on
Ford Thames 10, 12, 15 cwt 1957-65
Ford Transit V4 1965 on
Ford Zephyr Zodiac Mk. 3 1962-66
Ford Zephyr Zodiac V4, V6, Mk. 4 1966-72
Ford Consul, Granada 1972 on
Hillman Avenger 1970 on
Hillman Hunter 1966 on
Hillman Imp 1963-68
Hillman Imp 1969 on
Hillman Minx 1 to 5 1956-65
Hillman Minx 1965-67
Hillman Minx 1966-70
Hillman Super Minx 1961-65
Jaguar XK120, 140, 150, Mk. 7, 8, 9 1948-61
Jaguar 2.4, 3.4, 3.8 Mk. 1, 2 1955-69
Jaguar 'E' Type 1961-72
Jaguar 'S' Type 420 1963-68
Jaguar XJ6 1968 on
Jowett Javelin Jupiter 1947-53
Landrover 1, 2 1948-61
Landrover 2, 2a, 3 1959 on
Mazda 616 1970 on
Mazda 808, 818 1972 on
Mazda 1200, 1300 1969 on
Mazda 1500, 1800 1967 on
Mazda RX-2 1971 on
Mazda R100, RX-3 1970 on
Mercedes-Benz 190b, 190c, 200 1959-68
Mercedes-Benz 220 1959-65
Mercedes-Benz 220/8 1968 on
Mercedes-Benz 230 1963-68
Mercedes-Benz 250 1965-67
Mercedes-Benz 250 1968 on
Mercedes-Benz 280 1968 on
MG TA to TF 1936-55
MGA MGB 1955-68
MGB 1969 on
Mini 1959 on
Mini Cooper 1961-72
Morgan Four 1936-72
Morris Marina 1971 on
Morris (Aust) Marina 1972 on
Morris Minor 2, 1000 1952-71
Morris Oxford 5, 6 1959-71
NSU 1000 1963-72
NSU Prinz 1 to 4 1957-72
Opel Ascona, Manta 1970 on
Opel GT 1900 1968 on
Opel Kadett, Olympia 993 cc 1078 cc 1962 on
Opel Kadett, Olympia 1492, 1698, 1897 cc 1967 on
Opel Rekord C 1966-72
Peugeot 204 1965 on
Peugeot 304 1970 on
Peugeot 404 1960 on
Peugeot 504 1968 on
Porsche 356A, B, C 1957-65
Porsche 911 1964 on
Porsche 912 1965-69
Porsche 914 S 1969 on
Reliant Regal 1952-73
Renault R4, R4L, 4 1961 on
Renault 5 1972 on
Renault 6 1968 on
Renault 8, 10, 1100 1962-71
Renault 12, 1969 on
Renault 15, 17 1971 on
Renault R16 1965 on
Renault Dauphine Floride 1957-67
Renault Caravelle 1962-68
Rover 60 to 110 1953-64
Rover 2000 1963-73
Rover 3 Litre 1958-67
Rover 3500, 3500S 1968 on
Saab 95, 96, Sport 1960-68
Saab 99 1969 on
Saab V4 1966 on
Simca 1000 1961 on
Simca 1100 1967 on
Simca 1300, 1301, 1500, 1501 1963 on
Skoda One (440, 445, 450) 1955-70
Sunbeam Rapier Alpine 1955-65
Toyota Carina, Celica 1971 on
Toyota Corolla 1100, 1200 1967 on
Toyota Corona 1500 Mk. 1 1965-70
Toyota Corona Mk. 2 1969 on
Triumph TR2, TR3, TR3A 1952-62
Triumph TR4, TR4A 1961-67
Triumph TR5, TR250, TR6 1967 on
Triumph 1300, 1500 1965-73
Triumph 2000 Mk. 1, 2.5 PI Mk. 1 1963-69
Triumph 2000 Mk. 2, 2.5 PI Mk. 2 1969 on
Triumph Dolomite 1972 on
Triumph Herald 1959-68
Triumph Herald 1969-71
Triumph Spitfire, Vitesse 1962-68
Triumph Spitfire Mk. 3, 4 1969 on
Triumph GT6, Vitesse 2 Litre 1969 on
Triumph Stag 1970 on
Triumph Toledo 1970 on
Vauxhall Velox, Cresta 1957-72
Vauxhall Victor 1, 2, FB 1957-64
Vauxhall Victor 101 1964-67
Vauxhall Victor FD 1600, 2000 1967-72

Continued on following page

Vauxhall Victor 3300, Ventora 1968-72
Vauxhall Victor FE Ventora 1972 on
Vauxhall Viva HA 1963-66
Vauxhall Viva HB 1966-70
Vauxhall Viva, HC Firenza 1971 on
Volkswagen Beetle 1954-67
Volkswagen Beetle 1968 on
Volkswagen 1500 1961-66
Volkswagen 1600 Fastback 1965-73
Volkswagen Transporter 1954-67
Volkswagen Transporter 1968 on
Volkswagen 411 1968-72
Volvo 120 series 1961-70
Volvo 140 series 1966 on
Volvo 160 series 1968 on
Volvo 1800 1960-73